Insider's Guide to Passing the Washington Real Estate Exam

5ᵀᴴ Edition

Rockwell Publishing Company

Copyright© 2016
By Rockwell Publishing Company
13218 N.E. 20th
Bellevue, WA 98005
(425)747-7272 / 1-800-221-9347

Fifth Edition, Second Printing

ISBN: 978-1-939259-75-2

PRINTED IN THE UNITED STATES OF AMERICA

Table of Contents

Chapter 17: Real Estate Careers and the Real Estate License Law 253

How to Improve Your Score on a Multiple Choice Exam

Prepare!

While almost anyone can improve his or her score by using our test-taking techniques, nothing replaces good, sound preparation. Without question, the number one reason applicants fail the license exam is the failure to adequately prepare. Even the brightest students can't guess their way through the state examination.

Make sure you're ready BEFORE your exam date. Don't make things more difficult by overlooking any of the following:

- **Bring a hand-held calculator to the exam.** If you don't already have one, buy one and learn how to use it before the day of the exam. The most elementary calculators are more than adequate. Calculators that are silent, hand-held, battery operated, without paper tape printing capabilities, and without an alphabetic keypad are permitted. Solar calculators are discouraged because test room lighting may be insufficient to power them. A malfunctioning calculator is not grounds for challenging your exam results.

- **Fill your car with gas the day before the exam.** Don't be frantically looking for a service station just before you're scheduled to sit for the exam.

- **Know where the exam site is.** Take a trial run, if necessary.

- **Keep a miscellaneous fact sheet.** Jot down details you have trouble remembering from one day to the next. For instance, if you can't remember the number of square feet in an acre, write it down on your fact sheet. But don't overdo it. Don't use more than one sheet of paper, and include only those facts you believe are relevant to the exam. Study your fact sheet for the half hour before entering the exam room so they'll be fresh in your mind when the test starts.

- **Don't try to memorize the information.** Try to understand it instead. You're taking a multiple-choice exam. The correct answer is in front of you. If you understand the subject you'll recognize the answer. If you attempt to memorize questions and learn by rote, you won't be able to recognize the answer unless the test questions are asked in precisely the same way you memorized the information.

Improve Your Score

There are a number of techniques that can help you score higher on any multiple-choice exam. Many students who fail the license exam do so by five or fewer percentage points. The student who has the patience to employ these test-taking techniques from beginning to end can increase his or her score by at least 5%—enough to make the difference between passing and failing.

- **Take the test one question at a time.** Once you understand how to use the electronic testing device, move to question one and concentrate on answering it. Don't start scrolling through the test to see what's ahead of you. If you do, you'll focus on the most troubling questions, which will only demoralize you.
- **Read the question carefully.** Make sure you understand the question before you consider the options. Don't hurry; you'll have plenty of time to finish. If you misread the question the first time, you'll tend to misinterpret it the same way every time you read it.
- **Conceal the options while you read the question.** An incorrect option can influence the way you read the question. Cover the options with your hand or with a piece of paper until you're satisfied that you understand what's being asked.
- **Eliminate obviously wrong answers and work back to the right one.** There is less risk of making a careless error if you work backwards to the right answer. You may be able to eliminate only one or two of the options. Even so, you have raised your odds from 1 in 4 to 2 or even 3 in 4, and that's a big improvement.
- **Pay attention to words like ALWAYS, NEVER, or EXCEPT.** Few things in life are "always" or "never." Greet these words with suspicion. The word "except" can turn a question around, and when you see the word in either the question or one or more of the options, make a mental note of it.

    Example: Each of the following is an essential element in a valid contract, EXCEPT:
    A.   constructive notice
    B.   mutual consent
    C.   consideration
    D.   legality of object

    In the example above, the question is brief and the word "EXCEPT" is conspicuous. But in longer questions it's easy to forget you're looking for an exception. Option "A" is the exception. If you forget you're looking for an exception, you will instinctively search for an accurate statement.

    You may be tempted to choose the first correct answer you read. If you do, you'll answer incorrectly even though you are familiar with the subject. There will be enough difficult questions on your test; don't give any away.

- **Double-check each answer.** And do it as you go along. When you select an answer, quickly go over both question and answer to be certain that you wanted to choose that particular option.
- **Don't change an answer.** There will be times when you're unsure of the answer you selected. However, after three decades of experience with tens of thousands of students, we know that you are much more likely to change an answer from correct to incorrect instead of the reverse. Unless you're absolutely certain you marked the wrong answer, resist the temptation to change it.
- **Don't dwell on a question you can't answer.** As you work through the exam, skip the questions you can't answer. Don't waste time on questions you're struggling with until you've answered all the easy ones. For example, if you find math difficult, skip the math problems until after you finish the rest of the exam. The electronic testing system has several features that make it easy to find the questions you skipped.
- **Don't let a question beat you more than once.** If you spend too much time and energy working on, puzzling over, or worrying about a few difficult questions, it may affect your mental alertness and ability to concentrate. That might cause you to miss questions you would have otherwise answered correctly. When faced with a difficult question, many students form a mental block. The longer the student ponders the question, the more permanent the block becomes. If you struggle too hard over a tough question or get into an ego conflict with the testing service, you hurt yourself three ways:

  1. you miss that question;
  2. you lose valuable time, which causes you to rush through the remaining questions; and
  3. the mental block carries over to subsequent questions that you might have otherwise answered correctly.

- **Don't be afraid to select the same option several times in a row.** If, according to your best judgment, the answer to four or five consecutive questions is "A," then mark your answers accordingly. This can and does happen.
- **A later question might answer an earlier question.** Occasionally, an answer to an earlier question will be revealed in a later question. This is one of the few situations where changing an answer would be justified. Be alert to the possibility, but don't count on it.
- **Don't keep score as you go along.** This might discourage you and affect your overall performance. If you want to tally your score by counting the questions you think you answered correctly, wait until you finish the test. But what's the point? They're going to grade your exam for you moments after you finish.

- **Don't compete with other applicants.** You're allowed three and a half hours to complete the Washington exam and you should use as much of it as you need. Don't worry if other people finish before you do. Many students who finish quickly fail.

Improve Your Odds When You Guess

Regardless of how thoroughly you prepare, on every license exam there will be at least a few questions you can't answer. Of course, the less complete your preparation, the more guesses you'll have to make. Still, there are some rules to follow that will increase the odds when you have to guess. (We're referring to the "pure guess" as opposed to the "informed guess" here.) If you're guessing, follow these guidelines:

- When two of the choices are opposites, choose one of them.
- If one of the options is noticeably longer than the others, choose that one.
- If two of the four options are almost identical, choose the longer one.
- Don't select any answer that uses absolute terms such as "all," "never," "always," and "must."
- General terms such as "most," "some," and "usually" are more likely to be found in a correct statement.
- Distrust exaggerated or complex options.
- If you've never heard of it before, don't select it.
- Answer every question, even if you're guessing. Unanswered questions are marked wrong. There is no penalty for guessing.

Don't Give Up

There will be questions you're absolutely certain you answered correctly. Unfortunately, there will be others you're not so sure of. When the stakes are so high, it's easy to get discouraged. The best way to handle this is to attack each and every question as if it were the only question on the exam. Don't be fretting about question 11 when you're answering number 12. You're going to miss some questions, but you don't need anything close to a perfect score to pass. You're going to be in the exam room for several hours. Tough it out one question at a time.

Chapter 1

The Nature of Real Property

I. **What is Real Property?** – Real property is commonly described as land, anything *affixed* to land, and anything incidental or *appurtenant* to land. Sometimes real property is referred to as that which is immovable. Personal property (or *chattels*) is that which is movable.

   A. **Land** – In the legal sense, land is the solid part of the surface of the earth, everything affixed to it by nature or by man, and anything on it or in it, such as minerals and water.

   B. **Bundle of Rights** – The rights, privileges, and interests associated with land ownership are also considered part of the real property. Real property is the land plus a *bundle of rights*.

II. **Appurtenances** – An *appurtenance* is a right or interest that goes along with or pertains to a piece of land, including *air rights*, *water rights*, *mineral rights*, and *support rights*. Appurtenances are ordinarily transferred along with the land, but the landowner may sell certain appurtenant rights (such as mineral rights) separately from the land.

> Do not attempt to memorize the listed appurtenances. Try to understand why they are classified as appurtenances.

   A. **Water Rights** – The right to use water can be an appurtenance. There are two types of surface water rights: *riparian rights* and *appropriative rights*.

   1. **Riparian rights** – Riparian rights are the water rights of a landowner whose property is adjacent to or crossed by a watercourse that flows downstream, such as a stream or a river. A riparian owner has the right to make reasonable use of the stream's natural flow for domestic uses. However, a riparian owner may not divert water for use on non-riparian property.

> Riparian waters are flowing waters: a stream or a river.

   a. **Littoral property** – Land that borders on a stationary body of water, such as a lake, is littoral property. Ocean water is considered littoral water, and oceanfront landowners are littoral owners. Oceanfront landowners own property only to the high-water mark.

> Littoral waters are standing waters: a lake or an ocean.

   2. **Appropriative rights** – If a landowner isn't located next to a body of water, the landowner may still have the right to use water through *appropriative rights*. Appropriative rights are obtained from the government through a permit system.

B. Air Rights – In theory, a landowner's rights extend to the upper limits of the sky. In reality, a landowner has the exclusive right to use the lower reaches of airspace over the property, but may do nothing that would interfere with normal air traffic.

1. **Air lots** – Air lots (such as units in a multi-story condominium) must be described in terms of elevation (by referring to an established plane of elevation known as a *datum*), in addition to ground location.

C. Mineral Rights – Solid minerals under the surface of the earth are considered part of the real property until they are extracted, at which point they become personal property. The right to extract minerals may be sold separately from the real property.

D. Support Rights – Property owners own the right to support from the land beside and beneath their property: *lateral support* (from adjacent land) and *subjacent support* (from the subsurface).

Sample questions

The legal description of which of the following would include a reference to airspace above a datum?
A. Industrial park
B. Cemetery plot
C. Single-family home
D. Condominium

    D. The legal description of a condominium includes references to airspace in order to describe the elevation of the floors and ceilings.

The owner of property located along a stream or river may have which type of water right?
A. Alluvion
B. Riparian
C. Appropriation
D. Littoral

    B. Riparian rights are water rights that belong to owners of property that border a stream or river. (Littoral rights refer to water rights associated with property that borders stationary water, such as a lake.)

III. Attachments – An *attachment* is anything permanently attached to the land. Attachments are considered part of the land. There are two types of attachments: *natural* and *man-made*.

A. **Natural Attachments** – Natural attachments are things attached to the earth by roots, such as trees, shrubs, and crops. As a general rule, these are part of the real property to which they are attached.

    1. **Timber or crops** – When timber or crops are harvested, they become personal property. If they are sold separately from the land and are subject to a contract of sale before harvest, they are personal property even while still attached to the land.

    2. **Doctrine of emblements** – The *doctrine of emblements* is a special rule that applies to crops planted by a tenant farmer. In this case the land belongs to the owner but the crops are the personal property of the tenant.

B. **Man-made Attachments** – Articles attached to the land by people are called *fixtures*. Houses, fences, patios, and other man-made improvements are fixtures. Lumber stacked on a site in preparation for construction is personal property. Once a structure is complete, the lumber used to build it becomes real property.

> Objects that are not attached to the land will not be included as part of a survey.

C. **Distinguishing Fixtures from Personal Property** – When a buyer and seller disagree about what was included in the sale (and it is not clear in their written agreement), the court will apply a series of tests to determine whether the item(s) in dispute are real or personal property.

    1. **Fixture tests** – If the written agreement between a buyer and seller specifies what will be real or personal property, the agreement will be controlling and the court tests unnecessary. Otherwise, courts will apply the following four tests:

        a. **Method of attachment** – As a general rule, any item that a person permanently attaches to the land becomes part of the real estate. If the removal of an item will cause damage, it will likely be considered a fixture.

        b. **Adaptation of the item to the realty** – If an unattached article was designed or adapted specifically for use on a particular property, it is probably a fixture.

        Example: Pews in a church or customized removable storm windows made for a specific building. Also, keys to a house fall into this category, even though they are movable.

> Keys to a house are classified as real estate.

Intention of the annexor is the most important test.

Age, cost, or size of an item are not fixture tests.

Trade fixtures are removable by the tenant at the end of the lease; otherwise, they become the property of the landlord.

    c. **Intention of the annexor (installer)** – This is the most important of the tests. Courts try to decide what the installer intended. Each of the other tests is considered when trying to make this decision. For instance, embedding a birdbath in concrete indicates permanence, while simply resting it on the ground does not.

    d. **Relationship of the parties** – Intent is also indicated by the relationship between the parties. For example, it is generally held that a tenant who installs a new lighting fixture for his use and enjoyment probably intends to remove it at the conclusion of his lease, while the same fixture installed by a landlord/owner is seen as intended to improve the property.

2. **Trade fixtures** – Items installed by a tenant so she can carry on a trade or business are called *trade fixtures*, which are considered personal property of the tenant. They can be removed by the tenant at the conclusion of the tenancy, provided she restores the property to its original condition. If not removed, they become the owner's property.

3. **Bill of sale** – A *bill of sale* is a document that conveys title to personal property. A bill of sale must be in writing, identify the parties, and be signed by the parties.

4. **Mobile homes** – A real estate agent may take a listing for a mobile home if the mobile home has gone through the title elimination process and the sale of the mobile home includes the property to which it is attached.

Sample questions

A buyer purchases a rental home that is fully furnished. The document used to transfer title to the furniture is a:

A. quitclaim deed
B. bill of sale
C. special warranty deed
D. general warranty deed

    B.   *Deeds transfer title to real estate; a bill of sale is used to transfer title to personal property.*

A home owner listed his property with a real estate agent. The owner had personally carved intricate wooden light switch covers for every room in the house, which all the prospective buyers admire. Can he take them with him after the house is sold?

A. Yes, if their removal is written into the purchase and sale agreement
B. Yes, if the owner replaces them with standard covers from a home improvement store
C. No, because the owner failed to tell his agent he wanted to take them with him
D. No, because they were hand-made, and their removal would damage the property

> A. The agreement of the parties always takes precedence over the tests a court uses to determine whether an item is a fixture.

Of all the tests used to determine whether an item is a fixture, the most important is:

A. the method of attachment
B. the intention of the party who attached the item
C. the adaptation of the item to the property
D. the weight of the item

> B. The intention of the party who attached the item is the most important fixture test.

A business tenant attached some personal property items to the leased real estate. These items probably:

A. became part of the real property as soon as they were attached
B. still belong to the tenant, and can be removed when the lease expires
C. belong to the landlord during the term of the lease
D. must be interpleaded when the lease terminates, so the parties can determine ownership

> B. These items are referred to as trade fixtures, and they belong to the tenant (who can remove them when the lease expires).

A tenant farmer has occupied a farm on which she has grown crops for several years. The landowner sells the farm to someone else who immediately gives the tenant notice to vacate. The timing of the notice will mean the crops currently in the ground will not be ready for harvest before the end of her lease. Who do the crops belong to?

A. The tenant
B. The former owner
C. The new owner
D. The tenant and the new owner

> A. A special rule, called the doctrine of emblements, applies to crops planted by a tenant farmer. If the lease is terminated through no fault of the tenant before the crops are ready for harvest, the tenant has the right to re-enter the land and harvest the first crop that matures after the tenancy is terminated.

Metes and bounds descriptions give the distance and direction of each boundary line.

Metes and bounds descriptions must specify a definite starting point, the point of beginning.

Once the point of beginning has been determined, boundary lines are described until the land being surveyed has been completely enclosed.

IV. **Methods of Legal Description** – When real property is transferred from one party to another, an accurate description of the land being conveyed is essential. There are three major methods used to describe land in legal documents: *metes and bounds*, *government survey*, and the *lot and block* method.

A. **Metes and Bounds** – The metes and bounds method describes a parcel by establishing its boundaries. Metes are distances and bounds are directions. The description may also reference *monuments*, which can be either man-made objects like roads or natural objects like rivers.

1. **Point of beginning** – A metes and bounds description begins at a well-defined point called the *point of beginning*. The description continues with a series of courses and distances, until the parcel's boundaries have been described all the way back to the point of beginning.

B. **Government Survey** – The government survey system, also called the rectangular survey system, describes land by reference to a series of grids.

1. **Principal meridian and base line** – The grids are composed of two sets of lines, one set running north/south, the other running east/west. Each grid is identified by a *principal meridian* and its *base line*.

2. **Township lines and range lines** – Grid lines run parallel to the principal meridian and base line at intervals of six miles.

a. **Township lines** – The east/west lines are called *township lines*, and they divide the land into horizontal rows called township tiers.

b. **Range lines** – The north/south lines, called *range lines*, divide the land into vertical columns called ranges.

3. **Townships** – A particular area of land that is located at the intersection of a range and a township tier is called a *township*. Because range lines and township lines are placed at six-mile intervals, each township measures six miles by six miles, or 36 square miles.

A quarter-section is 160 acres. A quarter-quarter-section is 40 acres.

A section is one mile (5,280 feet long) on each side.

4. **Sections** – Each township contains 36 sections. Each *section* is one square mile, or 640 acres. The 36 sections are numbered 1 through 36, starting in the northeast corner, then moving west, and snaking back and forth until ending in the southeast corner.

C. **Lot and Block** – The lot and block method of land description is sometimes referred to as the recorded map method, or the maps and plats system. Most subdivisions within city limits are described using this method.

1. **Plat maps** – When land is subdivided, lots and blocks (groups of lots surrounded by streets) are mapped out by a surveyor on a subdivision map, called a *plat map* or just a *plat*. The plat is recorded in the county where the land is located. For each lot, the plat will include the lot's dimensions, boundary lines, and utility easements.

A survey establishes a property's boundary lines.

Sample questions

A section of land is equivalent to:

A. one square mile
B. 36 square miles
C. 460 acres
D. 43,560 acres

    A. A section of land, under the government survey system, is one square mile, or 640 acres.

A survey has been completed, and stakes have been placed marking off the property. The survey can be used to:

A. construct fences and driveways
B. measure soil stability
C. perform a percolation test
D. verify known liens

    A. A survey may be used to determine where exactly a property's boundary lines fall. This would be an important consideration in the placement of fences and driveways, to avoid encroaching on a neighbor's property.

Meridians and base lines relate to the:

A. lot and block method
B. metes and bounds method
C. recorded map method
D. rectangular survey method

    D. The rectangular survey system, also known as the government survey system, divides the land into a series of grids, identified by meridians and base lines.

Chapter Quiz

1. A buyer and seller were inspecting a property, prior to the buyer making an offer. The property was occupied by a tenant at the time of inspection. The seller told the buyer that the garden furniture would be included in the sale. However, the buyer discovers upon possession that the garden furniture belonged to the tenant, not the seller. Is the buyer entitled to the garden furniture?

   A. No, because the garden furniture was the tenant's real property
   B. No, because the seller didn't have the right to include the tenant's personal property in the deal
   C. Yes, because garden furniture is a fixture included with the sale of real property
   D. Yes, because the buyer relied on the seller's representation

2. A property owner has riparian rights. This suggests that her property is next to:

   A. a river or stream
   B. a road or street
   C. agricultural property
   D. oil or mineral deposits

3. You have just purchased a prime parcel of oceanfront property. You probably have what type of water rights?

   A. Reliction rights
   B. Riparian rights
   C. Littoral rights
   D. Avulsion rights

4. A commercial tenant leases retail space for $1,500 per month. A few months later, the owner of the complex adds new counters, and increases the rent to $1,750 per month. At the end of the lease term, the commercial tenant:

   A. cannot take the counters with her, because the owner installed them
   B. can take the counters with her if she reimburses the owner for the fair market value of the counter
   C. can take the counters with her if she reimburses the owner for any damage caused by removal
   D. can take the counters with her without any charge

5. Mineral rights associated with real property are always:

   A. conveyed along with the surface rights to the property
   B. separable and divisible
   C. sold separately from the property
   D. an interest in personal property

6. Unless otherwise stated, a property buyer should receive:

   A. air rights and mineral rights
   B. air rights and surface rights
   C. mineral rights and subsurface rights
   D. air rights, surface rights, and subsurface rights

7. A tenant farmer had a heart attack, and decided to terminate his lease and retire. However, his last crop was still growing in the field and he wanted the right to come back and harvest it when it was ripe. The crops are considered to be:

   A. emblements, which belong to the tenant farmer
   B. fixtures, which belong to the property owner
   C. real property, which belongs to the property owner
   D. trade fixtures, which belong to the farmer

8. Which of the following is an example of an emblement?

   A. An orange grove
   B. An apple orchard
   C. A field of corn
   D. A vineyard

9. Josephine, a real estate agent, is showing a house to a buyer. The buyer loves the house, but wants certain appliances and pieces of furniture to stay with the house. Josephine should advise the buyer:

   A. to make an offer that includes the appliances and furniture (which would be reflected in a higher purchase price)
   B. that the furniture and appliances are fixtures and will automatically transfer to the buyer along with the house
   C. that it's illegal to say anything about the appliances and furniture in an offer for real property
   D. to refuse to make an offer unless the seller agrees to throw in the appliances and furniture for free

10. Chin, a home seller, is talking to his real estate agent. He mentions that he rents the backup generator; it doesn't belong to him. The generator would be considered:

    A. a fixture
    B. a natural attachment
    C. a trade fixture
    D. personal property

11. A test that a court might apply to determine whether an item is a fixture or personal property is:

    A. age
    B. expense
    C. size
    D. use

12. If a court were deciding what type of property house keys were, it would likely decide that they were:

    A. personal property, because they are so small and light
    B. real property, because all sales contracts stipulate that they transfer to the buyer
    C. personal property, because they are not attached to the property in a permanent way
    D. real property, because they are "adapted" to the real property

13. Which of the following is NOT a fixture test?

    A. Method of attachment
    B. Intent of the person who attached the item
    C. Size of the item
    D. Adaptation of the item

14. The owner of a small store leased a retail space and installed his own shelving by bolting it to the walls. At the end of his lease, he wanted to take the shelving with him to his new location. Which of the following is true?

    A. The shelves are fixtures, and must be removed by the tenant
    B. The shelves are fixtures, and must remain as part of the building
    C. The shelves are trade fixtures, and may be removed by the tenant
    D. The shelves are trade fixtures, and must remain as part of the building

15. A tenant has agreed to build out the space to meet the needs of her business. She is paying for all the expenses. Any "chattel fixtures" she adds to the property during this process belong to the:

    A. tenant, as long as she removes them from the property on or before the expiration of the lease, and she repairs any damage caused by their removal
    B. tenant, because she paid for them
    C. landlord when the lease expires, because they have been physically attached to the property
    D. landlord, as soon as they are added to the premises

16. The property description in a deed reads: "Starting at the old stone well, then going south 120 feet, west 400 feet, north 80 feet, and east 210 feet." This description is:

    A. invalid, because it doesn't return to the point of beginning
    B. invalid, because it uses a point of beginning that is man-made
    C. valid, because it returns to the point of beginning
    D. valid, because all descriptions must start with a man-made point of beginning

17. The best description of the boundary lines for a property located in a subdivision would be found on:

    A. a plat map
    B. the deed
    C. the mortgage
    D. the purchase and sale agreement

18. One side of a section (in a government survey) is how many feet long?

    A. 100
    B. 2,640
    C. 5,280
    D. 43,560

19. A parcel occupies the NW 1/4 of the SE 1/4, and the S 1/2 of the SW 1/4 of the NE 1/4 of Section 4. How many acres is this parcel?

    A. 40
    B. 60
    C. 80
    D. 100

20. A real estate agent takes a listing for a mobile home. He may do this if:

    A. the mobile home contains a minimum of 1,500 square feet
    B. he holds a real estate securities license
    C. the listing agreement is clearly identified as a personal property listing
    D. the listing includes the land on which the mobile home rests

Answer Key

1. **B.** Since the garden furniture belongs to the tenant, the seller cannot promise it to the buyer. The buyer is not entitled to receive the garden furniture, but the seller might be liable to the buyer for damages for the misrepresentation, if the buyer relied on the seller's promise.

2. **A.** Riparian rights allow property owners who have flowing water, such as a river or stream, next to or across their property to take reasonable amounts of water for use on the property.

3. **C.** Littoral rights attach to property that borders a stationary body of water, such as a lake or ocean.

4. **A.** A commercial tenant may take a trade fixture with her at the end of the lease. Note, however, that the counters were added by the owner, not the tenant, so they would not be considered a trade fixture.

5. **B.** Mineral rights may be sold separately from the land. However, they are appurtenant to the land and will be conveyed with the land unless there is an agreement otherwise.

6. **D.** Unless noted, a property buyer should receive all the normal appurtenances that go along with the land: air rights, surface rights, and subsurface rights.

7. **A.** The doctrine of emblements applies to crops planted by tenant farmers. If a tenancy is terminated through no fault of the tenant before crops are ready to harvest, the tenant may re-enter the land and harvest the first crop after the tenancy ends.

8. **C.** Emblements are crops that are produced annually by the labor of the cultivator. Fruit trees and vineyards don't require planting every year, but crops such as corn and wheat do.

9. **A.** The buyer and seller can agree in the purchase and sale agreement that certain items of personal property will be included in the sale. Because the furniture is personal property, though, a separate document in addition to the deed, known as a bill of sale, will be necessary to transfer the personal property.

10. **D.** The generator is the personal property of the company that owns it. While it might remain on the property after possession of the property changes hands, it still belongs to the company and they could reclaim it according to the terms of their contract.

11. **D.** A court might inquire into the item's use, for instance, to decide whether it is specifically adapted to the property, or what the intention of the annexor was. Age, cost, and size of the item are not at issue.

12. **D.** Adaptation to the property is one of the fixture tests, and house keys would fit into this category of adaptation.

13. **C.** The size of the item is irrelevant to whether it is a fixture.

14. C. Items installed by a commercial tenant involved in a trade or business are a special category of fixtures, known as trade fixtures. The tenant may remove trade fixtures, even if permanently attached to the property, as long as the property is restored to its original condition (or the landlord is compensated for any damage).

15. A. Trade fixtures belong to the tenant and they may be removed when the lease terminates, but the property must be left in good repair.

16. A. The property description is invalid, because it does not return to the point of beginning. A property description may be based on a man-made object as its point of beginning (although it doesn't have to be), but it must enclose the property's full perimeter.

17. A. Subdivided property is usually described by reference to a map of the subdivision and its individual lots, prepared by a surveyor. This is known as a plat map.

18. C. A section is one square mile, with each side being one mile long. One mile equals 5,280 feet.

19. B. A section is 640 acres, so a quarter-section is 160 acres (640 ÷ 4 = 160) and a quarter-quarter section, like the NW 1/4 of the SE 1/4, is 40 acres (160 ÷ 4 = 40). Half of a quarter-quarter section, like the S 1/2 of the SW 1/4 of the NE 1/4, is 20 acres (40 ÷ 2 = 20). Add the two parts together to find the parcel is 60 acres (40 + 20 = 60).

20. D. If the listing includes the sale, exchange, or lease of the land on which the mobile home sits, the real estate agent is not required to have any additional kind of license. The real estate agent would be able to list a mobile home where the listing does not include the sale, exchange, or lease of the land if the agent also held a mobile home dealer's license.

Chapter 2
Estates in Land and Methods of Holding Title

I. **Estates** – The word *estate* refers to an interest in land that is or may become possessory. In other words, someone has now, or may have in the future, the absolute and exclusive right to possess the property. The right to possess the property is the right to occupy and use it. Estates fall into two categories: *freehold estates* and *less-than-freehold estates*.

"Estate" refers to the degree of interest a person has in land.

A. **Freehold Estates** – A freehold estate is an interest in real property with an indeterminable (not fixed or certain) duration. The holder of such an estate is usually called an owner. There are two types of freehold estates: fee simple estates and life estates.

1. **Fee simple estates** – The fee simple estate is also called a *fee estate*. It is the greatest estate in land. It is of potentially infinite duration and represents the whole "bundle of rights." A fee simple estate may still be subject to encumbrances, such as a mortgage.

A fee simple is also referred to as a fee simple absolute or a fee.

a. **Inheritable and transferable** – A fee simple is sometimes called an *estate of inheritance*. It can be owned forever by the titleholder and his heirs. A fee simple estate is either *absolute* or *qualified*.

i. **Fee simple absolute** – When a grantee receives title in fee simple, it is assumed to be a *fee simple absolute* estate (unconditional).

ii. **Qualified fee simple** – If the deed is conveyed on the condition that the property be used only as a church, a failure to use it as a church could result in a reversion of title to the grantor. This is also known as a *possibility of reverter*, or *right of re-entry*. Such an estate may also be known as a *qualified fee* or *defeasible fee*.

A qualified fee estate is a legal interest in land that is subject to one or more limitations placed on the estate by the grantor (former owner).

A qualified fee simple is also called a qualified fee or a defeasible fee.

2. **Life estates** – An *estate for life* is a freehold estate because it is an ownership interest of uncertain duration. However, the estate is limited to the lifetime of a specified person or persons; it is not a perpetual estate, nor an estate of inheritance.

A life estate is a freehold estate, since it is a possessory estate of indefinite duration. But it is not an estate of inheritance.

If the measuring life is someone other than the life tenant, the life estate is called a life estate *pur autre vie*.

If a life tenant dies before the measuring life does, the estate will pass to the life tenant's heirs until the end of the measuring life.

a. **Life tenant** – The person who owns the property is called the *life tenant*.

b. **Measuring life** – The person whose lifetime is used to measure the length of the life estate is called the *measuring life*. This is often the same person as the life tenant (she will own it for her lifetime), but it doesn't have to be. A grantor may deliver title to "Smith for Olson's lifetime."

c. **When the measuring life ends** – When the person whose life is the measure of the estate dies, title will pass to someone else. That other person is said to have an estate in reversion or an estate in remainder.

    i. **Estate in reversion** – If the deed that delivered title to the life tenant states that title shall revert to the grantor on the death of the measuring life, then while the measuring life is alive, the grantor has a future possessory estate called an *estate in reversion*.

    ii. **Estate in remainder** – If the deed states that title shall pass to a third party on the death of the measuring life, that third party has a future possessory estate called an *estate in remainder*. Upon the death of the measuring life, the remainderman receives a fee simple interest in the property.

d. **Sale or lease** – A life tenant may sell or lease his interest in the property, but the life tenant may sell or lease only the interest that he has. For instance, a lease given by a life tenant will terminate upon the end of the measuring life; the property's new owner does not have to honor the lease.

Waste is the improper use or abuse of real property by a person in possession who holds less than a fee simple interest, such as a life tenant.

e. **Waste** – A life tenant cannot commit *waste*. This means the life tenant must not engage in acts that permanently damage the property and harm the interests of the reversionary or remainder estate.

Sample questions

Which of the following is true regarding an estate in land?

A. A certificate of occupancy must be issued to the estate owner
B. A patent must be issued by the government to the estate owner
C. A valid deed must be delivered to the estate owner
D. An interest in land must be conveyed that is possessory or may become possessory in the future

    D. An estate is possessory, either now or in the future.

A right held by one or more persons to use and possess property to the exclusion of others is a/an:

A. covenant
B. easement
C. fee simple estate
D. right of equity

    C. An estate is an interest in land that is or may become possessory. A fee simple estate specifically is a freehold estate of potentially infinite duration. (An easement allows the use of property, but is not a possessory right.)

Of the following, which is the best definition of a fee simple estate?

A. Title and ownership without limitations
B. An estate for years
C. A leasehold interest in property that is supported by consideration
D. The greatest interest one can own in land

    D. A fee simple estate is the highest and most complete form of land ownership. A fee simple estate may still be subject to other limitations, like liens or encumbrances.

A life estate is:

A. conveyed by one party to another party for the duration of that second person's life
B. created by homestead law
C. created by holographic will
D. subject to a condition subsequent

    A. A life estate is an ownership interest that lasts as long as the measuring life is alive.

Which of the following can a conventional life tenant do?

A. Sell, lease, or mortgage the life estate
B. Devise the life estate to his children
C. Deliberately fail to pay the property taxes when they come due
D. Let the property fall into disrepair (commit waste)

    A. A life tenant can do many things with his property interest, such as lease it, sell it, or mortgage it, but whatever he does has no legal effect beyond his death. He cannot commit waste (destroy, damage, or materially alter the property), or expose the property to the risk of foreclosure.

Pam gave a life estate to her aunt, naming her cousin Sylvia as the remainderman. Almost immediately Pam's aunt sold the property to her neighbor, Fred. What is the result of the sale to Fred?

A. The sale is valid only as long as Pam's aunt is alive
B. The sale is valid only as long as Sylvia is alive
C. The sale is valid only as long as Fred is alive
D. The sale is valid only as long as Pam is alive

    A. In this case, Pam's aunt is the measuring life (since no other measuring life is mentioned). The sale would be valid only for as long as the aunt is alive.

The landlord's (lessor's) interest is called a leased fee estate. The tenant's (lessee's) interest is called a leasehold estate.

A lease is both a contract and a transfer of an interest in property.

Even though a lease concerns real property, the lease itself is considered personal property.

No notice is required to terminate an estate for years.

Periodic tenancies may be created by express agreement, but they are often created by implication. For example, at the end of a 12-month estate for years, the tenant may continue to make monthly payments, which the landlord accepts.

An estate at will terminates on the death of either the landlord or the tenant.

Even though the tenant at sufferance is wrongfully in possession of the property, she is not a trespasser because she originally entered the land with the landlord's permission.

B. Less-than-Freehold Estates (Leasehold Estates) – Less-than-freehold estates are more commonly called *leasehold estates*. There are two parties to a lease: the *lessor* (or *landlord*) and the *lessee* (or *tenant*). The tenant receives a *leasehold estate*, while the landlord retains an interest called a *leased fee estate*.

1. **Nature of lease.** A lease is both a contract and a transfer of an interest in real property. But even though a lease concerns real property, the lease itself is classified as personal property.

2. **Types of leasehold estates.** There are four types of leasehold estates:

   a. **Estate for years** – An *estate for years* (or *term tenancy*) is a tenancy for a fixed period of time. Thus, the name "estate for years" is misleading; a one-week lease is an estate for years. It must be formed through an express agreement. The lease terminates automatically upon the end of the term, or else upon mutual consent by the parties (called *surrender*).

   b. **Periodic tenancy** – Sometimes called a *periodic estate*, this type of lease has no definite termination date. It is for a specific period, such as a month, and will continue from month-to-month until one party or the other gives notice to terminate. Failure to give proper notice of termination results in the automatic extension of the lease for an additional period.

   c. **Estate at will** – An *estate at will* often arises when a lease has expired and the parties are in the process of negotiating the terms of a new lease. They have no agreement, but the tenant remains in possession at the will of the landlord. The estate terminates when either party gives notice of termination, or on the death of either the landlord or tenant.

   d. **Tenancy at sufferance** – A *tenancy at sufferance* is the lowest form of estate. In fact, though it's sometimes called an "estate at sufferance," it isn't an estate at all. A tenant at sufferance (or *holdover tenant*) is one who comes into possession of land lawfully, but who holds over after the lease ends, at the "sufferance" of the landlord.

Sample questions

Raul manages a commercial property, overseeing day-to-day operations and maintenance. Raul is the agent of the building's:

A. lessee
B. lessor
C. lessor and lessee
D. vendor

> B. *In a leasehold, the lessor is the owner of the property, and the landlord. A property manager represents the owner and thus the lessor.*

Martinique is renting an apartment, and she has an estate for years. This means:

A. she has a freehold estate
B. her lease has a definite beginning and ending date
C. she can sublet the apartment for up to one year
D. her lease term is at least one year

> B. *An estate for years has a definite beginning and ending date; it does not have to last for one or more years.*

The CEO of a large bank rented a stadium for a five-day company meeting. The rental started on August 1 and ended on August 5. This is a/an:

A. periodic estate
B. estate from year to year
C. estate for years
D. recurring tenancy

> C. *An estate for years both begins and ends on a definite date.*

A tenant has an automatic renewal clause in his lease. He probably has a/an:

A. defeasible estate
B. periodic tenancy
C. estate for years
D. possibility of reverter

> B. *Periodic tenancies generally contain automatic renewal clauses.*

A tenancy at will:

A. is created by a testator under the terms of a will
B. expires on a certain date
C. is created when a life tenant dies
D. is created with the consent of the landlord

> D. *A tenancy at will depends on the consent of the property owner.*

Most corporations hold title to real property in severalty.

II. Methods of Holding Title – Title to real property may be held by one person, known as ownership in *severalty*; or it may be held by two or more persons at the same time, called *concurrent ownership*.

A. Ownership in Severalty – When one person (or a corporation or a city) holds title to property individually, the property is owned in *severalty*. The term is derived from the word "sever," which means to keep separate or apart.

B. Concurrent Ownership – Concurrent ownership exists when two or more people own the property at the same time. There are three forms of concurrent ownership in Washington, each with its own distinctive legal characteristics.

Each co-tenant is entitled to the undivided possession of the property, and cannot be excluded from or confined to a specific portion of the property.

If the method of holding title is not specified in the deed, it is presumed to be a tenancy in common.

Unlike some other types of co-ownership, when a tenant in common dies, her interest passes to her heirs, or to beneficiaries named in her will, not to the surviving co-tenants.

A tenant in common may will his share in the property to his co-owners.

1. **Tenancy in common** – In a *tenancy in common*, two or more individuals each have an undivided interest in a single piece of property. This means that each tenant in common has a right to share possession of the whole property (as opposed to a right to possess only a specified part of it). This is referred to as *unity of possession*. If the method of taking title is not specified in a deed, tenancy in common is assumed.

   a. **Unequal interests** – Tenants in common can have equal or unequal interests. But no matter how small the interest of a tenant in common is, he is still entitled to share possession of the whole property.

   b. **Death of a tenant in common** – A tenant in common may will her interest to someone besides the other tenant(s) in common (and if she dies without a will, the interest passes to her heirs). A tenancy in common may also be terminated through a *partition* suit.

Joint tenancy is an interest in real estate that is owned by two or more natural persons with rights of survivorship. There is only one title and it is equally shared by all of the joint tenants.

On the death of a joint tenant, the surviving joint tenant holds the property free from the debts of the deceased joint tenant.

2. **Joint tenancy** – In a *joint tenancy*, two or more individuals are joint and equal owners of the property. The key feature that distinguishes joint tenancy from tenancy in common is the *right of survivorship*: on the death of one of the joint tenants, his interest automatically passes to the other joint tenant(s). The survivors take title free from the claims of the deceased tenant's creditors and from any liens against his interest. The disadvantage is that a joint tenant cannot will his interest in the property.

   a. **Creating a joint tenancy** – To create a joint tenancy the four unities of title must exist. These unities are:

      i. **Unity of interest** – The interests of the joint tenants must be equal;

      ii. **Unity of title** – The joint tenants must have received their title in the same document (usually a deed);

      iii. **Unity of time** – The joint tenants must have received their interests at the same time; and

      iv. **Unity of possession** – Like tenants in common, joint tenants must have an equal right of possession.

  b. **Termination of joint tenancy** – A joint tenancy terminates automatically if any of the four unities is destroyed. A joint tenant may convey her interest to someone else, but this terminates the joint tenancy with respect to the ownership of the conveying joint tenant.

      i. **Mortgaging an interest** – Executing a mortgage against a joint tenant's interest does not break the unity of title. The joint tenancy would still be valid.

3. **Community property** – In a community property state such as Washington, all the property owned by a married couple is classified as either (a) the *separate property* of one spouse, or (b) the *community property* of both spouses. Each spouse has an undivided one-half interest in the community property.

  a. **Separate property** – A spouse's separate property is the property he or she acquires before the marriage, plus property acquired during marriage by inheritance, will, or gift.

  b. **Community property** – All other property that either spouse acquires during the marriage is community property. For this reason, it is advisable to have both spouses sign a deed when conveying real property, even if they consider it separate property, in order to release any possible community interest in the land.

4. **Tenancy by the entireties** – In some states that do not have community property laws, married couples may hold title to property as *tenants by the entireties*. This is similar to joint tenancy, but is restricted to married couples. Tenants by the entireties have survivorship rights, but do not have the right of partition.

A joint tenant's sale of her interest does not necessarily defeat a joint tenancy.

If J, T, and F own property as joint tenants and J sells her interest to Q, Q would become a tenant in common with T and F, but T and F would remain joint tenants with survivorship rights as to each other.

Sample questions

Which of the following would characterize a tenancy in common?

A. Only available to married persons
B. Requirement of equal interests
C. Right of survivorship
D. Tenants can will a partial interest in the property

> D. Unlike a joint tenant, a tenant in common can deed or will his share of the property to someone else. There is no right of survivorship and no requirement of equal interests in a tenancy in common.

Harry, Taylor, and Warren own property as joint tenants. Harry sells his interest to Davis. The property is now owned by:

A. Taylor, Warren, and Davis, as joint tenants
B. Warren and Davis as joint tenants, and Taylor as a tenant in common with them
C. Taylor and Warren as joint tenants, and Davis as a tenant in common with them
D. Taylor, Warren, and Davis, as tenants in common

> C. When Harry sold his interest to Davis, he broke the joint tenancy as to his interest only. Taylor and Warren are still joint tenants, and Davis—the new owner—is a tenant in common.

Jesse, Kim, and Diane own a home together as joint tenants. If Jesse dies, her property interest:

A. will be inherited by her children according to the provisions of her will
B. must be bequeathed to Kim and Diane in her will
C. will be automatically devised to her heirs
D. will be automatically transferred (conveyed) to Kim and Diane

> D. Joint tenancy includes the right of survivorship, which means that upon the death of one joint tenant, title passes immediately to the remaining joint tenant(s). The property interest is not subject to probate; the transfer of title is automatic.

Which of the following is true regarding community property?

A. Property paid for during marriage with the earnings of one spouse is generally separate property
B. Property a spouse receives as a gift during marriage is usually community property
C. All property owned by a married person is community property
D. Property accumulated prior to marriage is generally separate property

> D. Property accumulated before someone is married is usually her separate property.

Regarding a tenancy by the entirety:

A. if the co-owners can't agree on the use of the property, it must be partitioned
B. the Torrens system is used to record title to the property
C. when one co-tenant dies, his interest in the property automatically passes to his heirs
D. the owners must be a married couple

> D. *A tenancy by the entireties is a form of spousal ownership used in states that do not have community property.*

C. **Forms of Business Ownership** – Real property may also be owned by a business entity. Business entities may be organized as: *general partnerships*, *limited partnerships*, *corporations*, *limited liability companies*, *joint ventures*, and *real estate investment trusts*. Any of these entities may be referred to as a **syndicate**: a group of individuals who pool their resources to carry out an enterprise.

1. **General partnerships** – A general partnership is formed by contract. The partnership agreement can be oral, but it's better to have it in writing. Each partner shares equally in the partnership's profits and in management responsibilities, and can be held personally liable for the debts of the partnership.

   > General partnership agreements need not be in writing.

   a. **Taxation** – The partnership itself is not taxed, but each partner's earnings are taxed individually.

   b. **Property ownership** – Each partner has an equal right to possess and use partnership property for partnership purposes. The partnership entity holds title to partnership property, and a partner has no transferable interest in the property.

2. **Limited partnerships** – A limited partnership is also formed by contract, but the contract must be in writing. A limited partnership has at least one general partner and one limited partner.

   > Limited partnership agreements must be in writing.

   a. **General partners** – Each general partner has unlimited liability for the partnership's debts and obligations.

   b. **Limited partners** – By contrast, each limited partner has limited liability (cannot be held liable for partnership debts).

3. **Corporations** – Corporations are owned by shareholders (stockholders). They have the following characteristics:

   a. **Artificial persons** – Corporations are *artificial persons* and can own property, taking title in severalty.

   > A corporation is an artificial person.

Security: an ownership interest representing an investment over which the investor has no managerial control.

State laws regulating the sale of securities are often called "blue sky laws."

A licensed securities broker, not a real estate broker, handles transactions involving securities.

LLC interests may also be considered securities.

REITs combine the flow-through tax advantages of a partnership with some of the attributes of a corporation, such as limited liability for the investors.

b. **Perpetual existence** – In theory, a corporation cannot die; it lives forever. Because of this, it cannot take title in joint tenancy.

c. **Debts** – Just like a natural person, a corporation can incur debts and is fully responsible for those debts. An individual shareholder's liability is limited to the value of the stock owned.

d. **Double taxation** – Corporations are subject to *double taxation*, which means any corporate profits are taxed before dividends are distributed to shareholders. When the dividends are distributed, they are taxed as ordinary income to the shareholders.

e. **Securities** – Shares in a corporation are *securities*. A security is an ownership interest that represents only an investment in an enterprise, without managerial control over it. Securities are regulated by the federal government through the Securities and Exchange Commission.

f. **Management** – Stockholders elect a corporation's board of directors. The board, in turn, appoints and supervises the officers of the corporation, who are responsible for day-to-day operations.

4. **Limited liability company** – A limited liability company (LLC) insulates all of its co-owners (called *members*) from liability for the company's debts.

5. **Joint venture** – A joint venture is similar to a partnership, but created only temporarily, such as for a particular transaction.

6. **Real estate investment trusts (REITs)** – In a real estate investment trust (a REIT), one or more *trustees* manage real property for the benefit of its investors, the *beneficiaries*. REITs must have a minimum of 100 investors and are subject to federal securities laws.

   a. **Tax advantages** – REITs are not subject to double taxation.

   b. **Limited liability** – Beneficiaries are shielded from liability for the debts of the REIT. Liability is limited to the amount of their investment.

Sample questions

Chin, Harrison, Juarez, and Regalio decided to pool their money in order to make some investments. This is known as:

A. a limited partnership
B. hypothecation
C. a long-term portfolio
D. syndication

> D.   Syndication is the process of pooling resources for investment purposes.

How would a limited partner's role in a limited partnership be best described?

A. Ability to appoint corporate officers
B. Anonymity but subject to double taxation
C. Authority over decisionmaking process and personal liability for company debts
D. Limited personal liability

> D.   The main advantage of the limited partnership arrangement, for a limited partner, is that liability for the entity's debts is limited.

Patricia establishes a real estate venture, and sells limited partnerships in it. All purchasers are residents of the same state where Patricia is licensed and where the partnership will operate. This offering will be regulated under:

A. blue sky laws
B. the federal Securities and Exchange Commission
C. IRS laws
D. fair-weather laws

> A.   A sale of securities that does not fall under federal jurisdiction would be regulated under state laws concerning sales of securities, which are often known as "blue sky laws."

Max owned an apple orchard, which he decided to divide into smaller parcels and sell. Once all of the parcels had been sold, though, Max decided he would enter into agreements with the buyers, in which he would continue harvesting apples on the properties and distribute proceeds from the income to the buyers. Concerning the second set of transactions, Max has sold:

A. real estate, because this concerns agricultural land
B. real estate, because the land had been subdivided prior to selling the investments
C. securities, because the apples are considered personal property
D. securities, because the buyers are investors who expect to make a profit off their investment in Max's business

> D.   The property buyers have entered into agreements that represent an ownership interest in an enterprise, without having day-to-day managerial control over it. These would be considered securities.

D. Condominiums and Cooperatives – *Condominiums* and *cooperatives* are properties that combine elements of both individual ownership and co-ownership.

1. **Condominiums** – Someone who buys a unit in a condominium receives a deed and owns a fee simple interest in the airspace inside the unit in severalty, but shares ownership of the *common elements* with other owners as tenants in common. Other types of properties that involve this same combination of sole and co-ownership include *townhouses* and *timeshares*.

   a. **Common elements** – Also called *common areas*, common elements are aspects of the condominium property that all of the unit owners have the right to use, such as the driveways or the elevators. *Limited common elements*, such as a unit's balcony or an assigned parking space, are owned in common, even though they are under the control of only one unit. A limited common element is appurtenant to ownership of the unit in question.

   b. **Each unit owner obtains her own financing** – She also purchases her own title insurance policy and receives and pays a separate property tax bill based on the value of her interest in the condominium. Unpaid taxes will result in a lien against only the unit, not the entire condominium project.

   c. **Governing board** – An elected governing board usually manages the condominium and establishes its bylaws. The owner's rights are defined in the *condominium declaration* (or *master deed*).

   d. **Conversion** – The process of changing apartments into condominiums, known as *conversion*, is regulated by state law.

2. **Cooperatives** – In a cooperative, ownership of the entire project is vested in a single entity, which is usually a corporation.

   a. **Residents own shares** – Residents of the cooperative own shares in the corporation proportionate to their own interests. They do not own the real estate itself. Residents do not pay property taxes or title insurance on their units.

   b. **Leasehold estate** – Residents are tenants with long-term proprietary leases on their units. They have *leasehold* estates.

Common elements typically include the land, exterior walls, elevators, swimming pools, parking lots, roof, clubhouses, and other shared amenities on the property.

A limited common element is appurtenant to a particular unit even though it is physically outside the unit.

The condominium declaration must be recorded, together with a copy of the bylaws governing the operation of the property, a survey map of the land, and a set of plans of the buildings.

   c.   **Tenants pay rent** – The rents paid to the corporation are a pro-rata share of the mortgage, taxes, operating expenses, and other debts for the whole property. If one tenant fails to pay rent, the other tenants must cover the unpaid rent to avoid having the mortgage on the entire project foreclosed on.

3.   **Timeshares** – A timeshare, also known as *interval ownership*, allows an owner to purchase a fractional interest in a property that allows her to use the property for a designated period each year.

> Persons buying into a cooperative sign a subscription agreement for stock, and in return they receive a proprietary lease. In the subscription agreement, a buyer agrees to pay his share of the cooperative's operating expenses.

Sample questions

Which of the following does not apply to condominium ownership?

A. Each unit owner has a proprietary lease on his unit
B. Each unit owner has an undivided interest in the common areas of the condominium project
C. Before the first unit can be sold, a declaration must be filed with the state
D. Each unit owner makes a separate mortgage payment and receives a separate tax statement

> A.   *Cooperative owners, rather than condominium owners, have proprietary leases on their units.*

An assigned parking space in a lot at a condominium development would be considered a/an:

A. common element
B. easement
C. limited common element
D. private restriction

> C.   *A feature outside of the airspace of a condominium unit, but that is reserved for the owner of a particular unit, is considered a limited common element.*

Jeff owns a new condominium. Which of the following statements best describes the nature of his ownership?

A. Jeff owns an undivided interest in the entire condominium project
B. Jeff owns the airspace in his unit in severalty and holds a tenancy in common in the common areas
C. Jeff has a separate interest in the common areas and an undivided interest in the unit
D. Jeff's ownership is held as a life estate

> B.   *A condominium owner owns the airspace separately, and has an undivided interest in the common areas with the other unit owners.*

Donald bought a condominium unit. Donald's interest in the unit would be a:

A. fee simple interest
B. leasehold interest
C. life estate
D. joint tenancy with other unit owners

> A. *Under the condominium form of ownership, an individual unit owner has a fee simple estate, just as she would with a single-family home.*

Sylvia owns some residential property. Her maintenance fee includes a proportionate share of the mortgage payment, property taxes, insurance, and maintenance expenses. She probably owns a:

A. condominium
B. cooperative
C. single-family home
D. loft

> B. *Unlike condo owners, each co-op owner pays a proportionate share of the mortgage payment, taxes, etc. She would not have an individual mortgage payment on her unit.*

The developer of a condominium project generally files:

A. a construction lien
B. a certificate of resale
C. a declaration
D. CC&Rs

> C. *A condominium developer files a declaration with the state.*

Chapter Quiz

1. An example of a freehold inheritable estate is a/an:
   A. life estate (not pur autre vie)
   B. leasehold estate
   C. estate at will
   D. fee simple defeasible estate

2. A real estate agent lists Harold's home, which he owns as a life estate. Harold's children hold the remainder interest. Which of the following is true?
   A. Anyone who buys Harold's life estate receives only the interest held by Harold
   B. Harold's children need to sign the listing agreement
   C. The buyer will automatically receive a fee simple absolute interest
   D. Since a life estate cannot be sold, the listing is invalid

3. Teresa gives her little brother, Mark, a life estate pur autre vie. Which of the following is true?
   A. Teresa is the life tenant
   B. Mark is both the life tenant and the measuring life
   C. Mark is the life tenant, but the measuring life is someone else
   D. Mark will have title to the property for as long as he lives

4. Jack receives a life estate in a property, for the life of Larry. When Larry dies, the property passes to Mary, rather than the grantor or the grantor's heirs. This is a:
   A. life estate pur autre vie, in remainder
   B. life estate pur autre vie, in reversion
   C. standard life estate, in remainder
   D. standard life estate, in reversion

5. Ben receives a life estate in a property, with his nephew Will designated as the remainderman. When Ben dies, what kind of interest does Will receive?
   A. Fee simple estate
   B. Life estate
   C. Remainder interest
   D. Reversionary interest

6. Maria has a lease that begins on June 1 and ends on December 1 of that same year. Maria has a:
   A. periodic estate
   B. tenancy at will
   C. term tenancy
   D. joint tenancy

7. A three-year lease ends. The tenant is allowed by the landlord to stay on and to continue to pay rent, on a month-to-month basis. This would be a/an:
   A. estate for years
   B. periodic tenancy
   C. term tenancy
   D. tenancy at sufferance

8. A corporation takes title to real property through a/an:
   A. estate in severalty
   B. joint tenancy
   C. tenancy at will
   D. A corporation may not take title

9. Five people buy an investment property. They take title so that they each have equal ownership shares, and so that if one of them dies, his share will pass to his heirs. How did they take title?
   A. Community property
   B. Joint tenancy
   C. Tenancy in common
   D. Term tenancy

10. A limited partnership is a preferable method of owning real estate investment properties because:
   A. all owners share equal control over the direction of the investment
   B. it allows persons with less capital to invest to still participate in real estate projects
   C. ownership is divided among the shareholders
   D. taxation is similar to that of a corporation

11. Mark and Kim's two-year lease on their apartment expires. Unhappy that the couple doesn't plan to renew the lease, the property manager charges them one month's rent for failure to give notice. If the lease is silent regarding this issue, in this case:

    A. no notice is required and no additional fee must be paid

    B. Mark and Kim owe one month's additional rent

    C. Mark and Kim owe one month's additional rent plus a nonrenewal fee

    D. Mark and Kim will lose the full amount of their security deposit

12. Two cousins want to buy a house together and arrange it so that if one dies, the other will receive full ownership of the property. They will probably take title to the property as:

    A. community property

    B. joint tenancy

    C. tenancy by the entireties

    D. tenancy in common

13. Erin entered into a lease that begins on February 1, and ends on January 31 three years later. This lease is a/an:

    A. estate for years

    B. tenancy at sufferance

    C. periodic tenancy

    D. estate from year to year

14. Jill and Julie are joint tenants. Jill sells her interest in the property to Sam. Julie and Sam:

    A. are automatically joint tenants

    B. do not own the property together, because the sale of property by a joint tenant is void

    C. are tenants in common

    D. are tenants in severalty

15. A tenancy in which the tenant is in possession with the permission of the landlord, but there is no definite rental period or duration of possession, is called a/an:

    A. estate in remainder

    B. estate for years

    C. periodic estate

    D. estate at will

16. Property held in tenancy by the entirety:

    A. cannot be transferred through the right of survivorship

    B. can be physically divided, by either party selling his or her interest separately from the other owner

    C. is owned by a married couple

    D. can be partitioned

17. A store owner would like to sell common stock in her business (a chain of stores) to investors. She asks an inexperienced licensee for help. The licensee should:

    A. ask her managing broker which listing agreement to use

    B. disclose her licensed status on the stock certificates

    C. hire an attorney to draft the listing agreement

    D. refer the client to a securities dealer

18. A popular downtown condominium project has many common facilities, such as a swimming pool, tennis courts, a gym, and a spa. These common elements are likely to be owned by:

    A. the owners of the units which are located adjacent to the amenities

    B. a corporation in which the unit owners own stock

    C. the unit owners, as an undivided percentage interest

    D. the condominium developer

19. An investor would like to invest in real estate, but without being involved in management or subjecting himself to any personal liability. He should invest in a:

    A. general partnership

    B. joint venture

    C. limited partnership

    D. sole proprietorship

20. A broker would need to have a securities license to participate in:

    A. a sale of both real and personal property

    B. a sale of a commercial building that is showing a profit

    C. a transaction involving an investment contract

    D. listing a property owned by a corporation

Answer Key

1. D. The fee simple estate is the highest and most complete form of owner-ship, and it is inheritable and of potentially infinite duration. Generally, life estates aren't inheritable.

2. A. A purchaser wouldn't be buying a fee simple absolute interest in the prop-erty, but rather, only the life estate held by the seller. The property would pass to Harold's children at the end of the life estate's measuring life.

3. C. In a life estate pur autre vie ("for another life"), the measuring life is some-one other than the life tenant.

4. A. A life estate pur autre vie is based on a measuring life that's someone other than the life tenant. An estate in remainder is one that passes to a third party at the end of the measuring life, rather than reverting to the grantor or the grantor's heirs.

5. A. The interest that passes to a designated person upon the death of the life tenant (or other measuring life) is a fee simple estate.

6. C. A term tenancy, also known as an estate for years, is a tenancy for any fixed term. This is true even if the term is for less than one year.

7. B. A lease that has no fixed termination date, but lasts for a specific period and continues until one party gives the other notice of termination, is a periodic tenancy.

8. A. A corporation cannot take title in joint tenancy, because of its potentially perpetual existence. Corporate property is owned in severalty by the corporation itself.

9. C. If co-owners are not married and are able to will their property to their heirs (instead of having it pass through right of survivorship), they hold title as tenants in common.

10. B. A limited partnership is open to limited partners, who may invest smaller amounts than its general partners, and in return receive limited liability, which keeps them from becoming personally liable for the partnership's debts.

11. A. The tenants have an estate for years: a lease for a specific period of time. The lease is presumed to terminate at the end of the period, unless the parties act to renew it. No notice, or penalty associated with not giving notice, is necessary.

12. B. Joint tenancy includes the right of survivorship, so that one joint tenant would own the entire property if the other joint tenant died. Unmarried persons cannot own property as community property.

13. A. An estate for years begins on a certain date and ends on a certain date.

14. C. The only possible way for Jill and Sam to hold title is as tenants in com-mon, because joint tenants must take title in the same deed at the same time, and Jill and Sam didn't do that. Ownership in severalty is title held by one person.

15. D. This is the definition of an estate at will (tenancy at will).

16. C. Tenancy by the entirety property is owned by married couples, in non-community property states.

17. D. A real estate licensee would not be involved in a sale of stock in a company that does not also involve the sale of real property. A licensed securities dealer would need to be involved instead.

18. C. Each unit owner owns an individual interest in the common elements.

19. C. A limited partner in a limited partnership is not personally liable for the partnership's debts and obligations. He cannot have a voice in management operations, though.

20. C. A securities license would be necessary in a transaction that involves sale of securities, without also involving the sale or lease of real property.

Chapter 3
Transfer of Real Property

I. **Alienation** – The process of transferring ownership of real property from one party to another is called *alienation*. Alienation may be either *voluntary* or *involuntary*.

II. **Voluntary Alienation** – *Voluntary alienation* occurs when property is transferred by its owner.

    A. **Patent** – Title to land passes from the government to a private party by a document known as a *patent*.

    B. **Deed** – Transfer by *deed* is the most common form of voluntary alienation. The *grantor* (current owner) transfers title to the *grantee* (prospective owner) with a deed. The act is called a *conveyance of title*. The deed provides evidence of the change in title.

        1. **Types of deeds** – Common types of deeds include the *warranty deed*, the *special warranty deed*, and the *quitclaim deed*.

            a. **Warranty deed** – A warranty deed (or general warranty deed) is the most common type of deed in Washington. It offers the greatest protection for a real estate buyer. The grantor warrants against all defects in title that arose either before or during the grantor's period of ownership.

No type of deed is a guarantee of receiving clear title to a property.

General warranty deed: grantor promises to defend against all adverse claims.

                i. **Covenants** – The covenants in a general warranty deed are the *covenant of right to convey* (which states that the grantor has title to an interest in the property or authority to transfer title), *covenant of seisin* (good faith belief in one's ownership), *covenant against encumbrances*, *covenant of quiet enjoyment*, and *covenant of warranty*.

            b. **Special warranty deed** – A special warranty deed contains the same warranties made in a general warranty deed, but it limits the grantor's warranties to the period during which the grantor owned the property. The grantor makes no assurances about earlier defects. This type of deed is most commonly used by corporations, which may not have the authority to make greater warranties.

Special warranty deed: grantor warrants title only against defects that may have arisen during her period of ownership.

Quitclaim deed: conveys any interest in a property that the grantor has at the time the deed is executed, without warranties. Creates the least liability for the grantor.

The primary purpose of a quitclaim deed is to cure clouds on title. "Clouds" are possible or actual encumbrances (liens, easements, etc.) or other claims affecting title.

c. **Quitclaim deed** – A quitclaim deed contains no warranties of any sort and, unlike a warranty deed, it does not convey after-acquired title. Compared with other deeds, a quitclaim deed creates the least liability for the grantor.

   i. **Interest conveyed** – A quitclaim deed conveys only the interest the grantor has when the deed is delivered. It conveys nothing at all if the grantor has no interest at that time. If the grantor does have an interest in the property, the quitclaim will convey title like any other deed.

   ii. **Curing clouds on title** – The primary reason for using a quitclaim deed is to *cure clouds on title*. In this capacity, a quitclaim deed may also be known as a reformation deed.

Sample questions

To be GUARANTEED of receiving good title at closing, a buyer should obtain a/an:

A. installment contract
B. quitclaim deed
C. general warranty deed
D. None of the above

   D. *While a general warranty deed gives the greatest protection to a real estate buyer, no deed can provide a 100% guarantee of good title. The best way for a buyer to protect his interest in a piece of property is to obtain title insurance.*

A buyer accepts a general warranty deed from a seller, believing that the seller is the sole owner of the property. The buyer later finds out that the seller is only a co-owner. Has a covenant in the general warranty deed been violated?

A. No, the only covenant in a general warranty deed promises that the previous owner didn't encumber the property
B. No, the principle of caveat emptor controls matters concerning a deed
C. Yes, there is a covenant providing equitable title
D. Yes, there is a covenant providing marketable title

   D. *The general warranty deed contains a covenant of the right to convey, meaning that the grantor either has title to the interest or is an agent of the owner with the authority to transfer the interest.*

A home was purchased and then later resold by a third party relocation company. Which type of deed would the business use in order to make no assurances about defects that may have existed before it obtained title?
A. Special warranty deed
B. General warranty deed
C. Reconveyance deed
D. Quitclaim deed

> *A. A special warranty deed makes no assurances about title defects that may have existed before the grantor obtained title, only those that arose during the grantor's ownership.*

At closing, a buyer refused to accept the deed. Of the following, which is the most likely reason?
A. The purchase and sale agreement stated that the seller would provide a general warranty deed, but a special warranty deed was presented instead
B. The deed lacked proper consideration
C. The deed had not been signed by the grantee
D. The deed hadn't been recorded

> *A. A general warranty deed gives the greatest protection to a real estate buyer. A special warranty deed doesn't offer as much protection, so if the seller planned to give the buyer a special warranty deed, it should have been stated in the purchase and sale agreement.*

Mary gave Juan a quitclaim deed when she sold him her lot. Juan can be sure that:
A. all of Mary's interests in the property as of the date of the quitclaim deed belong to Juan
B. Mary owned the property free of all encumbrances
C. there are no nonfinancial liens against the property
D. Juan's ownership interest is partial; it is subject to some rights of Mary

> *A. A quitclaim deed conveys any interest in a property that the grantor has at the time the deed is executed, without warranties.*

To cure a defect or cloud on the title to a piece of property, the parties should:
A. bring an action to cancel the title
B. bring an action to record the title with the state
C. obtain quitclaim deeds from any interested parties
D. have the property surveyed

> *C. The usual reason to use a quitclaim deed is to cure clouds or defects on the title. A quitclaim deed conveys only the interest the grantor has when the deed is delivered, and nothing more.*

---

2. **Deed requirements** – The following requirements must be satisfied for a deed to be valid:

   a. **In writing** – Washington's *statute of frauds* requires certain contracts to be in writing, including a deed.

   b. **Identify the parties** – A deed must adequately identify both the grantor and the grantee.

   c. **Signed by competent grantor** – The statute of frauds requires a deed to be signed by the party making the transfer (the grantor). All property owners (grantors) must sign the deed; the signatures of both spouses are necessary to convey community property. The grantor must be legally competent at the time he signs the deed.

      i. **Attorney in fact** – A deed can be signed by a grantor's *attorney in fact*. The authority to do this is created by a document called a *power of attorney*, signed by the grantor, which specifically authorizes conveyance of the property. An attorney in fact may not deed a property to himself.

      ii. **Deeds from corporations** – Deeds from corporations are usually signed by an authorized officer.

   d. **Living grantee** – The grantee does not have to be competent for the deed to be valid. He must only be alive and identifiable. Thus, an infant can receive title, as can a person who has been declared legally incompetent.

Words of conveyance are also called the "granting clause."

   e. **Words of conveyance** – The deed must contain *words of conveyance*, such as "grant" or "convey." Otherwise, the document will contain insufficient language to transfer title.

Property must be adequately described. A legal description is prudent, but not essential.

   f. **Description of property** – The deed must contain an adequate description of the property being conveyed. A legal description of the property is not required by law, but should always be included.

3. **Acknowledgment, delivery, and acceptance** – A proper conveyance requires *acknowledgment*, *delivery*, and *acceptance*.

Acknowledgment: occurs when a person who has signed a document formally declares to an authorized official (usually a notary public) that he signed voluntarily. The notary public does NOT acknowledge a document (she simply witnesses it).

   a. **Acknowledgment** – Acknowledgment occurs when the grantor swears before a notary public or other official witness that her signature is genuine and voluntary.

      i. **Notary public** – The *notary public* cannot have an interest in the transfer (as either grantor or grantee).

      ii. **Unacknowledged deed is valid** – Technically, a deed is valid even if it is not acknowledged. But an unacknowledged deed cannot be recorded.

    b. **Delivery** – The transfer of title occurs when the deed is delivered to the grantee. Delivery must take place while the grantor is alive (with the exception of "transfer on death" deeds).

> A deed must be delivered during the grantor's lifetime.

    c. **Acceptance** – Delivery is not complete until the grantee has accepted the deed. The deed may be accepted by an agent of the grantee (such as an escrow agent).

> A valid delivery occurs if the grantor delivers the deed to the escrow agent before she dies, even if she dies before the escrow agent delivers the deed to the grantee.

4. **Nonessential terms** – The following terms are not essential to the validity of a deed, but may be included:

    a. **Habendum clause** – A deed generally includes a *habendum clause* (or "to have and to hold" clause), which states the nature of the interest the grantor is conveying (such as a fee simple or a life estate).

> The habendum clause describes the owner's exact interest in the property.

    b. **Exclusions and reservations clause** – An *exclusions and reservations* clause is a list of encumbrances (easements, private restrictions, liens) that the grantee will take title subject to.

    c. **Recital of consideration** – A deed does not need to state the exact amount of consideration exchanged.

    d. **Grantee's signature** – The grantee ordinarily does not sign the deed. The date of conveyance is usually included, although not required.

> Grantee does NOT sign the deed.

Sample questions

A married couple decides to move to Italy and the wife quickly secures a job in the new country, leaving the husband to sell their home in the United States before he joins her. To transfer title to the property to a buyer, the husband should:

A. sign his wife's name to the documents, after showing their marriage certificate to the escrow agent
B. sign on behalf of his wife, since they are married anyway
C. obtain a power of attorney from his wife so that he can sell the property
D. sign by himself; her signature isn't necessary if she's out of the country

> C. *A power of attorney specifically authorizes a person to act on another's behalf. The wife's signature is required to transfer title to the buyer; if she cannot be present to sign the documents herself, then the husband should obtain a power of attorney from her, authorizing him to sign the documents on her behalf.*

Of the following documents, which is the only one signed by the sellers alone?

A. First right of refusal
B. Warranty deed
C. Listing agreement
D. Purchase and sale agreement

> B. To be valid, a deed must be signed by a competent grantor. It isn't neces-sary for it to be signed by the grantee. The other options are all contracts that require the signatures of both parties.

The document that would enable a listing licensee to sign a sales contract in the owner's absence would be known as a:

A. covenant of right to convey
B. habendum clause
C. power of attorney
D. power of sale

> C. A power of attorney is a document that appoints a person to act on another person's behalf. The person who receives that authority is an at-torney in fact.

A deed must be acknowledged before it's recorded to:

A. guarantee good title to the grantee
B. validate the identity of the grantee
C. verify that the deed was not signed under duress
D. clear a cloud on the title

> C. A person acknowledges a document by formally declaring to an autho-rized official (usually a notary public) that he signed voluntarily. A grantor would acknowledge a deed in the presence of a notary public, who would then attest that the signature is voluntary and genuine.

The provision in a deed that describes the type of estate the grantee will hold, which is sometimes referred to as the to have and to hold clause, is also called:

A. the habendum clause
B. the alienation clause
C. the exclusions and reservations clause
D. the transfer clause

> A. The habendum clause is often referred to as the to have and to hold clause.

Marty is selling his home to Phil, but doesn't want the deed to state the actual consideration paid for the house. Which of the following is true?

A. The deed doesn't need to state the actual price, but the price listed must be within 10% of the sales price
B. The deed can state the consideration as $10.00
C. The actual price may not appear in the deed under any circumstances
D. The actual price of the house must appear in the deed

> B. Although not required, a recital of consideration in a deed is helpful because it indicates that the transfer is a sale and not a gift. However, the recital of consideration usually names some small amount to accomplish this, rather than the actual sales price.

C. **Wills** – A *will* is a person's stipulation regarding how her estate should be disposed of after she dies.

   1. **Requirements for a valid will** – The following three requirements must generally be met for a will to be valid:

      a. **Writing** – A will must be in writing.

      b. **Signature** – A will must be signed by the person making it.

      c. **Witnesses** – A will usually must be witnessed by two competent individuals.

   2. **Will terminology** – The following will-related terms appear frequently on the real estate licensing exam.

      a. **Testator:** one who makes a will.

      b. **Bequeath:** to transfer personal property by will.

      c. **Legatee:** a person who receives bequeathed property.

      d. **Devise:** to transfer real property by will.

      e. **Devisee:** a person who receives devised property.

      f. **Executor:** a person appointed by the testator to carry out the instructions in a will.

      g. **Intestate:** a person who dies without leaving a will dies intestate.

      h. **Administrator:** a person appointed by the court to carry out the instructions in a will when no executor has been named, or to manage and distribute an estate when no will exists.

      i. **Probate:** procedure to prove a will's validity.

      j. **Holographic will:** a will written entirely in the testator's handwriting, which may be valid even if not witnessed.

> Holographic will: an entirely handwritten will. Valid in some states even if not properly witnessed.

      k. **Nuncupative will:** an oral will spoken by a terminally ill person before two witnesses.

> Nuncupative will: an oral will declared by a terminally ill person before two witnesses.

III. **Involuntary Alienation** – *Involuntary alienation* refers to the ways real property can be conveyed by operation of law, without any voluntary action by the owner.

A. **Dedication** – When private property is given to the public, the process is called *dedication*. Dedication may be involuntary, as when a county requires a land developer to dedicate land within a new subdivision for public streets. It may also be a voluntary gift of private land for a public use.

> Dedication can be voluntary or involuntary.

A person who dies intestate has died without a will. His estate will be distributed to lawful heirs according to state laws called statutes of descent and distribution.

B. Intestate Succession – A person who dies without leaving a will is said to have died *intestate*. The law provides for the distribution of the property of someone who has died intestate by a process called *intestate succession*.

    1. Heirs – Persons who receive property by court order through the intestate succession process are called *heirs*. Heirs take title by *descent* and *distribution*, rather than by bequest or devise.

Escheat: property reverts to the state after a person dies and no heirs can be located, or when property has been abandoned by its owner.

C. Escheat – If the probate court cannot locate any heirs or beneficiaries, the property of the person dying intestate will pass back to the state according to the laws of *escheat*. Since the state is the ultimate source of title to property, it is also the ultimate heir when there are no lawful heirs or beneficiaries. Abandoned property also passes to the state through escheat.

D. Condemnation – The government has the constitutional power to take private property for public use, as long as it pays just compensation to the owner of the condemned property. The government's power to condemn (take) property is called the power of *eminent domain*.

    1. Requirements – For eminent domain to be exercised, the use must be a *public use* and the owner must receive *just compensation*.

    2. Who may exercise – The power of eminent domain may be exercised by any government entity, and also by some semi-public entities, such as utility companies.

    3. Inverse condemnation – If a property owner feels that her property has been taken or damaged by a public entity, the owner may file an *inverse condemnation* action to force the government to pay the fair market value of the property.

A quiet title action is a lawsuit to determine who has title to a piece of property, or to remove a cloud from the title.

E. Quiet Title – A *quiet title* action is a court procedure to remove a cloud on title when the cloud cannot be cleared amicably with a quitclaim deed. The court decides questions of property ownership, and the result is a binding determination of who owns what.

A partition action is the court-ordered division of a property among its co-owners—called a *judicial partition*.

F. Suit for Partition – A suit for *partition* is a court procedure for dividing co-owned property when the co-owners cannot agree on how to divide it.

G. Foreclosure Actions – Persons holding liens against real property may bring a *foreclosure* lawsuit to force the sale of the property if the debts secured by their liens are not paid.

H. Adverse Possession – *Adverse possession* is a process by which the possession and use of property can mature into title.

1. **Requirements** – In Washington there are five basic requirements for adverse possession:

    a. **Actual** – Actual possession means occupation and use of the property in a manner appropriate to the type of property. For example, the adverse possessor does not have to reside on the property unless it is a residential property.

    b. **Open and notorious** – Possession of the land must be conspicuous.

    c. **Hostile to the interests of the true owner** – Hostile intent exists if the adverse possessor uses the property the same way as an owner would use it.

    d. **Exclusive** – The adverse possessor must have exclusive possession of the property. The true owner must be excluded from possession.

    e. **Continuous and uninterrupted** – In Washington, the possession must be continuous and uninterrupted for ten years. The period is only seven years if the possessor has color of title (an invalid deed and a good faith belief that she owns the property) and pays property taxes on the parcel. Successive adverse possessors may add together their periods of possession to equal the statutory time period, which is known as *tacking*.

2. **Perfecting title** – An adverse possessor's interest is not recorded, so she must take additional steps to obtain marketable title. Unless the true owner is willing to provide a quitclaim deed, the adverse possessor must file a quiet title action.

I. **Accession** – *Accession* is any addition to real property from natural or artificial causes. It can result in involuntary alienation. Accession includes:

1. **Accretion** – When riparian or littoral land is enlarged by waterborne soil (such as a river depositing additional soil, known as *alluvium* or *alluvion*, on land that borders it), the owner acquires title to the added soil.

2. **Reliction** – When a body of water gradually retreats, the newly exposed soil belongs to the landowner.

3. **Avulsion** – Avulsion occurs when land is torn away by flowing water and deposited elsewhere, or when land is exposed by a sudden change in a watercourse (such as when a river that acts as a boundary between two properties changes its direction after massive flooding). (Avulsion usually does not alter the ownership of the changed piece of land.)

Adverse possession involves acquiring title to real property that belongs to someone else by taking possession of it without permission, in the manner and for the length of time prescribed by law.

Perfecting title: taking the necessary steps to remove title defects and defeat claims against one's title.

The adverse possessor does not need to compensate the other party to take title.

Avulsion is a term to describe the sudden tearing away of land by the action of water, as with a flood.

Sample questions

Real property ownership comes with a bundle of legal rights. This bundle of rights includes the rights to do all of the following EXCEPT:

A. sell, lease, devise, and improve
B. mortgage, lease, drill for oil, and bequeath
C. trade, cultivate, lease, and sell
D. possess, enjoy, exclude trespassers, and control

> B. *The bundle of rights associated with real property doesn't include the right to bequeath personal property by will. In contrast, one does have the right to devise real property by will.*

Three friends own an old lakefront house together. One friend finds a developer who would like to buy and redevelop the property, but the other two friends don't agree. What can the friend who'd like to sell do?

A. File a partition suit in the hope the court will order the sale of the property and division of the proceeds
B. Request a court order for the eviction of the friends
C. Sell his interest in the property, but let the friends continue to live there as tenants
D. Unilaterally sell the property to the developer, and divide the proceeds with his friends

> A. *A partition suit is filed when co-owners cannot resolve a dispute regarding ownership of their property. The court will decide how to divide the property, or if it is too small to physically divide, the court may order the sale of the property and division of the proceeds.*

Chris owns land. How might title to his land be transferred?

A. Delivery of a deed
B. Involuntary alienation
C. Descent and distribution
D. All of the above

> D. *When someone dies without a will, his property will be distributed in a process called intestate succession. Those who receive property through intestate succession are said to have received property by descent.*

Abandoned private property can be claimed by the state under the doctrine of:

A. regression
B. escheat
C. subordination
D. eminent domain

> B. *The doctrine of escheat, which calls for property to revert to the state, applies both to property owned by individuals who died without a will and with no known heirs, and to property that has been abandoned by its owner.*

The process of acquiring title to property through open, notorious, hostile, and continuous use is known as:

A. adverse possession
B. condemnation
C. dedication
D. prior affiliation

A. Adverse possession allows a person who has put an otherwise unused property to productive use for a required number of years to obtain title.

A person takes control of an abandoned farmhouse and begins to modernize it. She notifies the property's owner of her intention to do so. Eventually she would be able to take title to this property through:

A. accession
B. adverse possession
C. escheat
D. partition

B. If a non-owner takes exclusive possession of a property without the owner's permission (the "hostile" requirement), in an open and notorious manner, and holds it for the required period of time, she can take title through adverse possession. Giving notice here helps satisfy the open and notorious element.

IV. **Recording** – Recording a document means filing it at the county recorder's office so that it will be in the public record and accessible to any member of the public. Documents concerning a property should be recorded in the county (or, for large parcels, counties) where the property is located.

A. **Recording Process** – Recording is accomplished by filing an acknowledged document according to policies and procedures established by state law. Recorded documents serve as the basis for *title searches*; a purchaser can search the grantor index to determine if the seller has already conveyed the interest to another party.

> State law establishes recording policies and procedures.

1. **What may be recorded** – Almost anything affecting title to property (deeds, mortgages, abstracts of judgments, lis pendens) may be recorded. Listing agreements and sales contracts (i.e., purchase and sale agreements) are ordinarily not recorded.

> An ordinary sales contract (not to be confused with a land contract) would not be recorded.

B. **Notice** – Notice may be either actual or constructive.

1. **Actual notice** – A party has *actual notice* of something if he actually knows about it.

2. **Constructive notice** – A person is presumed to have *constructive notice* (legal notice) of something when he should have learned about it through reasonable diligence or an inspection of the public record.

> Constructive notice is the knowledge that the law presumes a person has about a situation, even if he doesn't actually know about it.

A properly recorded deed serves constructive notice of its existence and of its contents, as well as the grantee's rights.

a. **Effect of recording** – Recording a document gives constructive notice to the world of the existence and contents of the document. Everyone has constructive notice of it, even those who don't check the public record.

b. **Failure to record** – A grantee who fails to record her deed can lose title to a subsequent good faith purchaser who did not have notice of the earlier conveyance. In a conflict between two purchasers, the one who records his deed first has good title to the property, even if the other purchaser's deed was executed first.

It is to the grantee's advantage to record the deed.

c. **Benefits of recording** – It is to the grantee's advantage to record a deed. It is to a mortgagee's advantage to record a mortgage.

Possession of property imparts constructive notice to the world of the rights of the party in possession.

d. **Possession as notice** – Possession of the land by someone other than the seller gives constructive notice to the buyer that someone may have an interest in the property, and the buyer has a duty to inquire further.

Sample questions

Peter bought a house but didn't record the deed. Which of the following is true?
A. The deed is invalid
B. The deed is invalid after one year
C. Peter's interest isn't fully protected against third parties
D. Peter's interest is protected because he holds the actual deed to the property

> C. *A grantee who fails to record his deed isn't protected against subsequent good faith purchasers who didn't have notice of the earlier conveyance.*

Constructive notice would include everything EXCEPT:
A. evidence that someone is in possession of the property
B. a legal notice printed in the newspaper
C. a recorded deed
D. an unrecorded lien

> D. *Recording deeds and liens gives constructive notice to anyone with an interest in the property. An unrecorded lien doesn't give constructive notice.*

Which of the following documents would ordinarily NOT be recorded?
A. Deed of trust
B. Purchase and sale agreement
C. Option agreement
D. General warranty deed

> B. *The sales contract would not usually be recorded since, by itself, it does not convey a right or interest in the property.*

Simone is from Carlyle County and buys a ranch that is located partially in Allen County and partially in Bower County. Where should she record the deed to the ranch?

A. In Allen County
B. In Bower County
C. In Carlyle County
D. In both Allen County and Bower County

> D. A deed should be recorded in the county where the property is situated. If the property is located in two counties, the deed should be recorded in both.

Bo purchased a home and took possession on closing. He did not record the deed. Which of the following is TRUE?

A. On taking possession, Bo served actual notice of his title
B. On taking possession, Bo served constructive notice of his title
C. Title will not pass to Bo until he records his deed
D. It's too late for him to record his deed; a deed can only be recorded at closing

> B. Bo could serve constructive notice of his interest in the property either by taking possession of the property or by recording the deed. A deed can be recorded at any time. (Recording the deed on the closing date is the best way to avoid trouble, however.)

V. **Title Insurance** – This form of insurance protects against losses resulting from undiscovered title defects. Title insurance provides only financial protection (also known as *indemnification*), not a guaranty of marketable title.

A. **Chain of Title and Abstract of Title** – A *chain of title* is a complete history of recorded interests in a property, while an *abstract of title* is a condensed history of the recorded interests. A history of title enables the buyer's attorney to make a more informed decision as to the quality of the title, but it does not guarantee title or even insure against losses due to title defects. As a result, almost all buyers purchase title insurance policies instead.

B. **Title Search** – A title insurance company will perform an inspection of public records to determine all rights and encumbrances affecting title to a piece of property.

C. **Title Report** – After a title search is completed, the title company issues a *title report* describing the condition of the title. The report lists all defects and encumbrances of record; if a title insurance policy is issued, these items will be excluded from coverage as *exceptions*. A title report should reveal any clouds on the seller's title.

A title report is supposed to reveal any clouds on the title.

An exception is a defect or encumbrance discovered in the title search that is specifically excluded from coverage under the policy.

Title insurance may protect a lender, buyer, or even lessee. It does not protect a seller.

D. Interest Protected – In most residential transactions, two title policies are purchased: an *owner's policy* and a *mortgagee's policy*.

1. **Owner's policy:** Protects the title of the home buyer (the new owner).

2. **Mortgagee's policy:** Protects the security interest of the buyer's lender. Also called a lender's policy. The amount of financial protection for the lender will decrease as the mortgage balance is reduced over time.

E. Types of Coverage – Title insurance companies offer three main types of coverage: standard, extended, and homeowner's.

1. **Standard coverage** title policy

   a. **Covered:** Standard coverage insures against defects in title, including hidden risks such as forgery, an improperly delivered deed, or a lack of capacity by a party to a transaction.

A standard coverage policy does not protect against problems that would be discovered only by a physical inspection of the property.

   b. **Not covered:** Standard coverage does not insure against defects known to the owner but not disclosed to the title insurer, the rights of an adverse possessor, encroachments, or other problems that would be discovered only by an inspection of the property.

   c. **Use:** Traditionally, an owner's policy protecting a home buyer was a standard coverage policy, but now it's typically a homeowner's coverage policy.

2. **Extended coverage** – A mortgagee's policy (protecting the lender) is almost always an extended coverage policy.

A mortgagee's (lender's) policy is almost always an extended coverage policy.

   a. **Greater coverage** – Extended coverage insures against any defects not in the public record, such as rights of adverse possessors, unrecorded mechanic's liens, and encroachments.

Extended coverage protects against problems that should be discovered by an inspection of the property.

   b. **Includes survey** – While a standard coverage policy relies only on an inspection of public records, an extended coverage policy will also include a survey of the property to ascertain boundary lines.

3. **Homeowner's coverage** – Available for residential property with up to four units. It covers most of the same title problems an extended coverage policy does, plus some additional ones.

No title insurance policy protects against losses caused by government action (condemnation, downzoning, etc.).

F. Government Action – Title insurance policies do not protect property owners from losses that result from governmental action, such as condemnation or zoning changes.

G. Premium – A title insurance premium is paid once, at closing.

Sample questions

Manny is buying property from Jackson, using a loan from ABC Bank. To protect its interest, the mortgagee will insist on title insurance which will:

A. indemnify the mortgagee against some title defects
B. protect Manny
C. protect Jackson
D. legally transfer the property from Jackson to Manny

> *A. The mortgagee is the lender, ABC Bank. When it insists on title insurance, it does so to protect itself against loss; the title insurance company agrees to indemnify (reimburse) ABC Bank for any losses sustained because of a defect or problem with the title.*

An abstract of title:

A. is necessary to sell a property
B. contains information obtained from the public record
C. can only be created by a lawyer
D. will identify unrecorded liens

> *B. An abstract of title is a condensed history of all the recorded interests in a piece of property. Recorded documents are part of the public record.*

A standard (owner's) policy of title insurance protects against losses resulting from any of the following, EXCEPT:

A. a forged deed
B. a recorded lien that the title searcher overlooked
C. government action
D. an incompetent grantor

> *C. Title insurance never protects a landowner from losses due to government action, such as condemnation or zoning changes.*

Which of the following is true about surveys?

A. They determine placement of improvements on a property
B. They identify setback lines from property boundaries
C. They protect against easements by prescription
D. They reveal encroachments not of public record

> *D. A survey may reveal matters that are not part of the public record and therefore would only be discovered through a personal inspection, such as encroachments. That is why a survey is often performed as part of obtaining an extended coverage title insurance policy.*

Chapter Quiz

1. A buyer received a general warranty deed when she took title to a property. The seller's cousin showed up several months later and claimed an ownership interest in the property. The buyer would be protected against this claim by the general warranty deed's:

    A. covenant against encumbrances
    B. covenant of hostile enjoyment
    C. covenant of seisin
    D. covenant of warranty

2. When part of the land is removed, but the boundaries of a property stay the same, it is known as:

    A. accretion
    B. adverse possession
    C. avulsion
    D. partition

3. The result of an unreleased lien is a/an:

    A. easement
    B. cloud on the title
    C. condemnation action by the city
    D. lis pendens

4. A quitclaim deed conveys:

    A. unencumbered title
    B. the grantor's interest in a given property, if any
    C. an estate for years
    D. fee simple title, including a covenant of quiet enjoyment

5. A deed that is not signed by the seller is still considered valid as long as it:

    A. is executed by a competent relative of the seller
    B. is delivered to the buyer
    C. contains a covenant of seisin
    D. is signed by an authorized attorney in fact

6. The closing date is fast approaching when the buyer's real estate agent learns that the seller's sister may have an interest in the property. The parties have already signed the purchase and sale agreement. The buyer's agent should:

    A. ask the agent to have the seller obtain a quitclaim deed from the sister
    B. ask the buyer to sue the seller for specific performance
    C. inform both buyer and seller that the transaction is void
    D. postpone the closing date

7. Deborah sells her property to Juan, but Juan fails to record the deed. Which of the following statements is true about unrecorded deeds?

    A. The conveyance is invalid
    B. The deed is still valid between Deborah and Juan
    C. The deed provides constructive notice that Juan is the owner
    D. The property with the unrecorded deed will escheat to the county where it is located when Juan dies

8. Bob builds a fence extending 20 feet onto the neighboring property. He uses the land for 15 years without the knowledge of the neighboring owner, who lives in another city. When Bob wants to list his property for sale, including the extra 20 foot strip, which of the following is true?

    A. Adverse possession does not apply because the neighboring owner did not know about Bob's possession of the land
    B. Adverse possession does not apply since Bob did not pay taxes on the land during those 15 years
    C. Bob has not proven hostile intent, because there has not been a confrontation with the neighboring owner
    D. The land is his to sell, having passed through adverse possession

9. A property owner dies without a will or any known heirs. The property passes to the state, under its:

   A. escheat power
   B. police power
   C. power of eminent domain
   D. taxation power

10. John, Kevin, and Lyle own a property as tenants in common, but only Kevin and Lyle live on the property. John would like to sell the property for redevelopment, but Kevin and Lyle refuse. What is John's best option?

    A. Charge Kevin and Lyle rent
    B. Create a trust to manage the property
    C. Evict Kevin and Lyle
    D. Obtain a court order to sell the property

11. A seller finds that he cannot provide marketable title because of a cloud on the title. To clear the title, he must file a/an:

    A. adverse possession claim
    B. quiet title action
    C. quitclaim deed
    D. partition suit

12. There's a strip of land that lies between two neighbors. One neighbor mistakenly believes the land is his, and he consistently cares for it by mowing it, fertilizing it, etc. At one point, he encloses the property with a chain link fence. After enough time passes, he might be able to obtain title to this strip of land by:

    A. escheat
    B. prescribed use
    C. eminent domain
    D. adverse possession

13. Sam takes possession of an unused farm and begins growing crops. He sends the farm's owner a letter describing his actions. Can Sam ever become owner of the farm?

    A. Yes, because he is putting the land to productive use
    B. Yes, as long as he maintains possession
    C. No, because adverse possession requires that the true owner be unaware of the possession
    D. No, because his possession is not hostile to the owner's interest

14. A seller partially finances the buyer's purchase of her property. What should the seller do if she wants to give public notice of her interest in the property?

    A. Ask the buyer to give her a quitclaim deed
    B. Record the deed
    C. Record the mortgage
    D. Secure the property by using a land contract

15. Who benefits the most from recording a warranty deed?

    A. Beneficiary
    B. Notary public
    C. Grantor
    D. Grantee

16. A buyer who records a deed is giving:

    A. constructive notice
    B. actual notice
    C. pending notice
    D. statutory notice

17. A buyer would like protection against any unknown encumbrances on the property she plans to buy. The greatest protection would come from:

    A. a home inspection
    B. a survey
    C. an abstract of title
    D. title insurance

18. If a buyer wants to protect herself against unrecorded encumbrances, she should:

    A. assume the seller's standard policy of title insurance
    B. order a survey
    C. purchase a title insurance policy that has the fewest exceptions possible
    D. have her attorney prepare an abstract of title

19. Sheila obtains a home loan from a commercial lender, and paid for a mortgagee's title policy. Who would this policy protect?

    A. Sheila (the buyer)
    B. Only the lender
    C. Both Sheila and the lender
    D. The seller

20. When title to property is lost but the property boundaries remain the same, it is:

A. acceleration
B. accretion
C. alienation
D. avulsion

Answer Key

1. C. The covenant of seisin protects the buyer in this case, in that it promises that the grantor actually owns the property interest being transferred to the grantee.

2. C. Avulsion is a form of accession, which is involuntary alienation of property due to natural causes. In the case of avulsion, an owner may lose title to land that has been torn away by flowing water and deposited elsewhere.

3. B. A cloud on the title is any claim, encumbrance, or apparent defect that makes the title to property unmarketable. A quitclaim deed is most often used to remove a cloud on title.

4. B. A quitclaim deed conveys any interest in a property that the grantor has at the time the deed is executed, without warranties.

5. D. The document used to assign legal rights to another person—for example, authorizing someone else to sign a contract and/or deed on one's behalf—is a power of attorney. The person who is appointed to act is known as an attorney in fact.

6. A. The agent's best bet is to suggest that the sellers seek a quitclaim deed from the relative who may have a claim. The agent should not presume that the transaction will have to be scrapped. Only the parties, not the escrow agent or a real estate licensee, can change the closing date.

7. B. A deed that is unrecorded is still valid. However, it exposes the grantee to the risk of other deedholders showing up with claims on the property.

8. D. Bob's possession of the land meets all of the criteria for adverse possession: he occupied the land, his use was open and notorious, it was exclusive, and it lasted for the required period of time. Hostile intent does not require confrontation. (Bob may need to file a quiet title action, though, to perfect the title before proceeding with the sale.)

9. A. The state's power of escheat means that property with no known owner, such as cases where an owner dies intestate and with no heirs, passes back to the state.

10. D. A partition suit can be used when co-owners cannot agree on how to divide a property. If there is no feasible way to physically divide the property, the court may order the property to be sold and the proceeds to be divided between the co-owners.

11. B. A quiet title action is a lawsuit that is used to remove a cloud on the title, by settling questions of who the proper owner of a property is.

12. D. Adverse possession allows a person who has occupied land in a manner that is actual, open and notorious, hostile, exclusive, and continuous and uninterrupted, to take title to the property after a specified period of time.

13.   B.   So long as Sam maintains continuous, uninterrupted possession for the required period of time, and meets the other requirements, he will be able to take title to the property (although he may need to file a quiet title action to perfect title). The owner does not need to know about the possession, but the possession must be obvious enough to put the average owner on notice that his interest in the property is threatened, and Sam's letter more than satisfies that requirement.

14.   C.   The seller would want to record the mortgage, to give notice to the world of her financial interest in the property. The buyer, of course, will want to record the deed, to give notice of his ownership interest.

15.   D.   The grantee is the one who has acquired an interest in the land, and she is the one who benefits the most from recording the deed to provide constructive (legal) notice of that interest.

16.   A.   A buyer who records a deed is giving constructive notice. Anyone who later acquires an interest in the property is held to know about all other recorded interests, even if he didn't check the records.

17.   D.   Title insurance offers protection against latent or undiscovered defects in the title. Buyers almost always protect their interests with a title insurance policy.

18.   C.   To protect against unrecorded encumbrances, a buyer would need something that goes beyond a standard title insurance policy, which is limited to certain defects in title. The buyer would probably want a homeowner's policy, which provides the greatest protection.

19.   B.   The mortgagee is the lender, and the mortgagee's title insurance policy (extended coverage policy) protects the mortgagee (the lender).

20.   C.   Alienation occurs when title to real property is transferred from one party to another. Unless the property is partitioned, the boundaries remain the same.

Chapter 4
Encumbrances

I. **Encumbrances** – An *encumbrance* is a nonpossessory right or interest in real property held by someone other than the property owner. The interest can be financial or nonfinancial. A financial encumbrance affects only title, while a nonfinancial encumbrance also affects the use of the property, which in turn affects its value.

II. **Financial Encumbrances (Liens)** – A financial encumbrance, commonly called a *lien*, is a security interest in real property. The creditor who holds the lien is called a *secured creditor*.

   A. **Foreclosure** – If an owner doesn't pay off the debt owed to a secured creditor, the lien allows the creditor to force the property to be sold to satisfy the debt. This is called *foreclosure*.

   B. **Taking Title** – A lien doesn't prevent a property owner from selling the property, but the buyer will take title subject to the lien if it isn't paid off by closing. Even though the property is no longer owned by the debtor, the creditor can still foreclose on the property if the debt remains unpaid.

   C. **Voluntary vs. Involuntary Liens**

      1. **Voluntary** – A voluntary lien is one the debtor voluntarily gives to the creditor. Examples include *mortgages* and *deeds of trust*.

      2. **Involuntary** – Sometimes called *statutory liens*, involuntary liens are given to creditors by operation of law, without the owner's consent. Examples include property tax liens and judgment liens.

   D. **General vs. Specific Liens**

      1. **General** – A *general lien* attaches to all of the debtor's real and personal property. A judgment is an example of an involuntary, general lien.

      2. **Specific** – A *specific lien* attaches only to a particular piece of property. A mortgage is an example of a specific lien.

   E. **Types of Liens**

      1. **Mortgage** – A *mortgage* is a specific, voluntary lien created by contract between the property owner (*mortgagor*) and the creditor (*mortgagee*).

2. **Deed of trust** – Also called a *trust deed*, a deed of trust is used for the same purpose as a mortgage.

3. **Construction lien** – Also called a *mechanic's lien*, a construction lien is a specific, involuntary lien recorded by a person who provides labor, materials, or professional services for the improvement of real property, if that person is not paid by the property owner within the agreed time. If the debt remains unpaid, the lienholder can foreclose in much the same way that a lender would foreclose a mortgage.

   a. **Materialman's lien** – A lien claimed by a person who provides materials (as opposed to labor) is sometimes called a *materialman's lien*.

   b. **Recording** – The construction lien must be recorded no later than 90 days after the claimant has stopped working on or providing materials for the project. A potential claimant who misses this deadline loses the right to a construction lien.

   c. **Priority** – A construction lien's priority is set according to the date the work began, not the date the lien was recorded.

4. **Judgment lien** – When the losing party in a lawsuit is ordered to pay money to the winning party, a *judgment lien* may be filed against her. A judgment lien is an involuntary, general lien and can be foreclosed in much the same way as a mortgage or a construction lien. The lien attaches to all property owned by the debtor in the county where the judgment was entered.

   a. **Writ of execution** – A debtor must pay the judgment to free the property from the lien. If not paid, the property can be sold to satisfy the judgment. To order this done, the court issues a *writ of execution*.

5. **Attachment lien** – Occasionally, someone who gets sued will sell off her property and skip town before a verdict is reached. To prevent this, the plaintiff can ask the court to issue a *writ of attachment* during the lawsuit, which directs the sheriff to seize enough of the defendant's property to satisfy the judgment, if one is entered against her. The writ of attachment is recorded and creates an involuntary lien.

   a. **Lis pendens** – As an alternative to the writ of attachment, the plaintiff may record a *lis pendens* (Latin for "action pending"). A lis pendens is not a lien but it does serve constructive notice of the pending lawsuit, and

The 90-day recording deadline does not apply in every state; therefore, it will not be tested.

Priority is set according to the date work began.

Lis pendens: action pending.

anyone who is thinking about buying the property will be bound by any judgment that results from the suit.

6. **Property tax liens** – When property taxes (also known as *ad valorem* taxes) are levied, a lien attaches to the property until the taxes are paid. Property tax liens are involuntary, specific liens.

Real estate taxes are also called *ad valorem* taxes.

7. **Special assessments** – *Special assessments* result from local improvements, such as road paving or sewer lines, that benefit some, but not all, property owners in the county. The properties that have benefited are assessed for their fair share of the cost of the improvement. A special assessment lien is involuntary and specific.

8. **IRS liens** – Liens for unpaid federal income taxes are involuntary, general liens that attach to all of a debtor's property.

Sample questions

A new subdivision requires payment of homeowners association dues. If unpaid, what type of lien do they create?
A. General lien applying to all property owned by the homeowner
B. Involuntary lien that does not pass to the next buyer of the property
C. Personal debt that is not secured by real property
D. Specific lien that will encumber the property

   D. *Homeowners association dues create a specific lien, meaning that the lien attaches only to a particular piece of property. A lien is an encumbrance, so it is not terminated by the sale of the property and would affect the next buyer's title.*

Green owes White money. Green has a parcel of prime real estate that's worth millions of dollars. The land is owned by Green free and clear of any liens. Green recently listed the property with a local real estate agent. White is worried that Green will sell the property before White can get a judgment against him (the judgment would allow White to place a lien on the property.) During the course of White's lawsuit against Green, White should:
A. seek an attachment on Green's property
B. tell Green's listing agent that he (White) has an interest in Green's property
C. ask the judge for a summary judgment
D. make sure that Green knows that if he sells the property before the end of the lawsuit, he will be committing fraud

   A. *White should seek an attachment on Green's property to protect his interests during the lawsuit.*

A lien on real estate would include a/an:

A. recorded mortgage
B. encroachment
C. gross easement
D. deed restriction

> A. *A lien is a financial encumbrance, and a mortgage is a type of lien. The other options are examples of nonfinancial encumbrances.*

A plaintiff files a lawsuit involving a property and also files a separate document intended to provide notice of the lawsuit. This recorded notice of a pending legal action is called a/an:

A. abstract of judgment
B. petition for alienation
C. writ of execution
D. lis pendens

> D. *A lis pendens is a recorded notice stating that there is a lawsuit pending that may affect title to the defendant's real estate and that could bind the purchaser of the property.*

All of the following are true, except:

A. Ad valorem taxes are tax deductible
B. Unpaid ad valorem liens may create a specific lien on the property
C. Unpaid ad valorem liens may create a general lien on the property
D. An ad valorem lien is also known as a property tax lien

> C. *Ad valorem liens (also known as property tax liens, or general real estate tax liens) are based on the value of real property. Unpaid liens create a specific (not general), involuntary lien against real property.*

If a lien is not removed when the property is sold, it remains a lien on the property.

F. Lien Priority – When a property is sold—voluntarily or involuntarily—the sale proceeds are not allocated among all the lienholders in a pro rata fashion. Instead, the liens are generally paid according to their priority; the lien with the highest priority is paid first, then if there is any money left, the lien with the second highest priority, and so on.

General rule: first to record, first in right.

1. **First to record, first in right** – Lien priority is usually determined by the date a lien was recorded. The lien that was recorded first will be paid first, even if another lien was created first (dated earlier).

2. **Exceptions** – Some types of liens offer special priority:

   a. **Property tax and special assessment liens** – Property tax and special assessment liens have priority over all other liens.

   b. **Construction liens** – Construction liens have priority from the date construction begins, regardless of when the construction lien is recorded.

Example: Construction begins June 1. The trust deed lien is recorded June 21. A mechanic's lien is filed September 29, eleven days following notice of completion. The mechanic's lien has priority over the trust deed lien.

   c. Judgment liens – A judgment lien's priority is set according to the date the court enters the judgment in the public record.

G. Homestead Laws – *Homestead laws* give homeowners limited protection against foreclosure; in Washington, they apply only to judgment liens. A creditor cannot foreclose unless the net value of an owner-occupied property is greater than the homestead exemption amount created by state law.

Sample questions

Juanita is purchasing an apartment building. To finance the purchase, she is obtaining both a first and a second mortgage, each from a different lender. The most important way that the first mortgage differs from the second mortgage is that:

A. the first mortgage would have a significantly higher interest rate than the second mortgage
B. the first mortgage would require a higher loan-to-value ratio than the second mortgage
C. the first mortgage would have a senior lien position, and the second mortgage would have a junior lien position
D. the first mortgage would be more likely to require a balloon payment than the second mortgage

   C. First mortgages have a senior lien position, compared to junior mortgages.

A homeowner has an unpaid hospital bill for $20,000. The hospital files suit and wins a judgment for the full amount. Is the homeowner's home (which he owns free and clear) at risk?

A. No, because the debt must be at least $25,000 to force a sale
B. No, because the debt must exceed the value of the homestead
C. Yes, but he may be partly or fully protected by state homestead laws
D. Yes, a court may always force a sale to fulfill a judgment

   C. Homestead laws are state laws that give limited protection against foreclosure of judgment liens. Generally, foreclosure is not allowed unless the net value of the property exceeds the homestead exemption amount.

III. Nonfinancial Encumbrances – While financial encumbrances affect only title to property, nonfinancial encumbrances affect the physical use or condition of the property itself; thus, a property owner could find the use of his property limited by a right or interest held by someone else.

An easement is not an estate.

A. Easements – An *easement* is a right to use another person's land for a particular purpose; it is a nonpossessory interest in land (the easement holder can use the land for the specified purpose but has no title or right of possession). An easement is not an estate.

 1. **Types of easements** – There are two types of easements: easements appurtenant and easements in gross.

    a. **Easement appurtenant** – An *easement appurtenant* burdens one parcel of land for the benefit of another. An easement appurtenant *"runs with the land"* like other appurtenances, meaning that the benefit or burden of the easement will pass to subsequent purchasers. An easement appurtenant doesn't enlarge the size of the dominant tenement, but it does increase its value. Ordinarily, an easement agreement or the deed mentioning the easement must be in writing and recorded to be valid. However, if it is immediately apparent that the easement is in use, the easement could run with the land even if not in writing or recorded.

An easement appurtenant increases the value of the dominant tenement, but it does not increase its size.

Dominant tenement benefits; servient tenement is burdened. The dominant tenement is sometimes called a dominant estate, and a servient tenement is sometimes called a servient estate.

      i. **Servient tenement** – The land burdened by an easement is called a *servient tenement*.

      ii. **Servient tenant** – The *servient tenant* is the owner of the burdened land.

      iii. **Dominant tenement** – The land benefited by an easement is called the *dominant tenement*.

      iv. **Dominant tenant** – The *dominant tenant* is the owner of the benefited land.

Ingress & egress: entering and exiting.

      v. **Ingress/egress** – The right to drive in is the right of *ingress*; the right to drive out is the right of *egress*. (A common easement is one in which the dominant tenant has the right to drive over a defined strip of the servient tenant's land to reach her home.)

Easement in gross: benefits a person, not a parcel of land.

Easements in gross usually benefit commercial tenants or utilities.

    b. **Easement in gross** – An *easement in gross* benefits a person (dominant tenant) rather than a parcel of land. With an easement in gross, there is no dominant tenement (land), only a servient tenement. Unlike appurtenant easements, easements in gross do not "run with the land," but instead terminate on the death of the dominant tenant.

       Example: Jones (dominant tenant) has a permanent right to fish in a small lake on Smith's land (servient tenement). Jones's right burdens Smith's land but does not benefit any land belonging to Jones.

2. **Creating an easement** – Methods of creating an easement include *express grant, express reservation, implication,* and *prescription.*

   a. **Express grant** – An easement is created by express grant when a property owner grants someone else the right to use the property. The grant must be in writing and comply with all other requirements for conveyance of an interest in land.

   b. **Express reservation** – A landowner who is conveying a portion of her property may reserve an easement in that parcel to benefit the land that is retained. The reservation of the easement must be made in writing.

   c. **Implication** – An easement by implication (sometimes called an *easement by necessity*) can be either an easement by implied grant or by implied reservation. It can be created by a court when a lot is subdivided into two or more lots and the grantor fails to grant or reserve an easement on one lot for the benefit of another.

   d. **Prescription** – An easement by prescription is created through long-term use of land without permission of the landowner. Acquiring a *prescriptive easement* is similar to acquiring ownership by adverse possession. A prescriptive easement requires all of the following:

      i. **Open and notorious use** – The use must be apparent to the landowner.

      ii. **Hostile use** – The use must be without the landowner's permission.

      iii. **Continuous use** – The use must be reasonably continuous for ten years.

         Note: Although adverse possession requires exclusive use of the property, a prescriptive easement may be created even if the true owner is also using the property.

> Requirements for prescriptive easements are set by state statute.

3. **Terminating an easement** – An easement can be terminated by *release, merger, failure of purpose, abandonment,* or *prescription.*

   a. **Release** – The holder of an easement (dominant tenant) may release his rights in the servient tenement. The release must be in writing, usually in the form of a quitclaim deed.

   b. **Merger** – If the dominant and servient tenements come to be owned by the same person, the easement is no longer necessary and therefore terminated. The ownership of the two lots has merged.

> Merger occurs when the dominant and servient tenements come under one ownership.

  c. **Failure of purpose** – If the purpose of the easement ceases to exist, the easement terminates. For instance, an easement created for railroad lines would terminate if the railroad company rerouted its line, tore up the tracks, and left the area.

  d. **Abandonment** – An easement is terminated if an easement holder abandons it. Mere non-use is not abandonment.

  e. **Prescription** – An easement may terminate by prescription if the servient tenant prevents the dominant tenant from using it for ten years.

Sample questions

Some encumbrances affect the use of property; others do not. Which of the following would affect the use of a property?

A. A construction lien
B. A tax lien
C. A mortgage
D. An easement

  D. Easements affect the use of property; liens generally do not.

A writ of attachment, an easement in gross, and a special assessment all have what in common?

A. They're court actions
B. They're encumbrances
C. They're restrictions
D. They're taxes

  B. Writs of attachment and special assessments are financial encumbrances (liens), while an easement is a nonfinancial encumbrance (one that affects the use of the property), but all three are encumbrances.

  B. **Profits** – A *profit* differs from an easement in that it allows a person not only to enter someone else's property, but also to take something of value (such as timber or gravel) from the property.

  C. **Licenses** – Like an easement, a *license* gives someone the right to use another person's land. However, easements and licenses are different in important ways. A license: (1) is temporary, (2) is revocable, (3) is not an interest in land, (4) does not encumber the land, (5) does not run with the land, and (6) can often be verbal. A license is not considered an encumbrance, because it is revocable.

  D. **Encroachments** – An *encroachment* is a physical object that lies wholly or partially on someone else's property. An example

Characteristics of a license:
• can be revoked,
• temporary,
• cannot be assigned.

would be a fence or garage built over the property line. It is considered a *trespass* rather than an encumbrance.

1. **Ejectment** – An owner damaged by the presence of a neighboring encroachment may file an *ejectment suit* in order to get the encroachment removed or to receive damages.

2. **Title insurance** – Standard title insurance policies do not cover encroachments. Extended title insurance policies cover encroachments and may require a property survey before the policy will be issued.

3. **Adverse possession** – If an encroachment is ignored for the statutory period, it may ripen into a prescriptive easement or title by adverse possession.

E. **Nuisances** – A *nuisance* is an activity or condition on neighboring property that interferes with a property owner's use or enjoyment of his own property. It could be an odor, noise, or interference with communication signals. Like an encroachment, a nuisance isn't an encumbrance, but rather a violation of an owner's possessory rights.

1. **Attractive nuisance** – The *attractive nuisance doctrine* holds that the owner of a property with a feature that is dangerous and attractive to children, such as an unfenced swimming pool, will be liable for any harm resulting from failure to keep out trespassing children.

F. **Private Restrictions** – Also known as *deed restrictions*, private restrictions are encumbrances imposed by a prior owner that restrict the use of the property.

1. **Run with the land** – Like easements appurtenant, private restrictions *run with the land* and are binding on all subsequent owners of the property.

2. **Cannot violate the law** – As long as a private restriction isn't unconstitutional, in violation of a law, or contrary to public policy, it can be enforced in court. The procedure for enforcing a restriction is known as an *injunction*.

   Example: An example of a void and unenforceable restriction is one prohibiting the sale of property to non-white buyers (a practice that was common before the civil rights legislation of the 1960s). Restraints on alienation, such as a restriction prohibiting resale to anyone other than a family member, may also be unenforceable.

> Encroachments are not covered by a standard title insurance policy. A title company may require a survey to determine if an encroachment exists before it will issue an extended coverage policy.
>
> An encroachment could ripen into a prescriptive easement.
>
> Private restrictions run with the land.
>
> Restrictions are enforced through private court action.

A homeowner may not choose to opt out of the CC&Rs, or out of the subdivision's homeowners association.

3. **CC&Rs** – Most subdivision developers impose a list of restrictions on all lots within a subdivision before they begin selling lots. This list is called a *declaration of restrictions* or *CC&Rs* (conditions, covenants, and restrictions). Restrictions may also be created by written agreement among neighbors after the subdivision has been developed.

   a. **Marketability of title** – The CC&Rs are intended to ensure that the subdivision will remain a desirable place to live. They do not affect the marketability of the property's title; in fact, they enhance the property's value.

   b. **Recording** – The CC&Rs are recorded and then referenced in the deeds used to convey the subdivision lots.

4. **Covenants vs. conditions** – A private restriction is either a covenant or a condition.

   a. **Covenant** – A *covenant* is a promise to do or not do something. A property owner who violates a covenant may be sued by any other affected neighbor subject to the same rules, leading to an injunction (a court order directing the owner to comply with the covenant) or, less often, an order to pay damages for failure to comply.

   b. **Condition** – Violation of a *condition* can have more serious consequences. A condition in a deed makes the grantee's title conditional, so that she owns a defeasible fee, rather than a fee simple absolute. Breach of a condition can result in forfeiture of title. Because of the harshness of this remedy, if it is unclear whether a restriction is a covenant or condition, it will be construed as a covenant.

5. **Termination of restrictions** – It is up to the owners within a subdivision to enforce the CC&Rs; if the residents have failed to enforce a particular restriction in the past, they may not be allowed to enforce it in the future. A private restriction will also terminate if its purpose can no longer be achieved.

   Example: Zoning changes and other forces have altered the character of a residential neighborhood. If there is a private restriction limiting a property to single-family residential use, but most of the surrounding properties are now used for light industry, the restriction is probably no longer enforceable.

Abandonment: CC&Rs may no longer be enforceable if subdivision owners have failed to enforce them in the past.

6. **Conflict between restrictions** – If there is a conflict between private restrictions and other restrictions (such as a zoning ordinance), the stricter restrictions will prevail.

Sample questions

Bart owns a piece of property. Which one of the following would not be an encumbrance on it?

A. A license
B. A pending foreclosure lawsuit
C. A gross easement for a utility company
D. Judgment in a suit for breach of contract

    A. A license is revocable, non-assignable permission to use another person's land for a particular purpose, and therefore is not an encumbrance. The other choices are encumbrances because they affect the physical use of or title to the property.

A neighbor's fence extends onto an adjoining property. This would be considered a/an:

A. easement
B. encroachment
C. encumbrance
D. license

    B. A physical object that is on someone else's property is an encroachment. It is not an encumbrance, because the encroacher doesn't hold a right or interest in the other property.

A deed restriction is a covenant that:

A. controls housing costs in a subdivision
B. lasts forever
C. prevents the property from becoming encumbered
D. restricts future owners of the property

    D. A deed restriction is a private agreement that limits uses of a property. It runs with the land, so it affects future owners of the property. While it potentially could last forever, there are a number of ways in which a deed restriction may be terminated.

Chapter Quiz

1. Encroachments are:
   A. spoken permission to use someone else's property
   B. activities that interfere with a neighboring owner's use of his property
   C. protected against by standard title insurance
   D. considered a trespass

2. What would result in a judgment lien being imposed on a landowner's property?
   A. Foreclosure
   B. Lawsuit
   C. Unpaid construction project
   D. Unpaid property taxes

3. Alex owns 35 acres of vacant land that he would like to deed to a local wildlife conservancy. However, a title search reveals that timber rights and an easement to use the property were sold to Giant Lumber Company in 1963. Since this lumber company went out of business in 1987, Alex should:
   A. cancel the transaction, because the lumber company went bankrupt
   B. seek advice from an attorney, since the easements may still be valid
   C. claim a prescriptive easement, since the requisite number of years has passed
   D. cancel the transaction, because the easements will still be valid

4. Allen begins providing construction services on May 2 and records a construction lien on May 5. Bart begins providing services on May 3 and records a construction lien on May 4. On May 10, a judgment lien against the property is recorded. The property's owner also receives notice on May 10 that he is in arrears on his property tax payments. Which lien has lien priority?
   A. Allen's lien
   B. Bart's lien
   C. Judgment lien
   D. Tax lien

5. Jones and Smith live across the street from each other in a subdivision that has deed restrictions prohibiting the keeping of large animals as pets. Jones realizes that Smith is keeping a pet Shetland pony in the backyard. Jones can:
   A. enforce the deed restriction against Smith via lawsuit
   B. do nothing, because Smith's ownership rights take precedence over deed restrictions
   C. do nothing, because only a next-door neighbor can enforce such a deed restriction against Smith
   D. notify the local zoning authority, who will investigate

6. K buys a piece of landlocked property from L on the condition that L provide an easement across the property for ingress and egress. The easement isn't recorded, but heavy use of the driveway is apparent. K later sells the property. Is the easement still valid for the new owner?
   A. No, because it wasn't recorded
   B. No, because it wasn't mentioned in the deed
   C. Yes, because an easement of this type runs with the land, rather than belonging to an individual
   D. Yes, because it is an easement in gross

7. An easement appurtenant is one that:
   A. can only be created by prescription
   B. is of more benefit to the servient tenant than the dominant tenant
   C. is given to a commercial tenant
   D. runs with the land

8. Moe has an appurtenant easement over Ray's land. Ray's land is called a/an:
   A. dominant estate
   B. servient estate
   C. encroachment
   D. license

9. Carl is housebound and never goes outside. Neighbor Salvador plants a vegetable garden on a corner of Carl's property that is not visible from the main house. After the required period of time, Salvador claims a prescriptive easement over this portion of Carl's land. This easement is:

   A. not valid, because Salvador had a duty to inform Carl of his intended use
   B. not valid, because Carl didn't know of the use and had no chance to formally object
   C. valid, because Salvador's vegetable garden is a productive use of the land
   D. valid, because the use was open, and Carl's knowledge of the use isn't considered

10. An easement for ingress and egress that is created by a court of law where it is reasonably necessary for the enjoyment of the property is an easement:

    A. appurtenant
    B. by necessity
    C. by prescription
    D. in gross

11. Three of the following are appurtenances that would transfer when the property is sold. Which of the following would not transfer?

    A. A deed restriction
    B. Water rights
    C. An easement
    D. A license

12. Branches from a neighbor's apple tree hang over the fence and overripe fruit falls into a homeowner's yard. This is an example of an:

    A. easement in gross
    B. emblement
    C. encroachment
    D. lien

13. Max would like to know if there's an encroachment on his boundary line. He should:

    A. examine the legal description
    B. order an appraisal
    C. order a spot survey
    D. do a title search

14. Each of the following is a typical subdivision rule or regulation, except:

    A. the property cannot be sold and used as a waste disposal site
    B. a tree house cannot be built on the property
    C. the walls and fences shall not exceed four feet in height
    D. no structure of a temporary character shall be constructed on any lot

15. A buyer is about to purchase a vacant lot in a new subdivision. The development plans for the subdivision state that all lots must be a minimum size of one acre. If the buyer goes through with the purchase, his deed would be subject to a/an:

    A. easement
    B. encroachment
    C. lien
    D. restriction

16. For how long is a deed restriction valid?

    A. Potentially forever
    B. Only as to the first purchaser of the property
    C. Only if the restriction is a covenant, not a condition
    D. Until a subsequent buyer and seller agree to release it

17. A property investor sells his 100-acre rural parcel of land with the restriction that the buyer may not divide the land into parcels smaller than one acre each. This restriction is:

    A. invalid; this restriction violates the rule against perpetuities
    B. invalid; one cannot put private restrictions on rural land
    C. valid; these kinds of restrictions are always valid on agricultural land
    D. valid; this restriction doesn't violate public policy

18. The deed restrictions in a subdivision prohibit homeowners from building fences. However, the city where the subdivision is located permits the construction of fences. Which of the following is true?

    A. Deed restrictions cannot be extended to cover matters such as fence construction

    B. The city's ordinances would take precedence, because it is a governmental entity

    C. The deed restrictions would take precedence, because they are more restrictive

    D. The deed restrictions would be found unenforceable as against public policy

19. A deed restriction is used to:

    A. control future uses of the property

    B. limit housing costs in a subdivision

    C. prevent housing from being encumbered

    D. require the use of high-quality building materials and construction techniques

20. A subdivision has deed restrictions that create a community nature trail from the rear ten feet of every owner's property. One owner decided that he wanted to use that part of his yard to have a storage shed instead. If the other owners want to keep him from doing that, they should:

    A. file an unlawful detainer action

    B. file for an injunction in the appropriate court

    C. not do anything, because they do not have authority to stop the owner

    D. request a cease and desist order from state real estate licensing authorities

Answer Key

1. D. An encroachment is considered a trespass if it violates a neighboring owner's right to possession, and can be the basis for an ejectment action.

2. B. A judgment lien may be placed on the property of the loser of a lawsuit. If the judgment debtor doesn't pay off the lien, the court can issue a writ of execution ordering the sale of the property.

3. B. Even though the easement holder is no longer existent, easements run with the land and may have passed to a successor company or other owner. It would be prudent to ask an attorney to investigate.

4. D. Property tax liens always take priority over other liens in Washington, including construction liens. Allen's lien still takes priority over Bart's lien, as construction liens take priority based on the date of the start of construction, but the tax lien takes priority over both.

5. A. Jones or any other homeowner in the subdivision can file a suit for an injunction against Smith; it isn't necessary to be a next-door neighbor. However, if other owners in the subdivision have also been violating the restriction for some time, the court might rule that the restriction has been abandoned and can no longer be enforced.

6. C. An easement for ingress and egress is a type of easement appurtenant. Easements appurtenant run with the land. Easements ordinarily need to be in writing and recorded in order to run with the land, but if the use is apparent, an easement can run with the land even if not recorded.

7. D. An easement appurtenant runs with the land; in other words, subsequent owners of the properties that benefit from or are burdened by the easement will also be subject to the easement. An easement appurtenant benefits the dominant tenant, not the servient tenant.

8. B. Moe is the dominant tenant and Moe's land is the dominant tenement (estate), benefited by the easement. Ray is the servient tenant and Ray's land is the servient tenement (estate), burdened by the easement.

9. D. A prescriptive easement requires a use that is open and notorious, meaning that it is reasonably apparent to the landowner. It doesn't inquire into whether the property's owner had specific knowledge of the open use, though.

10. B. A court may find that an easement by necessity (or easement by implication) is created where it is reasonably necessary for enjoyment of the property, and there was apparent prior use. This may occur where a grantor divides a property into more than one lot, and forgets to grant or reserve an easement for the owner of the new lot.

11. D. A license is not an appurtenance; it's a privilege that can be revoked, and it does not run with the land.

12. C. An object that extends over a property's boundary line is an encroachment. An encroachment is not an encumbrance because it is not a right or use held by the encroaching property owner; however, if it is in place long enough, it may ripen into an easement.

13. C. The best way to ascertain if a physical object encroaches on a boundary line would be through a survey.

14. A. Regulation of whether a property can be used for waste disposal is likely to occur through laws or ordinances. The other options, however, are common rules imposed by homeowners associations.

15. D. A limitation on the use of the land, such as a minimum lot size requirement that would prohibit partitioning the lot, would be considered a deed restriction. It is not an easement, as it does not benefit another property or person, and it is not a lien, as it is not a financial interest secured by the property.

16. A. Deed restrictions "run with the land," meaning they bind all subsequent owners of the property. A court may find that a deed restriction is no longer enforceable, for instance, if it violates public policy or hasn't been enforced by residents, but it will continue to remain part of the deed.

17. D. Deed restrictions are generally valid, so long as they aren't unconstitutional, a violation of a law, or contrary to judicial determinations of public policy. For example, deed restrictions prohibiting sale to non-white buyers are invalid on public policy grounds.

18. C. When deed restrictions and zoning regulations are in conflict, whichever is more restrictive will apply. In this case, the deed restriction is more restrictive (it prohibits fences, while the municipal ordinance allows them), so it takes precedence.

19. A. Deed restrictions are limitations on what property owners can and cannot do. As they run with the land, they limit the ways future owners may use the property.

20. B. Homeowners who wish to enforce a deed restriction against another owner who plans to violate the restriction may do so by filing for an injunction, which is a legal action that prohibits a person from taking a particular action.

Chapter 5
Public Restrictions on Land

I. **Land Use Controls** – The constitutional basis for land use laws is the *police power*—the state government's power to adopt and enforce the laws and regulations that are necessary to protect the public's health, safety, and general welfare. Zoning ordinances, building codes, and subdivision regulations are all examples of the exercise of the police power. The state may delegate its police power to local government bodies like cities and counties.

   A. **Limitations on Police Power** – An exercise of the police power must meet the following constitutional limitations:

   1. **Public health, safety, and welfare** – An exercise of the police power must relate to protecting the *public health, safety, and welfare*.

   2. **Nondiscriminatory application** – An exercise of the police power must not be discriminatory, which means it must apply in the same manner to all *similarly situated* property owners.

   3. **No confiscation** – An exercise of the police power must not reduce a property's value so much that the regulation amounts to a confiscation.

   4. **Protection from harm** – An exercise of the police power must protect the public from harm that would be caused by the prohibited use.

   B. **Comprehensive Planning** – Many cities and counties have a planning agency, usually called a planning commission, which is responsible for designing and adopting a comprehensive, long-term plan for all the development within the city or county. This is called a *master plan* or *general plan*. All future development and zoning laws must conform to the master plan.

   C. **Zoning** – *Zoning ordinances* divide a community into areas (zones) that are set aside for specific types of uses, such as agricultural, residential, commercial, or industrial. Neighboring zones with incompatible uses may be separated by undeveloped areas called *buffers*. Zoning ordinances regulate the height, size, and shape of buildings, as well as their use. The goal of zoning is to limit uncontrolled growth and ensure that neighboring properties have compatible uses.

The long-term growth plan for a city or county is called a master plan or general plan.

Rural cluster development is a type of zoning that allows rural subdivisions with small lots and open space.

One of zoning's primary purposes is to prevent uncontrolled growth.

Setbacks: provisions in a zoning ordinance or in the CC&Rs that do not allow structures to be built within a certain distance of the property line.

Planned unit development: a subdivision with reduced setback and sideyard requirements.

Nonconforming uses are also called pre-existing nonconforming uses or legal nonconforming uses.

Whether or not a use is profitable is not a consideration in allowing a nonconforming use.

Variance: permission from a zoning authority to use property or build a structure in a way that violates the strict terms of the zoning law.

Rezone: an amendment to a zoning ordinance changing the allowable uses.

Downzoning: rezoning land for a more limited use.

1. **Setback and sideyard requirements** – *Setback* and *sideyard* requirements set out the prescribed minimum distances between buildings (or other improvements) and the street and adjoining property lines.

2. **Exceptions and amendments** – There are four possible exceptions to zoning ordinances: *nonconforming uses*, *variances*, *conditional uses*, and *rezones*.

    a. **Nonconforming use** – A *nonconforming use* (or pre-existing nonconforming use) is a property use that does not meet current zoning requirements, but is allowed because the property was used that way before the present zoning ordinance was enacted.

        i. **Limitations** – Owners of a nonconforming use may not (1) enlarge the use, (2) rebuild it if it is destroyed, or (3) resume it if the use is abandoned. If the nonconforming use becomes a nuisance, it can be abated.

    b. **Variance** – A *variance* is the authorization to build or maintain a structure or use that is prohibited by the zoning ordinance. It is granted only if the owner faces severe practical difficulties or hardship because of zoning laws, not simply because an owner is prevented from the property's most profitable use. A variance would not be allowed that reduces the value of surrounding properties.

        Example: A variance may be granted if the irregular configuration of a lot makes it impossible to comply with setback and sideyard requirements.

    c. **Conditional use** – A *conditional use* permit allows an exception for a special beneficial use, such as a school or hospital, to operate in a neighborhood where it would otherwise be prohibited by zoning.

    d. **Rezone** – A property owner who believes that his property has been zoned improperly may petition the local appeals board for a *rezone* (sometimes called a zoning amendment).

        i. **Downzoning** – If an area is rezoned for a more restrictive use, it is known as *downzoning*.

3. **Conflicting restrictions** – When zoning ordinances (or building codes) and private restrictions conflict, the general rule is that the more restrictive law controls. (For instance, if a private restriction is more restrictive than a corresponding zoning ordinance, the private restriction would prevail.)

Sample questions

While being shown a property in the Oak Leaf subdivision, the buyers asked the agent if there was the possibility of commercial development nearby. The agent pointed out that the adjacent property was zoned for residential uses only. The buyers should verify the agent's statement by:

A. asking a neighbor
B. asking the agent's supervisor
C. checking the master plan
D. checking the plat map

> C. *A master plan or general plan describes a zoning authority's long-term plan for managing growth in an area. It would shed light on whether there were plans to change zoning laws in the future in a particular area.*

Some investors have requested permission to build a factory in Littletown. When deciding where the factory may be built, Littletown's zoning board will most likely consider:

A. how many employees the factory will need
B. how far employees will have to drive
C. impact of the factory's air, noise, and water pollution
D. the amount of taxes the factory will generate

> C. *Of the choices given, a zoning board is most likely to consider the factory's impact on nearby neighborhoods with regard to air, noise, and water pollution.*

Which of the following actions by a developer would require a zoning variance or a rezone, because it would result in a more intensive use of the land?

A. Deed restriction prohibiting further subdivision of individual lots
B. Deed restriction prohibiting painting houses non-earth-tone colors
C. Fewer outbuildings placed on each lot than allowed by law
D. Increase in number of lots per acre

> D. *An increased number of lots per acre would be a more intensive use. If the new number exceeds the maximum number of lots per acre allowed under zoning laws, it would require either a variance or a rezone.*

A new subdivision is built in a rural area, outside urban growth boundaries. It is set up so that houses are situated on small lots, with most of the subdivision's land taken up by green space that is held by all owners in common. This is an example of:

A. condominiums
B. rural cluster development
C. spot zoning
D. townhouses

> B. *Rural cluster development is a zoning practice that allows subdivisions in rural zoning districts to be made up of small lots and reserved green space, in order to conserve rural open space.*

Building codes, like zoning laws, are enforced by cities or counties, not the state.

D. Building Codes – *Building codes* protect the public from unsafe or unworkmanlike construction. They are generally divided into specialized codes, such as a fire code, an electrical code, and a plumbing code. These codes set standards for construction methods and materials.

1. **Enforcement** – Enforcement of building codes is usually accomplished through the *building permit system*. Before constructing, repairing, improving, or altering a building, the builder must submit plans and obtain a permit from the city or county. When the permitted construction has been completed, it is inspected and, if found satisfactory, the local building inspector will issue a *certificate of occupancy*.

2. **Historical landmarks** – Local ordinances may protect buildings designated as historical landmarks. They may prohibit demolishing or modifying such buildings without a permit.

E. Subdivision Regulations – Another way state and local governments control land use is by regulating subdivisions. A *subdivision* is a division of one parcel of land into two or more parcels.

1. **Requirements** – Someone who wants to subdivide a parcel of land must first notify county officials by submitting a plat map showing boundaries of the proposed lots and providing information about provisions for utilities and other public services. The plat must include the legal description of the land to be subdivided.

2. **ILSA** – The federal government also regulates the sale of subdivisions in interstate commerce, through the *Interstate Land Sales Full Disclosure Act (ILSA)*. Enforcement authority for ILSA has passed from the Dept. of Housing and Urban Development to the Consumer Financial Protection Bureau.

F. Environmental Issues – Many environmental hazards are addressed by federal and state laws. An agent should be aware of these hazards, but should contact an expert if any of the following types of contamination is suspected.

1. **Asbestos** – Asbestos is a carcinogenic material used for many years in insulation and roofing.

2. **Urea formaldehyde** – Urea formaldehyde can be found in new pressed wood building materials.

3. **Radon** – Radon is a cancer-causing gas that can enter a house through foundation cracks or floor drains.

4. **PCBs** – Polychlorinated biphenyls (PCBs) are cancer-causing chemicals that may leak from electrical equipment.

5. **Water contamination** – Properties that rely on wells for drinking water should have the water regularly tested by health authorities.

6. **Illegal drug manufacturing** – Manufacture of illegal drugs, such as methamphetamine, may leave behind dangerous toxic residues.

7. **Mold** – Mold can cause respiratory problems for sensitive persons, and requires careful inspection.

8. **Geologic hazards** – Buyers should exercise caution when considering property in flood plains or landslide hazard areas.

Sample questions

Which of the following is true about a building designated as a historical landmark?

A. All lead paint must be removed immediately
B. It may not be willfully destroyed without a permit
C. It may only be sold to family members
D. It must comply with all local ordinances

> *B. Historical preservation ordinances may protect existing buildings of historical value, and prohibit their destruction or modification without approval from an appropriate local authority.*

Which of the following best describes the difference between building codes and zoning regulations?

A. Building codes control the use of real property; zoning regulations affect improvements on the property
B. Building codes affect improvements on the property; zoning regulations control the use of real property
C. Building codes are enforced by municipalities; zoning regulations are enforced by the state
D. Building codes are enforced by the state; zoning regulations are enforced by municipalities

> *B. Building codes protect the public from unsafe or unworkmanlike conditions, through the building permit system. Zoning regulations, by contrast, regulate the use of properties, dividing communities into zones for specific types of uses. Both are enforced at the city or county level.*

A developer wants to subdivide a parcel and market it to potential buyers in other states. The property is divided into 135 vacant lots. He must register with the Office of Interstate Land Sales, which is administered by:

A. FNMA
B. HUD
C. the state real estate office in developer's home state
D. the state real estate office in state in which property is located

B. The Interstate Land Sales Full Disclosure Act requires the developers of subdivisions with more than 100 vacant lots who will market the lots through interstate commerce to register with the Office of Interstate Land Sales, a division of the Department of Housing and Urban Development. (Note: As of July 2015, responsibility for administration of ILSA has been transferred from HUD to the federal Consumer Financial Protection Bureau, but you may still encounter a question similar to this on the state exam.)

There are several environmental issues that would be likely to lead to a property being declared a toxic waste site. Which of the following is one of those issues?

A. A methamphetamine lab
B. Lead-based paint that is not chipped or damaged in any way
C. Mildew found in the kitchen sink
D. Low levels of radon gas

A. Manufacture of illegal drugs, such as methamphetamine, can leave behind toxic residues that are difficult to clean up.

Eminent domain is the right to take; condemnation is the process of taking.

II. **Eminent Domain** – The power of *eminent domain* is the federal or state government's right to take (as opposed to regulate) private property for a public purpose. A local government may use eminent domain to implement its general plan.

A. **Condemnation** – Eminent domain is the government's right to take property; *condemnation* is the process by which it is taken.

B. **Just Compensation Paid to Seller** – The owner must receive *just compensation* for the taken property. Just compensation is usually defined as the fair market value of the property. By contrast, compensation is not necessarily required if an exercise of the police power diminishes a property's value.

C. **Eminent Domain vs. Police Power** – Eminent domain is the government's right to *take* private property for a public purpose through the process of condemnation. Police power is the government's right to *regulate* private property for the public good (through zoning ordinances, building codes, subdivision regulations, and environmental regulations).

III. **Taxation** – There are three types of taxation that affect real property: general real estate taxes, special assessments, and the real estate excise tax.

A. **General Real Estate Taxes** – Real property is taxed *ad valorem*, which is Latin for "according to value." General real estate taxes are levied to support the general operation and services of government.

Assessed value means appraised value for taxation purposes.

1. **Assessment** – The appraisal of land for taxation purposes is called *assessment*. Properties in Washington are assessed

at 100% of their market value. To determine how much tax is owed in a year, multiply the property's assessed value by the tax rate.

2. **Exemptions** – All real property in Washington is taxed unless it is exempt, but there are numerous exemptions. For instance, general real estate taxes are not levied against publicly owned property, property used for church purposes, cemeteries, or non-profit hospitals and schools.

3. **Assessment appeals** – Property owners who disagree with an assessment may appeal to the county. The best evidence would be if comparable properties in the same neighborhood were assessed for less.

B. **Special Assessments** – *Special assessments*, also called *local improvement taxes*, are levied to pay for improvements that benefit particular properties, such as the installation of streetlights. Only the properties that benefit from the improvement are taxed, usually in proportion to the benefit that they receive. (For example, with an assessment for the construction of sidewalks, a particular property owner's share might be calculated based on the property's front footage.) This contrasts with general real estate taxes, which are levied on all properties in a municipality to pay for day-to-day government operations.

Special assessment: a tax levied against properties that have benefited from a public improvement to cover the cost of the improvement.

1. **One-time tax** – A special assessment is usually a one-time tax, although the property owners may be allowed to pay the assessment off in installments.

C. **Real Estate Excise Tax** – The *real estate excise tax* is a tax levied on each sale of real property in Washington. It is usually collected when the deed is recorded.

1. **Tax based on the property's selling price** – The state's share of the tax is 1.28% of the property's selling price. An additional amount (up to 0.75%) may be owed to the city or county government.

Sample questions

An involuntary alienation of property occurs when:
A. a quitclaim deed is signed
B. property is taken by eminent domain
C. property is received through an inheritance
D. property is received through a gift

   B. *Eminent domain occurs when a governmental entity takes private property for a public use.*

Special assessments levied against a property for local improvements, such as streetlights and sidewalks, are computed on the basis of:

A. the market value of the property
B. the benefit the property receives from the improvements
C. a recent appraisal of the property
D. the square footage of the land

B. As a rule, special assessments are allocated according to the benefits each property receives, instead of the market value of the property. Thus a special assessment is not an ad valorem tax. Sometimes the allocation is based on the front footage of the lot, if the assessment is levied to pay for storm drains, curbs, and gutters.

Chapter Quiz

1. The police powers of the government include:

   A. defeasance
   B. foreclosure
   C. lis pendens
   D. building codes and zoning regulations

2. The entity that determines the number of people who may live in a rental unit is the:

   A. Department of Housing and Urban Development
   B. state government
   C. local health department and zoning authority
   D. property owner

3. Cluster zoning, which allows smaller lot sizes and reduced frontages, is suitable if a development:

   A. includes both commercial and residential uses
   B. still has a density ratio consistent with the general plan
   C. abuts a wetland or other sensitive site
   D. abuts state- or city-owned land

4. Sylvia and Bob buy a house on two acres and want to keep cows on the property. Which determines if they can do so?

   A. Their neighbors
   B. Zoning ordinances
   C. State laws
   D. Federal laws

5. Maria buys a home in a subdivision that is subject to restrictive covenants. The city Maria lives in allows fences, but the subdivision's restrictive covenants don't. Of the following, which is true?

   A. Restrictive covenants only limit lot size; they don't limit fencing
   B. The city is a government entity, so its rules take precedence over private restrictions
   C. The deed's restrictive covenants take precedence over the city because they are more restrictive
   D. Maria owns the property, so she has a legal right to build a fence regardless of the deed's restrictions

6. An increasingly common land use pattern allows for subdivisions with smaller lot sizes and little or no setback and sideyard requirements. These are known as:

   A. horizontal property divisions
   B. integrated zoning
   C. planned unit developments
   D. spot zoning

7. Sonya buys a parcel of land and pays taxes on it for five years. After she builds a home on it, the taxes she'll pay are:

   A. special assessments
   B. ad valorem taxes
   C. estate taxes
   D. excise taxes

8. A movie theater was built 10 years ago. If the neighborhood is now zoned entirely residential, the movie theater:

   A. will have to be torn down
   B. must be remodeled to better conform to the neighborhood's intended use
   C. will be allowed to continue if the owner obtains a conditional use permit
   D. will be allowed to continue since it was built before the new zoning law went into effect

9. Jean has operated a store on a busy corner in a suburban area. The city decides to rezone the area from commercial to residential use. Which of the following is true?

   A. Jean is prohibited from operating the store and must stop doing business
   B. Jean must sell the store to residential buyers
   C. Jean must try to obtain a variance
   D. Jean now has a nonconforming use

10. Stanley would like an exception for his diner from new zoning regulations, in that it is a nonconforming use. He would want to argue all of the following to zoning authorities, except that:

    A. conforming to the zoning ordinance would create an undue hardship
    B. he would earn more by using the property for purposes that do not conform with the zoning ordinance
    C. the diner doesn't harm the public health, safety, and welfare
    D. the diner existed before the zoning regulation was passed

11. A homeowner in a recently built subdivision plans to build an extra bedroom extending from the back of his house. Nobody in the subdivision has added on to their houses in a similar manner yet. What would the homeowner need to obtain before he could begin work on this project?

    A. Building permit
    B. Certificate of occupancy
    C. Conforming use permit
    D. Variance

12. A woman owns a house in a subdivision that is zoned strictly residential. She would like to operate a preschool out of her house. She should seek to obtain a/an:

    A. HOA release
    B. conditional use permit
    C. nonconforming use
    D. variance

13. The purpose of a building code is to:

    A. support zoning objectives
    B. acquire land for public use
    C. establish lot size and setback requirements
    D. provide minimum standards for construction

14. Sara is interested in buying a home that is located next to a creek. Sara's agent should advise her to check whether:

    A. a death has ever occurred on the property
    B. the property has asbestos insulation
    C. the property is located in a flood plain
    D. the property is subject to radon

15. A licensee is helping her buyer purchase some property. The buyer would like to make an offer on a corner lot that may have once been used as a storage site for a heating oil company. The licensee should advise her buyer to:

    A. consult with an environmental expert
    B. have a survey done
    C. seek tentative approval from the Environmental Protection Agency
    D. use a condemnation clause in the offer

16. In spite of Delia's objections, the city took a portion of her lot as part of a street widening project. Which of the following is true about eminent domain?

    A. The city can only take vacant land by eminent domain
    B. The city can only take private property for recreational purposes
    C. Delia's property was taken through the process of condemnation
    D. Delia won't be compensated for her lost property

17. An apartment building is right where a new city park is going to be built. The city condemns it. Can the city terminate the leases of the building's tenants?

    A. No; this is a violation of the Federal Fair Housing Act
    B. No; if the government forces a landlord to breach a contract with a tenant, it is violating the Landlord-Tenant Act
    C. Yes; if notice is provided to the tenants, and they receive relocation assistance
    D. Yes; if the tenants receive just compensation from the city

18. By what right would a railroad company acquire private land necessary for a new railway line?

    A. Partition action
    B. Eminent domain
    C. Suit in federal court
    D. Condemnation

19. Which of the following would a landlord need to disclose to prospective tenants?

    A. Busy freeway is nearby
    B. One of the other tenants is a chronic alcoholic
    C. Presence of asbestos
    D. Similar units are available for lower rent in a nearby, more diverse neighborhood

20. Which of the following would be subject to real property taxes?

    A. A house and the land it's on
    B. Cars and motorcycles
    C. Household furnishings
    D. Only the land, but not the improvements

Answer Key

1. D. Building codes and zoning regulations are examples of the government's police power, which is its authority to adopt laws that are necessary for the protection of the public's health, safety, morals, and general welfare.

2. C. Among the many things that a local zoning authority might determine is the maximum occupancy of each dwelling and rental unit in a particular area.

3. B. Cluster zoning is an approach to zoning that allows developments in sub-urban or rural areas where a subdivision may have smaller lot sizes and higher density, but also more shared green space. A development cannot exceed the general plan's limits on density, though.

4. B. Local zoning ordinances allow only certain types of uses within each zone, and would most likely address whether farm animals are allowed on residential properties.

5. C. When zoning ordinances and private restrictions conflict, the more restrictive of the two prevails.

6. C. A planned unit development is a subdivision where lot sizes are smaller and dwellings are grouped closer together, compensated for with significant amounts of open space owned in common.

7. B. General real estate taxes are ad valorem taxes; the amount of tax owed is based on the value of the property. (Note that the taxes Sonya was paying on the land before she built a house on it were also ad valorem taxes.)

8. D. The movie theater is an example of a nonconforming use, which predates a zoning change. Nonconforming uses are generally allowed to continue, although they may not be enlarged, or resumed if they are stopped.

9. D. Certain established uses that were lawful before a rezone may be permitted to continue to operate. These uses, such as Jean's store, are known as nonconforming uses.

10. B. Whether or not a use is profitable does not enter into consideration when deciding whether a nonconforming use will be allowed to continue.

11. A. A property owner must obtain a building permit from the city or county before making significant alterations to an existing building.

12. B. A conditional use permit will allow certain beneficial uses (such as schools and churches) to operate in residential neighborhoods despite zoning laws.

13. D. Building codes set minimum standards for construction materials and methods, in order to protect the public from unsafe or unworkmanlike construction.

14. C. For properties that are located on or near a body of water, it is advisable to check whether the property is in a flood plain. It may affect the buyer's decision, and it should also factor into the decision whether to purchase flood insurance.

15. A. The buyer should consult an environmental expert, who might want to conduct tests to see whether the soil has been contaminated. While the EPA enforces CERCLA, which addresses liability for cleanup of contaminated sites, a buyer does not need EPA approval before buying a site that may have been contaminated.

16. C. Eminent domain is the constitutional power to take private property for a public use. Condemnation is the process by which the property is taken.

17. C. According to the Uniform Relocation Act, tenants whose leases terminate because of the condemnation of their residence are entitled to at least 90 days' notice and assistance with relocation, including payment of moving expenses. (A residential tenant is not likely to have a compensable interest in the property. The tenant does not have an ownership interest, and from an appraisal perspective a residential leasehold interest is unlikely to have any financial value.)

18. B. A state government may delegate the power of eminent domain to local governments, and to private entities that serve the public, such as utility companies and railroads. Eminent domain is the right; condemnation is the process.

19. C. Landlords must disclose the presence of asbestos and other environmental hazards on the property.

20. A. Real property taxes are assessed on the entire value of the property, taking into account both the value of the land and the improvements.

Chapter 6
Contract Law

I. **Legal Classifications of Contracts** – A contract is an agreement between two or more competent persons to do or not to do certain things in exchange for consideration. Every contract is express or implied; unilateral or bilateral; and executory or executed.

   A. **Unauthorized Practice of Law** – Only attorneys may draft contract language. A real estate agent who does so is engaging in the unauthorized practice of law, which is a crime.

   B. **Express vs. Implied** – An *express contract* is one that has been put into words. It may be written or oral. An *implied contract* is created by the actions of the parties, not by express agreement.

   C. **Unilateral vs. Bilateral** – A *unilateral contract* exists if only one of the contracting parties is legally obligated to perform, as with an *option* to purchase or an open listing. A *bilateral contract* is formed when each party promises to do something so that both parties are legally obligated to perform. Most contracts are bilateral.

   Most real estate contracts, including exclusive listings and leases, are bilateral.

   D. **Executory vs. Executed** – Contracts can be either executory or executed.

      1. **Executory contract** – An *executory contract* is one that has not yet been performed or is in the process of being performed.

      Executory contract: a contract in which one or both parties have not yet completed performance of their obligations.

      Example: A purchase and sale agreement is signed by the buyer and seller on May 13, with a closing scheduled for May 29. From May 13 until the closing, the contract is in an executory state.

      2. **Executed contract** – An *executed contract* is one that has been fully performed. When the sale mentioned above has closed, the contract is executed.

II. **Elements of a Valid Contract** – The four elements necessary for a valid contract to be enforceable in court are: capacity to contract, mutual consent, a lawful objective, and consideration. In addition, some contracts must be in writing.

   A. **Capacity** – To have the *capacity* to contract, a person must be 18 years old or older, and she must be *competent*. Contracts signed by someone under 18 are voidable by the minor and are *unenforceable* by the other party. A guardian, however, may sign a contract for a minor, and may ratify or disaffirm a voidable contract that a minor signs.

   Parties to a contract must be at least 18 years old and competent.

   A guardian may sign a contract on behalf of a minor.

1. **Competence** – If a person has been declared incompetent by a court, any contract he signs is void. An incompetent person may still take title to property through a gift or will, just not through a contract.

2. **Temporary incompetence** – If a person entered a contract while temporarily incapacitated (for instance, while under the influence of alcohol), the contract may be voidable by the incompetent party if action is taken to rescind the agreement within a reasonable period of time.

3. **Representing another** – An incompetent person may be represented by another person in contractual matters. This can include a court-appointed guardian or an attorney in fact.

Sample questions

In a bilateral contract:

A. a duty will be performed by one party only
B. one party can restrict the performance of another party
C. two parties have exchanged promises, and both parties are obligated to perform
D. all parties have fully performed their duties

> C. *In a bilateral contract, two parties have exchanged promises and both parties are obligated to perform.*

A contract signed by a person who was intoxicated at the time of the signature would be:

A. valid
B. void
C. voidable by the intoxicated party
D. voidable by the other non-intoxicated party

> C. *A contract signed by a person who is temporarily incompetent (through intoxication, for instance) may be voidable, if the person takes action to rescind the contract within a reasonable time after regaining competency.*

After a purchase agreement has been signed, but before the transaction closes, the buyer attempts to have the contract voided. It is likely he will be able to prove that, because of bipolar disorder, he was mentally incompetent at the time the contract was signed. Is the contract still valid?

A. Yes, because mental illness does not factor into questions of contractual capacity
B. Yes, because the deed has already been placed into escrow
C. No, because buyers are entitled to rescind contracts before closing
D. No, because his temporary incapacity allows him to rescind the contract

> D. *A contract signed by a person who was temporarily incompetent at the time may be voidable, if the person takes action within a reasonable period of time after regaining competency.*

W, age 17, enters into an installment contract to purchase a five-year-old car from S, an adult. From a legal point of view, the contract is:

A. void
B. voidable by W only
C. voidable by S only
D. voidable by either S or W

> B. *The contract is voidable by the minor, but not by the other party.*

Chris, a real estate agent, met with Zach, a property owner, to discuss listing the property. Zach told Chris that he was illiterate and that he needed Chris to read the listing agreement to him. Chris did so, plus he spent a long time explaining the various terms and answering Zach's questions. Zach agreed to everything, and signed the agreement with an "X". The listing agreement is:

A. valid, as long as Zach gets his attorney to verify what Chris told him
B. valid, because Zach fully understood the terms of the contract (he was illiterate, not incompetent)
C. invalid, because an illiterate person is not mentally competent
D. invalid, because Chris was guilty of the unauthorized practice of law when he explained the terms of the listing agreement to Zach

> B. *As long as an illiterate person understands the terms of the contract, he can give his consent to it.*

B. Mutual Consent – Each party must *consent* to the agreement. Once a contract is signed, consent is presumed; thus, no one should sign a contract until its contents are fully understood. Illiteracy or failure to read a contract does not excuse a person from fulfilling the contract.

> Illiteracy or failure to read a contract does not excuse a person from fulfilling the contract.

1. **Offer and acceptance** – Mutual consent is sometimes called *mutual assent*, *mutual agreement*, or a *meeting of the minds*. It is achieved through the process of *offer and acceptance.*

2. **Requirements** – An offer must express a willingness to contract, and must be definite and certain in its terms. An advertisement about a property is not considered an offer; it is only an invitation to negotiate.

3. **Terminating an offer** – If an offer terminates before it's accepted, the *offeror* (the person who made the offer) is entitled to have any deposit returned. There are a number of ways that an offer can terminate before it's accepted:

   a. **Revocation** – The offeror can *revoke* the offer at any time until she is notified that the *offeree* (the person to whom the offer was made) has accepted it. An offer may be revoked for any reason.

   b. **Deadline for acceptance** – If a deadline is set and acceptance is not communicated within the time allotted, the offer terminates automatically.

A counteroffer is a rejection of the original offer and the tender of a new offer.

The offer must be accepted without any changes; changes create a counteroffer.

Constructive fraud: an innocent misrepresentation without the intention to deceive.

c. **Death or incapacity** – If the offeror dies or is declared incompetent before the offer is accepted, the offer terminates.

d. **Rejection** – A *rejection* terminates an offer. Once the offeree rejects an offer, he cannot change his mind and later accept the offer without the offeror's consent.

e. **Counteroffer** – Sometimes called a *qualified acceptance*, a *counteroffer* is actually a rejection of the initial offer and the tender of a new offer. The original offeror becomes the offeree, and can accept or reject the revised offer. If the counteroffer is rejected, the party making the counteroffer cannot go back and accept the original offer (that was terminated by the counteroffer).

4. **Acceptance** – The offeree must communicate his acceptance to the offeror within the time allotted and in the manner specified. A contract is not formed until the offeror receives written notice of the offeree's acceptance. The date of acceptance is the date of the contract.

5. **Negative influences** – The offeree's acceptance must be free of any negative influences, such as *fraud*, *undue influence*, or *duress*. If any of these negative influences occurred, the contract is *voidable*.

a. **Fraud** – *Fraud* is the misrepresentation of a material fact to another person who relies on the misrepresentation as the truth in deciding to enter into a transaction.

   i.   **Actual fraud** – *Actual fraud* occurs when the person making the statement either knowingly makes a false statement with the intent to deceive, or doesn't know if the statement is true, but makes it anyway.

   ii. **Constructive fraud** – *Constructive fraud* occurs when a person who occupies a position of confidence and trust, or who has superior knowledge of the subject, makes a false statement with no intent to deceive.

b. **Undue influence** – *Undue influence* is using one's influence to pressure a person into making a contract, or taking advantage of another's weakness of mind to induce him to enter a contract.

c. **Duress** – *Duress* is compelling someone to do something (such as enter a contract) against her will, with the use of force or constraint.

C. **Lawful Objective** – Both the objective of the contract and the consideration for the contract must be lawful.

> **Example:** Two parties agree to buy and sell cocaine. The objective of the contract is illegal and the consideration offered by the seller (the cocaine) is also illegal. A court would not enforce this contract. If either the objective of a contract or the consideration promised is illegal, the contract is void.

Charging an interest rate that exceeds the legal maximum is called *usury*.

D. **Consideration** – The parties to a contract must exchange *consideration*; each party must give something of value (such as money, goods, or services) to the other. The consideration given by one party does not have to be equal in value to the other party's consideration.

Consideration: anything of value given to induce another to enter into a contract, such as money, goods, services, or a promise.

E. **Writing Requirement** – For most real estate contracts there is a fifth element necessary for the contract to be valid. Real estate contracts must be in writing under the *statute of frauds*.

1. **Statute of frauds** – This is a state law that requires certain types of contracts to be in writing and signed. This includes real estate purchase and sale agreements, listing agreements, mortgage assumptions, and leases for more than one year.

The statute of frauds applies to real estate contracts.

    a. **Unenforceable** – If the parties fail to put a contract that falls under the statute of frauds in writing, the contract is *unenforceable*.

Sample questions

A contract to purchase property must include which essential element?
A. Equal bargaining power between the parties
B. A seal by a notary public
C. Mutual agreement
D. A three-day right to rescind

> C. *An unambiguous offer and an unqualified acceptance are essential to a valid contract of any kind. This is also called mutual acceptance (also known as mutual consent).*

A potential buyer gives a seller an offer that doesn't meet the seller's demands. What has the buyer given?
A. Contract of sale
B. Counteroffer
C. Offer to purchase
D. Option

> C. *An offer simply must express a willingness to contract, and be certain in its terms. It does not need to match the seller's terms. (An advertisement with the listing price is not a contract offer; it is only an invitation to negotiate. So the buyer's response to the ad is not a counteroffer.)*

When is an enforceable purchase and sale agreement formed?

A. When the buyer knows of the seller's written acceptance of the offer
B. When the seller has orally informed the buyer of her acceptance
C. When the seller has received the earnest money
D. When the transaction has closed

> A. *Formation of a contract occurs when the offeree communicates acceptance to the offeror in an acceptable method and within the proper time period. For a real estate contract to be enforceable, the agreement must be in writing.*

Which of the following does NOT terminate an offer?

A. An offer from a third party for a higher purchase price
B. A qualified acceptance (counteroffer) by the offeree
C. The offeror dies before the offeree accepts the offer
D. The offeror revokes the offer before it is accepted

> A. *An offer can be terminated through revocation by the offeror, death of the offeror, or a counteroffer. It is not terminated by a competing offer from another party.*

A real estate contract, in order to be valid, must include:

A. a contingency
B. a "time is of the essence" clause
C. an option
D. consideration

> D. *Any contract, whether for real estate or anything else, must include consideration as one of the four basic elements.*

To be enforceable, a contract for the sale of real estate must be in writing and signed by the parties. This is true because of which law?

A. Real Estate License Law
B. Uniform Commercial Code
C. Real Estate Settlement Procedures Act
D. Statute of frauds

> D. *The statute of frauds requires certain contracts, including virtually all real estate contracts, to be in writing.*

III. **Legal Status of Contracts** – Four terms are used to describe the legal status of a contract. They include:

A. **Void** – A *void* contract is no contract at all; it has no legal effect. This most often occurs because one of the essential elements (capacity, mutual consent, lawful objective, or consideration) is completely lacking.

B. Voidable – A *voidable* contract appears to be valid, but has some defect or contingency giving one or both of the parties the power to withdraw from the agreement.

    1. Negative influences – If a contract is formed as a result of fraud, undue influence, or duress, it is *voidable*, not void. The same is true for a contract entered into by a minor.

    2. Rescission and ratification – The contract party damaged by the fraud, undue influence, or duress can avoid having to perform, but she must *rescind* the agreement. If she doesn't take action in a reasonable period of time, a court might decide the contract was *ratified*. An injured party who decides to continue with the contract may also *expressly ratify* the contract.

C. Unenforceable – An *unenforceable* contract is one that can't be enforced in court because (1) its contents can't be proved (usually oral contracts); (2) the other party has a voidable contract; or (3) the *statute of limitations* has expired (for written contracts, six years from the breach of contract; for oral contracts, three years from the breach of contract).

D. Valid – If an agreement has all the essential elements, can be proved in court, and is free of negative influences, it's a *valid* contract and a judge will enforce it.

> A contract is voidable if signed:
> • as a result of fraud,
> • because of undue influence,
> • under duress, or
> • by a minor.

> The damaged party must rescind a voidable contract or it will become valid through ratification.

> Oral real estate contracts are unenforceable under the statute of frauds.

> If there is a conflict between two different valid contracts, the more recently signed one will take precedence.

Sample questions

A buyer failed to sign an offer to purchase her property. The contract is:

A. valid
B. voidable
C. void
D. enforceable

    C. When an offer has not been signed (accepted) by one of the parties, there is no contract at all.

There are written contingencies in a purchase and sale agreement. This contract is:

A. unilateral
B. voidable
C. executed
D. contrary to public policy

    B. Contracts with contingencies are valid, but they may be voidable if the contingency is not fulfilled.

Which of the following would NOT make a contract voidable?
A. It is missing an essential element
B. One party signed the contract as a result of fraud
C. The contract resulted from misrepresentation
D. One of the parties was subject to duress

    A.   If one of the four contract essential elements (capacity, mutual consent, lawful objective, and consideration) is totally missing, the contract is void, not just voidable.

IV. **Discharging a Contract** – Once there is a valid, enforceable contract, it may be discharged by full performance or by an agreement between the parties. A contract is not discharged by the death of one of the parties; it remains binding on the heirs.

    A. **Full Performance** – *Full performance* means that the parties have performed all of their obligations. The contract is *executed*.

    B. **Agreement Between the Parties** – The parties to a contract can agree to discharge it in any of the following ways:

        1. **Rescission** – Sometimes the parties may mutually decide to rescind the contract. The buyer and seller sign an agreement that terminates their original agreement and returns them (as nearly as possible) to their original positions. A *mutual rescission* is sometimes called a *contract to destroy a contract*.

> The damaged party can unilaterally rescind a voidable contract.

        2. **Cancellation** – In a *cancellation*, the parties agree to terminate the contract, but previous acts are unaffected. For example, money paid before the cancellation is not returned.

        3. **Assignment** – In an *assignment*, one party wants out of the contract and intends to assign his contractual rights and responsibilities to a third party. The new party (the assignee) assumes primary liability for the contractual obligations, while the withdrawing party (the assignor) remains secondarily liable.

> The assignor remains secondarily liable for the contractual obligations.

        4. **Novation** – *Novation* is the substitution of a new party into an existing obligation, or the substitution of a new obligation for an old one.

            a. **Assignment vs. novation** – After a contract is assigned there is continuing liability for the assignor; with a novation there is no continuing liability for the withdrawing party.

V. Breach of Contract – A *breach of contract* occurs when one of the parties fails, without legal excuse, to perform any of the promises contained in the agreement. The injured party can seek a remedy in court only if the failure is a *material breach* (a breach of an important clause in the contract). When a material breach occurs, there are four possible remedies available to the injured party:

> Breach: an unexcused failure to perform a contractual obligation.

> Material breach: when a promise that has not been fulfilled is an important part of the contract.

A. Rescission – A *rescission* is a termination of the contract resulting in the parties returning to their original positions. A rescission can be by agreement between the parties or by court order.

B. Liquidated Damages – The parties to a contract sometimes agree in advance to an amount that will serve as full compensation to be paid in the event that one of the parties defaults. This sum is called *liquidated damages*. In a real estate transaction, the buyer's earnest money deposit is often treated as liquidated damages.

C. Damages – A damage award is an amount of money that the court orders the breaching party to pay the other party. *Damages* are generally intended to put the non-breaching party in the financial position she would have been in if the breaching party had fulfilled the terms of the contract.

> Mediation is a dispute resolution process where parties to a dispute are helped by a mediator to find a mutually agreeable solution.

D. Specific Performance – *Specific performance* is a remedy that forces a defaulting party to perform the terms of the contract. For example, a court can order a defaulting seller to sign and deliver a deed to a buyer to complete a purchase.

  1. Limitations – Specific performance applies as a remedy only when monetary damages would be inadequate.

Sample questions

A provision in a sales contract that states that a sum agreed to in advance will serve as full compensation in the event of a breach is a:

A. liquidated damages provision
B. compensatory damages provision
C. punitive damages provision
D. default damages provision

  A. Most purchase and sale agreements require a forfeiture of the earnest money (called liquidated damages) if the buyer breaches the contract.

The Taylors sign an exclusive right to sell listing that expires in six months. A short time later they change their minds and decide not to sell. Can they terminate the listing?

A. No, they must wait for the listing to expire in six months
B. No, an exclusive right to sell listing is binding on both parties
C. Yes, by mutual consent
D. Yes, but only if the agent agrees

C. Both parties to a contract can mutually agree to rescind a contract before it is scheduled to expire.

John negotiated an option contract with Margaret, in which Margaret had three months to purchase John's property. In the second month, Margaret found another buyer. Margaret can probably transfer her right to purchase the property to another buyer because of the right of:

A. novation
B. assignment
C. first refusal
D. rescission

B. Margaret may assign the option contract to another buyer (unless there is a clause in the contract prohibiting assignment).

A homeowner with a mortgage sells his home to a purchaser who agrees to assume the mortgage. The purchaser applies for and obtains the lender's approval, and the seller is released from liability for the mortgage. This is an example of:

A. assignment
B. subrogation
C. subordination
D. novation

D. This is a novation, because the lender has accepted the purchaser and released the seller from liability. The purchaser has entered into a new loan agreement with the lender that replaces the original agreement between the seller and the lender.

A legal action brought in court to compel a party to fulfill the terms of a contract because the land is unique and money damages would not adequately compensate the party victimized by a breach is called a/an:

A. partition action
B. suit for specific performance
C. quiet title action
D. injunction

B. The legal premise that no two properties are alike is the basis of a suit for specific performance. In this type of suit, the plaintiff asks the court to order someone who has breached to actually perform the contract as agreed (deliver the deed to the buyer), rather than simply pay money damages.

VI. **Types of Real Estate Contracts** – The most common types of contracts relating to real estate are listing agreements, purchase and sale agreements, and leases, all of which we will discuss in later sections. In this section we will discuss *land contracts* and *option agreements*.

    A. **Land Contracts** – Under a land contract (also called a real estate contract, installment sales contract, agreement of sale, or contract for deed), the buyer purchases the seller's property on an installment basis.

        1. **Parties** – The parties to a land contract are the *vendor* (the seller) and the *vendee* (the buyer).

        2. **Title** – Periodic payments toward the purchase price are made over a span of years, during which time the vendor retains *legal title* to the property. The vendee receives a warranty deed when the full purchase price has been paid. In the meantime, the vendee has *equitable title* to the property, which includes the right to possess and enjoy the property.

    B. **Option Agreements** – An option agreement is essentially a contract to make a contract; it is an agreement that creates a right to buy, sell, or lease property for a fixed price within a set period of time.

        1. **Parties** – The parties to an option agreement are the *optionor* (the property owner who grants the option; the seller) and the *optionee* (the person with the option right; the buyer).

        2. **Option period** – The optionor is bound to keep the option open for the period specified in the option agreement. She is not allowed to sell or lease the property to anyone other than the optionee until the option expires. If the optionee fails to exercise the option and purchase the property within the specified time, the option expires automatically.

        3. **Unilateral contract** – An option agreement is considered a unilateral contract, because the optionee is not obligated to exercise the contract. Once exercised, it becomes a bilateral contract. Because it becomes the sale contract once the option is exercised, the option agreement must contain all of the terms of the sale (like price and financing).

        4. **Consideration** – Some consideration must pass from the optionee to the optionor; a mere statement of consideration in the agreement is not sufficient.

        Exception: In a lease/option agreement, the provisions of the lease are treated as sufficient consideration to support the option.

> Option money is typically not returned at the end of the option period if the optionee does not exercise the option.
>
> Lease/option agreement: provisions of the lease are sufficient consideration to support the option.

5. **Contract right** – An option agreement gives the optionee a contract right, but not an interest in real property. It is not a lien, and cannot be used as security for a mortgage. If the optionor dies during the option period, the option remains binding on the optionor's heirs.

6. **Assignment** – An option can be assigned, unless the agreement includes a provision prohibiting assignment.

   Exception: Assignment is not allowed when the consideration paid by the optionee is in the form of an unsecured promissory note. In such a case, the optionee must obtain the optionor's written permission before the option may be assigned.

7. **Recording** – An optionee can and should record his option agreement to give third parties constructive notice of the option. If an option is recorded and then exercised, its priority dates back to the date the option was recorded.

8. **Right of first refusal** – An option should not be confused with a *right of first refusal*, which gives a person the first opportunity to purchase or lease real property if it becomes available. For instance, a tenant may be given the right of first refusal to purchase the property if the landlord decides to sell it.

Unless there is language that prohibits it, an option can be assigned, as long as the option money is NOT in the form of an unsecured promissory note.

The optionee can and should record her option agreement.

Sample questions

An option:
A. transfers title immediately when it is signed by both parties
B. transfers legal title (but not equitable title) when it is signed by both parties
C. sets a time limit to keep an offer open
D. does not include the basic terms of the contract (such as the sale price); those are to be determined later

   C. An option basically keeps an offer open for a set period of time.

An optionee's rights can be assigned under all of the following circumstances, except when the:
A. option money is $10 or less
B. option money is in the form of a promissory note
C. optionor has died
D. optionee has died

   B. If the option money is in the form of a promissory note, the optionee cannot assign it (nor can his estate, if the optionee is dead).

A buyer and seller agree upon an option to purchase with a 60-day option period. When should the parties agree upon the purchase price?

A. Any point between the signing of the option agreement and closing
B. At closing
C. Before signing the option agreement
D. When the buyer decides to exercise the option

    C.   *An option agreement should contain all of the details that a purchase and sale agreement would contain. Once the option agreement is exercised, the option agreement serves as the sale contract.*

Two parties enter into an option agreement, scheduled to end in December. However, in October the optionee decides he doesn't want to buy the property. What should the parties do in order to terminate the option?

A. Execute a rescission of contract form
B. Exercise the option's contingency clause
C. File an interpleader action so a court can void the contract
D. Nothing; the option will expire automatically

    D.   *An optionee must take an affirmative step to exercise an option by giving written notice of acceptance to the optionor. If the optionee does not do so by the end of the option period, the option automatically expires.*

Of the following types of contracts, which one is a unilateral contract?

A. Escrow instructions
B. Exclusive right-to-sell listing
C. Lease
D. Option

    D.   *An option that has not yet been exercised is a unilateral contract: in other words, only one party is obligated to act. Once it has been exercised, it becomes a bilateral contract.*

Chapter Quiz

1. A real estate firm handles property management for a number of property owners. Rather than use one standard form, though, each lease must be separately drafted, based on individual negotiations. Which of the following statements is true?

   A. A lease agreement can be prepared by anyone
   B. An attorney must be engaged to draft each contract
   C. Any licensed real estate agent can draft these leases
   D. A real estate firm can draft the leases if both parties agree in writing

2. When can a minor enter into a binding contract?

   A. If a guardian co-signs
   B. If the contract is witnessed
   C. If the minor is a high school graduate
   D. Never

3. A minor purchases a home right before he turns 18. Immediately after he reaches the age of majority, he contacts the seller and rescinds the contract, demanding his money back. Which is true?

   A. This is possible if the home was purchased with a mortgage, because of the right of rescission under Regulation Z
   B. This is possible because he is doing so within a reasonable time after having reached the age of majority
   C. This isn't possible because buyers are subject to caveat emptor
   D. This isn't possible because a buyer can't rescind a voidable contract after closing

4. An offer is dated June 4. The offer is accepted on June 7. The buyers are approved for a loan and satisfy the financing contingency on June 9. The transaction closes on June 28. The date of the contract is:

   A. June 4
   B. June 7
   C. June 9
   D. June 28

5. A property is listed for $275,000. The buyers offer $265,000, and insist that the gourmet six-burner stove remain with the property. When the signed offer is presented to the sellers, the sellers accept the price, but want to take the stove with them. They cross out the item about the stove, sign the form, and return it to the buyers. Under these circumstances:

   A. there is now a valid contract that has been signed by all parties
   B. the offer has been invalidated and the parties will need to begin negotiating from the beginning
   C. the sellers can turn around and accept the original offer, if the buyer won't go along with giving up the stove
   D. the original offer is terminated, and the sellers have made a counteroffer

6. Mark is selling his property, which has an unfinished basement. He gets a full-price offer from Susan, but the offer requires Mark to finish the basement prior to closing. Do Mark and Susan have a binding contract?

   A. Yes, because both parties have made offers to each other
   B. Yes, because Susan made a full-price offer
   C. No, because a valid offer must be written and recorded
   D. No, because Mark has not accepted Susan's offer

7. Barker is declared incompetent by a court, and his daughter, Marge, is appointed to handle his affairs. After several years, Marge asks her sister Beth to take over her duties. Beth then lists Barker's property for sale. Would a sale of Barker's property be valid under these circumstances?

   A. No, any contract concerning real estate and an incompetent person is automatically void
   B. No, Beth hasn't been designated by a court to handle Barker's affairs
   C. Yes, but only if Beth gets Barker's written permission
   D. Yes, Marge has delegated her responsibilities properly

8. A and B sign a rental agreement in which A agrees to lease her property to B in exchange for rent. This contract is:
   A. bilateral
   B. implied
   C. unilateral
   D. voidable

9. The parties negotiate the sale of a property by writing letters to each other (in the old-fashioned way—by hand). Their agreement is:
   A. invalid; the parties must meet with each other in person
   B. invalid; the parties must use a pre-printed form
   C. invalid; each letter is only a counteroffer to the previous letter
   D. valid; under the statute of frauds, written contracts to sell real estate are enforceable if they are in writing

10. Which of the following is true regarding an oral agreement for the sale of real property? It is:
    A. unenforceable; it violates the statute of frauds
    B. void; it violates the statute of frauds
    C. voidable; it violates the statute of frauds
    D. valid; assuming both parties are above the age of majority

11. A 17-year-old purchased a house. He moved in, lived in it for a year, and then decided he didn't want the responsibility of owning a home. He refused to honor the contract. In this case, the contract:
    A. is valid; the buyer must abide by its terms
    B. is voidable; the buyer can choose whether or not to carry out its terms
    C. was voidable when signed; however, the buyer probably ratified it by living in the house
    D. is void; it was missing an essential contract element

12. A buyer and seller sign a contract for deed. Two weeks later, the buyer is declared mentally incompetent. The buyer's guardian contacts the seller and says that he can continue to make the buyer's payments as agreed. Which of the following is true?
    A. The buyer can disaffirm the contract within a reasonable period of time
    B. The buyer can finish out the contract as the buyer's guardian has proposed
    C. The seller can agree to receive payments from the guardian and if the payments become unreliable, the seller can then cancel the contract
    D. The contract is automatically voided because of the buyer's incapacity, regardless of what the guardian says

13. X and Y execute a properly drawn up option agreement for X to purchase Y's commercial property. X gives $5 in consideration. The option is:
    A. unenforceble
    B. valid
    C. void
    D. voidable

14. The listing agreement states that a property is 5.1 acres. The purchase and sale agreement states that it's 5.12 acres. The mortgage notes that the property is 5.22 acres, while the deed states that the lot's size is 5.21 acres. If there is a dispute, which of the documents will take precedence?
    A. Deed
    B. Listing agreement
    C. Mortgage
    D. Purchase and sale agreement

15. Jerry offered to buy some vacant land for $500,000. There were no contingencies in his offer, and it was accepted by the seller. Jerry was planning on building a shopping center on the property, but didn't mention this to the seller or his real estate agent. A few days before closing, Jerry learned that his financing for the shopping center had fallen through. The contract is:
    A. void
    B. voidable
    C. unenforceable
    D. valid

16. Which of the following people might bring a suit for specific performance?

   A. A buyer in a real estate transaction in which the seller backed out one day before closing

   B. A homeowner unhappy about a neighbor who painted her house purple in violation of the subdivision CC&Rs

   C. A real estate broker who didn't receive the commission she was promised

   D. A seller who was overcharged during escrow

17. Frank gives Stella an option. Stella, as the optionee, is obligated to:

   A. exercise the option at the end of the option period

   B. apply for a zoning change, if one is necessary in order to use the property in the way Stella wants

   C. pay consideration for the option right

   D. record the option

18. A contract gives a person the right to purchase property for a particular price within a certain timeframe. This contract is a/an:

   A. land contract

   B. lien agreement

   C. sale-leaseback

   D. option

19. In an option:

   A. no consideration is required

   B. the seller is the optionee and the buyer is the optionor

   C. the seller must apply the option money to the purchase price if the optionee exercises her option

   D. the option agreement must clearly state all the terms and conditions of the sale

20. Martha gave Hannah the right to purchase her vacant lot for $65,000. Hannah paid Martha $1,200 for this right. Hannah is the:

   A. mortgagor

   B. mortgagee

   C. optionor

   D. optionee

Answer Key

1. B. Only an attorney may draft a contract for someone else; for a real estate agent to do so would be the unauthorized practice of law. The agent may fill out preprinted forms, but not draft new contract language.

2. A. Affairs of minors or incompetent persons can be handled by parents or by court-appointed guardians. The authorized person can enter into a contract on behalf of the minor.

3. B. A person can typically rescind a contract he entered into as a minor, as long as he acts quickly after reaching the age of majority.

4. B. The date on which acceptance occurs is considered to be the date of the contract. In this case, that would be June 7.

5. D. Even though the sellers accepted the price change, they still changed the terms of the offer by altering the part about the stove. This had the effect of terminating the offer and creating a counteroffer. The sellers, in essence, become the new offerors.

6. D. For a valid contract to exist, there must be offer and acceptance. An advertisement (like a listing) is not considered an offer, only an invitation to negotiate. The buyer's offer is just that: an offer, without an acceptance.

7. B. An incompetent person's property may be sold, but the deed must be signed by a court-appointed guardian or a duly appointed attorney in fact. Beth doesn't meet either of these criteria.

8. A. Bilateral contracts are formed when each party promises to do something and both parties are legally obligated to perform. Lease agreements are bilateral contracts.

9. D. The statute of frauds requires contracts for the sale of real estate to be in writing. Simple notes or memoranda are sufficient to meet the requirement, so long as they identify the property adequately, indicate agreement between the parties, and are signed by the parties.

10. A. An oral agreement for the sale of real estate violates the statute of frauds. Such a contract is unenforceable, except in rare instances, such as when there is evidence that the party trying to enforce the contract performed her contractual obligations.

11. C. Generally, a contract entered into by a minor is voidable, which means it can be rescinded by the minor. However, if the minor does not act promptly, the contract may be deemed to have been ratified.

12. B. If a person is declared incompetent after signing a contract, the contract may be voidable at the discretion of a court-appointed guardian. As with any voidable contract, though, the person's guardian may decide to ratify the agreement and continue with it. (If the buyer has an appointed guardian, the buyer would not be the one who decides to disaffirm the contract.)

13. B. An option agreement, because it is a contract, must include consideration. The consideration can be a nominal amount (like $5), but it must actually be given to the optionor and can't be merely a recitation of consideration.

14. A. When there is a conflict between several different contracts, the one that was most recently signed is considered to take precedence. The deed would most likely be the final document signed of the four.

15. D. The contract is valid. Since it was not made contingent on financing for the shopping center, Jerry must go ahead with the purchase.

16. A. A suit for specific performance is used when the object of a sales contract is unique and monetary damages would not be sufficient to put the victimized party in the position she would have been in, had the contract been performed. That's the case with real estate, as well as items such as jewelry or artwork.

17. C. Some consideration must pass from optionee to optionor. A mere statement of consideration is not adequate. Recording the option is advisable, but not required.

18. D. An option is an agreement that gives one party the right to buy or lease property at a set price within a set period of time.

19. D. The option agreement also serves as the sale contract once the option is exercised, so all terms and conditions of the sale need to be included in the option agreement.

20. D. Martha gave the option to Hannah, so Martha is the optionor and Hannah is the optionee.

Chapter 7

Real Estate Agency Law

I. **Introduction to Agency** – An *agency relationship* arises when one person authorizes another to represent her. In Washington, agency relationships are governed by Washington's Real Estate Brokerage Relationships Act. Some aspects of general agency law that apply in most states do not apply in Washington because of this law, but it is important to know these concepts because they may be tested on the National portion of the exam.

A. **The Agency Relationship** – The parties to an agency relationship are the *agent*—the person authorized to represent another; and the *principal*—the party who authorizes and controls the acts of the agent. (For instance, in a listing agreement, the brokerage is the agent and the seller is the principal.) Persons outside the agency relationship who seek to deal with the principal through the agent are *third parties*. A principal who engages the agent's services is also known as a *client*, while a third party is known as a *customer*.

1. **Subagency** – There is an agency relationship between a brokerage and the licensees who work for that firm. An affiliated licensee is her firm's agent, and the firm is the licensee's principal. To the firm's principal (the buyer or seller), an affiliated licensee is a *subagent* (the agent of an agent).

B. **Agency Law** – For a third party, dealing with the agent can be the legal equivalent of dealing with the principal; for instance, when an authorized agent signs a document or makes a promise, it's as if the principal himself signed the document or made the promise.

II. **Creating an Agency Relationship** – Under general agency law, an agency may be formed in four ways:

A. **Express Agreement** – Most agencies are created by an *express* written agreement, such as a listing agreement or a buyer agency agreement. However, the agreement does not need to be in writing to create a valid agency, nor does the agreement have to be supported by consideration.

The agency agreement need not be in writing to be valid.

The agency relationship does not have to be supported by consideration.

Ratification: a principal's approval of a prior unauthorized act performed on behalf of the principal. Ratification gives the act validity and a legally binding effect.

Implied agency: one not expressed in words, but understood from actions or circumstances.

B. **Ratification** – An agency is created by *ratification* when the principal gives approval after the fact to acts performed by a person not acting as the principal's agent (or acts outside the agent's authority). Ratification may be made expressly or by accepting the benefits of the acts.

C. **Estoppel** – An agency can be created by *estoppel* when the principal has allowed a third party to believe there was agency authority and it would be unfair to the third party to deny the agent's authority.

D. **Implication** – An agency can be created by *implication* if a person behaves toward another in a way that implies that she is that person's agent.

E. **Creating an Agency Under Washington Law** – Under Washington law, an agency relationship between a licensee and a client begins when the licensee undertakes to provide real estate services for the client. An agency relationship with a seller begins with a written listing agreement. An agency relationship with a buyer begins automatically when a licensee performs real estate brokerage services for the buyer.

Exception: A licensee working with a buyer does not automatically become the buyer's agent if there's a written agreement to the contrary. This may include a listing agreement with the seller, a dual agency agreement with both parties, a subagency agreement with the seller, or a non-agency agreement. For example, an agent who shows a buyer one of his own listings does not become the buyer's agent, because of his listing agreement with the seller.

Sample question

Seller Sam is selling his property to Buyer Carol, who is represented by Agent Phil. To Agent Phil, Seller Sam is a:

A. customer
B. client
C. principal
D. subagent

    A. In this situation, Phil is the agent, Carol is the principal, and Sam is the customer (third party).

III. **Legal Effects of Agency** – Once an agency relationship has been established, the principal is bound by acts of the agent that are within the scope of the agent's authority.

    A. **Scope of Authority** – The extent to which the principal can be bound by the agent's actions depends on the *scope of authority* granted to the agent. There are three basic types of agents:

        1. **Universal agents** – A *universal agent* is authorized to do anything that can be lawfully delegated to a representative.

        2. **General agents** – A *general agent* is authorized to handle all of the principal's affairs in one or more specified areas. Property managers are considered general agents.

        3. **Special agents** – A *special agent* has limited authority to do a specific thing or conduct a specific transaction. In most cases, a real estate licensee is a special agent because she has only limited authority; for instance, she can only negotiate with third parties and cannot sign a contract on the seller's behalf. (She would need a power of attorney to bind the seller.)

    B. **Actual vs. Apparent Authority** – *Actual authority* is authority granted to the agent by the principal, either *expressly* (written or orally), or by *implication* (the implied authority to do what is necessary to carry out actions that were expressly authorized). A person has *apparent authority* when he has no actual authority to act, but the principal negligently or deliberately allows it to appear that the actions are authorized. The principal may be liable for acts committed by an *apparent agent* (or *ostensible agent*).

    C. **Vicarious Liability** – Under general agency law, the principal may be held liable for his agent's wrongful acts. This is known as *vicarious liability*. Thus, a buyer or seller may be liable for the acts of his real estate agent.

        1. **Washington law** – Under Washington real estate law, there is no vicarious liability between a real estate agent and a principal. A seller or buyer is ordinarily not liable for any act, error, or omission by a real estate licensee.

    D. **Imputed Knowledge** – Under general agency law, a principal is considered to have notice of information that the agent has, even if the agent never actually tells the principal. As a result, a principal could be liable for failing to disclose a problem to a third party, even if the agent never told the principal about the problem.

        1. **Washington law** – Under Washington real estate law, the *imputed knowledge* rule does not apply. A principal is not

Property managers are considered general agents.

automatically held to have notice of facts known by a real estate agent.

Sample questions

ABC Realty signed a property management agreement with XYZ Apartment Rentals. Do they have an agency agreement and, if so, what kind of agency authority has been created?

A. No; to create an agency relationship, they would have to sign a listing agreement
B. No; XYZ has only hired ABC Realty to manage the properties, not to be its agent
C. Yes; ABC has been hired by XYZ to be a special agent
D. Yes; ABC has been hired by XYZ to be a general agent

> D. *A property management agreement creates a general agency relationship, in which the agent (ABC Realty) is authorized to handle all of the principal's (XYZ Apartment Rentals) affairs in one or more specified areas.*

Gerald engages a licensee to find a buyer for his listed property. In this context, the licensee is acting as a:

A. general agent
B. power of attorney
C. property manager
D. special agent

> D. *When a licensee represents a seller in a single transaction, and is authorized to perform typical duties associated with listing a property, she acts as a special agent.*

Special, general, and universal agency all:

A. create a long-lasting relationship over multiple transactions
B. give the agent authority to act on the principal's behalf in all financial matters
C. originate with the principal
D. terminate with the end of a particular transaction

> C. *Special, general, and universal agency have varying lengths, and give the agent varying levels of authority. The common thread is that they all are created when a principal delegates to an agent the right to perform certain actions on his behalf.*

A home is built on a hillside with underground springs that cause the ground to soften from time to time. The owner, who has had the property for three years with no problems, sells the house without mentioning the underground springs. The listing agent is aware of the springs but says nothing. A year later, the buyer realizes that a corner of the house is sinking. She is entitled to sue:

A. the listing agent
B. the seller
C. both the listing agent and the seller
D. neither the listing agent nor the seller

C. *The agent's failure to tell the buyer about the springs (a known material fact) amounted to misrepresentation by omission, and the agent may be liable to the buyer. If the seller knew about the springs, the seller could also be liable to the buyer for misrepresentation. And even if the seller did not know about the springs, in many states the seller could be held vicariously liable for his agent's misrepresentation.*

A seller sells his house "as is" to a buyer. Shortly after the sale closes, the buyer finds a large hole in the ground next to the house. The hole, which has caused significant damage to the foundation, is concealed with leaves and branches. Which of the following is correct?

A. Only the licensee is liable
B. Only the seller is liable
C. Both the seller and the licensee may be liable
D. Neither is liable, because the house was sold "as is"

C. *Even when property is sold "as is," sellers and real estate agents have a duty to disclose any known latent defects or other material facts. Here, whoever concealed the hole—whether it was the seller, the licensee, or both of them—would be liable for misrepresentation. If only one of them covered up the hole, the other one could also be liable if he or she was aware of the deception and failed to say anything about it to the buyer. Also, even if the seller knew nothing about the problem, in many states the seller could be vicariously liable if it was the seller's agent who concealed the hole.*

IV. **Duties in an Agency Relationship** – An agent owes certain duties to her principal, and both the agent and the principal have certain responsibilities to third parties. An agency relationship is a *fiduciary* relationship. A fiduciary is a person who stands in a special position of trust and confidence in relation to someone else. The law holds the fiduciary (real estate agent) to high standards of conduct. As a fiduciary, an agent must serve the best interests of the principal.

> Fiduciary relationship: one party owes the other loyalty and a higher standard of good faith than is owed to third parties.

A. **Agent's Duties in General** – In addition to owing fiduciary duties to her principal, an agent owes certain duties to any party to whom he renders services. This applies whether it is a principal or a third party. Under Washington law, these duties include:

1. **Reasonable care and skill** – If an agent's negligence or incompetence harms a third party, the agent may be liable.

2. **Honesty and good faith** – Real estate agents must avoid inaccuracies in their statements to prospective buyers.

   a. **Opinions, predictions, or puffing** – Misrepresentations, which may be grounds for a lawsuit, should not be confused with opinions, predictions, or puffing. The latter are nonfactual or exaggerated statements a buyer should know he cannot rely on.

Copies of signed contracts must be given as soon as possible to all signing parties.

3. **Presenting all written communications** – A licensee is obligated to present all types of written communications, including all written offers, to and from either party in a timely manner. Offers and counteroffers must be presented regardless of how unacceptable they may appear. The party, not the licensee, will decide whether or not to accept a particular offer. The licensee should present offers even if the property is subject to an existing contract (although not if the listing has expired).

4. **Disclosure of material facts** – A licensee must disclose any material fact, if the fact is not apparent or readily ascertainable by the party.

   a. **Material fact** – Washington law defines a *material fact* as information that has a substantial negative effect on the value of the property or on a party's ability to perform her contractual duties, or that defeats the purpose of the transaction. A seller may not rely on the principle of *caveat emptor* ("let the buyer beware").

   Example: Anything that might make it difficult for the parties to complete the transaction (such as the bankruptcy of one of the parties) is a material fact and therefore should be disclosed.

If an agent is asked about the presence of a sex offender in the neighborhood, the best response is to refer the client to online sources where that issue can be researched.

   i. According to Washington law, the presence of a registered sex offender in the neighborhood does not need to be disclosed as a material fact.

   b. **Latent defects** – The seller and his agent have a duty to disclose any known *latent defects* in the property to the buyer, even if the property is listed "as is." A latent defect is one that would not be discovered in a typical inspection of the property by the buyer. This contrasts with *patent defects*: defects that are readily apparent, although they too must be disclosed. An agent should refuse to take a listing if the seller insists on concealing any defects.

Latent defects: defects that are not visible or apparent. They must be disclosed.

   Example: A leaky roof inspected by the buyer in the dry season is a latent defect. Defective plumbing or wiring, or environmental hazards, are other examples of latent defects.

   c. **Stigmatized property** – If a property is stigmatized, an agent should seek expert advice from an attorney or managing broker regarding what, under state law, must be disclosed.

Example: Properties where a death or crime occurred may be considered stigmatized. However, under Washington law, these are not material facts that must be disclosed, unless they affect the property's physical condition.

    d. **No duty to investigate** – Washington law states that a licensee has no duty to investigate any matters that she does not specifically agree to investigate. This includes inspecting the property, investigating either party's financial position, or verifying the seller's statements.

5. **Accounting for trust funds** – A licensee must account for any *trust funds*: money or valuable items received on behalf of a party to a transaction. The licensee must report to the party on the status of the trust funds and avoid *commingling* (mixing) them with her own money. The duty of accounting continues after the termination of the agency.

6. **Providing an agency law pamphlet** – A licensee must give an agency law pamphlet to each party she provides services to. The pamphlet sets forth provisions of Washington's agency law. The pamphlet must be given to parties before any written agreement is signed.

7. **Making an agency disclosure** – Before any party signs an offer in a real estate transaction, a licensee must disclose in writing to that party whether the licensee represents the buyer, the seller, both, or neither. An agent must always conduct herself in a manner consistent with the agency status that was disclosed.

Sample questions

A licensee represents the seller in a transaction. Which of the following duties does she owe to the buyer?

A. Confidentiality
B. Honesty
C. Loyalty
D. Recommend expert advice

    B. One of the duties owed to all parties (third parties as well as the principal) is the duty of honesty and good faith. Confidentiality, loyalty, and recommending expert advice are duties owed only to a principal.

A real estate agent is working with buyers who are interested in a house in a new rural subdivision. She tells the buyers that the developer will pave the streets. However, she didn't verify this statement; she assumed that was the case, based on the developer's previous subdivisions. If the buyers rely on this statement and decide to buy the house, and the streets never get paved, who is potentially liable?

A. The agent, for engaging in misrepresentation through an unverified statement
B. The county, which is ultimately responsible for rural roads
C. The developer, for not providing paving as expected
D. Nobody, as this is a "let the buyer beware" situation

> A. *A licensee owes all parties the duty of acting in honesty and good faith. Even an unintentional misrepresentation can be constructive fraud, which would allow the victimized party to sue for damages.*

Tina is representing the buyers in a transaction; she described the property's boundaries to her clients without clarifying that she was not sure that the boundaries were exactly precise. The buyers, upon taking possession, built a fence along the boundaries that she described, but the neighbors then filed suit because the fence didn't follow the actual boundaries and encroached on their land. Can Tina be held liable for misrepresentation?

A. Yes, because any offer must include a photocopied legal description of the property
B. Yes, because she reasonably knew that the described boundaries might not have been correct
C. No, because the description was not in writing
D. No, because the buyers were duty bound to perform their own survey

> B. *An agent's duty of honesty and good faith requires her to avoid inaccuracies in statements to all parties to a transaction. This includes even unintentional misrepresentation, which could still be considered constructive fraud.*

A real estate agent completed a listing agreement form, which the sellers signed. At what point should the agent give the sellers a copy of the form?

A. Immediately after they sign the listing form
B. Only after a buyer has made an offer
C. Once the listing has been entered into the local MLS database
D. When the sellers finish filling out the seller disclosure statement

> A. *Real estate agents should give copies of documents to all parties, as soon as possible after they sign.*

Late on a Friday afternoon, an agent receives an offer on a property that she has listed, for $10,000 less than the listed price. The sellers will be away all weekend. The agent should:

A. discard the offer since it is not for the desired amount
B. try to get the offer to them as soon as possible on Friday
C. wait in the hope that a full-price offer comes in
D. wait until Monday since the buyers will be away for the weekend too

> B. *Offers and counteroffers should be presented to the parties in as timely a fashion as possible. All offers and counteroffers should be presented, regardless of whether their terms seem acceptable.*

Under normal circumstances, a real estate agent may do which of the following on behalf of a principal?

A. Receive financial benefits from a sale without the principal's knowledge
B. Sign a contract on behalf of the principal
C. Submit all written offers
D. Withhold disclosure of known defects to protect the principal's interests

> *C. One of an agent's duties to his principal (and to all parties) is to present all written communications, including offers. The other options are not permissible.*

An agent performing brokerage services owes all of the following duties, except:

A. perform independent visual inspection of the property in question
B. give parties a copy of the agency law pamphlet
C. transmit all offers promptly
D. disclose all known material facts

> *A. In Washington, a licensee is under no obligation to perform an inspection of the property or investigate any other matters that she has not specifically agreed to investigate.*

After listing a property for sale, a licensee learns that the property was used as a beer hall during Prohibition, for illegal drug sales in 2003, and as a homeless shelter in 2009. What is the licensee's duty regarding property disclosures?

A. All of these uses must be disclosed
B. Only the most recent use must be disclosed
C. The drug sales must be disclosed
D. None of these uses must be disclosed

> *D. While any of these prior uses might stigmatize the property, none of them are material facts that would have to be disclosed by a seller or a seller's agent. There would be an exception if a prior use adversely affected the property's physical condition (for example, if the property had been used for illegal drug manufacturing, which may leave behind harmful chemical residues; however, the question refers only to drug sales, not drug manufacturing).*

Agent Ralph represents the sellers in a transaction. At the time he takes the listing, which of the following should he disclose to the sellers?

A. Current market conditions
B. Neighborhood's racial demographics
C. Presence of asbestos in a neighboring house
D. Presence of sex offender in neighborhood

> *A. When taking a listing, a seller's agent should disclose current market conditions to the sellers while discussing an appropriate listing price. (Note that the other options involve disclosures that might be made to prospective buyers, not to the sellers. And even if the question concerned disclosures to buyers, none of the other options is information that would have to be disclosed.)*

B. **Agent's Duties to the Principal** – In addition to the general duties that licensees owe to any party to whom they render services, there are specific duties that licensees owe to the parties they represent. If the agent represents the seller, these duties are owed only to the seller. If the agent represents the buyer, these duties are owed only to the buyer. If the agent is a dual agent, these duties are owed to both buyer and seller.

1. **Loyalty** – An agent must always comply with a principal's lawful instructions, and place the principal's interests above the interests of a third party. For instance, a seller's agent must negotiate with the buyer to get the highest price possible for the seller.

   a. **Secret profits** – An agent must not make any secret profits off the agency. A *secret profit* is a financial benefit that the agent receives without the principal's consent, such as a kickback from referring the principal's business to a contractor. An agent may still use the services of a contractor with whom she has an interest, so long as the interest is disclosed and the principal consents.

   A kickback is a secret profit.

2. **Conflicts of interest** – A licensee must disclose any potential conflicts of interest to the principal, such as any relationship between the agent and a prospective buyer. (For instance, if the buyer is a friend, relative, or business associate of the agent.)

   a. **Self-dealing** – An agent must inform the seller if the agent is buying the property herself. An agent should not list a property for less than it is worth, buy it, and then sell it for a profit; this is known as *self-dealing*.

3. **Confidentiality** – The agent must place the principal's interests above the interests of a third party by refusing to reveal confidential information. The duty not to disclose confidential information continues even after the agency relationship has ended; thus, a real estate agent could not tell subsequent clients information about a past client obtained while representing that past client.

   The duty of confidentiality continues even after the agency relationship ends.

   Example: In negotiations with a prospective buyer, a seller's agent should not reveal the seller's financial condition or willingness to accept less than the listing price, unless the seller has authorized such a disclosure.

   Exception: Latent defects should always be disclosed, even if a principal considers them to be "confidential." In addition, confidential information about a principal may be disclosed under court order or subpoena.

4. **Expert advice** – A licensee must advise the principal to seek expert advice on any matters relating to the transaction that are beyond the agent's expertise (such as matters best handled by a lawyer or a home inspector).

Agents should never give legal advice.

5. **Good faith and continuous effort** – Licensees must make a good faith and continuous effort to fulfill the terms of the agency agreement. For instance, a seller's agent must make a good faith and continuous effort to find a buyer for the property.

Sample questions

A seller complains that the seller's agent is showing other properties to buyers that compete with the seller's property. Which of the following is true?

A. Seller's agent is breaching duty of loyalty to seller
B. Seller's agent is not breaching the duty of loyalty
C. Seller's agent has created a conflict of interest
D. Seller's agent may do so, but only with the seller's express permission

> B. *A seller's agent has a duty of loyalty to the seller. However, a real estate licensee will most likely have other clients as well, so even if a dual agency doesn't exist, the duty of loyalty to one client must still be balanced against the need to work in other clients' best interests as well.*

Which of the following pieces of information must a listing agent convey to a seller?

A. A potential buyer confides that he plans to violate zoning restrictions
B. A potential buyer is a member of a racial minority
C. A potential buyer, who has asked for the seller to take back a purchase money mortgage, has abused his credit in the past
D. The neighborhood where the seller plans to move is seeing more minorities moving in

> C. *A listing agent owes the duty of loyalty to his principal, the seller. If the listing agent discovers information that suggests that selling to a particular buyer could be detrimental to the seller, that should be disclosed to the seller.*

Carrie owns an apartment building and is discussing marketing strategy with her property manager, Isabel. Isabel suggests that Carrie advertise in the local weekly alternative newspaper, but Carrie refuses to, because it's published by a former business partner with whom she's fallen out. Isabel argues that she's had great results advertising other properties in this publication, but Carrie still refuses. What should Isabel do?

A. Advertise in it, because the property manager is an independent contractor and has authority to make low-level administrative decisions
B. Advertise in it, to avoid potential discrimination claims
C. Do not advertise in it, because the property manager is an agent who must obey a principal's instructions
D. Do not advertise in it, because the property manager, as a special agent, does not have authority to make such decisions

C. A property manager, as an agent, is bound by the duty of loyalty to follow the lawful instructions of a principal, in this case the property's owner.

Sally lists her property for sale with Broker Al. Al learns that the property is about to be rezoned to a higher use. He tells Sally he would like to purchase the property himself. She agrees, and the sale closes. Six months later, Al resells the property for a significant profit. This is legal:

A. as long as before Sally agreed to the sale, Al informed her of the upcoming zoning change and what it would mean for the property's value
B. as long as he disclosed to Sally the profit he made off the resale, after his sale closed
C. only if Al shares his profits with Sally
D. under no circumstances

A. When Al decided to buy the property for himself, his duty to disclose conflicts of interest and material facts to his principal required him to let Sally know all of the circumstances. If he failed to do so, it was self-dealing and a breach of fiduciary duties.

A firm's managing broker requires agents to recommend a particular lender to buyers. However, the managing broker has a financial interest in this lender. What should an agent do about this?

A. Avoid any recommendations of lenders to buyers
B. Recommend only this lender, as per policy
C. Recommend this lender after disclosing the managing broker's interest, and recommend other lenders as well
D. Recommend whatever lender has the best rates

C. It is best for a real estate agent to recommend multiple lenders, so that a buyer can shop around for the best rates (and consider other factors, like the quality of service provided). If the licensee or the firm has a financial relationship to the lender, that business relationship should be disclosed.

A licensee can reveal confidential information about his principal:

A. under court order or subpoena
B. under no circumstances
C. when another party asks directly if a certain fact is true
D. when acting as a dual agent

A. While a licensee ordinarily has a duty to not disclose confidential information about the principal, it may be disclosed when the licensee is faced with a court order or a subpoena.

A home is listed for $200,000. A prospective buyer tells the listing agent that she may make an offer for $190,000. The listing agent tells her that the seller won't accept anything under $195,000. The buyer offers $195,000 and the seller accepts. Which is correct?

A. The listing agent violated her fiduciary duty to the seller by engaging in self-dealing
B. The listing agent violated her fiduciary duty to the seller by telling the buyer how low the seller would go
C. The listing agent did not violate her fiduciary duty to the seller because that is not information that the seller would expect to remain confidential
D. The listing agent fulfilled her fiduciary duty to the seller by facilitating a successful offer and acceptance

B.   *By telling the buyer that the seller's walk-away price is $195,000, the list-ing agent divulged information that the seller would expect to remain con-fidential and, if divulged, works to the seller's detriment. This is a violation of the agent's fiduciary duties.*

A home inspection revealed that black mold is present in a home. What should the buyer's agent tell the buyer?

A. That black mold is toxic, and that the buyer should not buy the house
B. That mold is commonplace, and can be cleaned up with bleach
C. To require the seller to remedy the problem
D. To seek expert advice

D.   *A buyer's agent typically does not have expertise in environmental hazards. The proper step, for matters in a transaction outside the agent's expertise, is to advise the principal to seek expert advice. In this case, that would be a mold remediation specialist.*

V. **Terminating the Agency** – The ways in which the parties can ter-minate an agency relationship include:

   A. **Mutual Agreement** – The parties may terminate the relation-ship by *mutual agreement* at any time. If the original agreement was in writing, the termination should be in writing.

   B. **Revocation by the Principal** – The principal may *revoke* the agency by firing the agent whenever she wishes. The principal may be liable for any damages caused by the breach.

   Exception: An *agency coupled with an interest* can't be re-voked. An agency is coupled with an interest if the agent has a financial interest in the property; for instance, the listing agent is a co-owner in the property.

   C. **Renunciation by the Agent** – An agent can *renounce* (quit) the agency at any time. The agent may be liable for any damages caused by the breach.

   D. **Termination by Operation of Law** – An agency relationship will terminate automatically if (1) the term of the agency ex-pires; (2) the purpose of the agency is fulfilled (property sold); (3) the principal dies, is declared incompetent, or declares bankruptcy, or the listing firm ceases to operate; or (4) the property is destroyed (for example, burns down).

Death of a listing licensee would not terminate an agency, as a listing agreement is between a seller and a firm, not an individual.

Sample question

Under which of the following circumstances would a listing be terminated?

A. Real estate agent who took the listing dies
B. Seller dies
C. Property is rezoned after listing is signed
D. Listing agent goes to work for another firm

> B. *According to agency law, if either the principal (in this case the seller) or the agent dies, the agency is terminated. However, the "agent" in an agency relationship is the real estate firm, not the individual who took the listing, so the listing is still in effect even if the individual real estate agent dies or moves to another firm.*

VI. **Buyer Agency** – A *buyer agency* relationship is often created through a contract between a buyer and a real estate agent called a buyer agency agreement. Like listings, they may be either open or exclusive.

VII. **Dual Agency** – *Dual agency* exists when an agent represents both the buyer and the seller in the same transaction. Dual agency is legal in Washington, although it is discouraged. To act as a dual agent, an agent must have the written consent of both parties to the transaction. He must also act impartially towards both buyer and seller and refrain from acting to the detriment of either party.

    A. **In-House Transaction** – The most common dual agency situation is an *in-house transaction*, in which two different affiliated licensees, representing the buyer and seller, both work for the same brokerage.

    B. **Designated Agency** – In some states (but not Washington), an in-house transaction may lead to a designated agency, where each agent is appointed specifically as an agent for a particular party.

    C. **Inadvertent Dual Agency** – Many dual agency lawsuits involve unintended dual agency, in which the seller's agent's conduct with the buyer created an agency by implication between the agent and buyer.

VIII. **Agency Disclosure Requirements** – Washington law requires real estate agents in residential transactions to make agency disclosures to both the buyer and seller informing them which party (or parties) they represent.

A. **Timing of Disclosures** – The agency disclosures must be made to the buyer before the buyer signs the offer, and to the seller before the seller signs the offer. The disclosure must be in writing, either in a separate paragraph in the purchase and sale agreement or in a separate disclosure document.

IX. **Brokerage/Affiliated Licensee Relationship** – A real estate licensee cannot act directly as the agent of a principal in a real estate transaction. Rather, the licensee acts as the agent of his brokerage, and it is the brokerage who acts as the principal's agent.

A. **Independent Contractor vs. Employee** – An *independent contractor* is hired to perform a particular job, and uses her own judgment to decide how the job should be completed. In contrast, an *employee* is hired to perform whatever tasks the employer requires, and is given instructions on how to accomplish each task.

1. **Agents are usually independent contractors** – Real estate agents are virtually always independent contractors in relation to their principals. And most affiliated licensees are independent contractors in relation to their brokerages, although in rare instances they're classified as employees.

Real estate agents are ordinarily independent contractors.

B. **Tax Withholding** – Important employment and tax laws apply when someone is classified as an employee, particularly those involving withholding income taxes and social security. Unlike employees, independent contractors do not have taxes withheld from their earnings. For tax purposes, an independent contractor must have a written independent contractor agreement.

C. **Brokerage Responsibility** – Even if an affiliated licensee is considered an independent contractor for tax purposes, the brokerage is still responsible for supervising that licensee's actions and may be liable for his misconduct.

X. **Brokerage** – The national exam may test a number of professional responsibility topics that fall under the scope of Washington's license law. For the most part, these laws and regulations are consistent from state to state. These may include:

A. **Licensure** – Anyone who is involved in listing real estate or other real estate transactions must be licensed. Licensees must work under the supervision of a broker or, in Washington, a licensed firm. If a firm's license is revoked, the licenses of the firm's licensees are suspended until they can begin working elsewhere.

B. **Regulatory Agency** – Notice must be provided to the appropriate state regulatory agency when there are changes in office locations, trust account locations, or in firm leadership. Notice must also be given if a licensee is terminated for violating the license law.

C. **Advertising** – Real estate licensees must include the name of their brokerage firm in advertisements, unless they are advertising their own property for sale.

D. **Trust Accounts** – Brokerages must maintain trust accounts for temporarily holding client funds, separate from their own business funds. Mixing client funds with business funds is a violation known as *commingling*.

E. **Commissions** – All commissions, including bonus payments from a seller to a licensee, must be paid through the licensee's brokerage, rather than directly to the licensee. The licensee's commission is whatever rate has been negotiated between the licensee and his firm. A licensee is entitled to a commission if he was licensed at the time of the transaction, had a written employment contract with the brokerage, and was the procuring cause of the sale.

F. **Client Relations** – A licensee may not negotiate directly with someone else's client. For instance, a buyer's agent may not reach out directly to a seller; she must make contact through the listing agent. Listing agents are not responsible for damage to or theft of a seller's property during an open house, but should inform sellers that they must remove or secure valuables.

Sample question

Which of the following is the best description of a real estate agent's status as an independent contractor?

A. The agent is currently licensed, and she is entitled to receive employee benefits from the brokerage firm
B. The agent is currently licensed; she is not entitled to receive employee benefits from the brokerage, but the brokerage withholds income tax and social security contributions
C. The agent is currently licensed, has a written employment contract with the brokerage, and agrees to work set hours at the firm's office
D. The agent is currently licensed and has a written contract of affiliation with the brokerage firm, and most of her income is commission income

> D. *In order to be treated as an independent contractor by the IRS, the agent must have a real estate license, have a contract with her brokerage which states that she will be treated as an independent contractor, and receive substantially all of her compensation in the form of commission income.*

Chapter Quiz

1. XYZ Realty has the exclusive right to represent a new subdivision. An agent working for XYZ shows a property to the Meyers, who are not working with their own agent. When the Meyers decide to buy, they have XYZ's agent help them prepare an offer. Which of the following is true?

   A. The agent owes the buyers the duty of loyalty

   B. The buyers are not represented by an agent

   C. The buyers are represented by this agent

   D. This has created a dual agency

2. An elderly woman gives a power of attorney to her son. In terms of his ability to handle her financial affairs, what sort of agency authority does he have?

   A. Ostensible agent

   B. Special agent

   C. Universal agent

   D. Unlimited agent

3. Ed knows that his basement leaks, but doesn't disclose this to Sally, the buyer. Ed has also instructed his agent to keep the information confidential. After the sale closes, Sally finds out that the basement leaks, and sues for fraud and misrepresentation. Sally can sue:

   A. the listing agent only

   B. the seller only

   C. both the listing agent and the seller

   D. no one, under the doctrine of caveat emptor

4. Peter plans to sell a number of different properties. He enters into an agreement with Agent Carla in which she agrees to act as Peter's special agent. Under this agreement, how many properties can Carla list for Peter?

   A. A special agent has no fiduciary obligations, so Carla can only list one property at a time

   B. A special agent may perform whatever legal acts have been authorized by the principal, so Carla can list as many properties are stated in the agreement

   C. A special agent acts as a dual agent, so Carla can only list two properties at a time

   D. None, because a special agent is in the business of appraising properties, not listing them

5. A real estate agent shows a listing to two different buyers. One buyer decides in the early morning to make an offer on the property for less than the listed price. The agent writes up the offer and plans to meet with the seller later in the day. The other buyer then contacts the agent and says that she'd like to make a full price offer. What should the agent do?

   A. Meet with the sellers but present only the first offer, and then present the second offer only if the first offer is rejected

   B. Present both offers to the seller at the same time

   C. Tell the second buyer that her offer is invalid because there is already an offer on the property

   D. Tell the second buyer that he can only present the first offer to the seller, but he'll present her offer if the first one is rejected

6. A buyer is looking at a house in a neighborhood with newly installed sidewalks. When the buyer asks about taxes, the seller assures her that the home isn't subject to any special assessments. The buyer's agent should:

   A. advise the buyer that the property may be subject to special assessments and recommend that the buyer look into it
   B. check the county records to see if the property has any special assessments pending against it
   C. contact an attorney to begin an investigation of the matter
   D. say nothing and take the seller's word for it

7. A buyer was considering purchasing a property sight unseen through a foreclosure auction. A friend warned him, "Caveat emptor." This expression means:

   A. Let the buyer beware
   B. Let the lender beware
   C. Neither a borrower nor a lender be
   D. Time flies

8. A buyer is planning to purchase a property where he can operate a small mechanic's shop out of his home. He eventually finds a property he likes, and tells the listing agent his plans. However, after closing he finds out that there are deed restrictions that prevent him from operating such a business from his home. Which of the following is true?

   A. Since the agent knew the buyer's intended use, the agent should have investigated whether it was feasible or informed the buyer that he or his agent should investigate it
   B. The agent represented the seller and did not have a duty of loyalty to the buyer
   C. The seller always has to disclose the zoning on a property
   D. The real estate agent was the one responsible for investigating deed restrictions

9. A real estate agent has assisted an investor with the purchase of a number of commercial properties. The investor will be out of the country for part of the year and asks the agent to manage all aspects of those properties during that time, including advertising and leasing. The real estate agent will be a/an:

   A. general agent
   B. implied agent
   C. special agent
   D. universal agent

10. A seller's agent knows that the seller intentionally failed to disclose on the property disclosure statement that the basement leaks during heavy rains. The seller's agent must:

    A. complete a new property disclosure statement himself
    B. inform the local housing authority
    C. inform the Department of Licensing
    D. inform the prospective buyer that there is misrepresented information on the disclosure form

11. The seller tells the buyer's agent that the home has never had flooding issues, but when touring the home, the buyer's agent notices a sump pump in the basement. The buyer's agent should:

    A. say nothing because the seller said there was no flooding
    B. advise the buyer that the sump pump may be a sign of flooding and that she should inquire into whether flooding is an issue
    C. contact the seller directly to ask about the sump pump/flooding
    D. instruct the buyer to stop considering the property

12. A seller tells a prospective buyer that the attic's insulation is 16 inches thick. The seller's agent, however, observes that the insulation is only 6 inches thick. The seller's agent should:

    A. consult with the seller and ask if he'd like to provide the correct information
    B. say nothing because of the duty of loyalty to the seller
    C. say nothing because this does not rise to the level of material fact
    D. tell the prospective buyer that there is six inches of insulation

13. Which of the following is a latent defect that would need to be disclosed?

   A. Decaying steps to back porch
   B. Leaking faucet
   C. A crack in the basement wall that is covered by paneling
   D. Worn out carpeting

14. Which is a list of duties owed to a principal by an agent?

   A. Loyalty, compensation, reasonable care, accounting
   B. Loyalty, confidentiality, reasonable care, accounting
   C. Performance, compensation, reasonable care, indemnification
   D. Performance, confidentiality, loyalty, indemnification

15. A seller and a brokerage sign a listing agreement. The listing will expire in three months, but after a few weeks, the seller decides she doesn't want to sell at all. Which is true?

   A. The listing can only be terminated with the mutual consent of both seller and brokerage
   B. The seller can revoke the listing and will not owe anything to the brokerage
   C. The seller can revoke the listing but may be liable to the brokerage for damages
   D. The seller can revoke the listing but can't list the property with any competing firm for three months

16. A seller has entered into a listing agreement with an expiration date of April 30. Under which of these circumstances would the listing NOT expire?

   A. The house burns down on April 25
   B. The licensee who took the listing is legally declared incompetent on April 26
   C. The seller revokes the listing on April 27
   D. The property has still not sold on April 30

17. A buyer enters into a buyer agency agreement with a real estate licensee. The buyer then enters into a purchase and sale agreement, but the property he agreed to buy is subsequently condemned. Which of the following is true?

   A. The agency is terminated
   B. They can immediately look for another property
   C. The agent may sue the buyer for damages, if any were incurred
   D. This creates a dual agency

18. The IRS issues rules that determine when a real estate agent is an employee and when he is an independent contractor. Which of the following statements on that topic is FALSE?

   A. The brokerage may pay an independent contractor primarily through commissions
   B. The brokerage may require an independent contractor to have a cell phone
   C. The brokerage will take taxes from an employee's paycheck
   D. The brokerage will tell an employee when to work

19. An independent contractor relationship between a real estate brokerage firm and a licensee requires that:

   A. the brokerage and licensee must enter into a written agreement
   B. the brokerage must consider the licensee an employee for tax purposes
   C. the brokerage must set the licensee's daily work schedule
   D. the licensee must be paid primarily based on number of hours worked rather than commission

20. A buyer asks the buyer's agent to write an offer on terms that don't match the listing agreement. The buyer's agent refuses to write the offer and then, in writing, unilaterally terminates the agency relationship with the buyer. Which is true?

A. Buyer's agent will be subject to disciplinary action

B. Buyer's agent is permitted to unilaterally terminate the agency relationship

C. Buyer's agent is allowed to terminate the agency, but must write the offer before terminating

D. Buyer's agent is not permitted to write such an offer

Answer Key

1. B. An agent can provide certain levels of assistance to customers without entering into an agency relationship with them, for instance, helping to fill out a purchase and sale agreement form. Since they are not working with any other agent, the buyers in this instance would be proceeding without any representation.

2. C. A power of attorney gives a person universal agency authority to take care of another person's affairs.

3. C. In this example, both the seller and listing agent acted to hide a latent defect from a buyer, and they are both liable to the buyer for any damages.

4. B. A special agent may perform whatever legal acts the principal has authorized the agent to perform. There is no limit on the number of listed properties that one agency agreement can cover.

5. B. A real estate agent has the duty of presenting all written communications to and from all parties in a timely manner. Failing to inform a party of any offer would be a breach of duty.

6. A. It would be proper (under the duty of loyalty) for the buyer's agent to let the buyer know that there is a possibility that a special assessment may be present and that the buyer should double-check. However, under Washington law, the agent is under no duty to investigate the matter himself (unless he specifically agreed to do so).

7. A. "Caveat emptor" is a Latin phrase meaning "let the buyer beware," suggesting that the duty of investigating a potential purchase ultimately falls on the buyer. While this phrase is generally applicable to most transactions, laws regarding real estate transactions limit this somewhat. For instance, sellers must, in most cases, disclose latent defects to buyers.

8. A. The seller's agent does not owe a duty of loyalty to the buyer, so he is not required to investigate anything on the buyer's behalf. However, the duty of honesty and good faith would likely compel him to at least recommend to the buyer that he or his agent should investigate the matter further.

9. A. A real estate agent acting as a property manager often is given authority as a general agent. This will enable the property manager to handle the day-to-day business associated with the property, such as hiring and entering into contracts.

10. D. A real estate agent has the duty to disclose all material facts to parties, regardless of whether the agent's principal would prefer that information not be disclosed. A leaking basement is a latent defect and certainly qualifies as a material fact.

11. B. An agent has a duty to disclose not just latent defects, but also red flags that indicate that a latent defect might be present (such as signs that flooding might be a hazard). It is up to the buyer, however, to decide if he wants to investigate further or not.

12.   D.   A licensee has the duty to disclose material facts to the appropriate party, even if the principal doesn't disclose that information himself. The insulation depth could be a material fact, since insufficient insulation could have a negative effect on the property's value.

13.   C.   A latent defect is a problem that would not be discovered by ordinary inspection. If a crack is obscured by paneling, it is not likely to be observed and therefore must be disclosed to prospective buyers.

14.   B.   Duties that an agent owes to all parties (including the principal) are reasonable skill and care, honesty and good faith, presenting written communications, disclosure of material facts, accounting, providing an agency law pamphlet, and making an agency disclosure. In addition, an agent owes the principal the duties of loyalty, disclosure of conflicts of interest, confidentiality, advising the principal to obtain expert advice, and good faith and continuous effort. Compensation, indemnification, and performance are not duties an agent owes the principal.

15.   C.   An agency relationship may be terminated by revocation by the principal, without the consent of the agent. Even so, the revocation of a listing agreement is often a breach of contract, in which case the principal (the seller) may be required to pay damages to the agent (the brokerage).

16.   B.   It wouldn't matter, for the purposes of agency law, whether the individual licensee who took the listing becomes incompetent or not. The listing agreement is between the seller and the brokerage firm, not an individual. Agency relationships can terminate because of seller revocation, expiration of term, or destruction of the subject property.

17.   A.   An agency is terminated by operation of law based on the extinction of the subject matter, such as the condemnation of the subject property. The buyer and agent can look for another property, but would need to form another agency relationship first. Note that this is the common law of agency tested on the national portion of the exam; in Washington, the rule is different. The agent could immediately start helping the buyer look for another property because this act itself would create an agency.

18.   B.   One of the key differences between employees and independent contractors is the level of supervision; an independent contractor uses his judgment regarding how to perform a task, while an employee receives specific instructions. An instruction to carry a cell phone indicates an employee. (Practically speaking, virtually all real estate agents do carry cell phones, but because it makes their job easier and not because they are instructed to do so.)

19.   A.   The Internal Revenue Service will consider a real estate licensee an independent contractor only if the brokerage services are provided under a written contract saying that the licensee is not treated as an employee.

20.   B.   An agent may unilaterally renounce an agency relationship. (Termination of the agency may involve a breach of contract; if so, the agent could be liable to the principal for damages resulting from the breach.)

Chapter 8
Listing Agreements

I. **Listing Agreement** – A *listing agreement* is a written employment contract; it is a contract between a property *owner* and a real estate *firm* (not the licensee), which creates a fiduciary relationship. The seller hires the brokerage to find a buyer who is ready, willing, and able to buy the property on the seller's terms. Though the listing is usually filled out and signed by the licensee on behalf of the firm, the agreement is always between the seller and the brokerage. The listing is the property of the firm; if the licensee who took the listing leaves that firm for another firm, the listing still remains with the original firm.

   A. **Authority** – A listing does *not* give the licensee the authority to accept offers on behalf of the seller or to transfer title to the seller's property (unless the licensee also has a written power of attorney authorizing those acts).

   B. **Compensation** – The standard form of payment for a real estate licensee is the *brokerage fee*, which is usually a percentage of the sales price (not the listing price). The percentage is determined by negotiation between the brokerage and seller. Neither party can set or change the commission unilaterally.

      1. **Requirements** – For a brokerage to be entitled to compensation, the parties must have had a written listing agreement, the brokerage must have been licensed at the time services were provided, and the brokerage must have fulfilled the terms of the listing agreement.

      2. **Lawsuit** – If a seller is unwilling to pay a commission, a brokerage must sue the seller to obtain the commission. The brokerage may not simply take the commission out of funds held in trust for the parties, such as an earnest money deposit, nor may it place a lien on the property.

   C. **Earning a Commission** – As a rule, a listing agreement obligates the seller to pay the listing brokerage a commission only if a *ready, willing, and able buyer* is found during the listing period.

      1. **Acceptable offer** – If the buyer makes an offer that meets the seller's terms (as stated in the listing agreement), the brokerage is entitled to a commission, even if the seller decides not to accept the buyer's offer. Terms include closing date and financing arrangements, as well as price.

2. **Unacceptable offer** – If the buyer makes an offer on terms other than those stated in the listing, the seller can turn down the offer without liability for a commission. However, if the seller accepts the offer, he is obligated to pay the commission.

3. **Able to buy** – A ready and willing buyer is considered "able" if she has the capacity to contract and the financial ability to complete the purchase.

4. **Commission without closing** – When failure to close is the seller's fault, the brokerage is still entitled to the commission. Once the seller accepts an offer, he is still liable for a commission if the sale fails to close for any of the following reasons:

   a. **Change of heart** – Seller has a change of heart and decides not to sell.

   b. **No marketable title** – Seller does not have marketable title.

   c. **Failure to deliver possession** – Seller cannot deliver possession of the property to the buyer.

   d. **Termination by agreement** – Seller and buyer mutually agree to terminate the contract.

D. **Types of Listing Agreements** – The circumstances under which a seller is required to pay a brokerage commission also depend on the type of listing agreement they have. The three basic types of listing agreements are: an *open listing*, an *exclusive agency listing*, and an *exclusive right to sell listing*.

   1. **Open listing** – Under an open listing agreement, the seller is obligated to pay a commission only if the brokerage was the *procuring cause* of the sale.

      a. **Procuring cause** – The procuring cause is the person who was primarily responsible for bringing about the agreement between the parties. This means the brokerage or one of its agents must have personally negotiated the offer from the ready, willing, and able buyer and communicated the offer to the seller.

      b. **Non-exclusive** – An open listing is non-exclusive, meaning a seller may give open listings to a number of brokerages. Only the brokerage who is the procuring cause of the sale earns a commission. If the seller sells the house herself, no brokerage receives a commission.

      c. **List of prospects** – A brokerage with an open listing should keep a list of prospects that it talks to, so that

Open listing: a non-exclusive listing, given by a seller to as many brokerages as she chooses.

Procuring cause: the real estate agent who is primarily responsible for bringing about a sale.

All brokerages with open listings may place signs on the property.

it has evidence of being the procuring cause if one of those persons winds up buying the property.

2. **Exclusive agency listing** – With this type of listing, the seller agrees to list with only one brokerage, but retains the right to sell the property himself without being obligated to pay a commission. The brokerage is entitled to a commission if anyone other than the seller (such as another broker) finds a buyer for the property.

3. **Exclusive right to sell listing** – Under the exclusive right to sell listing, the seller lists with only one brokerage, and that broker is entitled to a commission regardless of who sells the property, even if it's the seller.

    a. **Preferred by brokerages** – The exclusive right to sell listing is preferred by most brokerages, because it provides the most protection for the firm.

    b. **Exclusive vs. open listings** – An open listing is a *unilateral contract*, while exclusive listings are considered *bilateral contracts*. Because an open listing is one-sided, only the seller needs to sign it.

> Exclusive agency listing: a listing agreement that entitles the brokerage to a commission if anyone other than the seller sells the property.
>
> Exclusive right to sell listing: a listing that entitles the brokerage to a commission if anyone (including the seller) sells the property.
>
> A seller who terminates an exclusive right to sell listing before its termination date may still be liable to the brokerage firm for damages.

Sample questions

Theo takes an exclusive right to sell listing in early September, while working as a licensee for West Side Realty. In mid-October, he quits his job, surrenders his license, and moves out of state. What happens to Theo's listing?

A. It is converted to an open listing
B. It continues to be a valid exclusive listing with West Side Realty
C. It will be reassigned to another brokerage firm in the same multiple listing service
D. The agency relationship automatically terminates

> B. *A listing belongs to a brokerage firm, not to an individual licensee. It is a contract between a seller and a firm, so it would remain in place even if the seller's particular agent left the firm.*

A licensee locates what seems like a ready, willing, and able buyer. However, the deal falls through at closing because the buyer couldn't obtain necessary financing. At the same time, though, the seller turned out to be unable to provide marketable title. Does the seller still owe a commission to the listing agent in this case?

A. No, because the sale didn't close
B. No, because there was no ready, willing, and able buyer
C. Yes, because the licensee saw the transaction through to the closing date
D. Yes, because the seller has an absolute duty to provide marketable title at closing

    B.   *The most important rule in determining whether a seller is obligated to pay a commission is whether a ready, willing, and able buyer was found during the listing period. This would take precedence over the seller's failure to provide marketable title. A buyer who does not have the financial ability to complete the purchase does not qualify as "able."*

At closing, a sale doesn't go through because the seller's anticipated transfer to another city gets suddenly postponed, and the seller no longer wants to sell. Does the seller owe the listing agent a commission in this situation?

A. No, because the sale didn't close
B. No, because this was a circumstance outside the seller's control
C. Yes, because the seller won't provide marketable title, which is considered a default
D. Yes, unless the buyer and seller agreed to mutually cancel the transaction

    C.   *Once a seller has accepted an offer (which presumably has already happened if a sale is scheduled to close), the listing agent is entitled to a commission if the sale fails to close and the seller is at fault. This is true even if the seller and buyer mutually agree to terminate their contract, or if circumstances arise that make it unwise for the seller to sell. (Of course, in such a situation, the agent may choose not to demand a commission.)*

A property seller and a real estate agent entered into a listing agreement. Even though the seller found the buyer, the agent still collected a commission. What kind of listing agreement did they have?

A. Net listing
B. Open listing
C. Exclusive agency listing
D. Exclusive right to sell listing

    D.   *Under an exclusive right to sell listing agreement, the real estate agent is entitled to a commission regardless of who finds the buyer.*

An exclusive listing agreement is an example of a/an:

A. express contract
B. illusory contract
C. implied contract
D. unilateral contract

    A.   *A listing agreement must be an express contract, because it must be in writing to be valid. It is a bilateral contract, not unilateral.*

Prices in a local market are trending downward. A seller found that she had to lower the price of her house by $25,000 over the course of six months before she could find a buyer. Upset over selling at a loss, she informs her listing agent that she is going to lower the amount of commission that she pays. Which of the following is true?

A. A loss by the seller must be shared by the listing agent
B. Commission rates are negotiated and can be changed at any time
C. Commission rates are established by the local multiple listing service and cannot be changed
D. The commission rate, once established in the listing agreement contract, cannot be changed unless both parties agree

D. *A change to the commission rate could be made by both parties, as the listing agreement is a contract that could be amended. However, once the contract exists, it is not something that can be changed unilaterally by one dissatisfied party.*

II. **Elements of a Listing Agreement** – Under Washington law, there are three requirements for an enforceable listing agreement:

A. **Writing Signed by Seller** – A listing agreement must be in writing and signed by the seller. The signature of all owners is necessary; for instance, both spouses should sign a listing agreement. The affiliated licensee may sign the listing on behalf of the brokerage. An attorney in fact may sign on behalf of a party who cannot be present.

B. **Property Description** – A complete legal description is advisable, but any description that identifies the property with certainty is adequate.

C. **Promise to Compensate Brokerage** – A listing must include authorization to market the property and a promise to compensate the brokerage. The commission must be negotiable and is set by agreement between brokerage and seller. The commission is usually a percentage of the sales price, although it may be a set dollar amount.

1. **Net listing** – Under a *net listing*, a seller specifies how much he wishes to net from the sale, and the brokerage receives as its commission any money in excess of that amount. Net listings are discouraged, because an unscrupulous agent can use one to take advantage of a poorly informed seller.

> A net listing does not specify a commission rate.

2. **Extender clause** – An *extender clause* may be included to stop sellers from trying to avoid paying a commission by waiting until after the listing has expired to sign an offer.

D. **Other Elements** – There are a number of other elements which are common to most listing agreements.

1. **Brokerage's authority** – The listing agreement usually gives the brokerage the authority to hold the buyer's earnest money deposit on the seller's behalf. The listing agent agrees to use due diligence to find a buyer, but ordinarily will not agree to perform duties outside a typical transaction, such as preparing title for closing.

2. **Termination date** – All exclusive agency listings and exclusive right to sell listings should have a definite termination date. The law doesn't require this, however.

Listing agreements without a termination date terminate after a reasonable period.

If there are deed conditions, as with a fee simple defeasible, these should be described in the agreement.

3. **Terms of sale** – All listings should state the terms of the sale—most importantly, the listing price. While a seller will take into consideration the broker's advice, the seller is responsible for deciding on a listing price.

Sample questions

An owner has a fee simple defeasible title. She enters into a listing agreement with a real estate agent. Which of the following should be included in the agreement?

A. A description of both the house and the car
B. House and deed conditions
C. All the furniture that is in the house
D. Details about the house and the landscaping

   B. *If a property is subject to a qualified fee (such as a fee simple defeasible), the listing should make note of what the particular conditions are for the owner to continue to hold title.*

To be valid, a listing agreement may be signed by:

A. an attorney in fact
B. the buyer
C. the designated broker only, with the owner's authorization via telephone
D. the licensee only

   A. *A listing agreement needs to be signed both by the listing agent, on the listing firm's behalf, and by the seller. An attorney in fact, someone the seller has appointed in a power of attorney and granted the authority to convey the property, may sign the listing agreement on the seller's behalf.*

Chapter Quiz

1. After much persistence, real estate agent Zelda obtains an exclusive right to sell listing from the Quincys. This listing agreement is a contract between:

   A. Zelda and the listing firm
   B. Zelda's firm and the seller
   C. the firm, Zelda, and the seller
   D. Zelda and the seller

2. A listing agent writes a full price offer from a member of a minority group. The seller refuses to accept the offer. What can the agent do?

   A. Nothing, because no contract was formed between buyer and seller
   B. Nothing, because it was an exclusive agency listing
   C. File a complaint with the Real Estate Commission
   D. Sue for a commission

3. Some real estate contracts are between the real estate agent and the principal; others are between the buyer and the seller. All of the following contracts are between the agent and a principal, except a/an:

   A. multiple listing
   B. open listing
   C. exclusive right to sell listing
   D. net listing

4. Gail gives ABC Realty a listing that stipulates it is the only real estate firm authorized to sell her home. At the same time she insists on including a provision that would allow her to sell the home herself without paying a commission to ABC. Which of the following types of listings would serve that purpose?

   A. Non-exclusive listing
   B. Exclusive right to sell listing
   C. Exclusive open listing
   D. Exclusive agency listing

5. If a real estate agent receives a commission even if the sellers find the buyer, what type of listing agreement do they have?

   A. Open listing
   B. Exclusive agency listing
   C. Exclusive right to sell listing
   D. Net listing

6. Buyer Bob and Seller Sam decide to wait until Sam's listing agreement with XYZ Real Estate Agency has expired, to avoid paying a commission. Does the listing agent have any legal recourse?

   A. Yes, the listing agent can pursue criminal charges
   B. Yes, the listing agent can sue Bob under the listing agreement
   C. Yes, the listing agent can sue Sam under the listing agreement
   D. No; the listing agent has no further recourse

7. A real estate agent made a listing presentation to a property owner. The owner was impressed with the agent and signed a listing agreement. The owner told the agent that he was married, but his wife was in the hospital and could not sign the listing agreement. He asked the agent to proceed with the listing anyway, because they were in a hurry to sell the house. In these circumstances, the agent should:

   A. do as the seller asks; the agent can get the wife's signature later
   B. do as the seller asks, because dower rights give the husband the right to list the marital property
   C. refuse to take the listing, because the seller clearly has an ulterior motive for trying to sell the property while his wife is ill, and the agent should not get mixed up in a fraudulent transaction
   D. refuse to take the listing, but tell the seller that as soon as the wife signs the listing agreement they can proceed with trying to find a buyer

127

8. Harry and Samantha are living in a lovely home beside a lake. They decide they want to move closer to the city, so they set up an appointment with a real estate agent. Samantha is a doctor, and she's called out on a medical emergency shortly before the agent arrives. Harry chats with the real estate agent and decides he's ready to sign a listing agreement. Harry owns the house in severalty. The agent should have who among the following sign the listing agreement?

   A. Harry
   B. Samantha (when she's available)
   C. Harry and Samantha, as tenants by the entireties
   D. Harry and Samantha, as tenants in common

9. A licensee takes a listing for a house that is owned by a married couple. The husband is working overseas in the Middle East for the next two years. The wife can sign the listing agreement for her husband:

   A. as long as he has given her a power of attorney
   B. as long as he is overseas for work purposes and not for pleasure
   C. if they were originally married in a state that does not follow the law of community property
   D. under any circumstances

10. An agent is ready to list a farm that was previously owned by a deceased woman with four adult children. Two of the children contacted the agent to take the listing. Before taking the listing, the agent should:

   A. insist that all four children sign quit-claim deeds
   B. check the public records to see who owns the property
   C. have the two children sign a lien release
   D. examine the deceased woman's will

Answer Key

1. B. Even though it is prepared by an individual licensee, a listing agreement is a contract between a brokerage firm and a seller. A licensee is only allowed to act as her firm's agent, and cannot enter into a contract with a seller.

2. D. The firm has a listing agreement with the seller that calls for the payment of a commission if the firm finds a buyer who is willing to meet the seller's terms. In this instance the firm has done that. (Notice that the question didn't say the seller refused the offer because of the buyer's minority status.)

3. A. A multiple listing service is an organization of local brokerage firms who share listing information.

4. D. An exclusive agency listing is a listing agreement that entitles the brokerage to a commission if anyone other than the seller finds a buyer for the property during the listing's term.

5. C. Under the terms of an exclusive right to sell listing, the agent is entitled to a commission regardless of who finds the buyer.

6. D. If a listing agreement does not contain an extender clause, a licensee has no recourse against a buyer and seller who avoid paying a commission by waiting to close until after the listing has expired. For this reason, most listings contain an extender (or safety) clause. This question, however, does not mention that the listing contains one.

7. D. All of the owners of a property should sign the listing agreement. Even if the spouse of an owner doesn't have any ownership interest, he or she should sign the listing to avoid any doubt as to the agent's authority.

8. A. Since Harry is the sole owner, only Harry needs to sign the listing agreement. However, even if a married person owns property in severalty, it's safest to have the spouse sign too.

9. A. Ordinarily, all co-owners of a property need to sign an agreement to list the property. However, if the husband has given the wife power of attorney to sign documents on his behalf in his absence, the wife would be able to sign for him.

10. B. The agent can check with the county recorder's office to determine who owns the property. The agent will want all owners of the property, not just the two children who contacted her, to sign the listing agreement.

Chapter 9
Purchase and Sale Agreements

I. **Purchase and Sale Agreement** – A *purchase and sale agreement* is a contract in which a seller promises to convey title to real property to a buyer in exchange for the purchase price. The buyer will present a signed, written offer along with an earnest money deposit to the seller. If the seller accepts the offer, he signs the agreement, which then becomes a binding contract of sale (as well as a receipt for the earnest money deposit).

> Once a purchase and sale agreement has been signed, the buyer is considered to have equitable title.

   A. **Who May Prepare the Agreement** – As a general rule, only an attorney may prepare a contract for others. However, a real estate agent may prepare a routine purchase and sale agreement using standard printed forms that were originally written and approved by attorneys. Real estate agents should not draft additional clauses or give legal advice to parties.

   B. **Identification of the Parties** – Every owner of the property must sign the contract for it to be enforceable. If the property is community property, both spouses must sign. Even if property is considered to be held as separate property by one spouse, it is best for both spouses to sign and release any possible legal interest in the property.

> In a purchase and sale agreement, there is no discussion of what type of listing agreement was used by the sellers.

   C. **Property Description** – A purchase and sale agreement must contain an adequate description of the property. A complete legal description should always be used. If there is insufficient space on the form for the full legal description, a copy of the description, initialed by both parties, should be attached to the agreement.

   D. **Included Items** – Only personal property listed in the purchase and sale agreement will be transferred along with the real property. An "included items" paragraph in the agreement states that certain items are included in the sale unless otherwise noted in the agreement. The list usually includes carpeting, built-in appliances, window coverings, air conditioning equipment, and shrubs. Generally, these items would be considered fixtures anyway, but this provision prevents any disputes over this issue.

   E. **Possession Date** – Possession of the property is transferred to the buyer on the closing date unless the parties agree otherwise. If possession will be transferred either before or after closing, the parties should execute a separate rental agreement.

> Possession is usually transferred at closing.

If the property is not in the same physical condition at closing as when the offer was accepted, the buyer may not need to complete the transaction.

F. **Risk of Loss** – Unless the buyer has already taken possession of the property, the seller ordinarily bears the *risk of loss* until closing. (For instance, if the house burns down a week before the closing date, it's the seller's loss.) However, the parties may choose to allocate the risk differently in the purchase and sale agreement.

G. **Time is of the Essence** – A *time is of the essence* clause is found in most purchase and sale agreements and makes performance on the specified date an essential element of the contract. This clause states that the parties are legally required to meet all deadlines set in the contract, and failure to perform on time is a material breach. For instance, closing must occur on or before the exact date set in the agreement.

H. **Earnest Money Deposit** – The amount of the *earnest money deposit* is determined only by agreement between the buyer and seller. The purchase and sale agreement should state under what circumstances the earnest money deposit will be refunded to the buyer or forfeited to the seller.

1. **Liquidated damages** – It is common for a purchase and sale agreement to provide that if the buyer defaults, the seller may keep the earnest money deposit as *liquidated damages*. The amount of liquidated damages may be no more than 5% of the purchase price.

Most purchase and sale agreements state that if the buyer has incurred costs that were to have been paid at closing and the transaction fails to close, those costs will be deducted before the deposit is returned to the buyer.

2. **Buyer's costs** – If the buyer incurs costs that were to have been paid at closing (such as the cost of a credit report), these costs will be deducted from the deposit before it is returned to the buyer.

3. **Form of deposit** – The deposit is usually in the form of a check, but it may be in other forms, such as a promissory note. The agent must disclose the form of the deposit to the seller before she accepts the offer.

4. **Handling the deposit** – If the seller accepts the offer, the selling agent may turn the check over to the closing agent for deposit into escrow, or may place the deposit into the brokerage's trust account.

I. **Signatures** – Every purchase and sale agreement must be signed by the buyer and seller. The buyer's signature turns the agreement into an offer, and the seller's signature turns the offer into a binding contract.

J. Amendments – After the buyer and seller have signed the purchase and sale agreement, the terms of the contract can be modified only with a written instrument signed by all the parties who signed the original agreement. A change in terms is called an *amendment*.

Amendment: a written modification to a contract that occurs after both parties have signed the document.

    1. Amendment vs. addendum – An amendment is added after the contract has been signed. By contrast, an *addendum* is an attachment added to the agreement before it has been signed. (Parties should initial and date each page of an addendum as well.)

Addendum: an attachment to a contract that contains additional provisions that apply to the transaction.

K. Backup Offer – A buyer might be enthusiastic about a particular house to the extent that she wants to make an offer even after the seller has accepted a different offer. This is known as a *backup offer*, and it should be made contingent on the failure of the first contract.

Sample questions

A buyer's earnest money deposit can be kept by a seller in the event of a buyer's default only if the:

A. seller breaches the contract
B. seller can prove that she has suffered a financial loss
C. purchase and sale agreement includes a forfeiture clause for liquidated damages
D. purchase and sale agreement provides for specific performance

    C. *Liquidated damages are only available as a remedy for breach of contract if the contract contains a liquidated damages provision. Most purchase and sale agreements provide that the earnest money will be treated as liquidated damages if the buyer (not the seller) breaches the contract. The seller is allowed to keep the buyer's deposit, and generally is not required to prove that she has suffered a loss as a result of the buyer's breach.*

A buyer and seller enter into a purchase and sale agreement. The agreement provides that closing must take place by September 30. What is the name of this clause?

A. A habendum clause
B. A contingency clause
C. A time is of the essence clause
D. A closing clause

    C. *When the parties are required to fulfill a duty before a particular date, this is referred to as a "time is of the essence" clause.*

A seller accepts an offer, but then a second buyer makes an offer on the same property for a higher purchase price. A licensee should tell the second offeror that:

A. she will encourage the seller to breach the contract and accept the second offer
B. she will present the second offer as well and the seller will consider it
C. the second offer can be presented, but only as a backup offer
D. the second offer cannot be presented as the property is already under contract

> C. *Offers may continue to be presented after a seller has accepted an offer, but such an offer should be made contingent on the first sale's failure to close. Such an offer is known as a backup offer.*

Maria offered to purchase Alexander's house for $135,000. After talking it over with his agent, Alexander signed the offer and returned it to Maria. At this point, what type of title does Maria have to the house?

A. Legal
B. Indivisible
C. Equitable
D. Chattel

> C. *A buyer receives equitable title to the property once the sales contract has been signed.*

A buyer makes an offer that's accompanied by a deposit. The deposit is sometimes called:

A. escrow
B. option money
C. a referral fee
D. earnest money

> D. *An earnest money deposit is usually given by a buyer to a seller along with the offer to purchase, as an indication of the buyer's good faith.*

II. **Contingencies** – Most purchase and sale agreements are conditional; in other words, they are legally binding only if certain conditions are fulfilled. These conditions are called *contingency clauses* or simply *contingencies*. If a contract contains a contingency clause, the contract will be enforceable only if that contingent event occurs. If it does not occur, the contract is terminated, and the buyer is usually entitled to a refund of the earnest money deposit by the seller.

Contingency: a provision in a contract that makes the parties' rights and obligations depend on the occurrence of a particular event.

An inspection contingency may specify which party is financially responsible for correcting any problems found.

A. **Waiver of Contingency** – The party who benefits from the contingency clause (typically the buyer) usually has the right to waive it. For example, a buyer could waive a pest inspection, and the buyer would be bound by the agreement whether or not the results of the inspection were satisfactory, or even if no inspection were performed.

B. **Good Faith Effort** – The parties are obligated to make a reasonable effort to fulfill the condition. For example, with a financing contingency, a buyer must actually apply for financing. A buyer who changed his mind about buying a house after having signed a contract with a financing contingency couldn't escape the deal by failing to apply for a loan; if the buyer didn't make that effort, the contract would not terminate, and the buyer wouldn't get his deposit back.

C. **Financing Contingency** – The most common type of contingency is a *financing contingency*, which makes the sale contingent on the buyer's ability to obtain the necessary financing. If a buyer applies for financing but finds that no lenders are willing to make a loan on the buyer's terms, the buyer may terminate the agreement and receive a refund of the deposit.

1. **Financing terms** – It is important to describe the necessary financing arrangements in the purchase and sale agreement. The terms should include the downpayment amount, the deadlines for applying for the loan, and the party who will pay the loan fees.

III. **Seller Disclosure Statement** – Washington requires a seller of real property to give the buyer a *disclosure statement* when the purchase and sale agreement is signed.

A. **Time Frame** – The seller must give the buyer the disclosure statement within *five business days* of the signing of the purchase and sale agreement, unless the parties agree otherwise. The buyer then has *three business days* from receiving the statement to either "approve and accept" the disclosure statement or rescind the purchase and sale agreement.

> The seller's agent should not fill out the statement; that is the seller's job.

1. **Rescission** – If the buyer wishes to rescind, she must do so in writing within that three-day period. The choice to rescind is in the buyer's discretion; the buyer does not need to explain her decision or meet any particular objective standards.

B. **Modifications** – Information may later come to light that makes the disclosure statement inaccurate (for instance, a house may be damaged in a storm between the buyer's acceptance and the closing date). The seller must either give the buyer an amended disclosure statement or take corrective action so that the disclosure statement is accurate once again. If no corrective action is taken, the buyer may either accept the amended disclosure statement or rescind the purchase and sale agreement.

> Information that comes to light after closing does not need to be disclosed.

C. **Liability** – The information in the disclosure statement is based on the seller's actual knowledge of the property. It is not a warranty from either the seller or the agent. Neither the seller nor the agent will be liable for any inaccuracies in the statement unless they had personal knowledge of the inaccuracies.

D. **Inspection** – Regardless of the contents of the seller disclosure statement, it is always in the buyers' best interest to order a home inspection, especially if they will be unable to do a walkthrough before closing.

IV. **Lead-Based Paint** – In transactions involving housing built before 1978, sellers and landlords must disclose any known information about lead-based paint that is present. They must also give a pamphlet discussing lead-based paint hazards.

A. **Report** – If the property has already been inspected for lead-based paint, the seller or landlord must provide copies of any inspection report.

B. **Testing** – Buyers (but not tenants) are also required to be given a ten-day period in which to have the building tested for lead-based paint. The seller is under no obligation to correct any problems discovered. If there has already been offer and acceptance, the contract is not voidable upon discovery of lead-based paint, unless there was an inspection contingency to that effect.

V. **Home Warranty Plan** – A home warranty plan, or home protection plan, is a short-term insurance policy that protects a buyer against expensive repairs. The policy will reimburse an owner for the cost of repairing or replacing covered systems or appliances in the first few years of ownership.

Sample questions

Which of the following statements about the federal law on lead-based paint is false?
A. Purchasers or tenants must be given a pamphlet on the hazards of lead paint
B. Purchasers or tenants must be given reports from any earlier tests for lead paint
C. Tenants must be given ten days in which to conduct an inspection, although they may waive this right
D. A disclosure must be given when selling or leasing a residential property constructed prior to 1978

C. *Buyers, but not tenants, have a ten-day window in which to request an inspection for lead-based paint.*

A buyer would be protected from risk of loss due to a failed heating system through:

A. an agency disclosure statement
B. a home protection plan
C. mortgage insurance
D. title insurance

> B. *A home protection plan is a short-term warranty that a home buyer may purchase at closing. The buyer will be reimbursed for expenses related to the failure of covered systems or appliances, usually only during the first few years of ownership.*

In an apartment building that was built in 1960, an apartment is being rented to a couple with no children. Which of the following is true?

A. The rules concerning lead-based paint don't apply unless the tenants have children
B. The rules concerning lead-based paint don't apply to tenants, only purchasers
C. The tenants must be allowed a ten-day window in order to test for lead-based paint
D. The tenants should sign the lead-based paint disclosure and receive a pamphlet on lead-based paint

> D. *A landlord must disclose the location of any known lead-based paint, provide a copy of any report concerning lead-based paint if the property has been inspected, and give tenants a copy of the lead-based paint pamphlet. Unlike buyers, tenants are not entitled to a ten-day period in which to have the home tested for lead-based paint.*

Chapter Quiz

1. Siobhan listed her property with ABC Realty. She asks her agent, Robert, to draft deed covenants that will prevent a buyer from subdividing the land in the future. She'd also like the agent to create a trust from the sale, to benefit her disabled sister. Robert's reply should be:
   A. I can draft the trust, but an attorney will need to draft the covenants
   B. I can draft both of these documents
   C. I can draft the covenants, but an attorney will need to create the trust
   D. I can't help you with either of these things; you'll need to contact an attorney

2. A buyer makes an offer to purchase on May 2. The offer includes a promise to deposit $5,000 in earnest money within two business days after mutual acceptance. The offer is contingent on results of a soil feasibility report. On May 5 the seller accepts the offer. On May 11 the soil report is ordered. On May 17 the soil feasibility report comes back and is approved by the buyer. By what date does the earnest money need to be deposited?
   A. May 4
   B. May 7
   C. May 13
   D. May 19

3. The purchase and sale agreement has been signed and the seller has completed the seller disclosure form. A windstorm damages the property. The seller's agent is obligated to:
   A. contact the buyer's agent and inform him
   B. amend the seller disclosure form
   C. terminate the purchase and sale agreement
   D. subtract the cost of repairing the damage from the purchase price

4. A purchase and sale agreement is for $150,000, with 80% financing, closing in 30 days with possession at closing, and a rent for possession after closing. This is an example of a/an:
   A. acceptance
   B. contract with contingencies
   C. counteroffer
   D. unilateral contract

5. The buyer and the seller entered into the purchase and sale agreement. The sellers were moving out of state and vacated the property well before the closing date. On the day before closing, the buyers and their agent arrived at the property for a final inspection. When they entered the home, they realized that a pipe had burst and the house had flooded. There was water in the basement, the basement floor and walls were ruined, and the entire house smelled of mold. Are the buyers required to go through with the purchase?
   A. Yes, because the parties will not be able to agree on who gets the earnest money deposit
   B. Yes, as long as the agent agrees to return the earnest money deposit to the buyers to compensate them for the damages
   C. No, because the buyers are entitled to receive the property in the same condition it was in on the day the sales agreement was executed
   D. No, because the mold problem is a health hazard, which voids the contract

6. Legally, how much earnest money must be submitted with a valid purchase and sale agreement?
   A. 1% of the purchase price
   B. 3% of the purchase price
   C. 5% of the purchase price; but the amount over 3% cannot be retained as liquidated damages
   D. No earnest money is required

7. The purchase and sale agreement required the seller to order a pest inspection. The inspector found an infestation, and remedial action was required. Which party was responsible for paying to fix the problem?

A. Only the buyer

B. The brokerage

C. The buyer and seller were required to split the cost

D. Whichever party agreed to pay for the expense in the purchase and sale agreement

8. An owner-occupied property qualifies for its state's homestead exemption from property taxes. Shortly after closing, the new assessed value of the property is issued, and the property tax amount increases significantly. The selling agent is obligated to:

A. contact the closing agent and ask for details on the assessment

B. contest the increased assessed value with local authorities

C. do nothing

D. tell the buyer that the tax amount has increased

9. Agent Marcus is showing a property that was built in the early 1970s. The buyer asks about the presence of lead-based paint in the house. What should the agent say?

A. Any lead-based paint has been painted over, and is no longer a problem that should concern the buyer

B. Federal law requires sellers of houses built before 1978 to make disclosures concerning lead-based paint, and the buyer may request an inspection

C. Federal law requires sellers of houses built after 1978 to make disclosures concerning lead-based paint, but the buyer may still request an inspection

D. The buyer could request an inspection, although no law regulates this

10. A couple with children would like to buy a house that was built in 1950. The home was recently remodeled, with completely new paint and plumbing. What does the agent always have to do?

A. Ensure that the paint used during the remodel is lead-free

B. Make sure the buyers receive a pamphlet on lead-based paint

C. Provide them with a copy of a recent lead inspection report

D. Nothing; the house was remodeled so lead-based paint rules don't apply

Answer Key

1. D. A real estate licensee is limited to filling in the blanks on a pre-prepared form drafted by an attorney. Going beyond that, such as the drafting of covenants or a trust, would be considered the unauthorized practice of law.

2. B. Mutual acceptance occurs when the offeree communicates acceptance to the offeror. In this case, acceptance occurred on May 5, so the deposit would need to be deposited by May 7, two days later.

3. A. If the condition of the property changes or other new information comes to light that makes the original disclosure statement inaccurate, the seller must give an amended disclosure statement to the buyer or take corrective action so that the original statement is accurate again. The seller's agent isn't supposed to amend the disclosure statement himself, but the duty to disclose material facts would compel the agent to notify the other party.

4. B. The contract includes 80% financing as one of its conditions, so this is a contract with contingencies: a financing contingency, to be specific. A purchase and sale agreement is a bilateral contract, not a unilateral contract.

5. C. Buyers are always entitled to receive the property in the same condition it was in when the sales agreement was signed.

6. D. While almost all buyers will include an earnest money deposit along with the purchase and sale agreement, that is because of tradition (and because sellers are unlikely to consider offers without earnest money). There is no contractual or legal requirement of a particular amount, or any earnest money at all.

7. D. If a purchase and sale agreement is contingent on the results of an inspection, the parties also should specify in the contract how repairs will be handled.

8. C. New information that comes to light after the disclosure statement has been made should be disclosed in an amended statement if it is a material fact (and higher property taxes may be a material fact if the increase is great enough that the buyer might reconsider the transaction). However, material facts that are discovered after closing do not need to be disclosed, and the buyer no longer has a right of rescission.

9. B. The Residential Lead-Based Paint Reduction Act requires sellers of houses built before 1978 to disclose the location of any known lead-based paint. The buyer must be offered at least a ten-day window in which the house may be tested for lead-based paint.

10. B. A seller of a house built before 1978 must always give buyers a copy of a pamphlet on lead-based paint prepared by the Environmental Protection Agency. If (but only if) the property has been inspected for lead-based paint, the seller must also provide a copy of the inspection report. The agent is responsible for making sure that the seller complies with these requirements.

Chapter 10
Principles of Real Estate Financing

I. **Real Estate Economics** – At any given time and place, there may be a *buyer's market*, where few people are buying and homes sit on the market a long time, or there may be a *seller's market*, where many people are buying and homes sell rapidly.

   A. **Supply and Demand** – When demand for a product exceeds the supply (a seller's market), the price charged for the product rises, and the price increase stimulates more production. As production rises, more of the demand is satisfied, until supply outstrips demand and a buyer's market is created.

   B. **Interest Rates** – Interest rates represent the price of mortgage funds. They affect supply and demand and also fluctuate in response to changes in supply and demand. Interest is sometimes called the cost of money.

      1. **Interest rates and rental properties** – Demand for rental property will go up if market interest rates go up. Fewer people will be able to afford to buy homes, so those people will need to rent instead.

      Demand for rental homes for sale will increase if interest rates drop, since the pool of potential buyers will get larger.

   C. **Federal Reserve** – The government body with the greatest control over interest rates is the Federal Reserve. It can affect the money supply by setting the discount rate and establishing reserve requirements for banks.

II. **Real Estate Markets** – Mortgage loans can be bought and sold just like other investments—stocks and bonds, for example. The value of a loan is influenced by the *rate of return* compared to the market rate of return, as well as the *degree of risk* associated with the loan (the likelihood of default).

   A. **Primary Market** – The *primary market* for mortgage loans is the local mortgage finance market, made up of the various lending institutions in a community, such as a local savings and loan association or bank. The local economy has a significant effect on the amount of funds a local lender has available.

   B. **Secondary Market** – The *secondary market* is a national market consisting of government-sponsored enterprises and private investors (such as pension funds) that buy and sell real estate loans in all parts of the United States. The secondary market stabilizes local mortgage markets, allowing lenders to raise more funds when local funds are scarce by liquidating loans in the national market.

   Secondary market: the market in which investors purchase real estate loans from lenders. Also called the national market.

A mortgage sold by a lender to an investor may be said to have been assigned.

1. **Discounting** – Investors generally buy mortgage loans, for less than their face value (known as *discounting*).

2. **Seasoned loans** – A seasoned loan (one with a history of several years of timely payments by the borrower) is less risky than a new, untested loan, and thus worth more to an investor than a new loan for the same amount.

C. **Government-Sponsored Enterprises** – The major players in the secondary market are two government-sponsored enterprises: *Fannie Mae* and *Freddie Mac. Ginnie Mae*, a federal agency, is also involved.

1. **Fannie Mae** – The Federal National Mortgage Association (FNMA), often referred to as "Fannie Mae," started out as a federal agency in 1938. Its original purpose was to provide a secondary market for FHA-insured loans. Fannie Mae has now been reorganized as a private corporation, but it is still chartered by the government.

2. **Freddie Mac** – Congress created the Federal Home Loan Mortgage Corporation (FHLMC) in 1970 specifically to assist savings and loans. Freddie Mac buys conventional, FHA, and VA loans. Like Fannie Mae, it is a government-chartered corporation.

3. **Ginnie Mae** – The Government National Mortgage Association (GNMA) is part of the Department of Housing and Urban Development. Ginnie Mae provides secondary market funds for government-insured loans made through the FHA and VA loan programs.

Sample questions

A federal agency is charged with the tasks of regulating reserve requirements and setting the discount rate of interest. This is the:

A. Federal Housing Administration
B. Federal Trade Association
C. Federal Reserve
D. Federal Deposit and Insurance Corporation

C. *The Federal Reserve is responsible for all of these tasks.*

Morgan is buying a new home, and she needs to obtain a mortgage loan. She could apply to all of the following except:

A. a mortgage broker
B. Ginnie Mae
C. a savings and loan association
D. a commercial bank

B. *Ginnie Mae, Fannie Mae, and Freddie Mac are part of the secondary market for loans; they do not make loans directly to home buyers.*

Where can a lender sell one of its loans?

A. Primary market
B. Mortgage market
C. Secondary market
D. The Fed market

    C. *Primary lenders such as banks can sell their loans on the secondary market.*

Ginnie Mae (Government National Mortgage Association) and Fannie Mae (Federal National Mortgage Association):

A. are primary lenders
B. help make up the secondary market for mortgage loans
C. are both owned solely by the government
D. are private agencies

    B. *Ginnie Mae and Fannie Mae are major players in the secondary market; Fannie Mae is privately held, although heavily supervised by the government.*

III. Finance Documents – The legal documents used in conjunction with most real estate loans are the promissory note and a security instrument (either a mortgage or a deed of trust).

    A. Promissory Notes – A *promissory note* is a written promise to repay a debt, and the note serves as primary evidence of the debt. One person loans another money, and the other signs a promissory note, promising to repay the loan with interest. The borrower who signs the note is called the *maker*, and the lender is called the *payee*.

> A promissory note is the primary evidence of a debt.

        1. Basic provisions – A properly written promissory note contains the loan balance (called the *principal*), when and how the payments are to be made, the *maturity date* (when the loan must be paid in full), and the names of the borrower and lender. The note states the interest rate, and whether it is fixed or variable.

            a. Usury – State *usury* laws may prohibit the interest rate specified in the note from exceeding a specific amount.

> Usury: charging an interest rate that exceeds legal limits.

            b. No legal description – Because the note does not concern the property, it does not need to include a legal description and is ordinarily not recorded.

        2. Types of notes – There are various types of promissory notes, classified according to the way the principal and interest are paid off.

a. **Straight note** – Also called a *term loan*, a *straight note* calls for the payment of interest only. The full amount of the principal is due in a lump sum—called a *balloon payment*—when the loan term ends.

b. **Installment note** – An *installment note* calls for the payment of interest and principal. If a note is fully *amortized*, the periodic payments are enough to pay off the entire loan, both principal and interest, by the end of the loan's term. A borrower will pay less interest over the life of the loan with an installment note.

Note: Whether the payments are interest-only, partially amortized, or fully amortized, the interest paid on real estate loans is *simple interest*, meaning that it is paid on the principal only. Interest paid on both principal and unpaid accrued interest is known as *compound interest*.

3. **Negotiable instrument** – A promissory note is usually a *negotiable instrument*, which means the lender may assign the debt to someone else by endorsing the note, in much the same way a check is endorsed. The person who receives the note and obtains the right to future payments is known as the *assignee*.

B. **Security Instruments** – When someone borrows money to buy real estate, in addition to signing a promissory note in favor of the lender, she must also sign a security instrument, either a *mortgage* or *deed of trust*. A security instrument is a contract between the borrower and the lender, so the usual contractual requirements (such as capacity to contract) apply.

The security agreement makes the property collateral for the loan.

1. **Creates a lien** – The promissory note is the borrower's binding promise to repay the loan. The security instrument is a contract that protects the lender by making the real property collateral for the loan; it secures the loan by creating a lien on the property. Failure to repay as agreed in the note will result in foreclosure. A lender with a security interest is known as a *secured creditor.*

a. **Hypothecation** – Though the borrower offers the real property as security for a debt, he doesn't give up possession rights while the debt is being repaid. To give title to property as security for an obligation without giving up possession is called *hypothecation*.

C. **Mortgage vs. Deed of Trust** – Both the mortgage and the deed of trust are security instruments and both can be used in Washington. Legally, a mortgage allows a lender to place a lien while a deed of trust purports to transfer a title interest. However, the most important practical difference between a mortgage and

144

a deed of trust concerns the procedures for foreclosure if the borrower defaults.

1. **Mortgage** – There are two parties to a mortgage: the *mortgagor* (the owner/borrower) and the *mortgagee* (the lender).

   Mortgagor: borrower
   Mortgagee: lender

2. **Deed of trust** – Sometimes called a *trust deed*, this security instrument has three parties: the borrower (called the *trustor* or *grantor*), the lender (the *beneficiary*), and a third party (a *trustee*), who holds the deed in trust during repayment, and who will handle the foreclosure process if necessary. The trustee will *reconvey* the title to the trustor when the loan has been repaid.

   Beneficiary: lender
   Trustor/grantor: borrower
   Trustee: third party

   a. **Foreclosure** – Foreclosure can be considerably easier with a deed of trust than with a mortgage, which makes it the overwhelming favorite with lenders in Washington.

   b. **Holding title** – Washington is a "lien theory" state, where a mortgage or a deed of trust is considered to create a lien but not to convey title to the lender. Title passes to the buyer/borrower as soon as the transaction closes. By contrast, in a "title theory" state, the mortgage or deed of trust is considered to actually convey title to the lender.

   c. **Recording** – The recording of a security instrument is not a legal requirement, but it should be recorded to serve constructive notice of the lender's financial interest in the property.

Sample questions

Ernest purchased a home using a term mortgage. Which of the following is true?

A. Ernest must pay the entire loan principal at the end of the term
B. Ernest must pay all of the loan's interest at the end of the term
C. Ernest's loan will be fully amortized over the loan's term
D. State laws limit the term of Ernest's loan

   A. In a term mortgage, the borrower makes monthly interest payments, and must pay the entire principal balance at the end of the loan's term.

A real estate mortgage loan's repayment plan is based on a 30-year amortization schedule, but it calls for full payment by the loan's tenth anniversary. What kind of loan is it?

A. Term mortgage
B. Graduated payment mortgage
C. Balloon payment mortgage
D. Fully amortized mortgage

> C. The payments are structured for full payment over 30 years to keep the monthly payments down. The ten-year due date requires a balloon payment.

The law that sets interest ceilings on certain types of loans is:
A. Regulation Z
B. the Statute of Limitations
C. the Uniform Commercial Code
D. the state usury law

> D. Usury is the act of charging interest at a higher rate than the law allows.

Anna takes out a loan to purchase real estate by signing a note and a mortgage. Anna is the:

A. beneficiary
B. trustee
C. mortgagor
D. mortgagee

> C. A mortgagor (the borrower) gives the mortgage to the mortgagee (the lender).

Paul would like to make an offer on a house right away, but he doesn't have the cash available for an earnest money deposit yet. He is, however, expecting a large commission check from his sales job within several weeks, so he offers the seller a promissory note for $10,000 as the earnest money deposit. He will also be seeking conventional financing to pay for the rest of the home's price. Will the promissory note be tied to the buyer's mortgage?

A. Yes, the institutional lender will require both promissory notes to be collateralized
B. Yes, the promissory note is not valid unless it has been collateralized
C. No, the promissory note is a promise to pay a debt and is a contract on its own
D. Not relevant, because a promissory note may never be used as earnest money

> C. It is acceptable, though not always wise, to use a promissory note as earnest money. A promissory note is a complete contract and never needs to be tied to a mortgage or deed of trust, although institutional loans will always be collateralized with a mortgage or deed of trust.

Traditionally, the main difference between a mortgage and a deed of trust was that:

A. a mortgage was a security instrument; a deed of trust was not
B. a mortgage could be foreclosed upon; a deed of trust could not
C. a deed of trust transferred title, while a mortgage only created a lien
D. None of the above

> C. Traditionally, a deed of trust purported to convey legal title to the trustee. Now in lien theory states like Washington, both deeds of trust and mortgages only create a lien against the property.

D. Security Instrument Provisions – Below are five key provisions that typically appear in security instruments.

    1. Acceleration clause – An *acceleration clause* in the promissory note and/or the security instrument states that if the borrower defaults, the lender has the option of declaring the entire loan balance due and payable in full immediately (sometimes referred to as *calling the note*). If the borrower doesn't pay, the lender may sue on the note or foreclose.

> Acceleration clause: a provision in a note or security instrument that allows the lender to "call the note" if the borrower defaults on the loan agreement.

    2. Alienation clause – An *alienation clause* is also called a *due-on-sale clause*. This provision does not prohibit the sale of the property, but it does give the lender the right to accelerate the loan if the borrower sells the property. Its purpose is to protect the lender's security interest, by enabling the lender to reject the substitution of a new borrower.

> An alienation clause is also called a "due-on-sale" clause.

        a. No alienation clause in loan – If there is no alienation clause in the security instrument and the loan is not paid off at closing, the purchaser can either *assume* the loan or take title *subject to* the loan.

        b. Assuming the loan – In an *assumption*, the borrower sells the security property to someone who agrees to assume responsibility for the loan. The new owner becomes primarily responsible to the lender for repayment; the original borrower remains secondarily liable.

> Assumption: buyer takes on personal liability for paying off the seller's existing mortgage or deed of trust.

        c. Subject to the loan – When a buyer takes title "subject to" an existing mortgage or deed of trust instead of assuming it, the original borrower remains fully liable for the debt.

> Subject to: an alternative to assumption. Buyer is liable to the seller for payment, but she isn't liable to the lender for payment.

        d. Lender's approval – Even when a loan contains an alienation clause, the lender may still agree to an assumption of the loan by a creditworthy purchaser. The lender will usually charge an assumption fee and may also raise the loan's interest rate.

> If a lender approves the buyer's assumption of the loan, the seller receives a release of liability. This is a novation.

    3. Prepayment penalty – Sometimes a lender imposes a penalty if the borrower prepays the loan. The penalty is intended to compensate the lender for interest it expected to collect, but won't be collecting because of early repayment. An *open mortgage* allows prepayment.

> Prepayment penalty: a penalty charged to a borrower who pays off a greater percentage of the loan in any year than the loan agreement permits.

    4. Subordination clause – A *subordination clause* in a security agreement makes it possible for a security instrument recorded later to assume a higher priority position—usually a first lien position—even though the security instrument that contains this provision was executed and recorded first.

> Subordination clause: a provision in a security instrument that permits a later security instrument to have higher lien priority than the one containing the clause.

a. **Common in land development situations** – The subordination clause benefits the borrower by making it easier to obtain additional financing on the security property. For instance, the clause makes it possible for a borrower to obtain future construction loans (which must have first lien position) in land development projects.

5. **Defeasance clause** – A *defeasance* clause states that when the debt has been paid, the security instrument lien will be canceled.

a. **Deed of reconveyance** – If the security instrument is a deed of trust, the lien is removed through a *deed of reconveyance* given by the trustee to the trustor (the borrower). The deed of reconveyance doesn't have to be recorded, but it's in the trustor's best interest to do so.

A deed of reconveyance is given by the trustee (third party) to the trustor/grantor (borrower) when the deed of trust debt has been paid in full. The trustor/grantor has the deed of reconveyance recorded.

b. **Satisfaction of mortgage** – If the security instrument is a mortgage, a document called a *satisfaction of mortgage* (or *satisfaction piece*) is used to remove the lien. Either a deed of reconveyance or a satisfaction of mortgage may be referred to as a *lien release*.

Sample questions

Which of the following clauses relates to a mortgage loan default and requires immediate payment of the debt?

A. Alienation clause
B. Acceleration clause
C. Writ clause
D. Safety clause

    B. *The acceleration clause allows the lender to accelerate the loan if the borrower fails to pay as agreed or defaults on any other aspect of the loan agreement.*

A mortgage often includes a clause requiring the lender's consent before another borrower may assume the mortgage. This clause is called a/an:

A. power-of-sale clause
B. subordination clause
C. defeasance clause
D. alienation clause (due-on-sale clause)

    D. *An alienation clause (or due-on-sale clause) prevents assumption without the lender's consent by stipulating that the loan balance is due and payable in full if the property is sold.*

Joan is assuming Eric's mortgage. Which statement is true?

A. Eric will still be primarily liable if Joan defaults on the assumed mortgage
B. Joan can only assume the mortgage if it contains an alienation clause
C. Joan will be primarily liable for the debt, while Eric becomes secondarily liable
D. Eric will not be responsible if Joan defaults

> C. *In an assumption, the buyer takes on primary responsibility for the debt, and the original borrower retains secondary responsibility in case the buyer defaults.*

Vacant Land Financing Co. has first lien position on the property, but it agrees to move into a second lien position in exchange for a fee. This is:

A. subordination
B. subrogation
C. subprime lending
D. fraud

> A. *Subordination is the process of giving up higher lien status and accepting a lower lien status.*

Upon full payment by the mortgagor, the mortgagee must execute a satisfaction of mortgage, as required by which mortgage clause?

A. Alienation
B. Defeasance
C. Acceleration
D. Power of sale

> B. *The defeasance clause states that the borrower will regain title and the security instrument will be canceled when the debt has been paid.*

Which of the following would not create a cloud on the title?

A. Lis pendens
B. Mortgage release
C. Undisclosed lien
D. Forged document

> B. *A mortgage release (satisfaction of mortgage) is a document given by the lender to the borrower after the final loan payment has been made. The mortgage will remain a cloud on the borrower's title until the release has been recorded.*

IV. **Foreclosure Procedures** – If the borrower doesn't repay a secured loan as agreed, the lender may foreclose and collect the debt from the proceeds of a forced sale.

   A. **Mortgage Foreclosure** – Mortgage foreclosures are sometimes called *judicial foreclosures* because they are carried out through the court system. The lender files a lawsuit against the borrower in a court in the county where the collateral property is located.

1. **Decree of foreclosure** – If the court finds in favor of the lender (and it usually does), it will issue a *decree of foreclosure* ordering the property to be sold to satisfy the debt. The sale is called a *sheriff's sale*.

2. **Equitable right of redemption** – Between the time the lawsuit is filed and the sale of the property, the borrower may redeem the property by paying off the mortgage debt in full, plus any costs incurred. This is known as the *equitable right of redemption.*

3. **Statutory right of redemption** – After the sheriff's sale, the borrower has a right to redeem his property by paying off the entire debt, plus interest, costs, and fees. This period continues for *one year* after the sale, unless the lender has waived his rights to a deficiency judgment, in which case the period continues for *eight months*.

4. **Deficiency judgments** – If the proceeds of the sheriff's sale are insufficient to satisfy the debt, the lender can obtain a *deficiency judgment* against the borrower.

   a. **Non-recourse mortgage** – A mortgage with language that specifically prohibits the mortgagee from seeking a deficiency judgment against the borrower is called a *non-recourse mortgage.*

   b. **Surplus funds** – If there are surplus funds after the sheriff's sale and after all debts have been satisfied, they belong to the foreclosed owner (unless the owner is bankrupt, in which case funds pass to the bankruptcy trustee).

B. **Deed of Trust Foreclosure** – A deed of trust foreclosure is quite different from a mortgage foreclosure. Every deed of trust has a *power of sale* clause. If the borrower defaults, the provision authorizes the trustee to sell the property through a *nonjudicial foreclosure*. The trustee will sell the property at a *trustee's sale* and use the proceeds to pay off the debt owed to the lender.

   1. **Notice of default** – To foreclose, the beneficiary or trustee must first give the borrower a *notice of default*. And in some states, junior lienholders (i.e., those with lower lien priority than the deed of trust being foreclosed) may file a request to receive a notice of default in case another lienholder begins a foreclosure action. Foreclosure by a senior lienholder could destroy a junior lienholder's security interest.

Redemption: a mortgagor's (borrower's) right to regain his property either while it is being foreclosed or within a statutory period after it has been foreclosed.

Non-recourse mortgage: a mortgage in which the borrower is not held personally liable on the note because the lender is confident the collateral property is adequate security for the loan.

A deed of trust foreclosure sale is called a trustee's sale.

Junior lienholders may request a notice of default.

2. **Notice of sale** – A month after the notice of default is issued, the trustee will issue a *notice of sale* and record the notice in the county where the property is located.

3. **Reinstatement** – The borrower under a deed of trust has a period in which he can stop the foreclosure proceedings by curing the default and reinstating the loan. To do this, the borrower must pay all past-due installments, plus fees and interest. This reinstatement period ends shortly before the trustee's sale.

4. **Trustee's deed** – The successful bidder at the trustee's sale receives a trustee's deed, which terminates the borrower's interest in the property. In contrast to a judicial foreclosure, there is no post-sale redemption period.

5. **Lenders prefer nonjudicial foreclosure** – Lenders prefer nonjudicial foreclosure, because it is faster and less expensive. The disadvantage for lenders, however, is that deficiency judgments are not allowed through nonjudicial foreclosure.

6. **Deed in lieu of foreclosure** – A defaulting borrower who doesn't have the resources to cure the default or redeem the foreclosed property may opt to give the lender a *deed in lieu of foreclosure*, which transfers title immediately to the lender and prevents the cost and aggravation of a foreclosure. The lender will take title subject to any other liens that encumber the property.

> In some states, nonjudicial foreclosure may also be known as "foreclosure by advertisement."

> Deed of trust foreclosure usually takes less time than mortgage foreclosure. However, no deficiency judgment is allowed.

> Deed in lieu of foreclosure: a deed given by a borrower to the lender, relinquishing ownership of the security property, to satisfy the debt and avoid foreclosure.

Sample questions

ABC Mortgage is seeking a deficiency judgment against a borrower. The most likely reason is because:

A. the property has lost value in the local market
B. the borrower failed to pay the second part of his annual property taxes
C. the borrower was late making his mortgage payment
D. a foreclosure sale produced insufficient funds to satisfy the unpaid debt

> D. *Under some circumstances, a lender may seek a deficiency judgment when the proceeds of a foreclosure sale are insufficient to satisfy the borrower's unpaid debt.*

Sheila lives in a state where she can pay the debt after a foreclosure sale and regain the property. What is her right called?

A. Statutory right of redemption
B. Title redemption
C. Debt redemption
D. Equitable right of redemption

   A.   The right to redeem the property within a certain time period following the sale is the statutory right of redemption. The right to redeem the property prior to the foreclosure (sheriff's sale) is the equitable right of redemption.

Jacob defaults on his mortgage, but has the right to redeem the property before the foreclosure sale. Jacob has a/an:

A. default redemption
B. owner's right of redemption
C. statutory right of redemption
D. equitable right of redemption

   D.   With an equitable right of redemption, the defaulting borrower can redeem the property before the foreclosure sale by paying off the mortgage debt in full, plus costs.

A mortgage must include a power of sale clause in order to be foreclosed by:

A. advertisement (nonjudicial foreclosure)
B. judicial foreclosure
C. a writ of satisfaction
D. lis pendens

   A.   A mortgage or deed of trust that contains a power of sale clause can be foreclosed nonjudicially (referred to in some states as foreclosure by advertisement).

V. **Land Contracts** – Some transactions are financed by the seller. The seller may use a promissory note and mortgage as an institutional lender would. Alternatively, the seller may use a security instrument known as a *land contract*. It may also be known as a contract for deed, installment sales contract, real estate contract, or contract of sale.

   A. **Parties** – The parties to a land contract are the *vendor* (seller) and *vendee* (borrower). The vendee agrees to pay the purchase price, plus interest, in installments over a specified number of years.

   B. **Title** – The vendee takes possession of the property right away, but the vendor retains legal title until the full price has been paid. The vendee has equitable title to the property while paying off the purchase price. When the contract is fully paid off, the vendor delivers a warranty deed to the vendee.

C. **Recording** – The vendee should record the contract promptly after signing it, to protect her equitable interest.

D. **Forfeiture** – If a vendee defaults on a land contract, the vendor may foreclose judicially. Alternatively, the vendor may declare a *forfeiture*, which is a remedy available only with land contracts. The vendor terminates the contract without having to go to court and without having to refund any of the payments the vendee has made. Washington law allows forfeiture only if there is a forfeiture clause in the contract and the contract has been recorded.

The vendee (buyer) should record the contract for deed (land contract) to serve constructive notice to the world of her equitable interest in the property.

Forfeiture: loss of equitable interest in property, as a result of failure to perform according to the terms of a land contract.

Sample questions

Which of the following would MOST LIKELY happen in a land contract?

A. The vendor pays the property taxes, insurance, repairs, and upkeep on the property until the final payment is made
B. The vendor finances the property and makes installment payments
C. The vendor retains the title to the property until the final payment is made
D. The vendee receives possession and the vendor retains equitable title

C. *The vendor (seller) retains title to the property until the final payment is made. The vendee (buyer) receives possession and equitable title while making installment payments. The vendee is also usually responsible for property taxes, repairs, and upkeep during the contract.*

Legal title may be conveyed by all of the following, except:

A. a deed of trust
B. equitable title
C. a warranty deed
D. bargain and sale deed

B. *Equitable title offers some rights to the holder, but does not convey legal title to a property.*

A seller agrees to finance the purchase of a home using a contract for deed (land contract). Once the contract is signed, the buyer will have:

A. title by contract
B. title by deed
C. legal title
D. equitable title

D. *When a land contract (contract for deed) is used to purchase property, the buyer has equitable title until the contract has been paid in full, at which time the seller will transfer legal title to the buyer.*

VI. Types of Mortgage Loans – The terms "mortgage" or "trust deed" are often coupled with an adjective that describes the particular function of the security instrument or the circumstances in which it is used. For example, a "construction mortgage" describes a mortgage that secures a loan made to finance the construction of some kind of real estate improvement. Listed below are several loan types that are tested. Any one of them could be a mortgage or trust deed.

A. Purchase Money Mortgage – This term has two meanings:

1. **Mortgage used to finance purchase** – The term can mean any mortgage used to finance the purchase of property. When an institutional or private lender gives the borrower cash in return for a promissory note and mortgage, the security instrument is considered a *hard money mortgage*.

2. **Seller-financed transaction** – The term can be interpreted more narrowly to mean a *seller-financed transaction*, either for part or all of the purchase price. The security instrument is considered a *soft money mortgage* because the borrower receives credit instead of cash from the seller. The seller is said to "take back" or "carry back" the mortgage.

B. Budget Mortgage – With a *budget mortgage*, the monthly payments include not just principal and interest on the loan, but also part of the year's property taxes and hazard insurance premiums as well. Almost all residential loans are secured by budget mortgages.

C. Package Mortgage – A *package mortgage* is a loan that includes both real and personal property as security for the debt.

D. Construction Mortgage – A *construction mortgage* secures a loan to finance construction. Because it is a temporary loan, a construction loan is sometimes called an *interim* loan. On completion of construction, the loan will be replaced with a permanent *take-out* loan.

1. **Fixed disbursement plan** – A construction loan is not disbursed all at once. Instead, it is disbursed in increments over the period of construction, with interest beginning to accrue when the first installment is released. This is called a *fixed disbursement plan*. When and how the disbursements will be made are determined in advance and the disbursements themselves are called *obligatory advances*.

2. **Risks to lender** – Because of the risks associated with construction loans, most lenders insist on having first lien priority for construction loans. Also, the lender will often hold back the final 10% or more of the loan proceeds until

---

Budget mortgage: a loan in which the monthly payments include a share of the property taxes and insurance, in addition to principal and interest.

Package mortgage: a mortgage that is secured by certain items of personal property in addition to the real property.

the period for claiming mechanic's liens has expired, to protect against unpaid liens.

E. Blanket Mortgage – When a mortgage secures more than one piece of property it is called a *blanket mortgage*. For example, if one property does not provide sufficient collateral for a loan, the owner might offer a second property—secured by the same mortgage—as additional collateral.

> Blanket mortgage: a mortgage that covers more than one piece of property.

   1. Subdivision development – Blanket mortgages are commonplace in subdivision developments. One mortgage will secure the entire development and all the subdivided lots within it.

   2. Partial release clause – Typically, the lender releases individual lots from the blanket lien as they are sold. This is accomplished in accordance with a provision in the blanket lien called a *partial release* clause (or *partial satisfaction* clause).

> Partial release clause: allows lender to release individual lot from blanket lien when lot is sold. Also called a partial satisfaction clause.

F. Participation Mortgage – A *participation mortgage* allows the lender to share in the earnings generated by the mortgaged property, as well as collect interest payments on the principal. Large lenders who finance commercial projects, such as insurance companies, are most likely to offer participation mortgages.

> Participation mortgage: a loan made in exchange for a share of the borrower's equity in the property, and/or a share of its earnings.

G. Wraparound Mortgage – A *wraparound* is a new mortgage that includes or "wraps around" an existing first mortgage on a property. The wraparound loan is recorded later, making it junior to the existing loan (known as the *underlying loan*). Wraparounds are generally used only in seller-financed transactions.

> Wraparound financing usually, but not always, involves seller financing. The wraparound is a junior loan to the seller's senior underlying loan.

   1. Requirements – The underlying loan cannot have an alienation clause. Otherwise, the lender would require the seller to pay off the underlying loan at the time of the sale. Also, a wraparound should be designed so that the underlying loan will be paid off before the wraparound, so that the buyer's title is not encumbered with the seller's debt after the buyer has paid the full purchase price.

> The underlying loan must be scheduled to pay off before the wraparound loan.

H. Open-End Mortgage – An *open-end mortgage* sets a borrowing limit but allows the borrower to re-borrow, when needed, any part of the debt that has been repaid, without having to negotiate a new mortgage. It can be repaid in full at any time without a prepayment penalty.

I. Graduated Payment Mortgage – A *graduated payment mortgage* allows the borrower to make smaller payments at first and gradually step up to larger payments. For example, the payments

> Graduated payment mortgages may result in negative amortization.

might increase annually for the first three to five years of the loan, and then remain level for the rest of the loan term.

J. Swing Loan – A *swing loan* is used when buyers need to purchase a new home before they've succeeded in selling their current one. The loan is usually secured by equity in the property that is for sale, and will be paid off when the sale closes. This type of loan may also be called a *gap loan* or *bridge loan*.

K. Reverse Mortgage – A *reverse mortgage* (or *reverse equity mortgage*) is designed to provide income to older homeowners. The owner borrows against the home's equity, but will receive a monthly check from the lender rather than making monthly payments. The home usually must be sold when the owner dies in order to pay back the mortgage. Reverse mortgages are non-recourse loans.

L. Refinance – A borrower may choose to take out a new loan and use it to pay off his old loan. This is often done to take advantage of lower interest rates. As with any new loan, the borrower must qualify, the property will be appraised, and a title search will be performed.

M. Home Equity Loan – A borrower may obtain a loan, usually for home improvements, by borrowing against the equity in a home he owns. If it is for a fixed amount and with fixed payments, it is known as a *home equity loan*. If it is an open-ended revolving credit account, similar to a credit card but secured by real property, it is known as a home equity line of credit.

Sample questions

Pamela agrees to buy Cindy's home using a purchase money mortgage for part of the purchase price. Which of the following is true?

A. Cindy will deliver a promissory note at closing
B. Cindy will buy back the property if Pamela defaults
C. Cindy will remain in possession of the property until the loan has been paid
D. Cindy is financing a portion of the purchase price

> D. *A purchase money mortgage is one that the buyer gives to the seller in a seller-financed transaction.*

Many home purchase loans require the borrower to set up an escrow account for taxes and insurance. These are:

A. budget mortgages
B. blanket mortgages
C. participation mortgages
D. third mortgages

    A. *Many ordinary home purchase loans are budget mortgages. The lender requires the home buyer/borrower to pay a share of the property taxes and hazard insurance each month, along with the principal and interest payment on the loan.*

A developer places a mortgage on 40 acres of property and begins building a housing development. Whenever he sells a lot to a purchaser, a partial release is obtained for the lot the home buyer purchased. This type of mortgage is a:

A. package mortgage
B. net-equity mortgage
C. blanket mortgage
D. closed mortgage

    C. *Blanket mortgages and trust deeds frequently contain release clauses that permit the release of portions of the secured property on payment of a predetermined portion of the debt.*

Seller financing that involves taking back a loan secured by a mortgage that is in the amount of the seller's existing loan, plus all or a portion of the seller's equity, is known as a:

A. package loan
B. budget mortgage
C. wraparound mortgage
D. purchase money mortgage

    C. *The wraparound mortgage wraps the seller's existing loan(s), plus that portion of the seller's equity that remains after the buyer's downpayment. The wraparound mortgage is junior in priority to the seller's existing loan(s).*

Ryan needs to replace his roof; not having the cash available, he decides to borrow several thousand dollars through a home equity line of credit, which is a:

A. fully amortized fixed-term loan
B. loan financing the purchase of both real and personal property
C. loan with smaller payments at first and larger payments later
D. secured loan

    D. *A home equity line of credit is a revolving credit account rather than a loan with a fixed term and amount. Unlike a credit card, though, it is secured by the borrower's real property.*

The Thompsons, a retired couple, need more income. Their lender offers a type of loan in which the lender will send the couple a monthly check for as long as the couple lives on the property, in exchange for a lien against the equity in their property. The lender is referring to a/an:

A. shared appreciation mortgage
B. deed in lieu
C. open-end mortgage
D. reverse mortgage

    D. *A reverse mortgage (also called a reverse equity or reverse annuity mortgage) is designed for borrowers in their retirement years who need a cash flow. Instead of loaning the entire amount agreed upon all at once, the lender (mortgagee) makes monthly loan disbursements to the borrower (mortgagor) over a period of time.*

Chapter Quiz

1. As a result of Federal Reserve action, interest rates for residential loans go down. Which of the following is most likely to occur as a result?

   A. Fewer buyers will qualify for loans
   B. There will be a decrease in sale prices for homes
   C. There will be an increase in sale prices for homes
   D. There will be more homes for sale

2. Which of the following entities would participate in the primary market for mortgage lending?

   A. Commercial bank
   B. Federal Home Loan Mortgage Corporation
   C. Federal Housing Administration
   D. Federal National Mortgage Association

3. Mortgage interest rates are primarily influenced by the:

   A. assessed value of the property
   B. condition of the money market
   C. credit history of the borrower
   D. value of similar mortgaged properties in the area

4. What is a final mortgage payment that is larger than all of the other payments called?

   A. Advanced
   B. Amortized
   C. Balloon
   D. Expanded

5. Interest on a loan for a home purchase is which type of interest?

   A. Annual
   B. Compound
   C. Complex
   D. Simple

6. A loan's interest is best defined as:

   A. a charge paid by a borrower in exchange for use of the lender's money
   B. a penalty assessed against a borrower's debt
   C. a surcharge that increases a lender's yield
   D. compensation for the lender's potential loss

7. A mortgage, and the associated mortgage note, are both examples of:

   A. contracts
   B. deeds
   C. non-negotiable instruments
   D. option agreements

8. The mortgagee assigns its interest and the assignee records the assignment. The mortgagor now needs to make payments to the:

   A. assignee
   B. assignor
   C. beneficiary
   D. mortgagee

9. A borrower defaults on a mortgage. What does the acceleration clause in the mortgage allow the lender to do?

   A. Compel the borrower to sell the property and repay the debt
   B. Demand immediate payment of the entire loan balance
   C. Prevent the borrower from selling the property
   D. Report the borrower to a collection agency

10. Most conventional loans contain an alienation clause, which prohibits:

    A. the sale of the property
    B. prepayment of the loan
    C. the loan from being assumed
    D. increases or decreases in the loan's interest rate

11. Buyer Perry would like to assume Seller Joan's loan with ABC Mortgage Company, in a way that would mean no further liability for Joan. To accomplish this, Perry and Joan should use a/an:

    A. acknowledgment of the agreement from ABC Mortgage
    B. purchase contract signed by the buyer and seller
    C. release of liability signed by ABC Mortgage
    D. release of liability signed by Joan

12. A contract for deed wouldn't be a good idea if the seller's mortgage has a/an:

    A. acceleration clause
    B. alienation clause
    C. defeasance clause
    D. subordination clause

13. When a mortgagor regains property after foreclosure by paying whatever the foreclosure sale purchaser paid for the property, plus interest and expenses, it is called:

    A. recapture
    B. redemption
    C. reversion
    D. replevin

14. Once a sales contract is signed by the parties, the buyer immediately receives:

    A. a life estate
    B. legal title
    C. equitable title
    D. the right to lease the property

15. Sarita bought a home. She had poor credit so the owner agreed to finance the purchase. The parties agreed to a 20-year loan term. Sarita took title to the property, and the seller held a lien against the property. What type of financing instrument was used?

    A. Option to buy
    B. Land contract
    C. Purchase money mortgage
    D. Open mortgage

16. The developer wants a construction loan to build 20 homes. The lender requires a take-out commitment. This means the developer needs:

    A. a clause that allows individual lots to be released from the blanket lien when they are sold to purchasers
    B. a new mortgage that wraps around an existing first mortgage
    C. a permanent lender who will provide financing once construction is completed
    D. an interim contract guaranteeing that the property will be finished by a certain date

17. A mortgage that uses both real and personal property to secure the borrower's debt is a:

    A. reverse equity mortgage
    B. budget mortgage
    C. package mortgage
    D. deed of trust

18. A mortgage that would be used to purchase more than one parcel of land is a:

    A. blanket mortgage
    B. budget mortgage
    C. closed mortgage
    D. package mortgage

19. If you have a graduated payment loan, this means that your loan payments:

    A. decrease
    B. balloon in five years
    C. vary according to interest rates
    D. rise for a number of years and then remain level

20. Shelly takes out a new mortgage on her house, paying off her old mortgage with part of the proceeds. The new mortgage has a rate several percentage points lower than the old mortgage. This is called:

    A. alienation
    B. refinancing
    C. a home equity line of credit
    D. a reverse equity mortgage

Answer Key

1. C. Home sales prices are likely to go up in the event of lower interest rates. Lower interest rates will enable more buyers to get more house for their money, motivating more buyers and increasing demand, which will in turn drive up sales prices.

2. A. Commercial banks, savings and loans, mortgage companies, and other entities that make loans to consumers are all part of the primary mortgage market. The Federal Home Loan Mortgage Corporation (Freddie Mac) and Federal National Mortgage Association (Fannie Mae) are part of the secondary market instead.

3. B. Mortgage interest rates are affected by the supply of available funds in the money market. This is shaped by supply and demand for funds, as well as actions by the Federal Reserve.

4. C. A balloon payment is required if, at the end of a loan term, the borrower has not paid off the loan balance. Usually this will be much larger than any of the mortgage's regular payments.

5. D. The interest paid on real estate loans is simple interest.

6. A. Interest is charged to a borrower as compensation for the lender, in exchange for the lender allowing the borrower to borrow money.

7. A. A security instrument (such as a mortgage) and a promissory note are both contracts between borrower and lender. The promissory note is a promise to repay money, and the mortgage pledges the subject property as security for the loan.

8. A. A mortgagee (lender) can assign the mortgage debt to a third party, who is then referred to as the assignee. After the assignment the mortgagor (the borrower) is required to make the payments to the assignee.

9. B. An acceleration clause allows a lender to "call" a loan, or demand the repayment of the entire loan balance, in the event of a borrower's default.

10. C. The alienation clause, also called the due-on-sale clause, prohibits the assumption of the loan. It means that if the property is sold, the loan must be paid off (unless the lender agrees to assumption of the loan by a particular buyer).

11. C. If a seller in a loan assumption wants to be released from further liability, he should approach the lender and request a formal document known as a release of liability.

12. B. An alienation clause gives the lender the right to accelerate the loan whenever the borrower sells the property or otherwise alienates an interest in it. A contract for deed (or land contract) transfers equitable title to the buyer, so execution of the contract would allow the lender to accelerate the seller's mortgage, demanding immediate payment in full. Thus, a contract for deed would be ill-advised unless the seller has enough money to pay off the mortgage at closing.

13. B. The equitable right of redemption is the right of a mortgagor to redeem property prior to the foreclosure sale. The statutory right of redemption is the right of a mortgagor to get his property back after a foreclosure sale.

14. C. A buyer receives equitable title to the property once the sales contract has been signed.

15. C. A purchase money mortgage is one given by the buyer to the seller to secure credit extended by the seller.

16. C. Construction loans are interim loans used to finance construction of improvements. The construction loan is replaced by a permanent loan, sometimes called a take-out loan, when construction is complete.

17. C. A package mortgage includes both real and personal property as collateral.

18. A. A blanket mortgage is often used by subdividers. It is secured by a number of parcels, with each parcel released from the blanket lien as it is sold.

19. D. The graduated payments start at what is usually a below-market rate and then annually increase until they reach a predetermined level. After that, they remain constant for the remainder of the loan's term.

20. B. Refinancing involves taking out an entirely new mortgage loan to replace an existing one. It often is done when mortgage interest rates drop, allowing borrowers to have lower payments.

Chapter 11
Applying for a Residential Loan

I. **Lending Institutions** – Lenders from whom a borrower might obtain a mortgage loan include commercial banks, savings and loans, savings banks, and credit unions.

   A. **Mortgage Companies** – A mortgage company is not a depository institution like a bank. It usually acts as a *loan correspondent*: an intermediary between large investors and home buyers. Traditionally, there was a distinction between mortgage bankers (who actually made loans) and mortgage brokers (who simply brought together lenders and borrowers for a fee), but those distinctions have faded.

II. **Loan Costs** – In addition to the annual interest, lenders impose certain charges that significantly affect the cost of a loan. The most important are *origination fees* and *discount points*.

   A. **Origination Fee** – A *loan origination fee* is designed to pay administrative costs associated with making the loan. It is sometimes called a *loan fee* or a *loan service fee*. The borrower usually pays the loan origination fee at closing.

> Loan origination fee: a fee a lender charges a borrower to cover the administrative costs of making a loan.

   B. **Discount Points** – *Discount points* are used to increase the lender's upfront yield, or profit on the loan. The lender not only receives interest throughout the loan term but also receives an additional sum of money up front. In exchange, the lender will make the loan at a lower interest rate than if discount points had not been paid. One point equals one percent of the loan amount; for instance, on a $100,000 loan, one point costs $1,000.

> Buydown: when discount points are paid to a lender to reduce (buy down) the interest rate charged to a borrower.

   C. **Lock-in Fee** – A borrower may pay a *lock-in fee* to a lender in order to "lock in" an interest rate for a certain period. Otherwise, the interest rate may change at any time between the loan approval and the closing date.

> Lock-in: when a lender agrees to "lock in" an interest rate quote for a definite period of time.

III. **Truth in Lending Act** – The *Truth in Lending Act* (TILA) is a federal consumer protection act that requires lenders to disclose the complete cost of credit to consumer loan applicants. TILA is implemented by *Regulation Z*, a regulation issued by the Federal Reserve Board. TILA is enforced by the Consumer Financial Protection Bureau.

   A. **Consumer Loans** – A *consumer loan* is a loan that is to be used for personal, family, or household purposes. A consumer loan is covered by TILA if it will be repaid in more than four installments or is subject to finance charges, AND is either for $54,600 or less or secured by real property.

Agricultural loans are exempt from TILA.

B. Exemptions – Loans exempt from TILA include: (1) loans made to corporations, (2) loans for business, commercial, or agricultural purposes, (3) loans exceeding $54,600, unless the loan is secured by real property, and (4) seller-financed transactions.

C. Disclosure Requirements – TILA requires lenders to provide a written disclosure statement that discloses the finance charge and the annual percentage rate to the loan applicant. The disclosure must be given within three days of the loan application, and at least seven days before closing.

1. **Finance charge** – The *finance charge* is the sum of all fees and charges the borrower will pay in connection with the loan. The lender must also disclose the total amount financed and whether the loan has a prepayment penalty.

   a. **Included** – Items included in the finance charge are the interest paid, origination fee, discount points paid by the borrower, mortgage insurance premiums, assumption fees, finder's fees, and service fees.

The appraisal fee and credit report fee charged to the borrower are not included in the finance charge.

   b. **Not included** – Items not included in the finance charge are appraisal fees, credit report fees, discount points paid by the seller, document recording fees, property taxes, or title fees.

2. **Annual percentage rate** – The *annual percentage rate* (APR) expresses the total cost of the loan as an annual percentage of the loan amount. The APR is sometimes called the *effective rate*, as opposed to the *nominal rate*, which is the interest rate stated on the face of the promissory note. The APR is almost always higher than the nominal rate, because it includes loan fees as well as interest.

D. Right of Rescission – A borrower has the *right of rescission* for home equity loans and for refinancing with a new lender. The borrower may rescind the loan agreement up to three business days after signing the agreement, receiving the disclosure statement, or receiving notice of the right of rescission, whichever comes latest. The right of rescission does not apply to home purchase loans or to refinancing with the same lender.

Including the annual percentage rate in an ad does not trigger the full disclosure requirement.

E. Truth in Advertising – It is always legal to state the cash price or annual percentage rate in an ad without making any other disclosures. But if other specific figures (downpayment, monthly payment, loan fee, etc.) are mentioned, then the APR and the rest of the repayment terms must also be disclosed in the ad. General statements like "low downpayment" or "easy terms" do not trigger disclosure requirements.

Sample questions

Which of the following is a primary market lender?

A. Federal Housing Administration
B. Mortgage banking company
C. Mortgage broker
D. Veterans Administration

> B. *A mortgage banker is a primary market lender, meaning that it originates loans directly to property buyers. Under the traditional distinction between a mortgage banker and a mortgage broker, a mortgage broker negotiates loans, bringing borrowers and lenders together for a fee, but (unlike a mortgage banker) is not a lender.*

A buyer is unfamiliar with the concept of discount points and asks a licensee to explain. The licensee responds "Discount points are used to replace funds that are being held by the Federal Reserve, so that more funds are available to lend." Is this description correct?

A. No, discount points are used to increase the yield for lenders who will sell the loans on the secondary market
B. No, discount points are used to pay brokers' commissions
C. Yes, banks hold discount points in escrow until sufficient funds have been accumulated to make more loans
D. Yes, discount points lower interest rates, which make loans more affordable for everyone

> A. *Discount points are paid to a lender in order to increase the lender's upfront yield on a loan. Typically, the lender will compensate for this by charging a below-market interest rate.*

B purchases a small commercial property, and he finances it with a 65% loan. The lender charges 9.25% annual interest and three discount points. The discount points:

A. increase the mortgage payments
B. decrease the annual percentage rate
C. increase the lender's yield
D. increase the nominal interest rate

> C. *Discount points are a percentage of the principal amount of a loan, collected by the lender at the time the loan is originated, to give the lender an additional yield over and above the interest. While the discount points decrease the nominal interest rate, they don't decrease the annual percentage rate; the APR takes the discount points into consideration.*

An advertisement for a house includes the following phrase: "Assume the owner's original loan with only a $1,000 downpayment!" What is wrong with this advertisement?

A. It doesn't also include the loan's annual percentage rate
B. It doesn't also include the loan's original balance
C. It doesn't give the brokerage firm's name as advertised
D. Nothing, so long as it is the real estate licensee's own property

> A. *Under the Truth in Lending Act, if an advertisement contains a triggering term, such as the amount of a downpayment, then it must disclose other specific information about the loan. This includes the loan's annual percentage rate.*

A seller lists a 1.1 acre vacant residential lot, asking $10,000. His broker decides to offer the financing himself. The broker runs an ad saying, "A $3,000 downpayment will get you beautiful residential acreage." Is more credit information required?

A. No, because Regulation Z doesn't apply to vacant land
B. No, because the value was under $54,600
C. Yes, because a real estate broker is offering financing
D. Yes, because the downpayment amount was given

> D. *Under the advertising requirements of the Truth in Lending Act and Regulation Z (which apply to consumer loans secured by real property, including vacant land), if an ad contains a specific triggering term such as the downpayment amount, then the annual percentage rate and the other terms of repayment must also be disclosed in the ad.*

A builder plans to construct a single-family home on spec, which he will then sell himself. He needs to borrow $60,000 to do so, and he approaches the local bank for a construction loan. Is this loan subject to Truth in Lending Act disclosure laws?

A. No, because no disclosure is required for business loans
B. No, because TILA applies to loans of $54,600 or less
C. Yes, because the loan concerns a single-family residence
D. Yes, because TILA applies to loans of $54,600 or more

> A. *The Truth in Lending Act applies to consumer loans (those made for personal, family, or household purposes); it would not apply to a business loan, even if it will be used to construct a single-family residence.*

IV. **Underwriting** – In the underwriting process, lenders evaluate whether an applicant qualifies for a loan. A specialist known as an *underwriter* will help decide whether to approve the borrower based on her financial position.

  A. **Qualifying the Buyer** – The three main factors the underwriter considers are the borrower's credit history, stable monthly income, and net worth. The underwriter will measure the borrower's monthly obligations (*debt service*) against the stable monthly income to see if the borrower can afford the proposed monthly payments. The most common acceptable ratio of debt to income is 36%.

The debt to income ratio is also called the debt service ratio.

B. Preapproval – Today, many buyers are preapproved by going through the qualification process before looking at houses. This helps them focus only on the properties they're financially able to buy.

C. Fair Credit Reporting Act – The *Fair Credit Reporting Act (FCRA)* requires lenders to notify the loan applicant in writing if they deny an application based on information from the applicant's credit report.

D. Qualifying the Property – The lender will also want to qualify the property, to make sure it is adequate collateral for the loan. In addition to an appraisal, the lender may also want to see pest control inspections, a flood report, a survey, or a title report.

E. Predatory Lending – *Predatory lending* refers to lender practices that take advantage of unsophisticated borrowers, often by approving them regardless of whether they qualify as good risks.

V. Basic Loan Features – Key features of any loan include the loan term, the amortization schedule, the loan-to-value ratio, and whether the interest rate is fixed or adjustable.

A. Loan Term – The *loan term* (or repayment period) has an impact on the size of the monthly payment and the total amount of interest paid over the life of the loan. The longer the term, the lower the monthly payment and the more interest paid.

B. Amortization – Most institutional loans are *fully amortized*, meaning that they are completely repaid within a certain period of time by making regular payments that include a portion for principal and a portion for interest.

Amortization: the gradual repayment of a debt with installment payments that include both principal and interest.

   1. **How amortization works** – Although the payment amount remains the same, each month the portion applied to principal increases and the portion applied to interest decreases.

   2. **Partial amortization** – Some loans are *partially amortized*; there are regular payments of both principal and interest, but not enough to repay all of the principal by the end of the loan term. The borrower will need to make a *balloon payment*.

   3. **Interest-only loans** – With an *interest-only loan* (or *term loan*), the borrower pays only interest, not principal, each month. The borrower will be responsible for the entire principal balance at the end of the loan term.

An interest-only loan is also called a term loan.

Loan-to-value ratio: the ratio of the loan amount to the value of the property.

C. Loan-to-Value Ratio – The *loan-to-value ratio* for a given transaction defines the size of the loan in relation to the value of the property. The lower the loan amount, the bigger the downpayment and the larger the equity.

1. **Risk** – The loan-to-value ratio (LTV) represents the lender's *risk*. The higher the LTV, the greater the lender's risk, so lenders use loan-to-value ratios to set maximum loan amounts. Higher LTVs are allowed for residential loans than for other types of loans, such as commercial or agricultural loans. Lenders base the maximum loan they're willing to make on the sales price or the appraised value, whichever is less.

D. Fixed-Rate Loans – *Fixed-rate loans* are popular when interest rates are low and stable. With a fixed-rate loan, the lender bears the risk of interest rate increases. A fixed-rate loan becomes gradually easier for the borrower to afford; the payments remain the same throughout the loan term, while the borrower's salary increases because of inflation and advancement.

Because an ARM's rate will fluctuate, it is impossible to calculate a lifetime APR for an ARM.

E. Adjustable-Rate Mortgages – An *adjustable-rate mortgage* (ARM) permits the lender to periodically adjust the loan's interest rate so that it accurately reflects changes in the cost of money. With an ARM, the borrower bears the risk of interest rate increases. If rates climb, the borrower's monthly payment goes up; if they decline, the payment goes down. ARMs are more popular when interest rates are high and volatile.

1. **Index** – An *index* is a published statistical rate that indicates changes in the cost of money. An ARM's interest rate will be adjusted periodically in response to changes in the selected index. The interest rate is not adjusted every time the index changes, but rather according to the loan's *rate adjustment period* (most commonly once per year).

Margin: the difference between the index rate and the interest rate charged to the borrower.

2. **Margin** – The lender will add a *margin* to the index to cover administrative expenses and profit. While the index will fluctuate, the margin remains the same throughout the loan term.

3. **Caps** – An ARM usually has *caps* that limit how much the borrower's interest rate and payment amount can increase. This is to prevent the payments from increasing so dramatically that the borrower can no longer afford them.

Negative amortization: when unpaid interest on a loan is added to the loan balance, increasing the amount owed.

4. **Negative amortization** – *Negative amortization* is a potential problem for ARM borrowers; it occurs when the monthly payments aren't sufficient to pay all the interest due each month. This causes the principal balance to increase instead of decrease.

Sample questions

A buyer's agent has repeatedly seen sales collapse at the last minute because the buyers weren't able to obtain financing. How could he best limit this in the future?

A. Qualify all prospects himself
B. Refer buyers to a specific lender
C. Require prospects to be approved first
D. Show lower-priced properties

> C. *Getting preapproved for a loan, before beginning the house hunting process, has become the standard procedure for buyers. This way, the buyer knows in advance the maximum amount he can spend on a house.*

Income, net worth, and credit history are all factors involved in determining the:

A. buyer's qualifications
B. seller's qualifications
C. sales price for a property
D. loan-to-value ratio

> A. *These three factors are evaluated in determining whether a buyer qualifies for a mortgage loan.*

Ben is applying for a loan. Of the following, which will the lender consider MOST important when evaluating the loan's risk?

A. The sales price of other homes in the area
B. The property's appraised value
C. The loan's interest rate
D. Ben's income and financial stability

> D. *Although the loan underwriting process will also consider the security property's appraised value, of the choices given Ben's income and financial stability are likely to be the MOST important factors the lender will take into consideration.*

XYZ Lending needs some paperwork before it can give final approval to Karen's loan. Which document is XYZ least likely to request from Karen?

A. A copy of the listing agreement
B. Termite inspection results
C. The results of a boundary survey
D. Title report

> A. *A loan underwriter will not be concerned with the listing agreement.*

When a borrower makes payments on a fully amortized loan, her debt service payments will cover:

A. only principal on the loan
B. only interest on the loan
C. both principal and interest on the loan
D. principal, interest, taxes, and insurance

    C. A fully amortized loan is repaid through regular payments that include both a portion of the principal and interest. The final payment will pay off the principal balance, leaving no need for a balloon payment. (Most home purchase loans are budget mortgages, which include taxes and insurance in each payment, but this is not a characteristic of all fully amortized loans.)

The interest rate on Mike's loan can fluctuate, based on an index, causing a periodic adjustment in the monthly principal and interest payment. Mike's loan is most likely:

A. interest-only
B. unconventional
C. adjustable-rate
D. fixed-rate

    C. An adjustable-rate mortgage (ARM) ties the interest rate (and, therefore, the size of the monthly payment) to the fluctuations in a chosen index.

Which of the following loans would result in the borrower paying the least interest over the life of the loan?

A. 15-year loan at 10% interest
B. 15-year loan at 11% interest
C. 20-year loan at 10% interest
D. 20-year loan at 11% interest

    A. The shorter the loan term is, the less interest the borrower will pay. A shorter loan may not always be the best option for a borrower, though, as a shorter loan for the same loan amount will mean higher payments and may limit what properties the borrower can afford.

VI. Residential Financing Programs – Residential financing programs can be divided into two main groups: *conventional loans* and *government-sponsored loans*.

    A. Conventional Loans – Conventional loans are loans made by institutional lenders and are not insured or guaranteed through government programs (such as FHA or VA loans).

        1. Private mortgage insurance – *Private mortgage insurance* (PMI) is commonly used with conventional loans that have high loan-to-value ratios. It is usually required on conventional loans with downpayments of less than 20% that will be sold in the secondary market. Private

Conventional loan: an institutional loan that is not insured or guaranteed by a governmental agency.

Private mortgage insurance: insurance provided by private companies for loans with loan-to-value ratios over 80%.

mortgage insurance protects the lender against the higher risk of default by the borrower.

B. FHA-Insured Loans – The *Federal Housing Administration (FHA)* was created in 1934 as part of the *National Housing Act*. The FHA is now a division of the Department of Housing and Urban Development. The FHA insures loans; it does not build homes or make loans.

1. **Mutual Mortgage Insurance Plan** – The FHA's primary function is insuring loans through its *Mutual Mortgage Insurance Plan*. The FHA charges the borrower a mortgage insurance premium called the *mutual mortgage insurance premium* (MIP). The borrower will pay a one-time premium and then pay annual premiums as well.

2. **Application to lender** – The FHA does not accept applications from borrowers; instead, borrowers apply to an institutional lender for an initial FHA loan commitment. A lender that underwrites its own FHA loans is known as a *direct endorsement lender*.

3. **One to four units** – The standard FHA loan program (the *203(b) program*) provides insurance for residential properties with one to four units, as long as the borrower occupies one of the units.

4. **Low downpayment** – The downpayment for an FHA loan is often much less than would be required for a comparable conventional loan. Lenders also typically charge lower interest rates on FHA loans because the FHA insurance reduces the lender's risk. The interest rate is not set by the FHA, but by agreement between the lender and the borrower.

5. **Loan-to-value ratios** – Another advantage of FHA loans is that they have higher maximum loan-to-value ratios than conventional loans. For most transactions, the LTV can be as high as 96.5%. An FHA borrower would need less cash at closing than a conventional borrower would.

6. **Assumption** – FHA loans can be assumed subject to credit approval of the new owner and payment of an assumption fee. If the new owner is creditworthy, the seller will receive a release of liability. The new owner must intend to occupy the property as a primary residence.

7. **Appraisal** – FHA loans require an appraisal by an appraiser who has met the educational and certification requirements necessary to be included on the FHA's roster of approved appraisers.

A government-backed loan may sometimes be referred to as an unconventional loan.

The FHA insures loans; it does not make loans.

The FHA's standard home loan is called a 203(b) loan.

An FHA loan allows either a buyer or seller to pay discount points on the loan.

When an FHA loan is assumed, a document known as a certificate of reduction is issued; it confirms the loan balance.

Sample questions

Monica has been preapproved for a loan of up to $250,000 to buy her first house. She has good credit, and plans to make a downpayment of at least 20%. Which type of loan is she most likely to use?

A. Blanket mortgage
B. Conventional loan
C. Swing loan
D. Wraparound mortgage

> B. *A conventional loan would typically be used for a purchase of a first home, especially if an FHA or VA loan can't be used in the transaction. While conventional loans can have smaller downpayments than 20%, no private mortgage insurance is needed when the downpayment is 20% or more.*

With an FHA-insured loan:

A. there is no origination fee
B. discount points may be paid by the seller or the buyer
C. the term is usually 15 years
D. None of the above; the FHA doesn't insure loans

> B. *Any discount points may be paid by the buyer or the seller.*

Shelly is buying Burt's property and assuming Burt's existing loan. As part of this process, Burt's lender issues a certificate of reduction to verify the remaining loan balance. The type of loan Shelly is assuming is a/an:

A. home equity loan
B. conventional loan
C. VA loan
D. FHA loan

> D. *When an FHA loan is assumed, a certificate of reduction is used to verify the loan balance. Buyers who assume FHA loans must meet FHA underwriting standards, and must intend to occupy the home as their primary residence.*

C. **VA-Guaranteed Loans** – The *VA-guaranteed home loan* program was established at the conclusion of World War II to help veterans finance the purchase of their homes with affordable loans. VA-guaranteed financing offers many advantages over conventional loans.

Certificate of Eligibility: a document issued by the VA as proof of a person's eligibility for a VA loan.

1. **Eligibility** – To be eligible to apply for a VA loan, a vet must have served a minimum amount of time in the U.S. armed forces. The document issued by the VA confirming eligibility is called a *Certificate of Eligibility*. A surviving spouse of a veteran who was killed in action is also eligible, unless he or she has remarried.

2. **Certificate of Reasonable Value** – The Department of Veterans Affairs will want to appraise the home that is being financed. A VA appraisal is called a *Certificate of Reasonable Value* (CRV) or a *Notice of Value* (NOV). A home will not be guaranteed for more than its appraised value. If it sells for more than its appraised value, the buyer will need to cover the difference.

A VA appraisal is called a Certificate of Reasonable Value (CRV) or Notice of Value (NOV).

3. **One to four units** – A VA loan may be used to finance the purchase or construction of a residence with one to four units. The veteran must intend to occupy one of the units.

4. **No downpayment required** – Unlike most loans, a VA loan doesn't require a downpayment. The VA does not set a maximum VA loan amount; the loan amount can be as much as the sales price or the appraised value, whichever is less. This makes 100% financing possible, so VA loans have a higher LTV ratio than most other loans. There is a maximum guaranty, however, so a veteran may still need to use a downpayment when purchasing a particularly expensive home.

A VA loan can have a 100% loan-to-value ratio.

5. **No mortgage insurance** – Unlike the FHA, the VA does not charge insurance premiums. Instead, the VA acts as a *guarantor* of the loan. The VA guaranty covers only part of the loan amount. The maximum guaranty amount available to a particular veteran is known as that veteran's "entitlement."

Neither FHA nor VA loans allow prepayment penalties.

6. **Restoration of entitlement** – If a veteran sells a property financed with a VA loan and repays the loan in full from the sale proceeds, the veteran receives a full restoration of guaranty rights for future use. A selling veteran's entitlement may also be restored if the loan is assumed by another veteran buyer who agrees to substitute her own entitlement.

VA eligibility can be fully restored if the original VA loan has been paid in full.

Sample questions

Which of the following persons is eligible to receive a VA loan?

A. A veteran or a deceased veteran's children
B. A veteran or a deceased veteran's children or unremarried spouse
C. A veteran or a deceased veteran's unremarried surviving spouse
D. Only a veteran him or herself

   C. *A veteran's surviving spouse may be eligible for a VA loan if he or she has not remarried, and the veteran was killed in action or died of service-related injuries.*

Once a lender issues a veteran a VA-guaranteed loan, the veteran:

A. can never receive another VA loan
B. cannot prepay the principal on the loan
C. immediately becomes liable for the guaranteed amount
D. must purchase private mortgage insurance

    C. A VA loan borrower who later defaults may be liable to the VA in some situations; in all situations, his guaranty entitlement (allowing another VA loan) won't be restored until he reimburses the VA.

A veteran's guaranty benefits may be restored by a:

A. simple loan assumption
B. substitution of eligibility/entitlement by another veteran assuming the loan
C. wraparound mortgage
D. lender release

    B. If another veteran substitutes his eligibility, a veteran's guaranty may be restored.

Which of the following statements about prepayment penalties is true?

A. Both the FHA and VA loan programs impose prepayment penalties
B. FHA loans include prepayment penalties, but VA loans do not
C. VA loans include prepayment penalties, but FHA loans do not
D. Neither the FHA nor VA loan programs allow prepayment penalties

    D. Prepayment penalties are not allowed as part of either the FHA or VA loan programs. Borrowers are allowed to prepay part or all of their loans at their own discretion.

A buyer is purchasing a home using a VA loan. Which of the following is true?

A. The VA sets the loan's guaranty limit
B. The VA will determine the loan's terms
C. The VA will determine the loan's interest rate
D. The VA will require a 3.5% downpayment

    A. The VA guaranty covers only part of the loan amount, up to a maximum set by the government. A VA loan's interest rate and many of the terms are negotiable between the borrower and the lender. No downpayment is required.

Chapter Quiz

1. A mortgage company charges three points on a $250,000 loan. How much is the charge?

    A. $750
    B. $2,250
    C. $7,500
    D. $22,500

2. An investor wants to invest $250,000 in the development of a shopping mall by taking out a loan secured by a residential property that he owns. Will the Truth in Lending Act apply to this transaction?

    A. Yes, because the loan is for less than $500,000
    B. Yes, because the loan is secured by residential property
    C. No, because the loan is for more than $54,600
    D. No, because this is a commercial transaction

3. The requirements of the Truth in Lending Act would apply to a:

    A. construction loan for a builder to build a model home
    B. loan for the purchase of a mobile home that will be used as a principal residence
    C. loan to purchase space in a mini-mall
    D. loan to renovate a gas station

4. A borrower obtains a home equity loan on a property he already owns. The Truth in Lending Act allows the borrower to rescind the loan transaction within:

    A. three days after signing the agreement or receiving the disclosure statement
    B. three days after receiving the funds
    C. one week after signing the agreement or receiving the disclosure statement
    D. one week after receiving the funds

5. Which of the following loans would be subject to the Truth-in-Lending Act?

    A. A loan to a first-time home buyer
    B. A loan to a homeowners association
    C. A loan to a residential subdivision developer
    D. A loan to buy a 20-unit apartment complex

6. Of the following, which is true?

    A. TILA applies to all seller financing
    B. TILA applies to loans made to corporations as well as to individuals
    C. TILA requires lenders to provide a good faith estimate of closing costs (GFE)
    D. TILA requires the disclosure of credit costs to borrowers and regulates the advertising of consumer loans

7. The primary purpose of the Truth in Lending Act (Regulation Z) is to require the lender to:

    A. provide the borrower with a statement showing its aggregate interest charge for similar properties in today's marketplace
    B. include in any advertisement about available financing the annual percentage rate, plus the applicable finance charges
    C. disclose the complete cost of credit to consumer loan applicants
    D. reveal the true cost of all real estate loans, except purchase money loans

8. Buyers who are looking at a variety of properties should only be shown homes that:

    A. are listed by the agent's firm
    B. are located in neighborhoods where the residents are of a similar race as the buyers
    C. they are qualified to purchase, based on preapproval or qualification
    D. will result in the highest commission for their agent

9. What kind of property could a buyer purchase with an FHA 203(b) loan?

    A. Apartment building
    B. Commercial property
    C. Farm occupied by a tenant
    D. Four-unit dwelling where the buyer will occupy one of the units

10. A purchase and sale agreement contained a financing contingency. The buyers applied for a loan with a local lender, who orally informed them that their loan application was denied. The buyers' agent should:

   A. ask the sellers to provide a purchase money loan instead
   B. have the sellers extend the contingency deadline
   C. tell the buyers about their right to receive the denial in writing
   D. terminate the agency relationship

11. Amortization is defined as:

   A. declaring an entire debt due in the event of default
   B. mutual withdrawal from a contract
   C. paying both principal and interest on a loan on an installment basis
   D. use of secondary financing to complete the purchase of real estate

12. A loan is set up so that the borrower's payments are the same size each month. Each payment is partly interest and partly principal, and the loan's balance at the end of the loan term will be zero. Which type of loan is this?

   A. Fully amortized
   B. Partially amortized
   C. Reverse annuity
   D. Straight note

13. Carol is buying a home using a loan that requires her to make monthly payments of principal and interest for ten years, at which time she will have to make a final balloon payment of the remaining loan balance. This describes a/an:

   A. fully amortized loan
   B. partially amortized loan
   C. term loan
   D. interest-only loan

14. The interest rate on an adjustable-rate mortgage (ARM) is calculated using an index as well as a margin. The margin:

   A. remains constant throughout the loan term
   B. changes yearly or half-yearly
   C. follows changes in the index
   D. decreases as the loan is paid off

15. A buyer is getting a loan to purchase a five-acre apple farm with no residence on it. The Truth in Lending Act requires:

   A. a three-day rescission period if the borrower changes her mind
   B. disclosure of all settlement charges on a uniform settlement statement
   C. disclosure of the finance charge
   D. no disclosure, because the land is agricultural

16. A home buyer can seek an FHA loan from which of the following?

   A. Ginnie Mae
   B. Fannie Mae
   C. A qualified Federal Housing Administration lender (such as a bank)
   D. Federal Home Loan Mortgage Corporation

17. Which is true regarding a standard 203(b) FHA loan?

   A. An FHA appraisal is required
   B. No downpayment is required
   C. Secondary financing from an institutional lender may be used for the downpayment
   D. The maximum loan term is 20 years

18. Which type of government-backed loan is guaranteed against loss to the lender?

   A. VA mortgage
   B. FHA mortgage
   C. Conventional mortgage
   D. Subprime mortgage

19. Which of the following characteristics apply to both FHA and VA loans?

   A. FHA and VA loans require a certificate of reasonable value
   B. FHA and VA loans carry mortgage insurance
   C. FHA and VA borrowers are not permitted to pay points
   D. Prepayment penalties are not permitted on FHA and VA loans

20. If the mortgage amount is $80,000 and the borrower paid $4,800 in discount points, how many discount points were charged?

   A. 4
   B. 5
   C. 6
   D. 8

Answer Key

1. C. A point equals one percent of the loan amount. Three percent of $250,000 is $7,500 ($250,000 × 0.03 = $7,500).

2. D. The Truth in Lending Act covers consumer loans. A loan is a consumer loan if the borrower plans to use the proceeds for personal, family, or household purposes. Since this borrower is going to use the proceeds for a commercial purpose, TILA does not apply, even if the loan is secured using owner-occupied residential property. (By contrast, if he had borrowed against real property to send a child to college, then TILA would apply.)

3. B. The Truth in Lending Act applies to consumer loans (for family, personal, or household purposes), including the purchase of mobile homes and the land they're on. It does not apply to commercial loans, such as a construction loan for a developer.

4. A. The Truth in Lending Act gives home equity loan borrowers the right of rescission for three days after the loan agreement has been signed, the disclosure statement has been received, or the notice of the right of rescission has been received, whichever comes latest.

5. A. The Truth in Lending Act applies to consumer loans. It doesn't cover loans for business, commercial, or agricultural purposes, or loans to corporations or other organizations.

6. D. TILA is a federal consumer protection law that requires the disclosure of credit costs to borrowers and regulates the advertising of consumer loans.

7. C. The Truth in Lending Act requires the lender to disclose the true cost of financing for consumer loans, including real estate loans.

8. C. It is a waste of time and a source of frustration to show properties to buyers that they will not be able to afford. As a result, it's important to make sure buyers are preapproved or prequalified before showing properties.

9. D. A 203(b) loan is the standard type of FHA loan that most homebuyers will use. This type of loan may be used to purchase a property with up to four dwelling units, as long as one of the units will be the borrower's primary residence.

10. C. Under the Fair Credit Reporting Act, when a lender takes an adverse action on the basis of a credit report, the applicant or borrower must receive written notice of that action. The consumer must also be notified which consumer reporting agency provided the report, so that the consumer can verify and, if necessary, contest the information in the report.

11. C. An amortized loan includes payments for both principal and interest. A fully amortized loan will be entirely repaid at the end of the loan term, with the monthly payment remaining the same throughout.

12. A. A fully amortized loan includes both principal and interest in level monthly payments. At the end of the loan term, the balance will be paid off, meaning that no balloon payment is needed.

13. B. A loan that requires regular payments of both principal and interest is an amortized loan. A fully amortized loan will pay off the entire loan balance by the end of the loan's term. Payments under a partially amortized loan, the one described here, will not fully pay off the loan balance by the end of the loan's term, and will require a balloon payment at the end.

14. A. The interest rate of an ARM will change in response to changes in the particular index selected by the lender. The margin itself is fixed at the time the loan is made.

15. D. The Truth in Lending Act's disclosure requirements do not apply to loans made for business, commercial, or agricultural purposes.

16. C. Prospective borrowers do not apply to the FHA itself for a loan; rather, they make the application to an FHA-approved lender, such as a commercial bank, savings bank, or mortgage company.

17. A. FHA loans require an appraisal by an appraiser who has met the educational and certification requirements for inclusion on the FHA's roster of approved appraisers. Secondary financing provided by a close family member is allowed, but secondary financing from an institutional lender is not allowed.

18. A. VA loans are government-backed loans that guarantee lenders against default. While FHA loans are similar in that regard, an FHA loan insures (rather than guarantees) a lender against loss.

19. D. Prepayment penalties are not permitted on either FHA or VA loans.

20. C. Divide the points paid by the loan amount to find what percentage was paid in points ($4,800 ÷ $80,000 = 0.06). Since one point is one percent of the loan amount, the borrower paid six discount points.

Chapter 12
Real Estate Appraisal

I. **Introduction to Appraisal** – An appraisal is an *estimate* or *opinion* of value. It is not a precise or scientific determination of value. It is synonymous with *valuation*. An appraisal usually takes the form of a written statement called an *appraisal report*.

   A. **Competitive Market Analysis** – An appraisal—which may only be performed by an appraiser—should not be confused with a competitive market analysis (or CMA). A real estate licensee may perform a CMA to help a seller determine an appropriate listing price for a property. A CMA estimates value based on selling prices of comparable properties. Comparables of similar size, age, and quality should be chosen.

   B. **Appraiser's Fee** – An appraiser's fee is determined in advance, based on the expected difficulty of the appraisal and the amount of time it is likely to take. The fee should not be a percentage of the property's appraised value, or based on the client's satisfaction with the appraiser's findings. The appraiser's fee does not need to be stated in the appraisal report. The appraiser's client in most residential transactions is the lender, even though the borrower pays the fee.

   C. **Effective Date** – Because property values change constantly, an appraisal reflects a property's value on one particular date, called the *effective date*.

II. **Value** – Three common definitions of value are: (1) the present worth of future benefits; (2) the ability of an item or service to command other items or services in exchange; and (3) the relationship between a desired thing and the person who desires it.

   A. **Elements of Value** – There are four economic elements essential to the creation of market value:

      1. **Utility** – A product must render a service or fill a need in order to have value; this is called *utility*.

      2. **Scarcity** – The scarcer an item is, the greater its value.

      3. **Demand** – There is *demand* for an item if it produces a desire to own. Demand cannot exist unless it is coupled with buyers' purchasing power, however.

      4. **Transferability** – The item must, in addition to the above, be transferable from one person to another.

An appraisal is an estimate or opinion of value, not a determination of value.

Appraisal rules are established by the Uniform Standards of Professional Appraisal Practice.

The effective date of an appraisal is usually the date the appraisal is made.

Value is the present worth of future benefits.

Every parcel of land is unique. No two are alike.

Acronym for elements of value: STUD (scarcity, transferability, utility, demand).

Note: An easy way to remember the four elements is to remember the acronym STUD (scarcity, transferability, utility, demand).

B. Types of Value – For appraisal purposes, value falls into two general classifications: *value in use* and *value in exchange*.

    1. **Value in use** – Value in use is the *subjective value* (emotional value) placed on property by a particular person. Value in use may also be known as *utility value*.

    2. **Value in exchange** – Value in exchange is the *objective value* of a property as viewed by someone other than the property owner (the average person). Value in exchange is more often called *market value*.

        a. **Definition of market value** – *Market value* is "the most probable price which a property should bring in a competitive and open market under all conditions requisite to a fair sale, the buyer and seller each acting prudently and knowledgeably, and assuming the price is not affected by undue stimulus."

Price: amount paid for a property, regardless of its value.

        b. **Market value vs. market price** – *Market price* is the price actually paid for a property, which may have been too much, too little, or right on—depending on the circumstances of the sale. *Market value* is what should be paid in a sale under normal conditions.

Sample questions

One of the economic characteristics of real estate is:
A. immobility
B. location
C. scarcity
D. topography

    C. *The four elements of value are demand, scarcity, transferability, and utility.*

Agent Kelly is helping her seller decide a proper listing price for his property. The agent must do all of the following, except:

A. perform a comparative market analysis
B. encourage the seller to get an independent appraisal
C. examine the home's square footage and improvements
D. determine the amount of private mortgage insurance that will be necessary

    D. *PMI has no impact on the value of a property, and would not be considered when determining a property's value or listing price.*

An appraiser determines the most probable price that a buyer would be willing to pay for a property. This type of value is known as:

A. subjective or fair market value
B. objective or fair market value
C. liquidation value
D. assessed value

    B. The most probable price a buyer would be willing to pay describes the property's market value, an objective measure.

    C. Principles of Value – Over the years, appraisers have developed a reliable body of principles that take into account the forces influencing value and guide appraisers in making decisions in the valuation process. They include:

        1. Principle of highest and best use – *Highest and best use* refers to the most profitable use of a piece of property, the use that will provide the greatest *net return* over a period of time. The highest and best use must take into account zoning regulations, as well as the feasibility of alternate uses and how much income would be generated by alternate uses. Highest and best use is of particular concern when appraising vacant land.

> The anticipated highest and best use must be:
> 1) physically possible,
> 2) economically feasible, and
> 3) legally permissible.

        2. Principle of change – This principle holds that real estate values are constantly in flux, moving up and down in response to the various social, economic, and governmental forces that affect value.

            a. Economic life – Every property has both a physical life cycle and an economic life cycle. The *economic life* (or *useful life*) is the period when the land and its improvements are profitable. The economic life almost always ends before the physical life, usually because of changes in the characteristics of the surrounding neighborhood. As a result, the principle of change is most relevant to the appraiser's neighborhood analysis.

> A property's economic life is shorter than its physical life.

            b. Life cycle – A property or neighborhood goes through a four-step *life cycle*: integration (growth), equilibrium (stability), disintegration (decline), and rejuvenation.

        3. Principle of anticipation – One way to think of value is the present value of future benefits. Appraisers are most concerned with the anticipated future benefits of owning a property, since future benefits, not present benefits, arouse the desire to own.

A large new employer in an area would increase the number of potential homeowners, and thus demand for properties.

No one will pay more for a property than they would have to pay for an equally desirable substitute property.

When a home is surrounded by homes of much higher quality, its value is increased by the association with the other homes.

Contribution: the value an improvement adds to the overall value of the property.

Competition: profits tend to encourage competition, and excess profits tend to result in ruinous competition.

4. **Principle of supply and demand** – According to the law of *supply and demand*, values tend to rise as demand increases and supply decreases, and fall when the reverse occurs. Increasing demand will cause prices to rise. For instance, as properties within a subdivision sell, the last lots to sell may sell for considerably more than the first lots to sell.

5. **Principle of substitution** – This principle states that no one will pay more for a property than they would have to pay for an equally desirable substitute property, provided there would be no unreasonable delay in acquiring that substitute. This principle is the basis for all three methods of appraisal.

6. **Principle of conformity** – The maximum value of land is achieved when there is an acceptable degree of social and economic conformity in the area. Conformity should be reasonable, not carried to a monotonous extreme.

   a. **Progression/regression** – The principle of *progression* states that a lower quality property gains value because of proximity to properties of higher quality, and the principle of *regression* states that a higher quality property loses value because of proximity to properties of lower quality.

7. **Principle of contribution** – Contribution refers to the value an improvement adds to the overall value of the property. Some improvements add more value to a property than they cost, while others may cost more than they add value. An owner deciding whether or not to add an improvement should consider how much the improvement would contribute to the property's value.

8. **Principle of competition** – Competition can have a major impact on the value of property, especially income-generating property. A property generating high income may find its income, and therefore its value, greatly reduced if competing properties appear nearby.

Sample questions

Lawrence is planning to buy a home. His ability to pay for the property is his first consideration, but he's also concerned about price. Which factor below will probably have the greatest impact on the price of homes he's looking at?

A. Style
B. Color
C. Age
D. Location

> D. The location of a property has one of the greatest impacts on the property's value. Buyers will be concerned with access to transportation, employment areas, and amenities, among other considerations, and will usually pay more for a similar home in a more favorable location.

A small house is situated on a large lot in a mixed-use neighborhood. The city decides that the area will, in the future, be zoned commercial. What will most likely happen to the property's value?

A. It will decrease, because of fears of new businesses being built nearby
B. It will increase, in anticipation of the changing uses
C. No effect, since the house is a nonconforming use
D. No effect, until the change actually occurs

> B. Under the principle of anticipation, a property's value may change based on expectations of what will happen to the property in the future.

The value of a property won't be affected by:

A. zoning regulations
B. title insurance
C. location near a major freeway
D. improvements to the land

> B. Title insurance won't affect the appraised value of a property.

Which of the following relates to the appraisal of real property?

A. Foreclosure value
B. Highest and best use
C. Deeded value
D. Operating expense ratio

> B. A property's highest and best use is the most profitable use it can be put to, the use that will provide the greatest net return to the owner over a period of time.

III. **The Appraisal Process** – Properly done, the appraisal process is orderly and systematic. While there is no official procedure, appraisers generally carry out the appraisal process in a series of steps: (1) define the problem; (2) determine the scope of work; (3) collect and verify the data; (4) analyze the data; (5) determine the site value; (6) apply the approaches to value; (7) reconcile the value indicators for the final estimate; and (8) issue the appraisal report.

A. Gathering General Data – *General data* includes both general economic data about the community and information about the subject property's neighborhood. An appraiser may use past economic data to "forecast" future trends that affect the property. Of all factors, local economic conditions tend to have the greatest impact on the property's value.

1. **Neighborhood analysis** – A property's value is inevitably tied to its surrounding neighborhood, or its *situs* (Latin for location). A neighborhood is a residential, commercial, industrial, or agricultural area that contains similar types of properties. Its boundaries are determined by physical barriers (such as highways and bodies of water), land use patterns, the age or value of homes, and the economic status of the residents.

2. **Economic-base analysis** – Appraisers may project employment and income trends in a market by looking at both basic industries (the foundation of the local economy) and non-basic industries (which support the basic industries); this is known as economic-base analysis.

B. Gathering Specific Data – *Specific data* has to do with the property itself, as opposed to the outside influences (general data) that affect the property's value. Specific data is broken down into *site analysis* (analysis of the land itself) and *building analysis* (analysis of the improvements).

1. **Site analysis** – Site analysis is largely concerned with determining the property's highest and best use. A thorough site analysis calls for accumulation of a good deal of data concerning the property's physical characteristics.

   a. **Frontage** – *Frontage* is the length of the front boundary of the lot—the boundary that abuts a street or a body of water. Frontage is important because it measures a lot's access to something desirable such as pedestrian traffic or water.

   b. **Excess land** – *Excess land* is land that does not contribute to a property's value and that does not support the existing improvements or the property's highest and best use. For example, a lot may be deeper than neighboring lots but be worth the same; the extra area would be considered excess land.

   c. **Plottage** – Two parcels of land, when combined, may be worth more than the sum of their individual values.

Neighborhood analysis: gathering data on home sizes and styles, topography, features, and amenities in a neighborhood, as part of the appraisal process.

Excess land: that portion of a parcel of land that does not add to its value.

(This is especially common when the larger parcel would have a different highest and best use than the two smaller parcels, such as a commercial use.) The resulting gain in value is called *plottage*.

    d. Percolation test – An appraiser may need to order a *percolation test* if a septic system will need to be constructed. This measures the soil's ability to absorb water.

  2. Building analysis – The improvements built on the site must be analyzed, along with any *amenities* (attractive features such as nice landscaping or a pool).

    a. Square footage – Square footage of a building is determined by measuring the outside dimensions of the building. The square footage includes the improved living area but not the garage, basement, or porches.

C. Selecting Methods of Appraisal – Once the appraiser has accumulated the necessary general and specific data, she will begin applying one or more of the three methods of appraising property: (1) sales comparison approach; (2) cost approach; and (3) income approach.

  1. Which approach to use – Each approach lends itself best to different types of property. The sales comparison approach is used for valuing older residential properties, vacant land, and properties with unusual amenities. The cost approach tends to be used for newly constructed properties, or for special purpose properties that tend not to be sold on the open market (a church or a school, for example). The income approach is used to value income-producing properties.

IV. Sales Comparison Approach – The *sales comparison approach* (also known as the *market data* or *market value* approach) is the best method for appraising residential property and the most reliable method for appraising raw land. It is also the basis for performing a competitive market analysis.

A. Comparable Sales – The sales comparison approach involves comparing the subject property to similar properties that have recently sold, which are called *comparables*. An appraiser needs at least three comparable sales to have enough data to evaluate a residential property. An appraiser is most likely to obtain data about recent sales activity from multiple listing service records.

B. Elements of Comparison – To be certain a property qualifies as a comparable, the appraiser will check the following aspects of the comparable transaction:

> The sales comparison method is the best method for appraising single-family homes and raw land.

> Nearby recent sales are the most reliable comparables.

> The sales comparison approach is based on the principle of substitution: no buyer would pay more for a property than she would have to pay for an equally desirable property.

1. **Date of comparable sale** – A comparable sale should be recent, within the past six months, if possible. The appraiser is more concerned with the date of the sale contract than the closing date.

   a. **Inactive or volatile markets** – If the market has been inactive, and adequate comparables do not exist, an appraiser may use comparables older than six months after making adjustments for inflation. An appraiser should also hesitate to use comparables sold in an economically volatile period, when prices are fluctuating.

2. **Location of comparable sale** – Whenever possible, comparables should be selected from the subject property's neighborhood.

3. **Physical characteristics** – To qualify as a comparable, a property should have physical characteristics (construction quality, design, amenities, etc.) that are similar to those of the subject property.

4. **Terms of sale** – An appraiser has to take into account the influence the terms of sale may have had on the price paid for a comparable property. For instance, if the seller offered the property on very favorable seller financing terms, the buyer may have been willing to pay more for the property than its true market value.

5. **Conditions of sale** – A comparable sale can be relied on as an indication of what the subject property is worth only if it occurred under normal conditions: when the sale is between unrelated parties (an "arm's length transaction"), both the buyer and the seller are informed about the merits and shortcomings of the property, both are acting free of unusual pressure, and the property is offered for sale on the open market for a reasonable length of time.

6. **Not considered** – Note that neither the original price paid for the property nor the cost of building any improvements is a consideration in the sales comparison approach.

C. **Comparing Properties and Making Adjustments** – In the sales comparison approach, the entire property is the basis of comparison. Since no two properties are alike, a proper comparison between the subject property and each comparable is essential to an accurate estimate of value. Making adjustments is the most difficult and subjective part of the sales comparison approach, so the more similar the properties, the easier the comparison.

1. **Adjust for differences** – Most of the time there will be some significant differences between the comparables and the subject property. The appraiser has to make adjustments that take into account differences in time, location, physical characteristics, and terms of sale in order to arrive at the *adjusted selling price* for each comparable.

Differences in physical characteristics between the subject property and a comparable result in adjustments to the comparable's selling price.

   a. **Too many differences** – When there are too many differences, a selected property cannot be considered comparable to the subject property and must be discarded.

2. **Make adjustments to comparable** – Adjustments are made to the comparable's selling price, not to the subject property.

Example: If a comparable and the subject property are alike in every respect, except the subject property has four bedrooms and the comparable has three bedrooms, the appraiser would adjust the price paid for the comparable upward to reflect what it would have sold for with four bedrooms instead of three. The result would serve as an indication of the subject property's value. If the subject property has three bedrooms and the comparable has four bedrooms, the appraiser would adjust the price paid for the comparable downward.

Adjusted selling price: the sales price of a comparable property after it has been increased or decreased to reflect what the comparable would have sold for if it had been identical to the subject property.

Sample questions

A percolation test will examine the:

A. likelihood of landslides or subsidence
B. presence of toxic contamination in soil
C. roofing material's ability to repel rain
D. soil's ability to absorb and retain water

   D. A percolation test measures the soil's ability to absorb and retain water. The test is usually performed to determine whether a property is suitable for a septic system that will meet applicable health standards.

An appraiser makes projections about how the population of a metropolitan area will grow and how much residents' income will increase, using data about both basic and non-basic industries. This is known as:

A. anticipation
B. economic-base analysis
C. economic life analysis
D. highest and best use

   B. Economic-base analysis looks at economic activity in both basic industries (those that drive a local economy) and non-basic industries (those that support the basic industries), in order to predict employment and other economic trends.

The comparable has a two-car garage and the subject property only has a one-car garage. The appraiser estimates that space for a second car contributes about $800 to the value of a home. To take this into account, the appraiser will:

A. add $800 to the sales price of the subject property
B. add $800 to the sales price of the comparable property
C. subtract $800 from the sales price of the comparable property
D. subtract $800 from the sales price of the subject property

C. *Since the comparable has a feature the subject property lacks, the appraiser will subtract the value of that feature ($800) from the sales price of the comparable property. The resulting figure will suggest what the comparable might have been worth if it, like the subject property, only had a one-car garage. (Note that the sales price of the subject property is not an appropriate consideration in appraising its market value.)*

V. Cost Approach to Value – The *cost approach* to value is based on the premise that the value of a property is limited by the cost of replacing it. This is a prime example of the principle of substitution (since if the asking price of a home was more than it would cost to build a new one just like it, no one would buy it). The estimate of value reached through the cost approach will usually represent the highest of the three different appraisal methods.

> The cost approach is the only appraisal method for public buildings and churches. It is also a reliable method for appraising newly constructed properties.

A. Steps in Process – There are three steps to the cost approach: (1) estimating the cost of replacing the improvements; (2) deducting any accrued depreciation; and (3) adding the value of the land. The appraiser does not account for inflation or the appreciation of the property. The original cost of building the structure is not considered.

B. Estimating Cost of Replacing Improvements – Appraisers are almost always concerned with the building's *replacement cost* (the cost of constructing a building with equivalent utility using current construction techniques and materials) rather than its *reproduction cost* (the cost of constructing an exact replica of the building using the same techniques and materials). Unless the building is very new, reproduction cost will be higher than replacement cost. There are three ways to estimate the replacement cost of a building:

> Replacement cost: the cost of building a replacement with equivalent utility.
>
> Reproduction cost: the cost of building a replica.
>
> The original cost of a property to its owner is irrelevant to its current value.

> The number of square feet in a home is calculated by measuring the outside dimensions of each floor of the structure, excluding the garage. Square footage below grade is usually not included.

1. **Square foot method** – The square foot method (or *comparative cost* method) is the simplest method. The appraiser analyzes the cost per square foot of recently built comparable homes and then multiplies that average cost by the number of square feet in the subject property. A smaller building may cost more per square foot than a larger building because of the rules of volume purchasing.

2. **Unit-in-place method** – The *unit-in-place method* involves estimating the cost of replacing specific components of the building, such as the floors, roof, plumbing, and foundation.

3. **Quantity survey method** – The *quantity survey method* involves a detailed estimate of the quantities and prices of construction materials and labor, which are then added to the indirect costs (building permit, survey, etc.). This is generally regarded as the most accurate replacement cost estimate.

C. **Estimating and Deducting Depreciation** – When a property being appraised is a used home, the presumption is that it is less valuable than a comparable new home because it has depreciated in value. *Depreciation* is defined as a loss in value due to any cause. Because depreciation is greater in older properties, the cost approach is less reliable for older properties.

1. **Land does not depreciate** – All improvements on the property—fences, sidewalks, landscaping, as well as the house—depreciate over time. However, land does not depreciate; it is considered indestructible.

2. **Types of depreciation** – There are three types of depreciation: *physical deterioration, functional obsolescence*, and *external obsolescence*.

    a. **Physical deterioration** – Sometimes called *deferred maintenance* (if it is curable), physical deterioration is physical wear and tear resulting from age or poor maintenance.

    b. **Functional obsolescence** – Functional obsolescence is a loss in value due to functional inadequacies such as a poor floor plan, unappealing design, over-improvement, or outdated equipment or fixtures. A common example is too few bathrooms in relation to the number of bedrooms. Functional obsolescence occurs when a building lacks functional utility, which includes attractiveness as well as actual usefulness.

    Functional obsolescence: loss in value due to inadequate or outmoded equipment, or as a result of a poor or outmoded design.

    c. **External obsolescence** – Also referred to as *economic obsolescence*, external obsolescence is caused by conditions outside the property itself, such as zoning changes, neighborhood deterioration, traffic problems, or exposure to nuisances like noxious odors from nearby industrial plants or noise from a nearby airport. An oversupply of similar properties on the market or the proximity of less-expensive houses, may also be considered external obsolescence. An

    External (economic) obsolescence: a loss in value resulting from factors outside the property itself, such as close proximity to an airport.

A simple method of estimating depreciation called the straight-line method assumes that an equal amount of depreciation happens each year.

Land can't be depreciated because (in economic theory) land is indestructible.

appraiser is on the lookout for external obsolescence when performing a neighborhood analysis.

3. **Curable or incurable** – Physical deterioration and functional obsolescence may be curable or incurable, depending on whether the cost of correcting the problem could be recovered in the sales price when the property is sold. External obsolescence is always incurable, since it is outside the property owner's control. External and functional obsolescence, rather than physical deterioration, are the sources of most declines in property value.

D. **Adding Land Value** – The last step in the cost approach is to add the value of the land to the depreciated value of the improvements. Because the cost approach involves estimating the value of land and buildings separately, then adding the two estimates together, it is sometimes called the *summation method*. The value of the lot is usually estimated based on the sales prices of comparable lots, using the sales comparison method.

Sample questions

Which of the following is an example of functional obsolescence?
A. Boards need to be replaced on deck
B. House downwind from paper mill
C. Only bathroom can be accessed only through bedroom
D. Worn-out carpet in hallway

C. *A design flaw, such as a bathroom that is accessible only through a bedroom, is functional obsolescence. Items that need to be replaced because of wear and tear are physical deterioration, while problems outside the property's boundaries (such as a nearby factory) are external obsolescence.*

A property has lost value because its maintenance and upkeep have been neglected. This would be an example of:
A. external obsolescence
B. functional obsolescence
C. internal obsolescence
D. physical deterioration

D. *A loss in value due to wear and tear or other damage is called physical deterioration.*

Charles takes very good care of his home, but recently discovered that some termites have made a nest in the floor. This type of depreciation is probably:

A. curable external obsolescence
B. curable functional obsolescence
C. incurable physical deterioration
D. curable physical deterioration

> D. Provided that the termite damage is recent, this is probably an example of curable physical deterioration. The damage might be incurable if the owner had not maintained his property in good condition, however.

Which of the following actions would most likely create the largest increase in the value of a property?

A. Installing a second bathroom in a house with four bedrooms and only one bath
B. Putting a swimming pool in the yard of a small house
C. Replacing an obsolete, inefficient furnace
D. Repairing a leaking basement

> A. Installing a second bathroom in a house with four bedrooms and only one bathroom would rectify a serious case of functional obsolescence. An owner who adds a swimming pool to a lower-end house is not likely to recoup the costs of the addition, and the other options are maintenance issues more oriented toward preserving, not increasing, the property's value.

The value of a property will NOT be reduced by the fact that the home:

A. is next to a local playground
B. has several large cracks in the basement walls
C. is located a few blocks from a new factory
D. has only one bathroom for five bedrooms

> A. Location next to a playground or park will not cause a loss of value in the property.

Regional growth leads to the addition of a third runway at the airport. The increased airplane noise causes nearby houses to suffer:

A. external obsolescence
B. functional obsolescence from poor design
C. curable depreciation
D. functional obsolescence from airport noise

> A. This is an example of obsolescence caused by something outside the property.

VI. **Income Approach to Value** – The income method, also known as the *capitalization method*, is based on the idea that there is a relationship between the net income a property generates and its market value to an investor. The income method seeks to determine the present value of a property's future income. It is best suited for commercial properties and residential rental properties; it cannot be used for properties that do not generate income.

A. Gross Income – When using the income method, the appraiser first finds the property's *gross income*. She does this by estimating what the property would earn if it were available for lease in today's marketplace. What it would earn on the open market is called the *economic rent*. This contrasts with the property's *contract rent* or *historical rent*, which is what the property is currently earning.

    1. Potential gross income – The property's economic rent is also called its *potential gross income*. This is what the property would earn if it were fully occupied and all rents owed were collected.

B. Effective Gross Income – An investor knows that vacancies must be expected and that there are tenants who won't pay their rent. So the appraiser must make a deduction from the potential gross income to allow for occasional vacancies and bad debts. The allowance is called a *vacancy factor*. Once the vacancy factor is deducted, the result is the *effective gross income*, which the investor can realistically expect to collect.

Effective gross income: the income remaining after subtracting a vacancy factor from the economic rent.

C. Operating Expenses – From the effective gross income, the appraiser deducts the expenses connected with operating the building. The operating expenses include:

Operating expenses include management fees, hazard insurance, property taxes, maintenance expenses, and utilities.

    1. Fixed expenses – Real estate taxes and hazard insurance are examples of fixed expenses.

    2. Maintenance expenses – Maintenance expenses include payments for utilities, supplies, tenant services, repairs, and management expenses.

    3. Reserves for replacement – Reserves include money set aside for replacing long-lived items such as roofs and heating systems.

    Note: Certain expenses related to owning investment property are not operating expenses and are NOT deducted from gross income. They include: principal and interest payments (also called *debt service*), depreciation, and the property owner's income taxes.

Mortgage payments (debt service), depreciation claims, and income taxes are not operating expenses.

D. Net Income – The income left when operating expenses are deducted from effective gross income is called *net income*. Net income is then capitalized to determine the property's value. Determining net income can be difficult since estimating future operating costs is highly subjective.

E. Capitalization – The process of converting net income into a meaningful value is called *capitalization*. The goal of capitalization is to measure the future benefits of property ownership, discounted to their present-day value. The mathematical procedure is expressed in the formula: *Annual Net Income ÷ Capitalization Rate = Value*.

1. **Rate of return** – The capitalization rate is the *rate of return* an investor would want to receive on money invested in the property (i.e., the purchase price). An investor willing to accept greater risk would select a higher capitalization rate. By dividing the net income by the desired rate of return, the investor can determine how much to pay for the property and still receive the desired return.

2. **Relationship of capitalization rate and value** – Capitalization rate and value are inversely proportional. If the income stays the same but the capitalization rate goes up, the property's value will go down. Interest rates affect capitalization rates, so if interest rates go up but a building's income doesn't go up, the building's value will go down.

F. **Gross Income Multiplier Method** – Single-family residences generally aren't thought of as income-producing properties, so traditional income analysis techniques do not apply. If a residential appraiser uses an income method at all, he will use a simplified version called the *gross income multiplier method* or the *gross rent multiplier (GRM) method*. As a rule, this method is applied only when appraising residential rental properties.

1. **Gross income multiplier** – A *gross income multiplier* is a figure which is multiplied by a rental property's gross income to arrive at an estimate of the property's value.

2. **Comparables** – The appraiser uses multipliers of comparable rental properties to determine an appropriate multiplier for the subject property, adjusting for similarities and differences between the properties. To find a comparable's gross income multiplier, the appraiser will divide its sales price by its gross income. The appraiser may use monthly multipliers (based on gross monthly income) or annual multipliers (based on gross annual income).

VII. **Reconciliation and Final Estimate of Value** – Appraisers refer to the assembly and interpretation of all the facts that influence a property's value as *reconciliation*. The *final value estimate* is not simply the average of the results yielded by the three appraisal methods; it is the figure that represents the appraiser's expert opinion of the subject property's value after all the data are assembled and analyzed. If the property has already sold, the appraiser does not consider the sales price of the property.

> Capitalization: appraising real property by converting the anticipated net income from the property into the present value.

> When cap rates go up, property values go down.

> When cap rates go down, property values go up.

> Reconciliation: the final step in an appraisal, when the appraiser assembles and interprets the data to arrive at a final value estimate.

A. Report Formats – The results of the value estimate will usually be disclosed in one of two types of appraisal reports:

Narrative report: a thoroughly detailed appraisal report; more comprehensive than a form appraisal report.

1. **Narrative report** – A *narrative report* is a thorough, detailed, written presentation of the facts and reasoning behind the appraiser's estimate of value; it is the most detailed type of report.

2. **Form report** – A *form report* is a brief standard form used by lending institutions and government agencies (such as the FHA and VA), presenting only the key data and the appraiser's conclusions. This is the most common type of report.

Sample questions

In what order would these steps be performed when using the income approach to value? 1. Apply the cap rate to the net income. 2. Estimate the potential gross income. 3. Determine the net operating income. 4. Calculate the effective gross income.

A. 3, 1, 4, 2
B. 1, 3, 2, 4
C. 2, 4, 3, 1
D. 2, 3, 1, 4

   C. This is the order of steps involved in the income approach. (Note that selecting and applying the cap rate may be viewed either as one step or as two separate steps.)

Which of the following is the proper method for determining the gross income multiplier?

A. Divide monthly income by sales price
B. Divide annual income by sales price
C. Divide sales price by gross income
D. Divide assessed value by gross income

   C. The gross income multiplier method involves dividing a comparable's sales price by its gross income to determine the multiplier.

Mike is appraising a property for a lender. Which of the following will he consider when conducting the appraisal?

A. The cost to update the subject property
B. The original price paid for the property
C. The average value of all available comparables
D. A reconciliation of values if more than one appraisal method has been used

   D. A reconciliation represents the assembly and interpretation of all the facts that influence a property's value, based upon whatever methods of appraisal have been used.

ABC Mortgage just received an appraisal report. Which of the following will not be in the report?

A. Condition of the property
B. Date of the appraisal inspection
C. Adjustments to the subject property
D. Reason for the appraisal

> C. An appraiser makes adjustments to comparable properties, not to the subject property.

The reconciliation process in an appraisal:

A. involves calculation of the average value of comparable properties
B. represents the appraiser's comparison and conclusion from the results of the appraisal methods used
C. is a determination of the highest possible value
D. is the calculation of the capitalization rate

> B. The final value estimate represents the appraiser's reconciliation of the value indicators arrived at through one or more of the approaches to value. Reconciliation is a matter of judgment, not a mathematical procedure like averaging.

A four-unit building rents for $1,500 a month per unit. If the GRM (gross rent multiplier) is 127, what is the value of the property?

A. $190,500
B. $381,000
C. $762,000
D. $914,400

> C. $1,500 x 4 units = $6,000. 127 x $6,000 = $762,000.

Chapter Quiz

1. What principle underlies competitive market analysis?

   A. A property's highest and best use is the most profitable use it can legally be used for
   B. A property's selling price can be estimated using selling prices of comparable properties
   C. Competition within the marketplace leads to lower interest rates
   D. Market value can only be determined precisely through an appraisal

2. When performing a competitive market analysis, a real estate agent should:

   A. disregard current and expired listings
   B. consider land and improvements separately
   C. pick comparables similar in age and quality to the subject property
   D. use the gross rent multiplier method

3. A seller wanting to get an estimate of the value of her property before settling on a listing price should obtain a/an:

   A. abstract of title
   B. assessment
   C. fee appraisal
   D. title search

4. Of the following factors, which one is the most significant in influencing value?

   A. Building materials
   B. Annual property tax bill
   C. Location
   D. Style of building

5. While preparing a competitive market analysis, an agent has four comparables to choose from. Comparable #1 sold for $180,000 13 months ago under normal conditions. #2 sold for $190,000 14 months ago under normal conditions. #3 sold for $175,000 10 months ago as a foreclosure. #4 sold for $180,000 16 months ago as a foreclosure. The agent should use:

   A. the oldest two
   B. the newest two
   C. all four
   D. None, because they are all older than nine months

6. An agent is performing a competitive market analysis for a potential client, working with four comparables. Which of the following comparables would require an upward adjustment in its sales price?

   A. Comparable W: is on a larger lot size than the subject property
   B. Comparable X: lacks a garage, which the subject property has
   C. Comparable Y: has a swimming pool, which the subject property lacks
   D. Comparable Z: is in a superior neighborhood compared to the subject property

7. Of the following, which would have the greatest effect on the supply of real estate in a particular market?

   A. Demographic change
   B. Employment rates
   C. Local amenities
   D. Size of labor force

8. Which of the following situations would cause prices for residential real estate to go up in a particular area?

   A. A large new factory that will employ thousands
   B. Interest rates are going up
   C. There is a large supply of recently built homes on the market
   D. Zoning change allowing more commercial uses

9. A buyer who is concerned with whether a property's soil is suitable for construction of a septic system would, as part of the inspection process, order a/an:

   A. absorption test
   B. geological inspection
   C. percolation test
   D. toxic waste report

10. Which of the following methods would be most appropriate for valuing a recently built, single-family home?

    A. Replacement cost and income approach
    B. Income approach and cost approach
    C. Market analysis and replacement cost
    D. Income approach and cap rate

11. A seller asks an appraiser to help determine a realistic listing price for her single-family, owner-occupied house. Which approach to value would the appraiser rely on when making this decision?

A. Cost approach
B. Gross rent multiplier method
C. Income approach
D. Market data approach

12. A real estate licensee is performing a competitive market analysis. He locates a comparable property that is slightly older than the subject property. The age of the comparable makes it worth $2,000 less. The comparable has a small porch worth $1,000 that the subject property lacks. If the comparable sold for $269,500 recently, what is the estimated value of the subject property?

A. $266,500
B. $268,500
C. $270,500
D. $272,500

13. What information does an appraiser need in order to calculate a capitalization rate?

A. Price and gross income
B. Price and net income
C. Value and gross income
D. Value and net income

14. A licensee who is taking a listing on a property finds a number of problems that need to be fixed, such as several leaking faucets and an electrical system that intermittently cuts out. This would be an example of:

A. economic obsolescence
B. external obsolescence
C. functional obsolescence
D. physical deterioration

15. An older retail building has narrow hallways, and window air conditioning units rather than central AC. These would be examples of:

A. economic obsolescence
B. external obsolescence
C. functional obsolescence
D. physical deterioration

16. An appraiser does a neighborhood analysis to determine:

A. functional obsolescence
B. external obsolescence
C. deferred maintenance
D. racial composition of the neighborhood

17. When determining the value of a vacant lot, an appraiser will typically use the:

A. cost approach
B. income approach
C. sales comparison approach
D. summation approach

18. An appraiser is valuing a commercial property that contains a restaurant run by the property owner. Which method of valuation would be most appropriate?

A. Cost
B. Income
C. Market data
D. Sales comparison

19. A former mansion has been divided into three apartments. The best approach to finding the property's value is:

A. cost
B. income
C. reconciliation
D. sales comparison

20. An appraiser is trying to estimate depreciation when valuing an older residential rental property, but is finding it difficult because no comparables have sold recently. However, the appraiser can find sufficient data on rental rates in the same market, and a capitalization rate can be supported. Which approach to value should the appraiser use?

A. Cost
B. Income
C. Market data
D. Sales comparison

Answer Key

1. B. Competitive market analysis is a process similar to the sales comparison approach to appraisal, where a real estate agent uses the sales prices of similar properties to estimate what a property might sell for.

2. C. A competitive market analysis should be based on comparables that are as similar as possible to the subject property, including size, age, and quality, as well as a nearby location. A CMA can also include current or expired listings, as well as recently sold properties.

3. C. An appraisal is an estimate of a property's value, as of a given date. A homeowner prior to a sale would work with a fee appraiser, rather than an appraiser who works for a lender.

4. C. A property's location is usually the most determinative factor in terms of its value. A view or a prestigious neighborhood can boost the value of an otherwise unremarkable property.

5. D. The general rule for choosing comparables is that the sale should have occurred within six months. A sale older than six months is allowable if necessary and if adjustments for inflation are made, but sales older than one year should never be used. In addition, only comparables that sold under normal conditions should be used, which would rule out foreclosed properties. Comparables 1 and 2 are too old, Comparable 3 is a foreclosure, and Comparable 4 is both, so none of them can be used.

6. B. When performing an appraisal or CMA, you would adjust a comparable's sale price upward if it does not have a feature that the subject property has. The object is to make each comparable as similar as possible to the subject property. In this case, you would want to know what the comparable's sale price would have been if it, in fact, had a garage.

7. D. The size of the labor force has the greatest influence on supply and demand for real estate. The size of the labor force determines how many people are able to afford to purchase homes within the local market.

8. A. If a new large employer arrives in the area, that will increase the population seeking to buy homes. The increased demand will cause prices to go up. Higher interest rates, on the other hand, will lower demand and thus lower prices, while an oversupply of houses will also lower prices.

9. C. A percolation test measures the soil's ability to absorb water. It is often performed when there are questions about the suitability of the property for meeting health and safety standards concerning septic systems.

10. C. The sales comparison approach (also known as the market data or market analysis approach) is the best method for appraising residential property. Replacement cost, which is based upon the idea that a property is not worth more than it would cost to replace it, may also be suitable for a newer residential property.

11. D. The market data approach, or sales comparison approach, is most commonly used when estimating the value of a single-family residence.

12. C. To estimate the value of the subject property, adjust the comparable's sale price to reflect what it would sell for if it were identical to the subject property. Add $2,000 to the comparable's sale price (to make it more like the subject property, which is newer), and then subtract $1,000 from the comparable's sale price (to make it more like the subject property, which lacks a porch). The result is $270,500.

13. D. In order to calculate a property's value, an appraiser using the income approach would need to know the property's net income and capitalization rate. So, conversely, if the appraiser wanted to know an appropriate capitalization rate, he would need to know the property's value and net income.

14. D. Physical deterioration is a loss in value caused by wear and tear, or by damage. Most likely, these are examples of curable physical deterioration, as the cost of correcting the problems could be recovered in the sales price.

15. C. Functional obsolescence includes both undesirable, out-of-date design elements (such as the narrow hallways) and fixtures or appliances (such as the window units).

16. B. External obsolescence is also called economic obsolescence. It is a loss in value resulting from factors outside the property itself, such as proximity to an airport. It is also referred to as external inadequacy.

17. C. An appraiser will estimate the value of vacant land using the sales comparison approach, referring to the value of similar lots.

18. B. For a commercial property that generates income for its owner, the most appropriate method of valuation would be the income approach.

19. B. The income approach is appropriate for properties that are oriented toward generating income for the property's owner. That would be true even if the property originally was intended as a single-family residence.

20. B. If sales comparables are not available and the cost of depreciation is difficult to estimate, but the data necessary to use the income approach are available, then it is appropriate to use the income approach.

Chapter 13
Closing Real Estate Transactions

I. **Closing** – Once a purchase and sale agreement has been signed and all of the contingencies have been satisfied, preparations are made to finalize the transaction. Finalizing a real estate transaction is called *closing* or *settlement*.

   A. **Escrow** – *Escrow* is an arrangement in which money and documents are held by a third party (*escrow agent*) on behalf of the buyer and the seller until the transaction is ready to close. The escrow agent is a *dual agent*, who represents both buyer and seller and owes fiduciary duties to both parties.

   B. **Escrow Instructions** – The parties usually give the escrow agent written instructions that determine under what conditions and at what time the agent will distribute the money and documents to the proper parties. Both parties must agree on the choice of escrow agent and the terms and conditions of the escrow.

   C. **Purpose of Escrow** – Escrow protects each party from the other's change of mind. For instance, if the seller suddenly doesn't want to sell the property as agreed, he can't just refuse to deliver the deed to the buyer. Once the signed deed has been given to the escrow agent, if the buyer fulfills all of the conditions of the escrow instructions and deposits the purchase price into escrow, the escrow agent must deliver the deed to the buyer.

      1. **Brokerage not a party** – The brokerage is not a principal in the transaction and cannot direct an escrow agent during the process of closing the transaction.

      2. **Death or incapacity doesn't terminate escrow** – If a seller dies shortly after depositing the deed in escrow, and the buyer fulfills the terms of the escrow instructions, the escrow will close as agreed.

   D. **Escrow Agents Must Be Licensed** – Escrow law requires all escrow agents to be licensed by the state *Department of Financial Institutions*. Only corporations may be licensed as escrow agents; individuals are not eligible. Individuals who pass an exam may be licensed as escrow officers, in order to be employed by an escrow agent.

Settlement statement: a document that presents a final, detailed accounting for a real estate transaction, listing each party's debits and credits and the amount each will receive or be required to pay at closing. Also called a closing statement.

A selling agent should always provide a prospective purchaser with an estimate of the prospect's closing costs.

1. **Real estate agents** – Real estate agents are exempt from escrow license requirements when handling escrow in a transaction in which they are an agent or a party. Real estate agents may not charge a fee for such services. For a real estate licensee to charge a fee for escrow services, he must also be licensed as an escrow officer.

E. **Roundtable Closing** – In some other states, rather than using escrow, closing usually involves all the parties meeting together to sign and exchange documents. This is known as a roundtable closing, or "passing papers." The real estate agent will be present as well, to collect her commission.

II. **Closing Costs and Settlement Statements** – For each transaction, the escrow agent prepares a *settlement statement*, which sets forth all of the financial aspects of the transaction in detail. The settlement statement shows exactly how much the buyer will have to pay at closing and exactly how much the seller will take away from closing.

A. **Preparing a Settlement Statement** – Preparing a settlement statement involves determining what charges and credits apply to a given transaction and making sure each one is allocated to the proper party. It is important for an agent to understand the process of preparing a settlement statement, because agents will use a simplified version of this process to provide buyers or sellers with estimates of their closing costs.

B. **Debits and Credits** – A *debit* is a charge payable by a particular party; the purchase price is a debit to the buyer, for example, and the sales commission is a debit to the seller. *Credit* items are payable to a particular party; the buyer is credited for her new loan and the seller for the purchase price.

1. **Purchase price** – The purchase price is paid by the buyer to the seller. It is listed as a debit to the buyer and a credit to the seller.

2. **Earnest money deposit** – The earnest money deposit appears as a credit to the buyer. No entry is made on the seller's side of the statement.

3. **Commission** – The real estate agent's commission is a debit to the seller.

4. **New loan** – A new loan is listed as a credit to the buyer. The buyer's loan is part of the purchase price already credited to the seller, so no entry is made on the seller's side of the statement.

5. **Assumed loan** – If a buyer assumes a seller's existing loan, it is part of the money used to finance the transaction, so (like a new loan) it is credited to the buyer. The assumed

loan balance is a debit to the seller. Any interest due on an assumed loan would be the seller's responsibility as well.

6. **Seller financing** – If a seller accepts a mortgage from the buyer for part of the purchase price, it shows up as a buyer's credit, just like an institutional loan. The seller financing arrangement reduces the amount of cash the seller will receive at closing, so it is listed as a debit to the seller. This also applies when the parties use a wraparound mortgage; however, the underlying loan will not appear on the settlement statement.

7. **Payoff of seller's loan** – The loan payoff is a debit to the seller. No entry is made on the buyer's side of the settlement statement. If the seller has a loan to pay off, the escrow agent requests an *estoppel certificate* from the seller's lender. This document states the loan's remaining principal balance. If the loan is being assumed, the document is known instead as a *certificate of reduction*.

8. **Prepayment penalty** – If a prepayment penalty is charged by the seller's lender, it is listed as a debit to the seller.

9. **Seller's reserve accounts** – During the loan term, the lender requires the borrower to make regular payments toward recurring costs. These payments are kept in a *reserve account* (also called an *impound account*). At closing, any unused balance is refunded as a credit to the seller.

   a. **Recurring costs** – *Recurring costs* include property taxes, insurance, assessments, and homeowners association fees. (Principal and interest payments are not considered recurring costs and do not go into reserve accounts.)

10. **Discount points** – Discount points are a debit to the buyer, unless the seller has agreed to a buydown on the buyer's behalf, in which case the points would be a debit to the seller.

11. **Hazard insurance** – The lender may require the buyer to pay for hazard insurance in advance; this would be a debit to the buyer. If the seller has paid in advance for hazard insurance beyond the closing date, the unused portion of the premium would be a credit to the seller.

12. **Excise tax** – The *excise tax*, a sales tax paid to the state on the selling price, is typically a debit to the seller. In some states, it may instead be known as a transfer tax or stamp tax.

The person who benefits from the recording of a document pays the recording fee.

13. **Recording fees** – Recording fees are paid by whichever party benefits from having the document recorded. For instance, the fee for recording the new deed is paid by the buyer, while the fee for recording the deed of reconveyance is paid by the seller.

C. **Prorations** – Certain periodic expenses, such as property taxes, mortgage interest payments, and hazard insurance premiums, are usually *prorated* between the buyer and the seller. The seller is responsible for these expenses during her period of ownership. The buyer is responsible for these expenses after he takes title.

1. **Proration formula** – Divide the annual expense by 360 or 365—depending on whether you're using a *banker's year (360 days)* or a *calendar year (365 days)*—to establish a *per diem* cost, then multiply by the applicable number of days to determine the prorated cost. You will be told whether to use a banker's year or a calendar year on your license exam.

Example: Annual taxes are $3,449.25. The transaction closes on April 24th. The seller has paid the taxes through the end of the tax year (June 30). What is the prorated charge to the buyer? Base your computations on a 365-day year.

Answer: $642.60 – Divide $3,449.25 by 365 days = $9.45 per day (per diem). There are 7 days remaining in April, including the day of closing, 31 days in May, and 30 days in June. 7 + 31 + 30 = 68 days charged to the buyer. 68 × $9.45 = $642.60.

2. **Prorated taxes** – The seller is responsible for the property taxes up to, but not including, the day of closing. The buyer becomes the owner of record on the day of closing and is responsible for taxes for the day of closing and afterward.

3. **Prorated interest** – The interest on the seller's mortgage accrues up to and including the day the transaction closes. Interest is paid *in arrears*, so if a transaction closes in the middle of a payment period, the seller will owe the lender some interest. For instance, the mortgage payment for the month of April would be due on May 1, and if closing occurred in mid-April, the seller would need to pay at closing for interest accrued in the first part of April.

Rent paid in advance: credit buyer; debit seller.

4. **Rent** – When the property being purchased and sold is rental property, the rent paid by the tenant at the beginning of the month is prorated and the buyer is entitled to a per

diem rent credit for the days of rent paid in advance. The seller will be debited for the same amount.

    a. Security deposits – Note that security deposits are never prorated; they must be transferred to the new owner (the buyer). They are listed as a credit to the buyer and a debit to the seller.

Security deposits are transferred to new owner at closing; they are not prorated.

D. Final Settlement Statement Balances – The totals in the buyer's debit column and buyer's credit column must be the same. Likewise, the seller's total debits and total credits must match. The totals in the buyer's column do not need to match the totals in the seller's column.

    1. Balance due from buyer – To determine the amount the buyer needs to provide in cash at closing, the escrow agent would subtract the buyer's total credits from the buyer's total debits. This amount would be entered at the bottom of the buyer's credit column, so that the final amount of buyer's credits matches the final amount of the buyer's debits.

Balance due from buyer is a credit to the buyer.

    2. Balance due to seller – Likewise, to determine the amount the seller receives at closing, subtract the seller's total debits from the seller's total credits.

Sample questions

State or local sales tax on the transfer of property is used as a way to generate revenue. On the uniform settlement statement, it is normally listed as a debit to the seller. It goes by a variety of names, such as the documentary stamp tax or the:

A. ad valorem tax
B. assessment fee
C. environmental tax
D. transfer tax

    D. *One name for the tax paid by the seller based on a percentage of the selling price is the transfer tax (or documentary transfer tax). It may also be known as a stamp tax or excise tax.*

All of the following charges are usually prorated between buyer and seller at closing, except:

A. property taxes
B. recording fees
C. special assessments
D. utility bills

    B. *Recording fees are usually paid by both parties at closing, but rather than prorating, each party pays the costs associated with recording the documents that benefit that party. (For instance, the buyer pays to record the deed, while the seller pays to record the lien release.)*

The Barkers have entered into an agreement to sell their house. Their property is subject to a special assessment for neighborhood improvements. The buyers will not assume the special assessment, as per the purchase and sale agreement. $1,500 of the assessment remains unpaid at closing. This will show up on the settlement statement as a:

A. credit to the buyer
B. credit to the seller and a debit to the buyer
C. debit to the seller
D. debit to the seller and a credit to the buyer

    C. *Because the buyers are not assuming the special assessment, the Barkers must pay off any remaining balance on the special assessment. This will be a debit to the sellers, and it will not affect the buyers' side of the settlement statement.*

III. Income Tax Aspects of Closing – The escrow agent has primary responsibility for reporting *gross proceeds* from the sale to the IRS using a *1099-S form*. If the escrow agent and mortgage lender fail to report the sale, it becomes the real estate agent's responsibility.

    A. Form 8300 – An escrow agent must use *Form 8300* to report having received more than $10,000 in cash in a transaction.

IV. Real Estate Settlement Procedures Act (RESPA) – *RESPA* is a federal law that affects how closing is handled in most residential transactions that are financed with institutional loans (from banks, savings and loans, credit unions, etc.).

    A. Two Main Purposes – The purposes of RESPA are: (1) to provide borrowers with information about their *closing costs*; and (2) to eliminate *kickbacks* and *referral fees* that unnecessarily increase the cost of settlement.

    B. Transactions Covered by RESPA – RESPA applies to *federally related* loan transactions. A loan is federally related if:

        1. Type of property – The loan is secured by a mortgage/trust deed against: (1) an existing residential property or one in which the loan proceeds will be used to build a residential property with four or fewer units; (2) a condominium unit or cooperative unit; or (3) a lot with (or on which the loan proceeds will be used to place) a mobile home; AND

        2. Type of lender – The lender is federally regulated, has federally insured accounts, or sells loans to Fannie Mae, Freddie Mac, or Ginnie Mae.

        NOTE: In short, RESPA applies to almost all institutional lenders and to most residential loans. RESPA does NOT apply to seller-financed transactions or commercial transactions.

Seller-financed transactions are not subject to RESPA.

C. **RESPA Requirements** – RESPA has seven requirements for federally related loans:

1. **Documentation** – Within three days after receiving a written loan application, the lender must give all loan applicants: (1) a copy of a *HUD booklet* about settlement procedures ("Shopping for Your Home Loan"), which explains matters related to closing; (2) a *good faith estimate of closing costs*; and (3) a *mortgage servicing disclosure statement*.

2. **Required providers** – If the lender requires the borrower to use a particular attorney, credit reporting agency, or appraiser, that requirement must be disclosed to the borrower.

3. **Referrals** – If the lender refers the borrower to an affiliated service provider, their business relationship must be fully disclosed, along with the fact that the referral is optional.

4. **Uniform settlement statement** – The closing agent must itemize all loan settlement charges on a *uniform settlement statement*. The uniform settlement statement must be provided to the borrower, seller, and lender on or before the closing date. If the borrower requests it, the closing agent must allow the borrower to inspect the statement one business day before closing. The statement must contain the name and address of the buyer, seller, and lender.

   > The uniform settlement statement will contain the names and addresses of the buyer, seller, and lender.

5. **Impound account** – The lender cannot require excessive deposits (more than necessary to cover expenses) into an impound account.

6. **Settlement services** – A lender or provider of *settlement services* (such as a title company) may not: (1) pay or receive kickbacks or referral fees (fees from one settlement service provider to another) for referring customers; (2) pay or receive unearned fees (for services not actually provided); or (3) charge a fee for the preparation of the uniform settlement statement, an escrow account statement, or the disclosure statement required by the Truth in Lending Act.

7. **Title company** – The seller may not require the buyer to use a particular title company.

D. **Integrated Disclosures** – Truth in Lending Act and Real Estate Settlement Procedures Act disclosures are made on the integrated disclosure forms.

1. **Loan estimate** – The initial TILA disclosure and RESPA's good faith estimate of closing costs are set forth on the *loan estimate* form, which must be given to the applicant within three days of submitting a loan application.

2. **Closing disclosure** – The final TILA disclosure and the uniform settlement statement are given on the *closing disclosure* form, which must be given at least three days before closing.

Sample questions

The primary purpose of the Real Estate Settlement Procedures Act is to:
A. ensure that the seller receives the purchase price, the buyer receives clear title to the property, and the lender's security interest in the property is perfected
B. require lenders to disclose the complete cost of credit to consumer loan applicants
C. promote uniformity and accuracy in the closing process by requiring closing agents to be state-certified
D. provide borrowers with information about their closing costs and to eliminate kickbacks and referral fees

> D. *RESPA is a federal law that requires certain information about closing costs to be disclosed to loan applicants, and also prohibits kickbacks and referral fees that unnecessarily increase the cost of settlement.*

A federal law requires lenders to give the booklet "Shopping for Your Home Loan" to all prospective borrowers within three business days of loan application. What law is this?
A. Regulation Z
B. Home Loan Disclosure Act
C. RESPA
D. Truth in Lending Act

> C. *RESPA requires, among other things, that all lenders give prospective borrowers a copy of the booklet about settlement procedures, entitled "Shopping for Your Home Loan."*

Which of the following transactions is NOT subject to the Real Estate Settlement Procedures Act?
A. An FHA-insured loan
B. A contract for deed used in a seller-financed residential sale
C. A conventional loan to finance the purchase of a three-unit residential building
D. A VA-guaranteed loan

> B. *RESPA applies to loans used to finance residential properties with up to four units. Seller financing, including a contract for deed, is not subject to the act.*

Chapter Quiz

1. A $4,500 earnest money check bounces because of insufficient funds. The first thing the broker should do is:

   A. notify escrow to charge this amount, plus the bounced check fee, to the buyer
   B. notify the borrower
   C. notify the principals
   D. write a personal check for $4,500 to cover the shortage

2. At closing, the buyer and seller receive settlement statements that list expenses related to closing. Every expense will show up on the settlement statement as:

   A. credits to both buyer and seller
   B. debits to both buyer and seller
   C. credits to either the buyer or the seller, or both
   D. debits to either the buyer or the seller, or both

3. Which statement about real estate settlement is FALSE?

   A. An escrow agent is a third party who acts on behalf of both the buyer and seller to orchestrate the closing of the transaction
   B. In an assumption of a loan, the lender will provide the buyer with an estoppel certificate that verifies the loan balance
   C. In some states, closing involves all of the parties meeting face-to-face to sign documents, rather than using escrow
   D. The terms and conditions of closing are set forth in a contract between the parties and the escrow agent, known as escrow instructions

4. Bronson agreed to sell his house to the Hatchers. Closing is scheduled for May 15. Bronson already paid the taxes for the entire year, but the Hatchers are assuming responsibility for the taxes as of the closing date. The settlement statement will prorate the taxes as a:

   A. credit to the buyer, and debit to the seller
   B. debit to the buyer, and credit to the seller
   C. debit to the seller
   D. credit to the buyer

5. On a settlement statement, the seller's net proceeds are calculated by:

   A. subtracting closing costs from the purchase price
   B. subtracting the buyer's credits from the seller's credits
   C. subtracting the seller's debits from the buyer's debits
   D. subtracting the seller's debits from the seller's credits

6. The Johnsons are buying a home and will be using $30,000 in cash to make the downpayment at closing. To comply with IRS rules, which form will need to be filed to report this transaction?

   A. 8300
   B. 8500
   C. 1099
   D. I-9

7. The Real Estate Settlement Procedures Act (RESPA) applies to:

   A. contracts for deed
   B. seller-financed transactions
   C. commercial and residential mortgages
   D. residential first mortgages

8. Terry is buying a house offered for sale by owner (FSBO) with the help of a real estate agent. The purchase and sale agreement is contingent on Terry receiving a loan from an institutional lender. Does RESPA apply to this transaction?

   A. No, because RESPA doesn't apply to FSBO properties
   B. No, because RESPA doesn't cover seller financing
   C. Yes, because Terry is purchasing a single-family home
   D. Yes, because a real estate agent was involved in the transaction

9. Which of the following statements regarding the Real Estate Settlement Procedures Act (RESPA) is true?

   A. It applies to residential and commercial transactions
   B. The borrower is entitled to a good faith estimate of the settlement costs within three days of submitting an application
   C. It covers all financed residential transactions, including seller financing
   D. It sets the maximum interest rate that the lender can charge

10. Under the terms of RESPA, all of the following are true EXCEPT:

    A. the borrower is given seven days to rescind (or back out of) the loan transaction after receiving the good faith estimate of closing costs
    B. the borrower must be given a good faith estimate of closing costs by the lender
    C. no party may receive any kickbacks in connection with the loan transaction
    D. a uniform settlement statement must be used at closing

Answer Key

1. C. Since both principals are party to the escrow instructions, the broker should notify both of them so they can decide how they want to proceed.

2. D. Expenses related to closing will show up on the settlement statement as a debit to either the buyer, the seller, or both. For example, the cost of an appraisal will show up as a debit to the buyer, but not the seller. But the cost of the escrow fee will probably show up as a debit to both buyer and seller, as it is usually a fee that is shared equally between the parties.

3. B. An estoppel certificate is used when a loan is being paid off. A document known as a certificate of reduction is used to report the loan balance in a loan assumption.

4. B. The seller has prepaid the taxes for the entire year, so he will be credited for the amount after closing. In turn, the Hatchers will be debited for the same amount.

5. D. To determine how much money the seller will take away from the transaction after closing (her net proceeds, in other words), start with the seller's credits and subtract the seller's debits.

6. A. Form 8300 is required by the IRS to report cash over $10,000 in a trade or business transaction.

7. D. RESPA applies to mortgages used to purchase a dwelling with up to four units. It does not apply to commercial transactions or seller financing.

8. C. RESPA applies to federally related loan transactions when the mortgage or deed of trust will be secured by a dwelling with up to four units.

9. B. Under RESPA, a lender is required to give a prospective borrower a good faith estimate of the settlement costs (closing costs) within three days after a written loan application is submitted. Neither commercial transactions nor seller-financed transactions are covered by RESPA, and RESPA does not limit the interest rate lenders can charge.

10. A. There is no seven-day right of rescission under the provisions of RESPA.

Chapter 14

Federal Income Taxation and Real Estate

I. **Basic Taxation Concepts** – The United States federal government taxes the income of individuals and businesses on an annual basis.

   A. **Progressive Tax** – A tax may be proportional, regressive, or progressive, depending on how its burden is distributed among taxpayers. Our federal income tax is a *progressive tax*. This means that the more a taxpayer earns in a given year, the higher his tax rate will be.

   B. **Deductions and Tax Credits** – A taxpayer who is entitled to a *deduction* can subtract a specified amount from his income before it is taxed. By reducing the amount of income that is taxed, the deduction also reduces the amount of tax the taxpayer owes.

      1. **Tax credits** – In contrast to deductions, *tax credits* are subtracted directly from the amount of tax owed. The taxpayer's income is added up, the tax rate is applied, and then any applicable tax credits are subtracted to determine how much the taxpayer will actually have to pay. Dollar for dollar, tax credits represent a greater tax benefit than tax deductions.

   C. **Gains and Losses** – The sale or exchange of an asset (such as real estate) nearly always results in either a gain or a loss. Gains are treated as income, so every gain is taxable unless the tax code specifically says otherwise. Losses may be deducted only if the deduction is authorized by the tax code.

      1. **No deduction for loss on principal residence** – A taxpayer may not deduct a loss suffered on the sale of the taxpayer's principal residence or other real property owned for personal use (such as a vacation home).

   D. **Capital Gains and Losses** – A gain or loss on the sale of an asset held for personal use or as an investment is considered a *capital gain* or a *capital loss*. When eligible property is sold for a profit, the capital gain is given favorable tax treatment. If capital gains exceed capital losses, the net gain is taxed as a capital gain.

   E. **Tax Basis** – For income tax purposes, a property owner's *basis* in the property is her investment in it. If the taxpayer sells the property for more than the basis, the amount received that exceeds the basis is a profit and is taxable.

Dollar for dollar, tax credits represent a greater tax benefit than tax deductions.

A *tax shelter* is any investment that generates income while taking advantage of credits or deductions to limit tax liability.

A real estate agent's commission is considered active income, rather than passive income, for tax purposes.

Basis: The amount of the owner's original investment in the property; what it cost to acquire the property, which may include closing costs, as well as the purchase price. Also called initial basis.

The basis can be increased through capital improvements and decreased through depreciation.

Adjusted basis = Initial basis + capital expenditures – depreciation.

1. **Initial basis** – In most cases, a taxpayer's *initial basis* (also called *cost basis* or *book value*) is equal to the original cost of acquisition—the cost of acquiring the property. A taxpayer who paid $475,000 for a property, plus $10,000 in closing costs, has an initial basis of $485,000.

2. **Adjusted basis** – The initial basis may be increased or decreased to arrive at an *adjusted basis*, which reflects any *capital expenditures* and any allowable *depreciation deductions*.

   a. **Capital expenditures** – Capital expenditures (or *capital improvements*) are expenditures made to improve the property, such as money a homeowner spends to add a room or to remodel a kitchen. The expenditures are added to the initial cost basis to determine the adjusted basis.

   Example: If the initial cost basis is $485,000 and remodeling the kitchen costs $48,000, the adjusted cost basis would be $533,000 ($485,000 + $48,000 = $533,000).

   b. **Maintenance expenses** – Maintenance expenses, such as painting or repairs, are not considered capital expenditures and do not affect the basis.

   c. **Depreciation** – Where depreciation deductions are allowed, the deductions are subtracted from the initial basis to determine the adjusted basis. Depreciation deductions are discussed later in this chapter.

F. **Realization** – A gain is not considered taxable income until it is *realized*. Ownership of an asset involves gain if the asset is appreciating in value. But for tax purposes, a gain is realized only when a sale or exchange occurs.

   1. **Calculating gain or loss** – To find the gain or loss realized in a transaction, start with the *net sales price* (called the *amount realized* in the tax code) and subtract the property's adjusted basis. The net sales price is the amount of money received in the sale less any selling expenses.

G. **Recognition and Deferral** – A gain is taxed the year it is *recognized*. A gain will be recognized in the year it is realized, unless there is a specific exception in the tax code that allows the taxpayer to *defer* payment of taxes until a later year.

H. **Classification of Real Property** – The tax code divides real property into the following classes:

1. **Principal residence** – A *principal residence* is the home the taxpayer owns and occupies as her primary dwelling. It may be a single-family home, a duplex, a condominium unit, a cooperative apartment, or a mobile home. If a taxpayer splits her time between two dwellings, one of them must be designated as the principal residence.

   A taxpayer can claim only one principal residence at a time.

2. **Personal use property** – *Personal use property* is property other than a primary residence that is owned for personal use, such as a second home or a vacation cabin.

3. **Unimproved investment property** – Vacant land that produces no rental income is considered *unimproved investment property*.

4. **Property held for production of income** – *Property held for production of income* includes residential, commercial, and industrial property used to generate rental income for the owner.

5. **Property used in a trade or business** – *Property used in a trade or business* includes land and buildings that the taxpayer owns and uses in his business, such as a factory owned by a manufacturer or a barber shop owned by the barber.

6. **Dealer property** – *Dealer property* is property held primarily for sale to customers rather than for long-term investment. Lots in a newly developed subdivision are dealer-owned properties.

Sample questions

A capital gain is the:
A. taxable profit that is realized when a capital asset is sold
B. taxable profit that is paid when investment property is sold
C. difference between the sale price and the operating expenses of investment property
D. difference between the sale price and the original purchase price of residential property

   A. When a capital asset is sold, the gain (profit) is called capital gain.

Adjusted basis is:
A. initial basis, less capital expenditures, plus depreciation
B. initial basis, less repair expenses, plus capital expenditures
C. initial basis, plus capital expenditures, plus repair expenses
D. initial basis, plus capital expenditures, less depreciation

D. *Adjusted basis is the initial basis, plus capital expenditures, less allowable depreciation.*

II. **Nonrecognition Transactions** – Nonrecognition transactions do not require the taxpayer to pay taxes on a gain in the year it is realized. These include *installment sales*, *involuntary conversions*, and *"tax-free" exchanges*.

A. **Installment Sales** – The tax code considers a sale to be an installment sale if less than 100% of the sales price is received in the year of sale. Nearly all seller-financed transactions are installment sales. Installment sale reporting allows the taxpayer/seller to defer recognition of part of the gain to the year(s) in which it is received. Taxes are paid only on the portion of the profit received each year. The gain is prorated over the term of the installment contract. Installment sale reporting is not usually available for dealer property.

B. **"Tax-Free" Exchanges** – Section 1031 exchanges are called "tax-free" exchanges but are really just tax-deferred exchanges. If unimproved investment property, income property, or property used in a trade or business is exchanged for *like-kind property*, recognition of any realized gain will be deferred indefinitely.

1. **Ineligible properties** – Certain properties are not eligible for tax-deferred exchanges, including a principal residence (your home), personal use property (your vacation home), or dealer property.

2. **Boot** – If only like-kind property is exchanged, no gain or loss is recognized in the year of the exchange. But if something other than like-kind property is included in the exchange, such as money to compensate for a difference in the values of the exchanged properties, the non-like-kind property is called *boot* and is taxable in the year of the exchange.

   a. **Mortgage relief** – In addition to cash, boot might be stocks, other types of personal property (like a boat), or *mortgage relief* (where there is a difference between the mortgage balances of the properties being exchanged).

3. **Requirements** – In a 1031 exchange, the taxpayer has 45 days after closing to identify the replacement property for the exchange. The taxpayer has 180 days after the initial closing to close the transaction for the replacement property.

Installment sales allow the seller to defer tax on the gain (profit) to the year in which it is received.

Boot is personal property given to balance the exchange when the two properties are of unequal value.

An agent who facilitates a 1031 exchange may be compensated by both parties.

Sample questions

Which of the following is not true?

A. A seller in a 1031 exchange must identify the replacement property within 45 days from close of escrow
B. A seller in a 1031 exchange must close on the replacement property within 180 days of close of escrow on the original property
C. A seller can exclude the capital gain from a 1031 exchange
D. A principal residence, personal use property, or dealer property is not eligible for a 1031 exchange

   C. A seller may defer the capital gain from a 1031 exchange, not exclude the gain.

Before the parties to a tax-deferred exchange can qualify for the tax benefit, they must provide notice of the exchange within:

A. 15 days
B. 30 days
C. 45 days
D. 90 days

   C. The notice period required by the IRS for tax-deferred exchanges is 45 days.

Agent Amy has a listing on an investment property where she will get a $4,000 commission if it sells. She has another listing on an investment property where she'll get a $5,000 commission if it sells. If she arranges an exchange of the two properties, her commission would be:

A. $4,000
B. $5,000
C. $9,000
D. None, because it was an exchange rather than a sale

   C. A real estate agent who arranges a section 1031 exchange (often referred to as a 1031 facilitator) may receive compensation from both parties to the exchange.

III. **Exclusion of Gain from Sale of Principal Residence** – Under current law, a taxpayer may exclude the entire gain on the sale of his principal residence, up to $250,000 if the taxpayer is filing a single return, or $500,000 if the taxpayer is married and filing a joint return. Any amount in excess of these limits will be taxed at the capital gains rate.

   A. **Eligibility** – To qualify for this exclusion, the seller must have both owned and used the property as a principal residence for at least *two years during the previous five-year period.*

217

IV. **Deductions for Property Owners** – There are a number of income tax deductions allowed to real property owners, including:

    A. **Depreciation Deductions** – When a taxpayer owns investment property or property used in a trade or business, she can claim annual losses due to depreciation. The amount that can be claimed is controlled by law and is spread out over a number of years; for instance, residential property is depreciated over 27½ years, while commercial property is depreciated over 39 years. (Depreciation deductions are sometimes called cost recovery deductions.)

> Straight-line depreciation is a depreciation technique that presumes that an equal amount of depreciation occurs each year.

        1. **Examples of depreciable property** – Rental property, business or factory equipment, and even commercial fruit orchards may be depreciated. But remember that principal residences, personal use property, and vacant land (or the land that depreciable buildings sit on) are not depreciable.

        2. **Subtracted from initial basis** – Allowable depreciation is subtracted from the property's basis upon its sale, whether or not the deduction was actually taken each year.

    B. **Repairs** – Deductions for repairs are allowed for properties other than principal residences and personal use property. Repairs, unlike capital expenditures, are oriented toward keeping the property in ordinary operating condition.

    C. **Property Tax and Special Assessment Deductions** – General real estate taxes are 100% deductible for any type of property. Special assessments for repairs or maintenance are deductible, but those for new improvements (like new sidewalks) are not deductible.

> General property taxes are 100% deductible.

    D. **Mortgage Interest Deductions** – For most real property, interest paid on a mortgage or deed of trust is deductible. Points paid on a loan are also deductible. Repayment of the loan's principal, however, is never deductible.

> Mortgage interest is 100% deductible on mortgage debt up to $1,000,000 used to buy, build, or improve a first or second residence.

        1. **Limitations** – A taxpayer may deduct interest paid on a mortgage or deed of trust debt up to $1,000,000 used to buy, build, or improve a first or second residence. The taxpayer may also deduct interest on a home equity loan of up to $100,000. If a loan amount exceeds this limit, interest on the excess is not deductible.

Sample questions

When depreciating property, which of the following statements is false?

A. Depreciation on a single-family home is done using the straight-line method
B. Depreciation deductions affect the taxpayer's eventual gain or loss on resale of the property
C. Vacant land cannot be depreciated
D. Depreciation may be known as cost recovery

> A. *Depreciation is only allowed on property used for the production of income or used in a trade or business.*

Miguel bought his home five years ago for $375,000, and made improvements worth $25,000. If he sells the property for $450,000 and pays a 6% commission on the sale, what capital gains can Miguel exclude?

A. $0
B. $23,000
C. $27,000
D. $75,000

> B. *First, add the cost of improvements to the original cost of the property. $375,000 + $25,000 = $400,000. Next, figure out the net sale proceeds after the selling commission is deducted. $450,000 - 6% = $423,000. Deduct the adjusted value of the home from the net proceeds to find the capital gain (which will be excluded under the principal residence exclusion rule). $423,000 - $400,000 = $23,000.*

All of the following are tax deductible, except:

A. property taxes
B. special assessments
C. repairs made to rental property
D. mortgage interest

> B. *Special assessments for new improvements are not tax deductible.*

A homeowner bought his home for $150,000. Ten years later, he refinanced his mortgage and borrowed $100,000. Which of the following is true for this type of property?

A. Interest on the difference between the original loan amount and the refinanced amount is not deductible
B. Interest on only half of the difference between the original amount and refinanced amount is deductible
C. Interest on loans such as this one for the purchase or refinance of a principal residence is deductible
D. Interest deductibility will depend on the borrower's tax bracket

> C. *For a principal residence, interest on a home equity loan of up to $100,000 is deductible, regardless of the size of the purchase loan, and regardless of the taxpayer's income.*

Chapter Quiz

1. Some investments allow the taxpayer to reduce her current tax bill by deducting losses from income from another source. These investments are often referred to as tax:

   A. brackets
   B. credits
   C. deductions
   D. shelters

2. An investor rents a property to a tenant. For tax purposes, depreciation on this property is based on:

   A. market value, plus capital improvements, minus land value
   B. market value, plus rental income, minus land value
   C. price, plus capital improvements, minus land value
   D. price, plus rental income, minus land value

3. If you make an improvement to property in order to extend its useful life or add to its value, it is referred to as a:

   A. capital depreciation
   B. capital gain
   C. capital basis
   D. capital improvement

4. A property owner would like to use a tax-deferred exchange. The owner's property would qualify if it was:

   A. a principal residence
   B. financed over a 30-year loan term
   C. owner-occupied
   D. used in a business or trade

5. After the sale of a property in a 1031 exchange, the seller must close on the new property within:

   A. 10 days
   B. 30 days
   C. 45 days
   D. 180 days

6. For income tax purposes, a homeowner can deduct:

   A. property taxes
   B. principal payments on a mortgage
   C. capital expenditures
   D. the adjusted basis

7. A single homeowner sells her home. Which of the following federal tax rules applies to her?

   A. The homeowner can depreciate the improvements on the property as long as the depreciation does not exceed $250,000
   B. The homeowner may defer the payment of capital gains tax if $250,000 or less is rolled over into the purchase of a new primary residence in the next two years
   C. The homeowner may exclude the payment of capital gains tax if she has lived in the home two out of the last five years and the exclusion does not exceed $250,000
   D. The homeowner must pay capital gains tax within one year of the sale of the property

8. The costs of which of the following could be deducted as expenses in the year incurred from the income taxes of the owner of an investment property?

   A. Adding a swimming pool
   B. Installing a new HVAC system
   C. Prepaying additional principal on the mortgage
   D. Repainting the building

9. Milo is filing his federal income tax return. He can deduct:

   A. capital improvements he's made to his home
   B. the interest paid on his mortgage
   C. the principal paid on his mortgage
   D. maintenance expenses for his home

10. Which of the following items would a residential homeowner be able to deduct on her income taxes?

    A. Depreciation
    B. Maintenance expenses
    C. Points paid on the mortgage
    D. The downpayment at the time of purchase

Answer Key

1. D. A tax shelter is an investment that generates income, while also offering offsetting credits or deductions, in order to minimize the taxes on the income.

2. C. Allowable depreciation deductions reduce the taxpayer's adjusted basis in the property. Adjusted basis is calculated by starting with initial basis (the cost of obtaining the property), adding capital expenditures, and subtracting depreciation deductions. The value of the land must also be discounted; land does not wear out, so it is not depreciable.

3. D. A capital improvement, or capital expenditure, is an expense incurred by the property owner to improve the property.

4. D. Tax-free exchanges may be used for unimproved investment property, income-producing property, or property used in a trade or business. Principal residences and personal use properties are not eligible.

5. D. Once a Section 1031 exchange (tax-deferred or "tax-free" exchange) has been arranged, the parties must close the transaction within 180 days.

6. A. A real property owner can deduct the property taxes she pays.

7. C. Under current federal law, a taxpayer filing singly may exclude the entire gain from sale of a principal residence, up to $250,000. The seller must have owned and used the property as a principal residence for at least two of the previous five years.

8. D. Repairs to keep an investment property in ordinary operating condition are deductible in the year they are performed. This would include repainting. Adding a pool or installing a new furnace would be considered capital expenditures, which have tax advantages too but are not deductible in the year they are made.

9. B. Interest paid on a mortgage is deductible. Principal payments are not. Capital improvements factor in when property is sold.

10. C. Points paid in connection with a mortgage loan are considered by the IRS to be prepaid interest, and therefore are deductible on a homeowner's income taxes just as mortgage interest is.

Chapter 15
Civil Rights and Fair Housing

I. **Civil Rights Act of 1866** – This law states that "All citizens of the United States shall have the same right, in every State and Territory as is enjoyed by white citizens thereof to inherit, purchase, lease, sell, hold, and convey real and personal property." The act prohibits discrimination based on *race*, with no exceptions.

The Civil Rights Act of 1866 prohibits discrimination on the basis of race only.

    A. *Jones v. Mayer* – The U.S. Supreme Court upheld the act in the landmark 1968 case of *Jones v. Mayer*. The Court ruled that the Civil Rights Act of 1866 prohibits all racial discrimination in the sale or rental of property, and that the act is constitutional based on the *13th Amendment*, which prohibits slavery.

II. **Federal Fair Housing Act** – Contained in *Title VIII* of the *Civil Rights Act of 1968*, the *Fair Housing Act* is intended to provide fair housing opportunity throughout the United States.

Title VIII of the Civil Rights Act of 1968 prohibits discrimination in the sale or lease of residential property.

    A. **Protected Classes** – The act makes it illegal to discriminate on the basis of *race, color, religion, sex, national origin, disability, or familial status* in the sale or lease of residential property, or in the sale or lease of vacant land for the construction of residential buildings.

        1. **Nonresidential transactions** – The act does not apply to nonresidential transactions, such as those involving commercial or industrial properties.

        2. **Real estate licensees are covered** – The law prohibits discrimination in real estate advertising and brokerage. An agent approached by a seller who wishes to violate the federal Fair Housing Act should decline the listing.

    B. **Exemptions** – While the Fair Housing Act applies to the majority of residential real estate transactions, there are four types of transactions that are exempt from the act:

        1. **Sale of home by owner** – The law does not apply to the sale or rental of a single-family home by its owner, provided that: (1) the owner does not own more than three such homes; (2) no real estate licensee is employed in the transaction; and (3) no discriminatory advertising is used.

        2. **Residential rental** – The law does not apply to the rental of a unit or a room in a dwelling with up to four units, provided that: (1) the owner occupies one of the units as her residence; (2) no real estate licensee is employed; and (3) no discriminatory advertising is used.

3. **Religious or nonprofit organizations** – In dealing with their own property in noncommercial transactions, religious societies or nonprofit organizations may limit occupancy or give preference to their own members, so long as membership isn't restricted on the basis of race, color, or national origin.

4. **Private clubs** – Private clubs with lodgings that aren't open to the public and that aren't operated for a commercial purpose may limit occupancy to, or give preference to, their own members.

C. **Prohibited Acts** – The Fair Housing Act prohibits a number of acts if they are done on the basis of race, color, religion, sex, national origin, disability, or familial status.

1. **Refusing to rent or sell** – The act prohibits refusing to rent or sell residential property after receiving a bona fide offer.

2. **Refusing to negotiate** – The act prohibits refusing to negotiate for the sale or rental of residential property, or otherwise making it unavailable.

3. **Changing terms** – The act prohibits changing the terms of sale or lease for different potential buyers or tenants.

4. **Discriminatory advertising** – The act prohibits using advertising that indicates a preference or intent to discriminate.

5. **Discriminatory misrepresentation** – The act prohibits representing that the property is not available for inspection, sale, or rent when it is in fact available.

6. **Discriminatory loan criteria** – The act prohibits using discriminatory criteria when making a housing loan.

7. **Blockbusting** – The act prohibits blockbusting. *Blockbusting* is the attempt to induce owners to list or sell their homes by predicting that members of another race, ethnic group, or minority will be moving into the neighborhood, and that this influx will have an undesirable effect on property values. This is also called *panic selling*.

8. **Steering** – The act prohibits steering. *Steering* is the channeling of prospective buyers or tenants toward or away from specific neighborhoods based on their race, religion, national origin, etc., in order to maintain or change the character of those neighborhoods. An agent should not disclose the racial composition of a neighborhood when discussing properties.

A landlord may collect information needed to determine whether a prospective tenant can afford the rent.

Note: An agent may refuse to show a property to a prospective buyer if the seller has asked the agent not to show the property while he is out of town.

9. **Redlining** – The act prohibits redlining. *Redlining* is a lender's refusal to make a loan because of the racial or ethnic composition of the neighborhood where the security property is located.

10. **Fair Housing poster** – HUD regulations require places of business that handle the sale or rental of dwellings to display a Fair Housing poster with the Equal Housing Opportunity logo.

D. **Disability and Familial Status** – Originally, the Fair Housing Act did not prohibit discrimination based on disability (referred to as "handicap" in the statute) or familial status; these classifications were added to the law in 1988.

1. **Disability** – It is illegal to discriminate against someone because he has a physical disability or mental impairment that substantially limits major life activities.

a. **Drug addiction excluded** – The definition of disability includes people with mental illness, chronic alcoholism, or AIDS. However, it does not protect those who are a direct threat to the health or safety of others or who are engaged in illegal activity, such as use of controlled substances.

b. **Modifications to unit** – A landlord must allow a disabled tenant to make reasonable modifications to the unit at the tenant's expense, so long as the modifications are necessary for the tenant's full use and enjoyment of the premises.

    i. **Restoration of premises** – The landlord may require the tenant to restore the premises to their original condition at the end of the tenancy.

c. **Exceptions to rules** – A landlord must make reasonable exceptions to rules to accommodate disabled tenants. For instance, a landlord with a no pets policy would be required to rent to a disabled person with a guide dog. The landlord could, however, charge that person for any damage caused to the apartment by the guide dog.

d. **Wheelchair accessibility** – Wheelchair accessibility rules apply to newer residential construction with four or more units. For multi-story units where there is no elevator, only the first-floor units need to be accessible.

225

2. **Familial status** – Discrimination on the basis of *familial status* refers to discrimination against a person because he has a child under 18 living with him. Parents, legal guardians, pregnant women, and those in the process of obtaining custody of a child are protected against discrimination on the basis of familial status.

   a. **Housing for older persons** – Generally, "adults only" complexes, or complexes separated into "adult" and "family" areas, are prohibited. However, children may be excluded from: (1) properties created under a government program intended to help the elderly; (2) properties intended for and solely occupied by persons 62 years or older; or (3) properties intended to house persons 55 years old or older, where at least 80% of the units are occupied by at least one person who is 55 years old or older.

   b. **Advertising** – Language in advertisements is considered a key indicator of whether or not a property is intended for older persons.

   c. **Number of occupants** – A landlord may refuse to rent to a family that is too large for the rental unit under consideration.

E. **Enforcement** – The Fair Housing Act is enforced by the *Department of Housing and Urban Development* (HUD) through its *Office of Fair Housing and Equal Opportunity*.

   1. **HUD conciliates** – If a discrimination complaint is filed with HUD, the agency will investigate the complaint, confer with the parties, and attempt to persuade the offender to abide by the law.

   2. **Administrative hearing** – If conciliation fails, HUD will conduct an *administrative hearing* with HUD attorneys litigating on behalf of the complainant.

   3. **Federal court** – If the parties wish, they can try the matter in federal court and bypass the administrative hearing. However, a federal court does not have the power to suspend or revoke a real estate license; only the Director of Licensing may do that.

A landlord may refuse to rent to a family that is too large for the rental unit under consideration.

The federal Fair Housing Act is enforced by the Department of Housing and Urban Development (HUD).

A complaint must be filed with HUD within one year of the alleged discrimination.

Sample questions

A developer lists 20 different properties in a subdivision, with four different licensees. Each licensee gets his or her own model unit to work from. Which of the following is true?

A. Each licensee must mention the other licensees' offerings to all visitors
B. Each model must display the Fair Housing logo
C. Each model must display the licensee's license
D. Each visitor must receive a copy of the Condominium Buyer's Handbook

> B. *HUD regulations require the display of a Fair Housing poster with the Equal Housing Opportunity logo in any place of business where the business involves the selling or renting of dwellings.*

Under Title VIII of the Civil Rights Act of 1968, some transactions are exempt. Which of the situations below would be exempted and not a violation of the act?

A. A church-owned apartment complex where language in the lease restricts tenancy to members of a specific national origin
B. Members of a certain ethnic group are denied lodging in facilities operated by a private club for commercial purposes
C. An unlisted home that is for sale by owner, where the only advertising is a sign in front of the property that reads simply "For Sale"
D. An absentee owner who rents units in a four-plex without the help of a real estate broker

> C. *The federal Fair Housing Act (Title VIII of the Civil Rights Act of 1968) does not apply to the sale or rental of a single-family home by its owner, provided that the owner doesn't own more than three such homes, no real estate broker is used, and no discriminatory advertising is used.*

Which of the following situations would be exempt under the Fair Housing Act?

A. A religious organization refuses to allow people of a particular national origin to spend the night in its temporary crisis housing
B. An elderly homeowner who rents out a room in her house asks that no people of a particular national origin apply, in her classified ad
C. The owner of a four-plex lives in one unit and refuses to rent the other three units to students because of their national origin
D. The owner of a house refuses to sell the property to buyers because of their national origin, after his real estate agent confirms that is allowed

> C. *The Fair Housing Act allows an exemption for the rental of a unit in a dwelling of up to four units, so long as the owner lives in one of the units, employs no real estate agent, and uses no discriminatory advertising.*

Which of the following pieces of information may an apartment property manager gather about applicants?

A. Age
B. Employment history
C. National origin
D. Social affiliations

B. *A property manager customarily gathers information about rental appli-cants' employment history, as a gauge of their financial stability and ability to pay the rent. National origin is a protected class under the Fair Housing Act, and asking about national origin would violate the act. While age and social affiliations are not protected classes in the Fair Housing Act, ques-tions about them are potentially problematic because they may implicate familial status and religion, which are protected classes.*

Which of the following rental transactions would be covered by the Fair Housing Act if no real estate agent were involved?

A. Owner-occupant rents a unit in a four-unit dwelling, using a nondiscriminatory ad
B. Owner-occupant of a duplex rents to a neighbor's son without advertising the unit
C. Rental of a unit in a triplex, using no discriminatory advertising
D. Owner rents out one room in her residence, without using any advertising

C. *A residential rental transaction can be exempt from the Fair Housing Act only if the property is a single-family home and the owner has no more than three such homes, or if the property has no more than four units and the owner is residing on the property. Option C does not indicate that the owner is occupying one of the units in the triplex, so the Fair Housing Act would apply to the transaction.*

Which of the following actions by a real estate agent would be illegal?

A. Asking a disabled client if there are special features he might need in a house
B. Showing only houses located in mostly Latino neighborhoods to a Latino family
C. Telling a client, during prequalification, that her bad credit score makes an affordable loan unlikely
D. Truthfully answering questions from a buyer about the demographics of a neighborhood

B. *If a real estate agent channels prospective buyers toward particular neighborhoods because of their national origin, that is considered steer-ing, which is a violation of the federal Fair Housing Act.*

The term "familial status" in the federal Fair Housing Act refers to the presence of:

A. adult children of tenants living on the property
B. children under the age of 18 living on the property
C. disabled persons living on the property
D. unmarried persons living on the property

B. *Discrimination based on familial status refers to discrimination against someone because a person under 18 years old is or will be living with him or her. This includes legal guardians, pregnant women, and people in the process of obtaining custody of a child, in addition to parents.*

A prospective tenant asks a licensee to show him only properties that do not al-low children. How should the licensee respond?

A. Say that only bona fide retirement communities may exclude children
B. Say that the law requires that all available properties must be shown
C. Say that to do so would be steering, and therefore illegal
D. Show properties that are billed as "adults only"

A. *The Fair Housing Act forbids "adults only" apartment complexes. There is, however, an exemption for properties that qualify as "housing for older persons," such as those intended for and solely occupied by persons 62 or older.*

III. **Equal Credit Opportunity Act** – The *Equal Credit Opportunity Act* applies to all credit transactions, including residential real estate loans. The act prohibits discrimination in lending based on race, color, religion, national origin, sex, marital status, age (as long as the applicant is at least 18), or because the applicant's income is derived partly or wholly from public assistance.

IV. **Home Mortgage Disclosure Act** – The *Home Mortgage Disclosure Act* requires lenders to make certain disclosures each year regarding the loans they issue. These disclosures are intended to help identify areas where few or no home loans are being made, in order to investigate whether lenders are engaged in redlining.

V. **Americans with Disabilities Act** – The *Americans with Disabilities Act* is a federal law intended to ensure that disabled persons have equal access to public facilities. The ADA requires any place of public accommodation (a private entity with nonresidential facilities open to the public, if the operation of the facilities affects commerce) or commercial facility to take readily achievable steps to make the building accessible to the disabled. For instance, the owner of a real estate office (or any other commercial building open to the public) may need to take steps such as adding a wheelchair-accessible entrance and grab bars in restrooms. Private clubs and religious organizations are exempt from the ADA.

Sample question

Which of the following describes a violation of the Americans with Disabilities Act?

A. A recently built one-story apartment complex with doorways too narrow for wheelchair users
B. A rental house that does not have a wheelchair ramp at its entrance
C. A shopping center without wheelchair-accessible restrooms
D. An older 40-unit apartment building without elevators

C. *The Americans with Disabilities Act requires public accommodations to be accessible to the disabled. This would include a shopping center, as it is open to the public and affects commerce. The ADA does not apply to residential properties (although the Fair Housing Act does impose some restrictions on new apartment construction).*

Chapter Quiz

1. Which of the following is true concerning federal fair housing laws?

   A. Enforcement may be brought about by filing a complaint with the Dept. of Housing and Urban Development
   B. Parts of these laws were overturned by the Supreme Court in the case of *Jones v. Mayer*
   C. They only apply to racial discrimination
   D. They preempt state-level antidiscrimination laws

2. Which law prohibits discrimination in real estate transactions based on race, with no exceptions?

   A. Civil Rights Act of 1866
   B. Civil Rights Act of 1964
   C. Civil Rights Act of 1968
   D. Fair Housing Act

3. A minority buyer with a disabled daughter makes a full-price offer on a property. The home doesn't have any grab bars in the bathroom and the front door isn't wide enough for a wheelchair. The seller informs the buyer's agent that the property wouldn't be suitable for the daughter, so he is going to refuse the offer. The buyer's agent should:

   A. explain the situation to the buyer, and advise her to consult an attorney and/or file a complaint with HUD
   B. instruct the seller to make those modifications at his own expense
   C. not say anything to the buyer about the circumstances, but help her find a more suitable property
   D. not say anything to the buyer, since a seller can choose who to sell his home to

4. A licensee hears that a religious group will be opening a commune in a neighborhood. He begins contacting neighbors and telling them about this, encouraging them to list their properties with him before property values decline. This would be:

   A. blockbusting
   B. redlining
   C. steering
   D. legal

5. A local bank refuses to make residential loans in a particular section of town because of the ethnic background of its residents. This is a discriminatory practice called:

   A. blockbusting
   B. redlining
   C. steering
   D. collusion

6. A prospective tenant applies to rent a unit in a 12-unit apartment building, where the owner lives in one of the units and handles all lease transactions on his own. The tenant is turned down, and believes he has been discriminated against on the basis of his race. This would be:

   A. lawful, because it is a 12-unit building
   B. lawful, because the owner lives on the premises
   C. lawful, because no real estate agent was used
   D. unlawful, because this is a violation of the Fair Housing Act

7. An Asian-American buyer asks to be shown homes that are located in primarily Asian neighborhoods. If a real estate agent complies with his wishes, this is:

   A. illegal, as it is blockbusting
   B. illegal, as it is steering
   C. legal, as it is done at the buyer's request
   D. legal, as the Fair Housing Act has an exception for single-family homes

8. A property manager of a ten-unit building shows an apartment to a woman who uses a wheelchair. The woman says that she would need to make some modifications, such as adding grab bars in the shower and removing some carpeting in the bedroom. The landlord:

   A. can refuse to rent to the tenant because of the tenant's proposals

   B. must allow the tenant to make the modifications at her own expense, but can require her to restore the property at the end of the lease

   C. must allow the tenant to make the modifications at her own expense, and cannot require the tenant to restore the property at the end of the lease

   D. must make the modifications and pay for the expenses himself

9. A seller tells a real estate agent that she has lived in the neighborhood for a long time and would like to be selective about who buys her house; she would like the agent to tell her the race and nationality of all prospective buyers. How should the agent respond?

   A. Agree to it, but avoid using any discriminatory advertising

   B. Agree to it, as the agent owes the seller the duty of loyalty

   C. End her agency with the seller, as the agent's duty is to find the most lucrative offer for the seller regardless of race

   D. End her agency with the seller, as it would be a violation of the federal Fair Housing Act

10. The manager of a 6-story, 18-apartment building carefully screens tenant applications, in order to make sure that tenants who use wheelchairs are assigned to the first floor. This:

    A. is allowed if there's no elevator to the upper floors

    B. is an example of a property manager making reasonable accommodations

    C. violates the Fair Housing Act

    D. violates of the Civil Rights Act of 1866

Answer Key

1. A. The Fair Housing Act is enforced through the Department of Housing and Urban Development's Office of Fair Housing and Equal Opportunity. *Jones v. Mayer* upheld the application of the Civil Rights Act of 1866 in sale or rental of real property. State laws are not preempted by federal antidiscrimination laws; in some cases, they may be stricter than federal law.

2. A. The Civil Rights Act of 1866 prevents discrimination based on race or color in any real estate transaction, without exception. The 1964 Act is limited to programs where the federal government offers financial assistance, while the Fair Housing Act (a part of the 1968 Act) is limited to residential transactions and has several exemptions.

3. A. The Fair Housing Act would prohibit the seller from refusing to sell a property after receiving a bona fide offer because of a buyer's family member's disability. The buyer's agent should let the buyer know about his options for legal recourse.

4. A. Blockbusting occurs when a licensee tries to induce homeowners to list their properties by predicting that persons from a protected class (usually on the basis of race, but also potentially on the basis of religion) will be moving into the neighborhood and that there will be undesirable consequences.

5. B. Refusing to make loans for discriminatory reasons is redlining, which is illegal.

6. D. If the rental application was in fact turned down because of the tenant's race, this would be a violation of the Fair Housing Act. There is no exemption that applies to this transaction: even though the owner lives on the premises and did not employ a real estate agent, the "Mrs. Murphy" exemption only applies to dwellings with four or fewer units.

7. C. It is legal for an agent to show a buyer homes in the neighborhoods that the buyer asks to be shown, even if the buyer has made decisions about neighborhoods based on race. Nothing in the Fair Housing Act requires an agent to show buyers houses against their will.

8. B. The Fair Housing Act says that a disabled tenant may make reasonable modifications to a leased property at his own expense. The tenant can be required to restore the premises at the end of the tenancy.

9. D. An agent faced with a client who wants her to violate the Fair Housing Act should refuse to follow the instructions and explain that following the instructions would be a violation of federal law.

10. A. The Fair Housing Act has wheelchair-accessibility requirements for apartment complexes built after 1988. However, apartments on the second floor or above in multi-story buildings are required to be wheelchair-accessible only if there is an elevator in the building.

Chapter 16
Property Management

I. **Investing in Real Estate** – An investment is an asset that is expected to generate a *return* (a profit). A return on an investment can take various forms, including interest, dividends, or appreciation in value.

   A. **Types of Investments** – Investment can be divided into two general categories:

   1. **Ownership investments** – With *ownership investments*, the investor takes an ownership interest in the asset. Real estate and stocks are examples of ownership investments. Ownership investments are often called *equities*.

      a. **Hedge against inflation** – Because equity investments appreciate instead of just paying interest like debt investments, they are considered a better hedge against inflation.

   2. **Debt investments** – A *debt investment*, such as a bond, is a loan to an investor. A lender loans money with the expectation that it will be repaid within a certain period of time at a prescribed rate of interest.

      a. **Portfolio** – Investors often choose to diversify their investments with both ownership investments and debt investments. The mix of investments, plus any cash reserves, is referred to as a *portfolio*. Portfolio income would include dividends, interest, and royalties.

   B. **Investment Characteristics** – An investor looks at three issues when considering any investment: *liquidity*, *risk*, and *return on investment* (yield).

   1. **Liquidity** – A liquid asset is one that can be converted to cash quickly. Cash in a bank is liquid. Mutual funds and stocks are liquid, but not as liquid as cash. Real estate investments are not liquid (turnover in real estate is slower than with other commodities).

      a. **Liquidity vs. rate of return** – The more liquid an investment, the lower the rate of return. Interest rates paid on savings accounts are small compared to other, less liquid, investments.

As a rule, the greater the investment risk, the higher the expected return; the lower the risk, the lower the expected return.

One advantage of investing in real estate is that it acts as a tax shelter.

Equity: the difference between the value of the property and the liens against it.

Leverage: the use of borrowed money to finance an investment such as real estate.

Cash flow: The residual income after deducting from gross income all operating expenses and debt service. Also called spendable income.

2. **Risk** – The most liquid investments are usually the least risky. Quick access to your investment (as with a savings account) makes for a safe investment. Higher risk investments (like mutual funds) are more difficult to convert to cash; it generally takes time. A non-liquid investment, like real estate, could take many months to liquidate, and this could prove costly in a falling market.

C. **Advantages of Investing in Real Estate** – While investing in real estate is riskier than placing your money in a savings account, it usually proves to be a profitable investment over the long run. The advantages of investing in real estate can be broken down into three categories:

1. **Appreciation** – *Appreciation* refers to an increase in a property's value due to changes in the economy or other outside factors. An asset appreciates in value because of inflation and may also appreciate because of a rising demand for the asset. Although real estate values may fluctuate, over a period of several years real estate usually increases in value at a rate equal to or higher than the rate of inflation.

    a. **Building equity** – Appreciation increases the property owner's *equity*. Equity is the difference between the value of the property and the liens against it, so an increase in the property's value increases the owner's equity in the property.

        i. **Net worth** – Equity adds to the net worth of the owner and can be used to secure a home equity loan. Thus, equity in real estate can be used to generate cash even though real estate isn't a liquid asset.

        ii. **Downpayment** – A buyer starts out with equity as soon as he buys a house; the buyer's downpayment instantly creates equity in the property.

2. **Leverage** – *Leverage* is the act of using borrowed money to invest in an asset. If the asset appreciates, the investor earns money on the money she borrowed as well as the money of her own that she invested.

3. **Cash flow** – Many real estate investments generate a positive *cash flow,* as well as appreciate in value. Cash flow is defined as spendable income—the amount of money left after all the property's expenses have been paid, including operating costs, mortgage payments, and taxes.

a. **Cash-on-cash ratio** – *Cash-on-cash* refers to a property's first year before-tax cash flow, divided by the initial investment. It pinpoints the ratio between cash invested (equity) and cash received.

Cash-on-cash: the first year before-tax cash flow divided by the equity invested.

b. **Sale-leaseback** – Another way in which a property can generate cash flow is through a *sale-leaseback*. In a sale-leaseback, the owner of a building (typically a commercial property) sells the building to an investor, but then (by prior agreement) leases the property back from the investor and continues to use it for income-producing purposes.

Sale-leaseback: A form of financing in which the owner of commercial or industrial property sells the property and leases it back from the buyer. The seller of the property has a leasehold interest, and becomes a lessee.

   i. **Deductible business expense** – The seller can deduct rent paid to lease the property from his income taxes as a business expense. The sale-leaseback also frees up capital and removes mortgage debt from the owner's balance sheet.

   ii. **Purchaser's concerns** – The purchaser in a sale-leaseback transaction would be concerned not only with the value of the property, but also with the terms of the lease and the lessee's credit.

   iii. **Buyback** – The agreement may contain the seller's right to repurchase the property at a later date. If such a provision isn't included, there is no guarantee the seller will be able to repurchase later.

D. **Profit and Loss Statements** – A profit and loss statement helps an investor determine net profit for a property. It helps the owner make projections for the future and decide what changes in management techniques should be made.

Sample questions

In a sale-leaseback:

A. the grantor becomes the grantee
B. the grantor becomes the lessee
C. the real estate agent has purchased the property
D. the property is sold at a loss

   B. The grantor (seller) sells the property, but retains possession of the land as a lessee (tenant).

A buyer would like to start out with a significant amount of equity invested in his house, so that he can reborrow against the equity if necessary. When structuring a loan, what should the buyer's highest priority be?

A. Largest downpayment possible
B. Longest loan term possible
C. Lowest interest rate possible
D. Smallest downpayment possible

    A. *Equity refers to the difference between the property's value and the loans against the property. Therefore, the larger the downpayment the buyer makes, the more equity in the property he will have initially.*

One tax advantage of investing in real estate is:

A. high liquidity
B. low risk
C. homestead protection
D. sheltering of income

    D. *Real estate investment is often thought of as a "tax shelter" because it serves to partially shelter investors from income tax liability.*

II. Property Management – A real estate investor may need to hire a property manager to oversee the day-to-day operations of a large property. Many brokerages engage in property management to some degree.

    A. Management Agreement – The first step in the management process is entering into a *management agreement*. The management agreement is a personal services contract that establishes a fiduciary relationship between the property manager and the property owner (the landlord). The property manager becomes the property owner's agent.

> A property management agreement ordinarily does not give the manager the responsibility of investing the owner's profits.

        1. Written agreement – The management agreement must be in writing and signed by both parties. It is very important for the written document to contain all the terms and conditions of the agreement. It is especially important that the exact *duties and powers* of the manager (i.e., the scope of his authority) be explicitly stated. It will, for instance, authorize the manager to pay for the property's operating expenses. The agreement should also state how the manager will be compensated. If a manager's duties change, the management agreement should be amended.

        2. Legal description – The management agreement should contain a legal description of the property.

3. **Description of manager's responsibilities** – The property manager will prepare a *summary statement* (on property operations and the property's financial status) on a regular basis. The manager will also inform the principal about the condition of the property and relevant changes in tax rates, zoning, building codes, local rental trends, and vacancy rates.

   a. **Day-to-day duties** – A property manager's most common day-to-day duties include supervising maintenance and repairs on the property, screening and qualifying tenants, handling tenant disputes, handling security deposits, and negotiating leases on the owner's behalf.

4. **Terminating the relationship** – The agreement should contain a termination date as well as a start date. The relationship between the manager and owner may be terminated by the same methods as any other agency relationship. If the relationship is terminated, the manager should deliver funds held in trust (such as security deposits) to the owner or new property manager.

5. **Compensation** – A property manager is most often compensated through a percentage of the property's gross income.

> Summary statement: the key portion of a property manager's statement of operations, which summarizes income and expenses.

Sample questions

A property manager decides to offer some additional services beyond what is specified in the property management agreement. She may do so after:

A. giving the tenants 30 days' notice
B. obtaining written authorization from the owner
C. providing notice to the Department of Licensing
D. the management agreement is amended in writing

> D. *Whenever the duties and powers of a property manager change, the property management agreement (the document that describes the scope of a property manager's authority) must be amended.*

Andrea owns a small apartment building. She is too busy to manage it herself, so she hired a property manager. The property manager is probably being paid a:

A. small percentage of the property's value
B. percentage of this year's gross income
C. flat fee, plus any kickbacks the manager is able to generate from service providers
D. flat fee, plus a percentage of the previous year's gross income

> B. *Most property managers receive a percentage of the current gross income as their compensation.*

Property management agreements generally include provisions on all of the following EXCEPT the:
A. amount of the security deposit that must be collected from each tenant
B. manager's authority to pay property expenses
C. starting and termination date of the agreement
D. manager's responsibility to provide the owner with management reports

> A. *Deposit amounts are found in the rental agreements, not the property management agreement.*

B. **Management Plan** – Once a manager has entered into a management agreement, the actual business of managing begins. The first (and often most important) step in managing a property is drawing up a management plan. A management plan outlines the manager's strategy for financial management and physical upkeep, and focuses on achieving the owner's goals.

1. **Market analysis** – The property manager will analyze the local market for residential rentals. In particular, she will study the supply of and demand for rentals, as this will help her establish a *rental schedule* (a list of rental rates assigned to the different units).

a. **Supply and demand** – An increase in interest rates will increase demand for rentals, as fewer people will be able to afford to buy. This will allow the manager to charge higher rental rates.

2. **Budget planning** – The property manager will set up a budget of income and operating expenses. *Operating expenses* include fixed expenses like management fees, property taxes, and insurance, as well as variable expenses like utilities, maintenance costs, and repairs. The budget will also take into account vacancies and bad debts, capital improvements, and reserves for replacement, though none of these are considered operating expenses. The budget should include a cash reserve fund for variable expenses. The operating budget does not take debt service into account.

C. **Management Functions** – Day-to-day functions include leasing and tenant relations, marketing, recordkeeping, and maintenance.

1. **Tenant relations** – A property manager will negotiate items like move-in date, length of lease, space requirements, and tenant alterations to the property as part of the leasing process. The manager should also discuss the property's rules and regulations with the tenant.

2. **Marketing** – Supply and demand for rentals, local economic conditions, and the location and type of property all affect the type of marketing used to attract tenants. Many managers offer inducements (like free first month's rent) to tenants. Inexpensive but effective techniques include getting referrals from satisfied tenants, and yard signs.

3. **Recordkeeping** – The manager has the duty to the owner to account for income and expenses. He also has the duty to tenants to properly account for security deposits; they should be placed in a trust account. If the property is sold, security deposits should be transferred to the new owner.

4. **Maintenance** – A manager is delegated the property owner's duties to keep the property habitable. He does so by supervising maintenance and cleaning of the building (although he's not responsible for fixing fixtures installed by tenants). This may take the form of corrective (repair work), preventive (keeping systems functioning), and routine (cleaning buildings and grounds) maintenance.

5. **Insurance** – A property manager must keep the property insured. In addition to hazard insurance (which is known as homeowners insurance when it's for residential properties), liability insurance (which pays for personal injury claims) is necessary. Alternatively, multi-peril coverage covers both hazard and liability. Flood insurance, if appropriate, must be purchased through a private insurer. An insurance underwriter will look at the property's loss history and the buyer's credit, as well as making sure the policyholder has an insurable interest. Insurance usually covers 80% of the value of the dwelling.

Sample questions

A property manager should always try to meet the property owner's specific goals. However, generally, most property managers try to:

A. set the highest rent feasible, and offer as many amenities as possible
B. generate the highest gross income possible (while still maintaining the property)
C. set the lowest rent feasible, and provide as many amenities as possible
D. generate the highest net operating income possible (while still maintaining the property)

    D. *Most owners want the highest net income possible, as long as the property is maintained (to preserve its value).*

A property manager can minimize the behavioral problems of a tenant by:

A. having a firm talk with the tenant about her behavior
B. giving a copy of the rules and regulations to the tenant when she first moves in, and making sure she understands them and agrees to abide by them
C. telling the tenant to mimic the behavior of the other tenants
D. waiting until there is a problem before intervening

> B. *Tenants should always be given a copy of the property's rules and regulations. It's best to go through them with the tenant, explaining them and getting the tenant to make a commitment to abide by them.*

As a property manager, you can best attract new tenants to the property by:

A. talking to other real estate agents in your locale
B. getting referrals from current satisfied tenants
C. developing an intense radio and television ad campaign
D. offering a free flat-screen TV to all applicants

> B. *Referrals from happy tenants is often the best way to find new tenants.*

You are managing a commercial property. When screening potential tenants, the most important thing to consider is:

A. the political affiliation of the potential tenant
B. the potential tenant's financial history, move-in date, and space requirements
C. how many parking spaces the potential tenant needs
D. whether the potential tenant has any special needs

> B. *You should be mostly concerned with the tenant's ability to pay the rent (financial history), how much space he needs, and the move-in date.*

A property manager is responsible for several types of maintenance. Keeping the common areas and the buildings clean, and maintaining the grounds is considered to be:

A. deferred maintenance
B. corrective maintenance
C. preventive maintenance
D. routine maintenance

> D. *Cleaning the building and maintaining the grounds would be considered routine maintenance.*

A property manager manages two large apartment buildings. They're older but well-maintained properties with a 96% occupancy rate. Based on analysis of market rates, the property manager should:

A. lower rental rates to get to 100% occupancy
B. maintain the status quo
C. raise rents, if competitive market analysis confirms this
D. refurbish the properties to improve desirability

> C. *When putting together a management plan, a property manager should perform a market analysis, examining rents at competing properties. This will help determine appropriate rents for her own property.*

III. Leases – A *lease* is both a method of conveyance and a contract. A lease conveys a less-than-freehold (leasehold) estate from the owner (the landlord or *lessor*) to the tenant (the *lessee*).

A. **In Writing** – A lease for any fixed term must be in writing. If the term is longer than one year, the landlord's signature must be acknowledged (notarized). The rental agreement for a periodic tenancy (such as a month-to-month lease) doesn't need to be in writing, unless the rental period is longer than one year.

B. **Only the Landlord's Signature Required** – While both parties to a lease usually sign the contract, only the landlord's signature is necessary. A tenant who takes possession of the property and pays rent is considered to have accepted the terms of the lease.

> Only the landlord's signature is required for a valid lease.

C. **Payment of Rent** – Rent is the consideration paid in exchange for the right to possess the property. Most leases require the rent to be paid at the beginning of the rental period. However, if the lease doesn't specify when the rent is to be paid, it isn't due until the end of the rental period.

> If a lease doesn't state when the rent is due, it is not due until the end of the rental period.

Example: If the tenant is renting on a month-to-month basis and no due date is specified, the rent is due at the end of each month.

D. **Security Deposit** – Most property managers require a security deposit from the tenant when the tenant signs the lease, especially in residential tenancies. This serves as protection against default. The landlord may keep the deposit to cover unpaid rent, cleaning the premises, or repairing damage. No portion of the deposit may be kept on account of reasonable wear and tear.

E. **Renewal** – A lease may contain a provision that gives the tenant an option to renew the lease at the end of its term. Usually the tenant must give notice of her intention to exercise the option before a specific date. The option to renew provision is not an essential lease term.

> An option to renew provision is not essential to a valid lease.

F. **Entry and Inspection** – Except in emergencies, the landlord must give notice before entering the unit. Two days' notice is required in most cases.

G. **Rent Control** – Local ordinances, known as rent control laws, may set limits on how much rent a landlord can charge.

H. **Uniform Residential Landlord-Tenant Act** – Most states have adopted the Uniform Act for their own landlord-tenant laws. The act does not allow a tenant to sign away (abrogate) her rights under the act, as part of signing a lease.

Sample questions

A one-year lease would require all of the following elements to be valid EXCEPT:

A. a description of the property
B. the signature of the landlord
C. notarization of the lease document
D. consideration

> C. A lease for one year or less does not need to be notarized to be valid. Notarization would be required for leases with a longer term.

Several new industries move into a region, making it difficult to find affordable apartments. Responding to the dramatic decrease in the supply of housing, the city council passes an ordinance that restricts the amount of rent that can be charged for certain apartments. This type of ordinance is known as:

A. the Uniform Landlord-Tenant Act
B. rent control
C. a home mortgage restriction law
D. a police power restriction

> B. Any law that limits the amount of rent a landlord can charge tenants is known as rent control.

Which of the following is a requirement for a valid lease?

A. Lease expiration
B. Pet exclusion policy
C. Service agreement
D. Witness

> A. A lease generally needs an expiration date, either the date an estate for years will end, or the date a periodic estate will renew unless proper notice of termination has been given.

I. **Transferring Leased Property** – Leased property may be transferred by *sale, assignment, sublease,* or *novation.*

1. **Sale of leased property** – A landlord can sell leased property to a third person during the lease term, but the property buyer must honor the lease to its conclusion. The new owner cannot cancel the lease or evict the tenant. Similarly, many mortgages contain a *nondisturbance clause,* which protects tenants in the event the mortgagor defaults on the loan.

Sale of leased property does not terminate the lease.

2. **Assignment** – In an assignment, the tenant transfers the entire leasehold interest for the entire unexpired term of the lease. The assignee (new tenant) becomes liable for paying the rent to the landlord, and the assignor (original

When a lease is assigned from one tenant to another, the original tenant (assignor) retains secondary liability; the new tenant (assignee) assumes primary liability.

tenant) becomes secondarily liable for the rent (if the new tenant fails to pay).

3. **Sublease** – A sublease is a transfer of the leasehold estate for a period shorter than the unexpired term. The original tenant retains part of the leasehold estate. An original tenant might take advantage of increased rental rates by subleasing and charging a higher rate to the subtenant than he is paying to the landlord. A tenant may sublease the property unless the lease specifically forbids doing so.

   Example: With 24 months remaining on his lease, the tenant subleases the property to a third party for the next 12 months. The new tenant has an exclusive right to possess the property for one year, at the conclusion of which the original tenant retakes possession of the property for the remainder of the lease term.

   Note: The subtenant is liable to the original tenant for the duration of the sublease. During this time, the original tenant remains liable to the landlord. This is sometimes called a *sandwich lease* because the original tenant is sandwiched between the new tenant and the landlord.

4. **Novation** – A novation occurs when a new lease contract is created and the old contract is extinguished.

   > Novation: when one party to a contract withdraws and a new party is substituted, relieving the withdrawing party of liability.

J. **Termination of a Lease** – A lease for a fixed term terminates automatically at the end of its term. It may also be terminated in a variety of ways before the end of its term.

   1. **Surrender** – A landlord and tenant may mutually agree to terminate their lease. This is called a (mutual) *surrender*.

   2. **Breach of implied covenant of quiet enjoyment** – This covenant exists in every lease, whether it's written or not. It is the landlord's promise that he will refrain from unlawfully interfering with the tenant's possession of the leased property and that no third party will lawfully claim a right to possess the property. The tenant is guaranteed exclusive possession and quiet enjoyment of the property.

      a. **Eviction** – The *covenant of quiet enjoyment* is breached when the tenant is unlawfully evicted from the leased property. There are two types of *eviction*: actual and constructive.

         i. **Actual eviction** – *Actual eviction* occurs when the landlord actually expels the tenant from the property.

Constructive eviction: when a landlord's act (or failure to act) interferes with the tenant's quiet enjoyment of the property, or makes the property unfit for its intended use, to such an extent that the tenant is forced to move out.

Implied warranty of habitability: a warranty, implied by law in every residential lease, that the property is fit for habitation.

Unlawful detainer action: a summary legal action to regain possession of leased property; a suit filed by a landlord to evict a defaulting tenant.

Fixed or gross lease: the rent is set at a fixed amount, and the landlord pays most or all of the operating expenses.

    ii. Constructive eviction – *Constructive eviction* occurs when the landlord causes or permits interference with the tenant's quiet enjoyment of the property (for example, if the roof leaks badly and the landlord refuses to repair it).

3. **Breach of the implied warranty of habitability** – The *warranty of habitability* is implied in every lease. It is the landlord's guarantee that the premises meet all building and housing code regulations that affect health and safety on the premises.

    a. **Failure to repair** – If the property does not meet the criteria, the tenant must notify the landlord, who in turn must correct the noted deficiency. If the landlord fails to correct the problem within certain time limits prescribed by statute, the tenant can terminate the lease on the grounds of constructive eviction.

4. **Failure to pay rent** – If the tenant fails to pay rent, the lease is not automatically terminated. The landlord must first give lawful notice of failure to pay rent. If payment is not forthcoming, she can file an *unlawful detainer* action, asking the court to order the eviction of the tenant.

    a. **Writ of possession** – If the court finds the tenant in default, it may issue a *writ of possession*, which requires the tenant to move out peaceably or be forcibly removed by the sheriff.

    b. **Tenant moves out** – Note that a lease isn't terminated if the tenant simply moves out; the tenant remains liable to the landlord for payments for the remainder of the lease term. However, the landlord must take steps to mitigate the tenant's breach, such as advertising to find a new tenant.

5. **Condemnation or destruction** – Condemnation of the premises by the government or destruction by natural disaster can also result in the premature termination of a lease.

IV. **Types of Leases** – There are five major types of leases:

    A. **Fixed Lease** – Also called a *flat*, *straight*, or *gross lease*, the *fixed lease* provides for a fixed rental payment. The tenant is required to pay a fixed sum of money, and the landlord pays most or all of the property's operating expenses (such as utilities, property taxes, insurance, and maintenance expenses). Fixed leases are most frequently used for residential apartment rentals. They are not commonly used for commercial properties, since the rent stays the same over the long term and can't be adjusted for inflation, which would depress income and lower the property's value.

B. **Net Lease** – A *net lease* requires the tenant to pay the landlord a fixed rent, plus some or all of the operating expenses, such as utilities or maintenance. (In a triple net lease, the tenant is responsible for both of these, plus property taxes.) A commercial tenant may, for tax purposes, write off the operating expenses as business expenses. A net lease does not include payment for the owner's debt service.

> Net lease: requires the tenant to pay some or all of the operating expenses in addition to the base rent paid to the landlord; a triple-net lease requires the tenant to pay all operating expenses.

C. **Graduated Lease** – A *graduated lease* (or *index lease*) is similar to a fixed lease, but it provides for periodic increases in the rent, usually set at specific future dates and often based on some kind of cost-of-living price index. These increases are called for in a graduated lease provision called an *escalation clause*. A graduated lease may be used as incentive for a hard-to-lease property.

D. **Percentage Lease** – A *percentage lease* is typically used for retail property, and the rent is usually based on a percentage of the gross sales from the tenant's business. This type of lease often provides for a minimum rent plus a percentage of the tenant's business income above a stated minimum gross.

> Percentage lease: the rent is often based on a percentage of the tenant's monthly or annual gross sales.

E. **Ground Lease** – When a tenant leases land for the purpose of constructing a building on that land, it is called a *ground lease*. This type of long-term lease is common in areas where land is scarce.

Sample questions

Which of the following is true regarding an assignment?

A. The assignor uses a "transfer lease" to assign the interest to the assignee
B. The lessee receives payments from the assignor
C. An assignment creates a life estate for the assignor
D. All the leasehold interests are transferred to the assignee

> D. With an assignment, the entire remaining term (and leasehold interests) are transferred to the assignee.

A landlord occasionally uses his master key to enter rental houses that he owns while residents are away. He's looking for undisclosed pets, any damage or physical problems, and the like. This would be:

A. allowed because of his duty to supervise tenants' use of the property
B. not allowed under the Fair Housing Act
C. not allowed under the implied covenant of quiet enjoyment
D. not allowed under the tenants' freehold estate rights

    C. A landlord may enter the leased premises only with advance notice or the tenant's permission. Entry without notice or permission is a breach of the implied covenant of quiet enjoyment, the landlord's promise that the tenant's exclusive possession of the property will not be disturbed.

A tenant comes home one day to find the heat turned off because the landlord failed to pay the electric bill as agreed. If the tenant decides to leave the apartment, this is known as:

A. statutory eviction
B. false eviction
C. actual eviction
D. constructive eviction

    D. Constructive eviction occurs when a landlord's act or failure to act interferes with the tenant's quiet enjoyment of the property, or makes the property unfit for its intended use, to such an extent that the tenant is forced to move out.

Martin buys a four-unit apartment building. When ownership transfers to him, what happens to the current leases on the four apartment units?

A. The leases are terminated
B. The leases are unaffected
C. The leases are still in force, but Martin can raise the rent
D. The leases are still in force, but Martin can cancel them within 30 days

    B. The existing leases remain valid, and Martin must abide by their terms.

A type of lease that allows the lessor to share in the increasing sales generated by a particular property is a/an:

A. percentage lease
B. graduated lease
C. index lease
D. net lease

    A. Percentage leases are frequently used in shopping centers and with other retail properties. They enable the landlord to share in the tenant's profits because of the pedestrian traffic assured by the leased property's location.

Marcia rents an apartment. She pays a fixed rent amount each month and her landlord pays all other expenses associated with the property. What type of lease do they have?

A. Percentage lease
B. Ground lease
C. Net lease
D. Gross lease

    D. The lease described is a gross lease (also known as a flat or fixed lease).

Chapter Quiz

1. Property management for residential property is different from property management for commercial property, in that a manager would be more concerned about:

   A. a written lease for a residential tenant than for a commercial tenant

   B. future space needs of a commercial tenant than of a residential tenant

   C. the credit rating of a commercial tenant than of a residential tenant

   D. the security deposit of a commercial tenant than of a residential tenant

2. A property manager bases the operating budget on:

   A. rental rates

   B. the rental market

   C. anticipated expenses and revenue

   D. state landlord-tenant law

3. A property management agreement must contain which of the following?

   A. A salary for the property manager

   B. What percentage of the property's net income will be used as the manager's commission

   C. Marketing plans

   D. The property manager's scope of authority

4. A property management agreement is amended to take into account some changing circumstances. The amendment must be signed by the:

   A. owner and the designated broker for the firm providing management services

   B. owner and the licensee who negotiated the management arrangement

   C. owner and tenant

   D. owner, tenant, and real estate licensee

5. A tenant signs a one-year lease. Four months later the owner sells the property to a third party, who wants to move in immediately. Which of the following is correct?

   A. The new owner takes ownership subject to the lease and must wait until the lease ends to move in

   B. The landlord (the previous owner) can force the tenant to move out as a matter of law

   C. The new owner holds title and can force the tenant to move out

   D. The lease automatically terminates whenever the property is sold

6. A landowner is negotiating the lease of his land to a developer who wants to build a mall there. They should use a:

   A. gross lease

   B. ground lease

   C. net lease

   D. percentage lease

7. What is the most important consideration for a property manager who is deciding on appropriate rental rates?

   A. How many units are in the property

   B. Proximity of the property to places of employment

   C. The number of units available in the city

   D. The rental rates for similar properties in the same market

8. A residential property manager should inform prospective tenants about:

   A. a neighbor who is an alcoholic

   B. the planned removal of a swimming pool

   C. the property's appraised value

   D. the racial composition of the tenants

9. As a property manager, you may:

   A. advertise that units are available, even when they're not

   B. use different application forms for minority applicants

   C. require credit checks for some applicants, but not for others

   D. offer inducements to prospective tenants

10. To avoid tenant problems, a landlord is best off using a standardized lease form that includes:

    A. a copy of the Uniform Landlord Tenant Act
    B. a warranty of quiet enjoyment
    C. a tenancy at will provision
    D. specific rules and regulations

11. A property manager is replacing the filters on the building's air conditioning units, which must be done quarterly. Which kind of maintenance is this?

    A. Corrective
    B. Deferred
    C. Housekeeping
    D. Preventive

12. A property manager usually:

    A. appeals tax assessments
    B. makes investment decisions regarding the property's income
    C. makes financing decisions
    D. oversees maintenance projects

13. Bartholomew leases several acres from Stan so he can grow strawberries. However, when Bartholomew arrives at the property to plant his strawberries, he realizes that the true owner of the property is already farming the acreage. Bartholomew does not have to pay rent to Stan because of the:

    A. covenant of quiet enjoyment
    B. covenant of right to convey
    C. covenant of seisin
    D. warranty of habitability

14. Which of the following is true regarding a sublease?

    A. The lessee is no longer liable to the lessor
    B. The lessee is still liable to the lessor if the sublessee defaults on the rent
    C. The sublessee is liable to the lessor during the sublease period
    D. The sublessee takes possession for the entire remainder of the rental period

15. TempWorks leased space from Consolidated Properties for an eight-year term. The lease did not include a provision regarding assignment of the lease. Two years later, SuperTemps bought out Temp-Works. TempWorks can:

    A. return the property to Consolidated with any penalties
    B. ask a judge to terminate its lease, on the grounds of unforeseen circumstances
    C. assign its leasehold estate to Super-Temps
    D. try to find a subtenant, but may not assign the space to anyone

16. Which of the following will terminate a lease?

    A. Lis pendens
    B. Mutual agreement
    C. Revocation
    D. Special assessment

17. A landlord enters an apartment without providing any advance notice to make sure everything is in working order. Is the landlord correct to do so?

    A. Yes, a landlord always has the right to enter a tenant's apartment
    B. Yes, a landlord may offer his potential liability for the tenant's safety as an affirmative defense
    C. No, the landlord would breach the covenant of quiet enjoyment
    D. No, the landlord would breach the warranty of habitability

18. A lease is likely to be a net lease if it requires the tenant to pay:

    A. a portion of the tenant's business income
    B. periodic rent increases based on a measure of inflation like the Consumer Price Index
    C. utilities
    D. property taxes

19. John leases a commercial property. In the lease, he agrees to pay part of the utilities and taxes, as well as a fixed monthly rent amount. This is a:

    A. net lease
    B. percentage lease
    C. ground lease
    D. graduated lease

20. John wants to rent a heated garage and is willing to pay a flat rate of $100 per month. Which type of lease would this be?

    A. Gross lease
    B. Ground lease
    C. Net lease
    D. Percentage lease

Answer Key

1. B. A commercial tenant may need to expand into remodeled adjacent units, if its operations grow, so a property manager will want to consider that possibility when helping a commercial tenant find the right space. However, this is not usually a concern for residential tenants. By contrast, a written lease, a security deposit, and a credit check are all common in both commercial and residential leases.

2. C. A property manager's proposed budget is based on what she expects income and operating expenses will be. The manager subtracts proposed expenses from projected revenues to determine expected cash flow.

3. D. Any property management agreement should include the scope of the manager's authority, such as whether he can collect and disburse funds. It should also discuss the manager's compensation, but the compensation does not specifically have to be either a fixed fee or a commission.

4. A. A property management agreement is a contract between a property owner and a real estate brokerage firm that provides the management services. It is not a contract between the property owner and an individual agent.

5. A. A landlord may sell leased property during the term of the lease, but the new owner must honor the lease for the remainder of its term.

6. B. A ground lease is used when a tenant leases land and constructs a building on that land.

7. D. A property manager will perform a market analysis to examine competing managed properties in the same market, which will help him to set rental rates at a competitive level.

8. B. A property manager should inform tenants about the property's amenities; however, he shouldn't misrepresent the amenities (for instance, if a pool were about to be removed, he would want to let a prospective tenant know that before the tenant signs the lease). Antidiscrimination laws would prohibit a manager from letting a prospective tenant know about an alcoholic resident (which would be discrimination on the basis of disability) or the race of the other tenants, and while he could legally tell the prospective tenant about the property's appraised value, that's likely to be of little interest to a tenant.

9. D. Property managers may offer inducements to attract tenants; a common example is waiving the first month's rent. A property manager should perform credit checks for all tenants, rather than only some tenants, as arbitrary enforcement of the rule could give rise to charges of violation of antidiscrimination laws.

10. D. The more specific and less vague a lease's rules are, the clearer the tenant's expectations. This means there will be fewer landlord/tenant disputes based on ambiguous lease language.

11. D. Preventive maintenance is all maintenance that is done on a routine basis, that helps to preserve the physical integrity of the property while preventing problems from cropping up that might require corrective maintenance instead.

12. D. It would depend on the scope of the authority given to the property manager in the management agreement, but investment decisions are not commonly made by property managers. Property managers are usually concerned with the building's maintenance, and may arrange with contractors to provide needed services.

13. A. Every lease includes an implied covenant of quiet enjoyment. This is the promise that the tenant's possession will not be disturbed, either by the landlord or a third party with a lawful claim to the property.

14. B. With a sublease, the lessee is the one who remains liable to the lessor for rental payments. The sublessee (the new tenant) is responsible for making payments to the lessee (the original tenant), who will then pay the landlord.

15. C. Absent a provision in the lease to the contrary, a tenant may assign or sublease the leased space.

16. B. One easy way to terminate a lease is by the mutual agreement of landlord and tenant, known as a surrender. A lease may also terminate because of a breach of the covenant of quiet enjoyment, a breach of the warranty of habitability, failure to pay rent, illegal use, destruction of the premises, or condemnation.

17. C. A tenant is guaranteed quiet enjoyment, which is freedom of possession without being disturbed by others, including the landlord. A landlord may enter the premises, but only by giving notice within the period required by law.

18. D. A lease that requires the tenant to pay all of the property's operating expenses, including the property taxes, is a triple net lease. (Although a net lease often requires the tenant to pay utility costs, that can also be true of a fixed lease. A tenant with a fixed lease does not pay property taxes, however, so option D is a better answer than C.)

19. A. The tenant's payments under a net lease include a share of the property's operating expenses, such as maintenance costs, taxes, and insurance.

20. A. A lease where the tenant pays a fixed flat rent and the landlord pays most or all of the operating expenses is called a gross lease or fixed lease.

Chapter 17

Real Estate Careers and the
Real Estate License Law

I. **Administration of the Real Estate License Law** – The *real estate license law* is administered by the *Department of Licensing*.

   A. **Director of the Department of Licensing** – The chief officer of the Department of Licensing is the *Director*. The Director is appointed by the Governor and serves at the Governor's pleasure.

   1. **Authority** – The Director has the power to adopt, amend, or repeal regulations necessary to enforce the license law. The Director also has the authority to enforce these regulations, including the power to grant or deny licenses, and to hold disciplinary hearings and impose sanctions.

   B. **Real Estate Commission** – The *Real Estate Commission* consists of the Director and six members who are appointed by the Governor. The Commission offers suggestions to the Director regarding the real estate industry and profession.

   1. **Requirements** – The commissioners are generally required to have at least five years of real estate experience. At least two members must be from west of the Cascades, and two from the east.

   2. **Examinations** – The Commission prepares and conducts the real estate license examinations.

   C. **Center for Real Estate Research** – The Center for Real Estate Research was created by the Commission to study statewide real estate concerns such as affordable housing. It provides scholarly information and may recommend changes to the license law and real estate education curricula.

   D. **Attorney General** – The Director is advised on legal matters by the state *Attorney General*.

II. **Real Estate Licenses** – By licensing real estate professionals, the state ensures that agents have at least the minimum level of competence necessary to carry out transactions. Licensing also facilitates enforcement of real estate regulations; an agent who violates the law may have his license suspended or revoked.

   A. **When a License is Required** – Anyone who performs real estate brokerage services must have a real estate license. To be compensated for assisting with a real estate transaction, that

The Director is appointed by the Governor.

Commissioners are usually required to have five years of real estate experience.

The Commission is responsible for preparing and conducting the real estate license examinations.

person must have been licensed at the time he engaged in real estate activities. A real estate license is required for all of the following activities when they are done on behalf of another and for compensation:

1. **Offering to sell, list, or buy** – Selling or offering to sell, listing or offering to list, or buying or offering to buy real estate on behalf of another.

2. **Negotiating sales, exchanges, or leases** – Negotiating or offering to negotiate the purchase, sale, exchange, lease, or rental of real estate on behalf of another.

3. **Business opportunity transactions** – Buying, selling, exchanging, or leasing of a business or *business opportunity*, if the transaction includes real estate.

4. **Negotiating sale of a mobile home on land** – Negotiating or offering to negotiate the purchase, sale, or exchange of a manufactured or mobile home in conjunction with the purchase, sale, exchange, rental, or lease of the land on which the manufactured or mobile home will be located.

5. **Advertising as real estate agent** – Advertising or holding oneself out to the public as someone who engages in activities requiring a license without actually having a valid license is prohibited.

6. **Performing property management services** – Marketing, leasing, or renting real property, including the physical and financial maintenance of rental property.

Sample question

The Real Estate Commission does all of the following except:
A. prepare licensing exam questions
B. set real estate transaction fees
C. advise the Director regarding new regulations
D. hold educational conferences for the benefit of the real estate industry

    B. The Commission does not set transaction fees. Fees are set by agreement between the agent and principal in each transaction.

B. **When a License is not Required** – There are several exceptions to the licensing requirements. The following persons are allowed to engage in real estate activities without a license in the situations described:

1. **Persons acting for themselves** – Someone buying or leasing property for himself or on behalf of a group to which he belongs, or selling property he owns or co-owns. (This would include land developers selling properties that they own.)

2. **Attorneys in fact** – An attorney in fact acting on behalf of her principal without compensation.

3. **Attorneys at law** – An attorney at law while performing her duties as an attorney.

4. **Persons acting under court order** – A receiver, bankruptcy trustee, executor, guardian, or any other person acting under court order.

5. **Persons performing clerical duties** – A secretary, bookkeeper, accountant, or other office personnel performing purely clerical duties.

6. **Referrals** – A person who provides a referral to a licensee, who is not involved in negotiating the sale and whose compensation is not contingent on the licensee being compensated.

7. **Property management employees** – Persons employed by a property owner or brokerage to perform limited property management tasks under direct supervision, such as receiving applications and rent payments, showing units, and providing clerical or maintenance services.

C. **Unlicensed Assistants** – A firm or a licensee may employ unlicensed assistants, but unlicensed assistants must carefully avoid performing any activities that require a license. Unlicensed assistants may not provide information about a listing or transaction, except by providing answers from printed material written by a licensee.

D. **Out-of-State Licensees** – A real estate licensee licensed in another state may handle transactions concerning commercial real estate in Washington without obtaining a Washington real estate license.

1. **Requirements** – The out-of-state licensee must have a written agreement with and cooperate with a Washington firm. The Washington firm's office must have custody of the records for the out-of-state licensee's Washington transactions, and should be given a copy of the out-of-state licensee's license. The Washington firm's name must be included in all advertising.

E. **Types of Licenses** – There are three basic types of licenses in Washington: *firm*, *managing broker*, and *broker*.

Land developers and building contractors who sell their own land don't need a real estate license to do so.

An attorney in fact can sell her principal's land without a real estate license when acting without compensation.

An out-of-state licensee working with a Washington firm on a commercial transaction must provide a copy of his license to the Washington brokerage.

1. **Firm** – A firm license may be issued to a business entity such as a corporation or partnership. The firm must name a managing broker who has control over the firm's operational or financial decision-making (such as a partner in the partnership) as its *designated broker.* The designated broker has ultimate authority over the firm.

   a. **Affiliated licensees** – A firm is authorized to employ managing brokers and brokers (known as the firm's *affiliated licensees*). Affiliated licensees are licensed to represent a firm in the performance of any acts for which a real estate license is required. A managing broker may be affiliated with only one firm at a time.

2. **Managing broker** – A managing broker's license can be issued only to an individual. The licensee is authorized to work with and represent her firm, to manage other licensees or a branch office of the brokerage, or to be the firm's designated broker.

3. **Broker** – A broker's license can be issued only to an individual. The license authorizes the agent to work with and represent his firm, but not to manage a branch office or other licensees or to be a designated broker. A broker with less than two years' experience is subject to a heightened level of scrutiny by a managing broker, including review of all transaction documents within five days of the client's signature.

4. **Designated broker** – There is not a separate designated broker's license; it is an endorsement on a managing broker's license. The designated broker must be licensed as a managing broker. The designated broker supervises and is liable for all brokerage activities, but may delegate duties to managing brokers, if the delegations are in writing and signed. A managing broker may act as designated broker of more than one firm, as long as he has control over operational or financial decision-making for each firm.

> Affiliated licensee: a broker or managing broker who is licensed under a particular firm.

> Designated broker: has full liability for the firm's activities; must have a managing broker's license and control over the firm's operational or financial decision-making.

Sample questions

A licensee hires another licensee, who works for the same firm, to be an assistant for negotiating and selling properties. The supervising licensee, in this relationship, must:

A. be a managing broker
B. be a member of the team
C. have a controlling interest in the firm
D. take a 30 clock-hour course on supervision

A. *A managing broker's license authorizes a licensee to manage other licensees. This applies even in the "team" context, not just to the management of branch offices.*

In Washington, a person licensed to act on behalf of a real estate brokerage is called:

A. an independent licensee
B. an affiliated licensee
C. an associate licensee
D. a designated licensee

B. *A person licensed to act on behalf of a real estate brokerage is called an affiliated licensee.*

F. **License Qualifications and Application** – Applicants for real estate licenses must satisfy specified age and educational requirements and pass an examination. Applicants for a managing broker's license must also satisfy experience requirements.

1. **Managing broker's license** – An applicant for a managing broker's license must satisfy all of the following requirements:

    a. **18 years old** – She must be at least 18 years old;

    b. **High school diploma or equivalent** – She must have a high school diploma or the equivalent;

    c. **Experience** – She must have at least three years of experience within the last five years as a full-time real estate broker in this state or another state with similar licensing requirements;

        i. **Substitution of experience** – An applicant who lacks three years' experience as a broker may take the managing broker's exam if the applicant has other education or experience that the Director considers an adequate substitute, such as one year of experience as a real estate attorney or five years' experience in property management.

    d. **90 clock hours** – She must have successfully completed 90 clock hours of approved real estate education courses in the previous three years (including 30 hours of advanced real estate law, 30 hours of brokerage management, and 30 hours of business management); and

    e. **Managing broker's exam** – She must pass the managing broker's license examination.

Other experience that may substitute for the three years of full-time real estate sales experience for managing broker eligibility: five years in any field allied to real estate OR one year as a real estate attorney.

2. **Broker's license** – An applicant for a broker's license must satisfy all of the following requirements:

    a. **18 years old** – He must be at least 18 years old;

    b. **High school diploma or equivalent** – He must have a high school diploma or the equivalent;

    c. **90 clock hours** – He must have successfully completed a 60 clock-hour course in real estate fundamentals and a 30 clock-hour course in real estate practices; and

    d. **Broker's exam** – He must pass the broker's license examination.

3. **Obtaining a license** – After passing the exam, the next step is to apply for the license itself. Examination results are valid for only one year. If someone passes the exam but doesn't become licensed within one year, she will need to take the exam again.

    a. **Fingerprint identification** – Applicants applying for a first broker's license must submit fingerprint identification on a form provided by the Department. Fingerprints must also be submitted every six years upon renewal.

    b. **Interim license** – An applicant for a broker's license who has been notified that she passed the exam may begin working on the date she mails or hand delivers the signed, dated, and completed application form and license fee to the Department. The completed form serves as an interim license for up to 45 days after the postmark or delivery date.

        i. **Brokers only** – There are no interim licenses for managing broker's license applicants.

G. **License Expiration and Renewal** – An individual's initial real estate license expires two years, to the day, after the issuance of the license. The licensee must apply for renewal and pay a renewal fee. Thereafter, the license must be renewed every two years on or before that same date. If the renewal application is late, the licensee must pay a penalty (in addition to the renewal fee). There is no fee if a licensee changes her license to account for a change in name or mailing address.

1. **Firms** – Firm licenses must also be renewed every two years. The renewal date for this type of license is the expiration date of the firm's registration or certificate of authority (as filed with the secretary of state).

Examination results are valid for one year.

An interim license can only be issued to a broker, and it is valid up to 45 days.

First license renewal occurs two years, to the day, after issuance.

2. **Continuing education requirements** – To renew their licenses, all brokers and managing brokers must submit proof that they have successfully completed a total of 30 clock hours of approved continuing education courses, including 3 hours of core curriculum.

   a. **Broker's first renewal** – The first time a broker renews his license, he must submit proof of completion of a 30 clock-hour course in advanced real estate practices, 30 clock-hours of real estate law, and 30 hours of a continuing education elective.

3. **Cancellation and reinstatement** – If a license isn't renewed within *one year* after it expires, the license is *canceled*. A license can be *reinstated* within *two years* after cancellation if the licensee: (1) successfully completes 60 clock hours of approved real estate courses within one year before applying for reinstatement (including a 30 hour real estate law course); (2) pays all back renewal fees, plus penalties; and (3) pays a reinstatement penalty. (If the licensee renews within one year after the license expires, only the back renewal fees and penalty fee are necessary.)

   a. **More than two years** – If it has been more than two years since the license was canceled, the former licensee cannot be reinstated unless he satisfies the requirements for initial licensure again (such as retaking the exam).

4. **Inactive licenses** – An inactive license is a license that has been turned over to the Director for any reason. The holder of an inactive license is considered to be unlicensed. She cannot engage in activities requiring a license, but is still subject to disciplinary action for license law violations.

   a. **Renewal** – Although an inactive license must be renewed on its renewal date, the holder is usually not required to comply with the continuing education requirement for renewal. Failure to renew an inactive license results in cancellation, just as with an active license. A licensee may not renew an inactive license if there are disciplinary proceedings pending against the licensee.

   b. **Education requirement** – Before reactivating a license that has been inactive for more than three years, the licensee must complete a 30 clock-hour real estate course. This may be used to both activate an inactive license and satisfy the first renewal requirements for an active license.

> All licensees must complete 30 clock hours of approved courses prior to each renewal.

> If a license isn't renewed within a year after it expires, it is CANCELED.

> The holder of an inactive license is generally deemed to be unlicensed.

259

5.   **License Fees** – Fees collected for licensing (application fees, renewal fees, etc.) are placed in the Real Estate Commission Account in the state treasury.

Sample questions

J passes the license exam on March 20. How much time does J have to apply for his license before being required to retake the license examination?

A. Six months
B. 12 months
C. 18 months
D. Two years

> B.   *J has 12 months. If the license fee is not paid and the license placed on an active or inactive status within that time, the applicant will have to retake the exam and meet any additional licensing requirements that have been adopted in the interim.*

L's broker's license was issued on October 16, 2014. L's license will expire on:

A. December 31, 2014
B. December 31, 2015
C. October 16, 2015
D. October 16, 2016

> D.   *L's license will expire two years after its issuance: October 16, 2016.*

A Washington real estate licensee's license has expired because he did not pay his license fee as required. His license can be reinstated if:

A. he completes an additional 30 hours of continuing education electives
B. he obtains special permission from the Director of the Department of Licensing
C. he pays back renewal fees, plus penalties
D. he retakes the real estate examination

> C.   *A license that hasn't been properly renewed will expire. It can be renewed within one year of the expiration, if the licensee pays a penalty and any back fees.*

Who needs to submit continuing education credits with each license renewal?

A. Active brokers only
B. Active managing brokers only
C. All active licensees
D. All active and inactive licensees

> C.   *Both brokers and managing brokers must take continuing education courses, so long as they are actively licensed. Inactive licensees do not need to comply with the continuing education requirement, although a 30-hour class is required in order to reactivate a license that has been inactive for more than three years.*

At what minimum point must an inactive licensee take a 30 clock-hour course in order to reactivate her license?

A. Six months
B. One year
C. Three years
D. Five years

> C. A licensee must take a 30 clock-hour continuing education course in order to reactivate a license that has been inactive for more than three years.

III. Regulation of Business Practices – State and federal laws govern the day-to-day business practices of licensees and firms in many matters, including relationships between licensees and clients, relationships between firms and affiliated licensees, trust accounts, and business records.

   A. Agency Relationships – Washington's real estate agency law describes how agency relationships are created.

   1. **Seller agency** – A *seller's agent* forms an agency relationship with his client when a listing agreement is signed.

   2. **Buyer agency** – A *buyer's agent* forms an agency relationship with the buyer as soon as she performs any real estate brokerage services for him, unless there is a written agreement to the contrary.

   3. **Dual agency** – A *dual agency* results if the seller's agent and buyer's agent are employed by the same brokerage firm. Dual agency is unlawful without the written consent of both parties.

   4. **Agency disclosure** – An *agency disclosure* must be made to each party before the party signs an offer in a transaction handled by the licensee. It must be either a separate paragraph entitled "Agency Disclosure" in the purchase and sale agreement, or a separate document entitled "Agency Disclosure." A licensee must always conduct herself in accordance with the agency disclosure she has made.

   An agency disclosure must be made in writing before a party signs a purchase and sale agreement.

   5. **Agent's duties to all parties** – An agent owes all parties the duties of reasonable care and skill, honesty and good faith, presentation of all written communications, disclosure of all material facts, accounting, providing a real estate agency law pamphlet, and making a written agency disclosure. The agent does not owe any duty of independent inspection of the property, investigation of the truth of statements made by her principal, or an estimate of the property's value.

The duties of confidentiality and accounting do not expire with the agency.

Vicarious liability: a legal doctrine under which a principal can be held liable for harm to third parties resulting from an agent's actions; no longer applies to real estate agency relationships in Washington.

6. **Agent's duties to the principal** – An agent also owes his principal the duties of loyalty, disclosure of conflicts of interest, confidentiality, advising the principal to seek expert advice, and good faith and continuous effort.

7. **Vicarious liability** – Under Washington's real estate agency law, a principal is not liable for harm caused by any act or omission of an agent or subagent. (Holding someone liable for the acts of another is known as *vicarious liability*.)

8. **Imputed knowledge** – Under Washington's real estate agency law, a principal is not held to have notice of any facts known by an agent but unknown by the principal. (The agent's knowledge is not *imputed* to the principal.)

9. **Penalties** – Washington's real estate agency law does not address penalties for failure to disclose agency status.

B. **Designated Broker's Supervisory Responsibilities** – A designated broker must supervise all of his affiliated licensees, whether they are independent contractors or employees. If a firm has branch offices, both the designated broker and branch office manager are responsible for the brokers and managing brokers working at a particular branch.

1. **Liability for licensees' violations** – A designated broker who fails to supervise her brokers and managing brokers may be held responsible for their actions. If an affiliated licensee violates the license law, the Director may suspend or revoke the designated broker's license.

A designated broker must cooperate with an investigation into an affiliated licensee's conduct by providing access to records and responding to written requests for information, but does not need to respond to a subpoena that does not specifically name the designated broker.

2. **Investigations** – A designated broker must cooperate with an investigation of an affiliated licensee's conduct by providing access to records and responding to written requests for information, but does not need to respond to a subpoena that does not specifically name the designated broker.

3. **Fee broker** – A designated broker may not act as a *fee broker*, which is a licensee who allows another person to operate a brokerage using his firm's name and license, usually for a fee.

C. **Affiliations and Termination** – A broker or managing broker must be affiliated with a firm for his license to be active. A broker or managing broker is not allowed to engage in real estate activities except under the supervision of and as a representative of a firm. The firm's designated broker has custody of the licenses of her affiliated licensees.

1. **License surrender** – The relationship between a firm and affiliated licensee may be terminated at any time by either party. When an affiliation is terminated, the designated broker must notify the Director and surrender the license immediately. (It is not necessary to notify the Real Estate Commission.)

2. **Termination date** – The designated broker will sign the license and mail or hand deliver it to the Department of Licensing. The termination date is the postmark or hand-delivery date. The license remains inactive until the licensee has found a new firm to work for and a new license is issued.

3. **Failure to surrender** – A designated broker's failure to surrender a license promptly is grounds for disciplinary action against the designated broker. The designated broker cannot place any conditions on its surrender, such as repayment of money to the firm.

4. **Grounds for disciplinary action** – When a broker or managing broker has been terminated because of conduct that would be grounds for disciplinary action under the license law, the designated broker must send the Director a written statement of the facts surrounding the termination.

When an affiliated licensee is terminated, the designated broker must return the license to the DOL immediately.

Sample questions

Washington state's real estate agency law does not address which of the following?
A. Definition of dual agency
B. Creation and termination of agency relationships
C. Vicarious liability of principal and licensee
D. Penalties for not disclosing agency status

    D. *Washington's real estate agency law is found in the Real Estate Brokerage Relationships Act (RCW chapter 18.86). There is no reference in the law to penalties for not disclosing agency status. Penalties are found in the license law (RCW chapter 18.85).*

When a licensee is terminated, the date of termination is the:
A. postmark date or the date the license is hand-delivered to the Department of Licensing
B. moment the termination is understood and agreed upon by both the designated broker and the affiliate
C. date the termination notice is tendered by either the designated broker or the agent
D. date the terminated license is received by the Department of Licensing

    A. *The termination date is the postmark date or the date the license is hand-delivered to the Department of Licensing.*

If a designated broker wishes to terminate an affiliated licensee, or an affiliated licensee wants to terminate employment with a brokerage, which of the following statements is TRUE?

A. Either party may act unilaterally to end the relationship
B. An affiliated licensee may terminate only after the agent pays all debts incurred to the brokerage
C. A designated broker may terminate an affiliated licensee only if there is good cause for termination
D. Only the affiliated licensee can terminate employment

    A. *Either a designated broker or an affiliated licensee may act unilaterally in order to terminate their employment relationship.*

D. Office Requirements – A firm licensed in Washington must maintain an office or records repository in this state that is accessible to the Director's representatives.

> An agent's license must be prominently displayed in the office where she works.

1. **Display of licenses** – The firm's license must be prominently displayed at its office, along with the licenses of all affiliated licensees. If the firm has more than one office, its license and the designated broker's license are displayed in the main office, and the licenses of affiliated licensees are displayed in the office where they work (the address shown on the license).

2. **Change of location** – If the location of a firm's office changes, the designated broker must promptly submit a change of address application to the Director, return all licenses, and pay a fee. The Department will issue licenses for the new address.

3. **Two businesses in same office** – A firm may operate two businesses out of the same office if the other business is compatible with real estate brokerage activities. The brokerage business must be carried out apart from other business activities, and brokerage records must be kept completely separate from other records.

4. **Branch offices** – Every branch office must be licensed and must have a branch manager, who must be a managing broker. A separate license is not required for a branch office where sales activity concerns only a particular subdivision or tract, and the subdivision is within 35 miles of a licensed office.

5. **Dual state agents** – Licensees who are actively licensed in another state as well as Washington and have a full-time office in that other state are not required to have an office in Washington. However, they must maintain a trust account in a Washington depository and keep records of

their Washington transactions at a registered location in this state.

E. **Advertising** – Advertising by real estate licensees must be truthful and not misleading, and must include the firm's name as licensed (or assumed name). An ad without the firm's name (called a *blind ad*) violates the license law.

Blind ad: an advertisement placed by a real estate licensee that does not include the firm's name.

1. **Exception for own property** – If a licensee is advertising his own property for sale or lease, the firm's name does not have to appear in the ad. The ad must disclose that the seller or landlord has a real estate license, however.

2. **Assumed name** – With the Director's permission, a firm may do business under a name other than the name on its license, as long as there is no intent to mislead the public.

When selecting an assumed name, a firm must choose a name that isn't deceptively similar to the name of another brokerage.

3. **Advertising online** – A licensee should be careful to disclose his licensed status in all Internet communications. The Real Estate Commission's Internet advertising guidelines include rules on disclosures concerning licensees and the firms they're affiliated with.

A licensee should fully disclose his licensed status in all Internet communications.

a. **Licensee disclosure**– Advertising on a website must always disclose the licensee's name, the name of the firm with which he is affiliated, the city and state where the licensee's office is located, and the states in which the licensee is licensed.

Full disclosure includes:
- the licensee's name and firm,
- the city and state of the licensee's office,
- the city and state of the licensee's firm, and
- the states in which the licensee and the firm are licensed.

b. **Licensed firm disclosure** – The website must also disclose the firm's name as registered with the Department of Licensing, the city and state where the firm is located, and the states where the firm is licensed.

c. **Other requirements** – The licensee should remove his website or any information on that website when it is no longer current or has expired. The licensee should have the written permission of other licensees to post those licensees' listings.

4. **CAN-SPAM Act** – The CAN-SPAM Act is a federal law that regulates unsolicited emails, including those that a real estate licensee might send as advertisements. It requires that any unsolicited email contain instructions on how the recipient can opt out of receiving further emails from the sender.

5. **Do Not Call Registry** – A real estate agent may not cold call people listed on the Federal Trade Commission's Do Not Call Registry. And agent may make calls to someone with whom she already has a business relationship, but only for 18 months after the last transaction.

Trust accounts must be opened in the name of the firm, as licensed, and designated as trust accounts.

Trust funds must be deposited in a trust account no later than the close of the next business day, excluding Saturday.

Real estate firms must put earnest money deposits of $10,000 or less in a pooled interest-bearing account.

Property management trust funds are exempt from the pooled account requirement.

Any commissions earned by the property manager that accrue in the trust account must be removed from the account at least monthly.

F. **Trust Accounts** – Every firm must maintain one or more trust accounts for funds held on behalf of clients and customers. The accounts must be in a recognized financial institution in the state of Washington.

1. **Requirements** – Trust accounts must be kept separate from the firm's general business and personal accounts, so that trust funds (such as earnest money deposits) will not be commingled with the firm's own money. Trust accounts should be opened in the name of the firm as licensed and specifically designated as trust accounts.

   a. **Commingling** – *Commingling* means mixing trust funds with personal funds. It is different from *conversion*, which occurs when a licensee actually uses others' funds for his own purposes.

2. **Trust fund handling** – As a general rule, trust funds must be deposited no later than the *first business day* following receipt of the funds. For purposes of this rule, Saturday is not considered to be a business day.

   a. **Earnest money** – If authorized to do so in the offer, a firm may hold a buyer's earnest money check (instead of depositing it) pending the seller's acceptance of the offer.

3. **Interest-bearing accounts** – With the exception of property management trust accounts, firms' trust accounts must be interest-bearing accounts and allow the designated broker to make withdrawals without delay (other than the minimum notice period required by banking regulations).

4. **Pooled accounts** – The firm must put all deposits of $10,000 or less into a *pooled account*. Interest paid on this account, after deducting bank charges, must be paid to the state treasurer. This money is divided between the Washington Housing Trust Fund (which receives 75%) and the Real Estate Education Account (which receives 25%).

   a. **Larger deposits** – For deposits of more than $10,000, the client or customer may choose to have the money deposited into the pooled account, or into a separate account with interest paid to the client or customer who owns the funds.

5. **Property management trust accounts** – Property management trust funds (chiefly, rents or tenant security deposits) don't need to be placed in the firm's pooled account, so the owner may receive the accrued interest. If any commissions or property management fees are to be paid out of the trust account directly to a firm, they must be removed from the trust account at least once a month.

6. **Trust account procedures** – Only trust funds may be kept in the trust account, except that a minimal amount of the firm's own money can be deposited if necessary to open the account or maintain a minimum balance.

7. **Firm's expenses** – A firm may not pay its business expenses directly out of a trust account. If the client owes the firm money, the funds must first be transferred from the trust account to the firm's general business account before the firm can use them for business expenses.

8. **Commissions to firm** – Commissions payable to the firm and to other cooperating firms may be paid directly from the trust account.

9. **Commissions to affiliated licensees** – Commissions the firm owes to its affiliated licensees may not be paid directly out of the trust account. These commissions are handled like any other business expenses; the funds must be transferred to the firm's general business account, then the affiliated licensees are paid out of that account.

10. **Transferring trust accounts** – If a firm purchases another brokerage, the other brokerage's trust accounts will pass to the new firm. This will require a consent form signed by the designated brokers of both the selling and purchasing brokerages.

> Commissions a firm owes to its affiliated licensees may NOT be paid directly from the trust account.

Sample questions

A licensee, with permission from his designated broker, sets up his own subsection S corporation, which he calls M Realty. He then rents a billboard and advertises a listing on it, using only the M Realty name. Is this legal?

A. No, because ads must give the name of the firm
B. No, because the firm must be the one that rents the billboard
C. Yes, because he had the designated broker's consent
D. Yes, because he used the exact corporation name that was registered with the Secretary of State

> A. *Under Washington's real estate license law, every advertisement placed by a licensee on behalf of others must contain the name of the real estate firm as licensed. This is true even if a licensee conducts his own operations under a separately named business entity.*

If a real estate agent is sending out emails offering his services, the federal CAN-SPAM Act requires the agent to:

A. avoid emailing persons on the "do not call" list
B. include the brokerage firm's name as licensed
C. make sure that a licensee, not an unlicensed person, was responsible for the content
D. tell recipients how to opt out of receiving future emails

D. The CAN-SPAM Act is a federal law that places limits on unsolicited emails. One requirement is that an email must give information on how recipients can avoid receiving further emails.

Transaction records must be kept for a minimum of three years.

A firm must make records available to DOL auditors upon demand.

G. Records – The license law requires real estate firms to keep adequate records of the transactions they handle for at least *three years after closing*. The designated broker may delegate recordkeeping activities, but the designated broker is responsible for the custody and accuracy of all required records.

1. **Available upon demand** – The firm must make the records available to auditors from the Department of Licensing and provide copies to the Director upon demand.

2. **Transaction folder** – For each transaction, the firm must maintain a *transaction folder* that includes the listing agreement, the purchase and sale agreement, all modifications and addenda, the settlement statement, and any other relevant documents.

3. **Trust account records** – A firm should keep a *client's ledger* for trust funds, summarizing all receipts and disbursements for each transaction or property management account. The firm should retain duplicate deposit slips, canceled checks, and reconciled bank statements, but does not need to retain photocopies of checks.

4. **Location** – A firm must keep all records at a location where the firm is licensed to have an office. Records from transactions that have been closed for at least one year may be kept at one central location, so long as it is in Washington. A list of those transactions must be kept at the firm's licensed offices. Records may be stored on disk or microfilm so long as the media are non-erasable and cannot be modified.

H. Commissions – Listings belong to the brokerage, not the individual licensee; if a licensee changes firms, a listing that she took but that has not closed remains with the brokerage. A person who provides brokerage services must have a valid real estate license in order to collect a commission (or any form of compensation). A licensee cannot sue for a commission without proof that he was properly licensed before he offered to perform any act that requires licensure, or obtained a promise or contract for the payment of compensation for performing such an act.

1. **When commission is earned** – The commission is earned when the sale is made, not at closing. If a licensee is no longer licensed or no longer employed by the same firm

at the time of closing, the licensee is still entitled to the commission.

2. **Commission sharing** – A firm may share a commission with or pay compensation to any firm that is licensed in the U.S. or Canada. The firm may also share the commission with its own affiliated licensees. This includes transactions with licensed manufactured or mobile home dealers, if purchase or lease of land is part of the sale.

3. **Payment to affiliated licensees** – A firm may not pay compensation directly to a managing broker or broker licensed with another firm. The firm pays the other firm, which then pays the affiliated licensee.

4. **Affiliated licensees** – Brokers and managing brokers may receive compensation only from their firm. They cannot collect a commission directly from a client or from another firm. Nor can they share their commission with other licensees; any commission split must be handled by their firms.

A licensee can pay a referral fee to another licensee (through the second licensee's firm) or to an unlicensed person for finding a buyer or seller.

Sample questions

Real estate transaction records should be kept for a minimum of:

A. one year
B. two years
C. three years
D. four years

   C. Transaction records should be kept for at least three years after the transaction closes.

To be entitled to sue for a commission, a licensee must be able to prove that at the time the real estate activities were performed, she:

A. was licensed
B. had passed the real estate exam
C. had at least a verbal promise of compensation
D. was under the supervision of a mentor

   A. A licensee must have been validly licensed at the time she engaged in the real estate activities for which a commission is claimed.

A real estate agent sold a home for $275,000. Prior to closing, the agent's license was revoked on grounds of moral turpitude. With respect to his eligibility for the commission, which of the following statements is true?

A. He is eligible for the commission because he was duly licensed when the sale was made

B. He is eligible for the commission because he is technically licensed until all appeals have been exhausted

C. He is not eligible for a commission because he was not licensed at the time the commission was paid

D. He is not eligible for a commission because a license revocation automatically nullifies any right to commissions that are yet unpaid

    A. *The commission is earned when the sale is made, not when it is paid (at closing). The license was revoked after the sale was made.*

If Licensee D works out of a home office, for how long is she required to maintain records of closed transactions?

A. 1 year

B. 3 years

C. 7 years

D. Affiliated licensees are not required to maintain records of closed transactions

    D. *Real estate firms must maintain records of closed transactions for at least three years. The firm is responsible for the custody and accuracy of the required records, and they should be kept at a main office or branch office.*

An affiliated licensee rarely works in the firm's main office. The records for the licensee's transactions must be kept in:

A. the licensee's personal files

B. the firm's office

C. both the licensee's personal files and the firm's office

D. the licensee's personal files until closing, then at the firm's office

    B. *A firm must keep all records at its main office or a branch office. While it may be advantageous for a licensee who is rarely in the office to keep copies of the records for personal reference, the law makes the firm ultimately responsible for the custody and accuracy of all required records.*

A licensee writes a successful transaction while working for Designated Broker X. Before the transaction closes, though, the licensee starts working for Designated Broker B. How is the licensee's commission handled?

A. Designated Broker X will pay the licensee, even though she is working for another designated broker

B. Designated Broker X will keep the commission

C. Designated Broker X will pay the commission to Designated Broker B, who will pay the licensee

D. Designated Broker X must forfeit the commission

    C. *A licensee can only accept compensation from the designated broker for whom she currently works. So, if a licensee moves from one firm to another with a transaction pending, the licensee's new designated broker would accept the compensation from the old designated broker and then pay the licensee.*

An affiliated licensee owns a wholly owned S corporation, A Realty. He instructs an escrow agent to issue a commission check directly to A Realty. How has he violated the real estate license law?

A. A third party can't give instructions to an escrow agent
B. Commissions can be paid to licensees only via their firm
C. The licensee didn't first inform the principals
D. The licensee may charge for escrow services only if he is also a licensed escrow agent

> B. *A licensee may be paid a commission only by the real estate firm he is affiliated with. Affiliated licensees are not designated brokers; they work for a firm. "A Realty" cannot be a brokerage because no designated broker has a controlling interest in the entity. An affiliated licensee cannot receive compensation directly from a client or customer, or from another licensee, another real estate firm, or another business entity.*

A Washington real estate broker takes a listing for a waterfront bungalow while working for Firm A. However, before the transaction closes, she terminates her affiliation and begins working for Firm B. Which of the following statements is true?

A. The listing belongs to Firm A, but Firm A will still owe a commission to the original broker
B. The listing belongs to the firm, and will remain with Firm A
C. The listing belongs to the licensee, and will go with her to Firm B
D. The listing is canceled automatically, and the seller must re-list with the broker

> B. *Listing agreements are the property of a firm, not a licensee. If a licensee leaves a firm mid-transaction, the listing still will belong to the firm and will not follow the licensee to a new firm.*

Licensee A and Licensee B form a team, working together within the brokerage they work for. Licensee A is listed as the agent on a purchase and sale agreement, but it was Licensee B who negotiated the transaction. Which of the following is true?

A. Licensee A cannot be paid because B negotiated the transaction
B. Licensee B cannot be paid because A's name is the only one on the agreement
C. Licensee A, as team leader, will pay Licensee B
D. Licensee B must receive payment from the brokerage

> D. *An affiliated licensee may receive compensation only from the firm who employs him or her. If two affiliated licensees will split a commission, it must be handled by their firm or firms.*

I. **Handling Transactions** – The Director's regulations include several rules governing how licensees serve their clients and customers in a real estate transaction, from the negotiation process to closing.

1. **Copies of all documents** – A licensee is responsible for providing clients and customers with copies of any documents they sign within a reasonable time after execution.

A licensee must provide clients and customers with copies of anything they sign when they sign it.

2. **Earnest money deposits** – Sometimes buyers make an earnest money deposit by writing a check payable to the firm as licensed, so the firm can deposit it in a trust account.

   a. **Holding the deposit** – The firm may hold the earnest money check without depositing it for a specific length of time or until a particular event occurs (i.e., the seller accepts or rejects the offer), if that is what the purchase and sale agreement directs the firm to do.

   b. **Who receives the deposit** – In a transaction with more than one firm, the firm that first receives the earnest money deposit (and to which the check is payable) is the one responsible for handling the funds. This will be the selling brokerage if it receives an earnest money check when the buyer makes an offer.

It is a violation of the license law to accept earnest money in the form of a promissory note without noting it in the purchase and sale agreement.

   c. **Promissory note** – It is a violation of the license law to accept an earnest money deposit in the form of a promissory note (or some other non-cash equivalent), unless the licensee discloses that fact to the seller before the seller accepts the offer, and the purchase and sale agreement also states the form of the earnest money.

3. **Closing** – The license law allows a licensee to close a transaction in which she already represents the buyer or seller (or both), if the licensee is designated as the closing agent in the purchase and sale agreement. The licensee may not charge either party a fee for closing services, unless the real estate agent is also a licensed escrow officer.

A licensee can act as closing agent for her own transactions, but cannot charge a closing fee unless she is a licensed escrow officer.

4. **Property management agreements** – A firm must have a written *property management agreement* with the owners of each property it manages. The license law requires the agreement to state the manager's compensation, the type of property, the number of units or square footage, whether the manager may collect and disburse funds, whether the manager may hold and disburse security deposits, and how often the manager must provide *summary statements* to the owner. The condition of the property is not described in the agreement.

   a. **Copy of agreement** – The firm must keep a copy of the management agreement and all summary statements in its records. The management agreement may be modified only in writing, and any modification must be signed by both the firm's designated broker and property owners.

b. **Summary statement** – A summary statement is a brief report showing the property's financial status for a period of time, such as a month or a quarter. The firm must provide a summary statement as often as the management agreement requires. The summary statement includes the starting and ending account balances, total rent receipts, itemized expenditures, and owners' contributions.

c. **Provision of services** – The firm may provide other services to the owner of the property it manages, such as janitorial or repair services, with the owner's consent. The firm must make a full written disclosure of its relationship with the company providing the services, and state what fees are charged. A rebate from a service provider to the manager would be illegal, unless the property owner approved it in writing.

Sample questions

Who is ultimately responsible for the delivery of the earnest money?
A. Purchaser
B. Designated broker
C. Listing licensee
D. Licensee who receives funds

> B. *The designated broker is the licensee who is responsible for handling the deposit in compliance with the license law.*

The selling agent must NOT accept a promissory note as an earnest money deposit:
A. unless the agent knows that the buyer has an excellent credit history
B. unless the purchase and sale agreement discloses that the deposit is a note
C. unless the seller agreed during negotiation discussions to accept a promissory note
D. under any circumstances

> B. *When preparing the buyer's offer to purchase, the selling agent must disclose on the purchase and sale agreement form that the deposit is in the form of a promissory note (or any other form that is not the equivalent of cash). The seller can then take this into account in deciding whether or not to accept the buyer's offer.*

IV. **Disciplinary Action** – The Director has the authority to investigate the actions of any real estate licensees and impose sanctions (such as license suspension or revocation) for any violation of the license law. This is true regardless of whether the licensee was acting on behalf of another or for his own account, and whether the license was active or inactive.

A. **Grounds for Disciplinary Action** – A licensee or license applicant may be subject to disciplinary action either for engaging in unprofessional conduct or for engaging in one of the acts specifically listed in the license law as grounds for disciplinary action.

B. **Unprofessional Conduct** – Washington state's Uniform Regulation of Business and Professions Act (URBPA) lists several kinds of unprofessional conduct.

1. **Moral turpitude relating to real estate activities** – The commission of any act involving moral turpitude, dishonesty, or corruption relating to real estate activities, regardless of whether the act constitutes a crime.

2. **Deceptive advertising** – False, deceptive, or misleading advertising (including blind ads).

3. **Malpractice** – Incompetence, negligence, or malpractice that harms or may harm a consumer.

4. **Exceeding scope of practice** – Practice or operation of a business or profession beyond the scope of practice or operation as defined by law.

5. **Misrepresentation** – Any type of misrepresentation in the conduct of real estate activities.

6. **Inadequate supervision** – Failure to adequately supervise or oversee staff, whether employees or independent contractors.

7. **Unlicensed practice** – Aiding or abetting an unlicensed person in performing activities that require a license.

C. **Specifically Illegal Acts** – There are also a number of activities specifically listed as illegal in the license law:

1. **Conversion** – Converting trust funds to a licensee's own use.

2. **Contingent appraisals** – Accepting compensation for an appraisal contingent on reporting a predetermined value.

3. **Failure to disclose interest in appraised property** – Issuing an appraisal for property in which the licensee has an interest without reporting that interest in the appraisal report.

4. **Falsely claiming to belong to an association** – Falsely claiming to be a member of a state or national real estate association.

5. **Failure to disclose licensee status** – Buying, selling, or leasing property (directly or through a third party) without disclosing one's status as a licensee.

6. **Kickbacks** – A licensee may not accept or solicit anything of value from a title insurance company or agent. A licensee may also not give a fee or kickback to another licensee that will be passed to a title insurance company for referring business.

D. **Failure to Meet Obligations** – The Director may suspend the license of any licensee who has been certified by a lending agency for nonpayment of a federal or state educational loan, or by the Department of Social and Health Services for failure to comply with a child support or visitation order. License reinstatement is automatic upon repayment or compliance.

E. **Disciplinary Procedures** – The usual procedures for discipline include an investigation, a hearing, and depending on the outcome of the hearing, either no action or some form of sanctions against the licensee. Either party (the licensee or the Department of Licensing) may appeal the result.

1. **Statement of charges** – If, after investigation, the Director decides that there is reason to believe there has been a violation of the license law, the licensee will be served with a *statement of charges*.

2. **Request for hearing** – The licensee must file a request for a hearing within *20 days* of receiving the statement of charges. If there is no request, the licensee is considered in default and the Director may enter a decision based on the facts available at the time.

3. **Hearing** – Once a hearing has been requested, the Director will fix the time for the hearing. The time must be as soon as is convenient, but at least *30 days* after the statement of charges was given to the licensee. If a licensee fails to show up for a scheduled hearing, the hearing will still be held in the licensee's absence.

   A licensee must be given at least 30 days' notice before a disciplinary hearing is held.

   If a licensee fails to show up for a scheduled hearing, the hearing will be held in the licensee's absence.

4. **Ordering sanctions** – If the accusation is proved, the Director may impose any of the sanctions permitted by law. An order imposing the sanctions will be filed with the Director's office and immediately mailed to the licensee. The sanctions take effect as soon as the order is received by the licensee.

   Disciplinary sanctions take effect as soon as the order is received by the licensee.

5. **Appeal** – A licensee who is dissatisfied with the outcome of a disciplinary hearing may file an *appeal* in *superior court*. The appeal must be filed within *30 days* after the date of the Director's decision and order.

   The licensee has 30 days to appeal an adverse decision to superior court.

A licensee who files an appeal must post a $1,000 bond to cover court costs. The licensee must also pay for a certified copy of the hearing transcript, which is prepared by the Director and used during the appeal process.

Sanctions imposed by the Director remain in effect throughout an appeal process.

    a. **Appeal bond** – The licensee must post a *$1,000 appeal bond* to cover court costs, and must also pay for a copy of the transcript of the hearing that is certified by the Director.

    b. **Order not stayed** – Filing an appeal *does not automatically stay* the Director's order. So if the Director suspended the licensee's license, the suspension stands. But the Director may choose to stay the sanctions during the appeals process if conditions necessary to protect the public are imposed.

F. **Sanctions** – If the licensee (or applicant) is found to have violated the license law, the Director may revoke the license, suspend the license for a fixed or indefinite term, restrict real estate activities, issue a censure or reprimand, deny an initial or renewal license application, require education, and/or impose a fine of up to $5,000 per violation. The Director does not have the authority to attach a licensee's future earnings.

All fines are placed in the Real Estate Education Account and used for licensee education.

    1. **Real Estate Education Account** – All fines collected are placed in the Real Estate Education Account, to be used for licensee education.

In special circumstances, the Director can issue a temporary cease and desist order before a hearing is held.

    2. **Cease and desist order** – Following a hearing, the Director may issue a *cease and desist order* to stop a licensee (or unlicensed person) from violating the law. In special circumstances, the Director may issue a temporary cease and desist order even before a hearing is held, if delay would cause irreparable harm to the public.

        a. **Right to hearing** – The temporary cease and desist order must inform the licensee of her right to a hearing to determine if the order should be canceled, modified, or made permanent. If the licensee requests a hearing, the Director must hold one within *30 days* (unless the licensee requests more time).

The Director can file an action in superior court seeking an injunction ordering a licensee to stop a continuing violation.

    3. **Injunction** – The Director may ask a superior court to issue an *injunction* ordering a licensee or unlicensed person to stop an ongoing violation. The Director may also ask the court to appoint a receiver to take over or close a real estate office operating in violation of the law, until a hearing can be held.

Selling real estate without a license is a gross misdemeanor.

G. **Criminal Prosecution** – Violations of the license law (including acts committed by unlicensed persons) are *gross misdemeanors*. If the Director decides that criminal charges should be filed against a licensee, the prosecution would ordinarily be handled by the prosecuting attorney in the county where the violation is alleged to have occurred. However, it may be handled by the state Attorney General instead.

H. **Civil Liability** – The Director does not have the power to award compensation to the victims of real estate fraud or other wrongful actions. Compensation for injured parties is handled through the court system, and anyone who has been injured by a licensee's actions can file a civil lawsuit for damages.

The Director does not have the power to award damages to victims of real estate fraud.

I. **Notification of Legal Action** – A licensee is required to notify the Real Estate Program Manager *within 20 days* of learning of: (1) any criminal complaint, indictment, or conviction in which the licensee is named as a defendant; or (2) any civil court order, verdict, or judgment entered against the licensee if the case involves any of her real estate or business activities.

V. **Antitrust Laws** – Federal antitrust laws impose certain restrictions on a real estate agent's behavior toward clients, customers, and other agents. The principal antitrust law is the Sherman Act.

A. **Sherman Act** – The *Sherman Antitrust Act* prohibits any agreement that would unreasonably restrain trade, including conspiracies. A conspiracy occurs when two or more business entities participate in a common scheme, the effect of which is the restraint of trade. Four main categories of conspiracies are *price fixing*, *group boycotts*, *tie-in arrangements*, and *market allocation*.

The Sherman Act is the antitrust law that prohibits the unreasonable restraint of trade. It is designed to prevent monopolies.

1. **Price fixing** – Price fixing is the cooperative setting of prices or price ranges by competing firms. To avoid the appearance of price fixing, two agents from different brokerages should never discuss their commission rates. Publications that appear to fix prices are prohibited. For instance, an MLS may not publish a commission schedule or "recommended" rates for commissions.

2. **Group boycotts** – A group boycott is an agreement between two or more real estate licensees to exclude other licensees from fair participation in real estate activities.

3. **Tie-in arrangements** – A tie-in arrangement is an agreement to sell a product only on the condition that the buyer also purchases a different product (a *tied* product).

4. **Market allocation** – Market allocation involves two competitors who agree not to sell products or services in designated areas.

Sample questions

J is selling real estate without a license. J is guilty of a:

A. misdemeanor
B. gross misdemeanor
C. second degree felony
D. first degree felony

> B. *Selling real estate without a license is a gross misdemeanor, which in terms of seriousness is somewhere between a misdemeanor and a felony.*

The Director may impose all of the following penalties on a licensee for violating the license law, EXCEPT:

A. additional remedial education
B. license revocation
C. license suspension
D. requiring licensee to pay for costs of formal hearing

> D. *A licensee may have her license revoked or suspended, or be required to complete additional education. However, a licensee is never required to pay for the costs of a disciplinary hearing.*

Z has been certified by the Department of Social and Health Services as not in compliance with his court-ordered child support payments. What disciplinary action is available to the Director of the Department of Licensing?

A. Suspend Z's license
B. Revoke Z's license
C. File a cease and desist order
D. File a criminal complaint in superior court

> A. *The Director can suspend Z's license until Z has repaid the delinquency or otherwise complied with the order.*

A licensee fails to attend a scheduled disciplinary hearing. What happens?

A. The licensee's license is automatically revoked
B. The hearing is automatically delayed for up to 20 days
C. The hearing is held without the licensee present
D. The proceeding is referred to superior court

> C. *If a licensee does not show up for a disciplinary hearing, the hearing still proceeds without the licensee present.*

A licensee would not be disciplined for:

A. accepting compensation from both parties to a transaction without a written disclosure
B. failing to adequately supervise an employee who misrepresents a property to a prospect
C. failing to include the firm's name, as licensed, in an advertisement
D. offering to advertise a property, for a fee, for a "For Sale by Owner" seller

> D. *Generally, a licensee may assist a "For Sale by Owner" seller and receive compensation for her services without entering into a brokerage relationship with the seller.*

Under the Uniform Regulation of Business and Professions Act (URBPA), which of the following actions by a licensee would constitute unprofessional conduct?

A. Allowing an unlicensed assistant to submit property information to the multiple listing service
B. Being convicted of a gross misdemeanor related to a motor vehicle accident
C. Failure to include in an advertisement the designated broker's name and telephone number of the brokerage
D. Failure to provide a buyer with a property disclosure form

> D. *Depending on the circumstances, failure to provide a property disclosure form in a transaction where one is required could be considered incompetence, negligence, or malpractice that harms another; or it could be considered misrepresentation in the conduct of real estate activities. Either way, it is a violation of the Uniform Regulation of Business and Professions Act. An advertisement must include the firm's name as licensed, but not the name of the firm's designated broker or the telephone number. (Also, failure to include the firm's name would be purely a license law violation, not a URBPA violation.)*

When a broker attempts to renew his license, he intentionally lists a 3-hour course twice in order to reach 30 hours. The Director can:

A. grant a 45-day interim license until the course is completed
B. suspend the license and charge him with misrepresentation in obtaining or reinstating a license
C. audit the school administrator
D. refer the case to the Attorney General for prosecution

> B. *It is a violation of the license law, and grounds for disciplinary action, for a licensee to engage in misrepresentation or concealment of a material fact when obtaining or reinstating a license.*

The cost of an appeal from a final decision made by the Director of the Department of Licensing in an adjudicative proceeding is paid by the:

A. appellant
B. appellant's real estate brokerage
C. Real Estate Commission
D. state Attorney General

> A. *A licensee appealing the outcome of a disciplinary hearing must post a $1,000 appeal bond to cover court costs, in case the superior court judge decides against the licensee. Even if the licensee wins the appeal, the licensee will still be responsible for the cost of a transcript of the hearing.*

A licensee is a defendant in a civil suit stemming from real estate activities. When must the licensee notify the Real Estate Program Manager?

A. Immediately
B. Within 20 days of a verdict or judgment entered against licensee
C. Within 20 days of service of process
D. Within 90 days of the lawsuit being filed

> B. *A licensee must notify the Department of Licensing within 20 days of learning of any civil court order, verdict, or judgment entered against the licensee, if it involves real estate or business activities.*

Chapter Quiz

1. The following are all goals of the Washington Real Estate Research Center, except:
   A. recommending change to state statutes regarding licensing
   B. promoting growth and development in Washington
   C. determining low income vacancy rates
   D. writing real estate exam questions

2. An out-of-state real estate licensee (who is licensed in another state) may enter Washington to engage in which real estate activity?
   A. Property management
   B. Residential sales
   C. Commercial sales or leasing
   D. Contract collection

3. A real estate agent from Oregon is involved in a commercial property transaction in Washington. The agent from Oregon must do all of the following EXCEPT:
   A. associate with a Washington brokerage
   B. provide a copy of the out-of-state real estate license to the Washington firm
   C. deposit all records in the transaction with the firm in Washington
   D. register with the Department of Licensing at least 20 days before engaging in brokerage activities

4. A licensee is considering an employment offer from a brokerage firm. The position would involve control over the firm's operational and financial decisions. The type of license required would be:
   A. broker
   B. managing broker
   C. managing broker, with a designated broker endorsement
   D. supervisory broker

5. It is not necessary to complete 30 hours of continuing education in order to renew a/an:
   A. designated broker's license
   B. broker's license
   C. inactive license
   D. managing broker's license

6. A property manager handling a vacant building fails, for several months, to keep out vagrants who damage the property. Who is liable?
   A. The management firm's designated broker alone
   B. The property manager alone
   C. The property manager as well as the designated broker (for failing to properly supervise the licensee)
   D. No one is liable

7. A licensee is about to change her business location. Which of the following should she do?
   A. Move her license to the new location until the renewal date
   B. Notify the Director of the Dept. of Licensing by phone
   C. Notify the Real Estate Program Manager in writing
   D. Surrender her license, and apply for an updated license with the correct location

8. Addenda to a purchase and sale agreement must be:
   A. kept in the broker's home office
   B. kept in the brokerage's transaction file
   C. kept in the firm's trust account
   D. signed by the broker

9. Which of the following would not be considered a nominal earnest money deposit, subject to the pooled interest-bearing account requirement?
   A. $5,000 in the form of a personal check
   B. $7,500 in the form of cash
   C. $10,000 in the form of certified funds
   D. $11,000 in the form of a cashier's check

10. Prior to a licensee's first license renewal, she must complete how many hours of education in courses approved by the Director?
    A. 30
    B. 45
    C. 90
    D. 120

11. A licensee hires an unlicensed assistant. While the licensee is on a two-week vacation, the assistant helps negotiate contract addenda. The licensee could be disciplined under Uniform Regulation of Business and Professions Act for:

A. unlicensed practice
B. aiding and abetting unlicensed practice
C. incompetence, negligence, or malpractice
D. misrepresentation

12. Unless the purchase agreement or other contract states differently, an earnest money check given to a real estate licensee shall be made out to the:

A. licensee's firm, as licensed
B. closing or escrow agent
C. seller
D. appropriate multiple listing association

13. Licensees are required to keep the Director notified of changes in their:

A. home telephone number
B. marital status
C. mailing address
D. errors and omissions carrier

14. In preparation for appeal proceedings, the Director of the Department of Licensing prepares a full transcript of the original disciplinary hearing and, per the law, submits it to the court along with a bill for the cost of preparing the materials. Who is responsible for paying for this?

A. Buyer
B. Director
C. Licensee/appellant
D. Seller

15. A group of affiliated licensees forms a team, the XYZ Corporation, within the brokerage they work for (ABC Real Estate). ABC has a firm license, but XYZ does not. Whose name must appear in all the advertising of those affiliated licensees?

A. ABC Real Estate
B. XYZ Corporation
C. Both ABC Real Estate and XYZ Corporation
D. The name of each affiliated licensee

16. S's license is temporarily suspended by the Director for a violation of the license law. S is also fined $500. The money collected as a result of the fine is:

A. placed in the state's general fund
B. used to support existing auditing and investigation services
C. deposited in the Real Estate Education Account, to be used solely for education for the benefit of licensees
D. used to compensate victims of real estate fraud

17. A real estate agent would like to contact a buyer that he previously represented, to ask if that person would be interested in listing her home or if she has any referrals. Under what circumstances could the agent contact that person without having to consult the Do Not Call registry?

A. He represented the buyer within the previous 6 months
B. He represented the buyer within the previous 18 months
C. There is no limit; he can contact the buyer regardless
D. He may never contact the buyer

18. In a disciplinary action, the Director of the Department of Licensing can do any of the following, EXCEPT:

A. award damages to individuals defrauded by real estate licensees
B. revoke a license
C. deny a license
D. refer criminal violations to the prosecuting attorney in the county where the offense was committed

19. A licensee is criminally charged for stealing prescription drugs on July 2. He tells his designated broker about the charges on July 5. Who must notify the Real Estate Program Manager?

A. The licensee must provide notice within 20 days of conviction
B. The licensee must provide notice by July 22
C. The licensee must provide notice by July 25
D. The designated broker must provide notice by July 25

20. Price fixing (including setting commission rates in a community) is prohibited by the:
   A. state Usury Act
   B. federal Regulation Z
   C. Sherman Antitrust Act and state anti-trust laws
   D. federal Real Estate Settlement Procedures Act

Answer Key

1. D. The Real Estate Research Center does not write real estate exam questions; this is the job of the Real Estate Commission.

2. C. Washington law allows out-of-state licensees to perform duties that would require a license when engaged in commercial real estate transactions. The out-of-state licensee must have a written agreement to work in cooperation with a brokerage licensed in Washington.

3. D. An out-of-state licensee may handle commercial real estate transactions in Washington without a license if he works in cooperation with a brokerage in Washington. The Washington firm must have custody of the out-of-state broker's records concerning the in-state transaction, and must receive a copy of the out-of-state broker's license. The Department of Licensing doesn't require out-of-state licensees to register.

4. C. The person who has ultimate responsibility for a firm is a designated broker. There is no designated broker license, though; the designated broker must have a managing broker's license and must receive a designated broker's endorsement for the license.

5. C. The renewal fee must be paid every two years, but as long as the license remains inactive, there is no education requirement.

6. C. The property manager is liable for failing to exercise reasonable care in carrying out the duties she took on for her client. The property manager's designated broker may also be liable for failing to supervise the property manager adequately.

7. D. If a licensee plans to change her place of employment, the firm's designated broker will surrender the license. The Director of the Department of Licensing will then issue a new license for the new location.

8. B. A transaction file should include all modifications or addenda to any agreement. The transaction file should be kept where the firm is licensed to have an office, not in a broker's home office. The addenda will be signed by the buyer and seller, not the broker.

9. D. Nominal earnest money deposits are $10,000 or less.

10. C. She must complete 90 hours (30 hours in advanced real estate practices, 30 hours in real estate law, and another 30 in an elective).

11. B. A licensee may be disciplined under the license law for aiding or abetting an unlicensed person to perform real estate activities that require a license.

12. A. The question and answer correctly state the law; however, it is common practice for the buyer to name an escrow agent in the offer and make out the check to that entity.

13. C. When a licensee changes her mailing address, she is required to notify the Director of the Department of Licensing of that change. (If a licensee's name changes for any reason, including marriage, the licensee must notify the Director. But the licensee does not need to notify the Director simply because of a change in marital status.)

14. C. If a licensee is dissatisfied with the outcome of a disciplinary hearing, she may file an appeal in superior court. The licensee must post a $1,000 appeal bond to cover court costs, and must also pay for a copy of the transcript of the hearing.

15. A. The license law requires that all advertising must include the brokerage firm's name, as licensed, so the name of ABC Real Estate would need to appear in all advertising.

16. C. Fines are deposited in the Education Account and used for the education of licensees.

17. B. If an agent has an established business relationship with a previous client, he may call that person within the 18 months following that person's last transaction, even if that person has placed her name on the Do Not Call registry. (If that person then asks the agent to stop calling, though, the agent must honor that request.)

18. A. The Director cannot award damages to victims of real estate fraud. Many states have what is called a "recovery fund" from which victims of real estate fraud can recover at least part of their losses. Washington doesn't have such a remedy for the consumer, however.

19. B. A licensee must notify the Real Estate Program Manager within 20 days of learning of any criminal complaint or indictment in which the licensee is named as a defendant. A conviction has yet to occur in this situation, although if the licensee is convicted that will also require notifying the DOL.

20. C. The Sherman Antitrust Act and state antitrust laws prohibit price fixing, group boycotts, market allocation, and tie-in arrangements.

Chapter 18
Real Estate Math

I. Solving Math Problems – A simple, four-step approach can be used to solve most real estate math problems.

    A. Four-step Approach

        1. Read the question – Thoroughly read and understand the question so that you know what you want to find out.

        2. Write down the formula – Choose the correct formula and write it down.

        3. Substitute – Substitute the relevant numbers from the problem into the formula. (You may need preliminary steps, such as converting fractions to decimals.)

        4. Calculate – Perform the calculations to find the unknown component. Most formulas have the same basic form: $A = L \times W$. You'll have two of the three numbers (or the information to find two of the numbers) and you'll divide or multiply (depending on which component is unknown) to find the third number.

           a. Compare equation – Compare your equation to the calculation $2 \times 3 = 6$. If the unknown component of your equation is in the same position as the 6 in $2 \times 3 = 6$, then you need to multiply the two given numbers to find the unknown. If the unknown component is in the 2 position or the 3 position, you need to divide. You'll divide the given number in the 6 position by the other given number to find the unknown.

    B. Decimal Numbers – If a problem contains fractions or percentages, convert them into decimals to make the calculations easier.

        1. Converting fractions – To convert a fraction into decimal form, divide the top number of the fraction (the numerator) by the bottom number of the fraction (the denominator).

        2. Converting percentages – To convert a percentage to a decimal, remove the percent sign and move the decimal point two places to the left (add a zero if necessary). To convert a decimal into a percentage, move the decimal point two places to the right and add a percent sign.

      a. **Using a calculator** – The percent key on a calculator performs the conversion of a percentage to a decimal number automatically.

  3. **Decimal calculations** – To add or subtract decimals, put the numbers in a column with their decimal points lined up.

      a. **Multiply decimal numbers** – To multiply decimal numbers, do the multiplication first; then add in the decimal point. (The answer will have as many decimal places as the total number of decimal places in the multiplied numbers.) Add zeros if necessary.

      b. **Divide by decimal numbers** – To divide by a decimal number, move the decimal point in the denominator all the way to the right. Then move the decimal point in the numerator the same number of places to the right. (If necessary, add zeros to the numerator.)

II. Area Problems – Area is usually stated in square feet or square yards. The formula used depends on the shape of the area: square, rectangle, triangle, or some combination.

  A. **Squares and Rectangles** – The formula for finding the area of a square or a rectangle is $A = L \times W$.

  B. **Triangles** – The formula for finding the area of a triangle is: *Area = ½ Base × Height*.

  C. **Odd Shapes** – To find the area of an odd-shaped room, lot, or building, divide it into squares, rectangles, and triangles. Find the areas of those figures and add them up.

  D. **Lot Dimensions** – It is conventional, when giving the dimensions of a lot, to give the length of the property's frontage (along a road or body of water) as the first dimension.

  E. **Important Numbers** – Memorize these numbers:

      1 mile = 5,280 feet

      1 square mile = 640 acres

      1 acre = 43,560 square feet

      1 square yard = 9 square feet

III. Volume Problems – Volume (three-dimensional space) is usually stated in cubic feet or cubic yards.

  A. **Solving Volume Problems** – The formula for calculating volume is: *Volume = Length × Width × Height*, or $V = L \times W \times H$. (It's the same as the area formula, but with one extra element: H.)

Sample questions

Brian purchases two parcels of land, one measuring one square mile and the other containing five acres. If he paid $2,000 an acre, what was his total purchase price?

A. $1,208,000
B. $1,209,000
C. $1,280,000
D. $1,290,000

> D. *One square mile equals 640 acres. Add those to find the total acreage (640 acres + 5 acres = 645 acres). Multiply the acreage by the price per acre to find the total price (645 × $2,000 = $1,290,000).*

The owner of a lot that is 99' by 110' would like to sell it. Similar properties sell for $180,000 per acre. What is the likely selling price for this property?

A. $45,000
B. $54,450
C. $60,000
D. $90,000

> A. *First, find the square footage of the lot (99 feet × 110 feet = 10,890 square feet). Convert that to acreage (10,890 square feet ÷ 43,560 square feet per acre = 0.25, or one-quarter of an acre). Multiply that by the price per acre to find the selling price ($180,000 × 0.25 = $45,000).*

How many square feet are in a square yard?

A. 3
B. 9
C. 27
D. 81

> B. *There are nine square feet in a square yard (3 feet per yard × 3 feet per yard = 9 square feet).*

A warehouse is listed at 60 feet long by 90 feet wide, with 15 foot ceilings. The building rents for 5 cents per cubic foot per month. What is the amount of the monthly rental payment?

A. $270
B. $2,700
C. $4,050
D. $405,000

> C. *First, calculate the building's volume (60 x 90 x 15 = 81,000 cubic feet). Multiply that by the monthly rent rate to find the amount of the monthly payment (81,000 x $0.05 = $4,050).*

IV. **Percentage Problems** – Percentage calculations are involved in problems about commissions, loan interest, property appreciation/ depreciation, and capitalization.

A. **Solving Percentage Problems** – Percentage problems ask you to find a part of a whole. The general formula is: A percentage of the whole equals the part, or *Part = Whole × Percentage*, or *P = W × %*. (Whenever something is expressed as a percentage "of" another number, multiply that other number by the percentage.)

1. **Changing the formula** – If you're given the part and asked to calculate the whole or the percentage, you'll need to rearrange the percentage formula into a division problem. If the whole is the unknown, divide the part by the percentage: *Whole = Part ÷ Percentage*. If the percentage is the unknown, divide the part by the whole: *Percentage = Part ÷ Whole*.

2. **Converting** – Convert the percentage into a decimal number, calculate, and then convert the answer back into a percentage.

B. **Commission Problems** – Most commission problems can be solved with the general percentage formula: *Part = Whole × Percentage*. The part is the amount of the commission, the whole is the amount the commission is based on (usually the sales price), and the percentage is the commission rate.

C. **Loan Problems** – Interest problems and principal balance problems can be solved using the *Part = Whole × Percentage* formula. The part is the amount of the interest, the whole is the loan amount or principal balance, and the percentage is the interest rate.

1. **Interest rates** – Interest rates are expressed as annual rates—a certain percentage per year. When presented with monthly, quarterly, or semi-annual interest payments, multiply the payment amount to determine the annual amount before you substitute the numbers into the formula.

2. **Principal balance** – Some loan problems ask you to determine a loan's current principal balance at a certain point in the loan term.

3. **Effective yield** – Some questions may ask what the lender's effective yield is. This requires you to use the rule of thumb that one discount point is worth the same as one-eighth of one percent of an interest rate to the lender. In other words, one discount point is equivalent to 0.125%. The

effective yield for a lender for a loan at 6% interest with one discount point would therefore be 6.125%.

4. **Cash outflow** – You may also see problems asking what a lender's cash outflow is. Cash outflow is the amount the lender turns over to the borrower as part of the closing process. This is simply the loan amount, minus the cost of any discount points. For instance, a $100,000 loan where the borrower pays one discount point would result in a cash outflow of $99,000 for the lender.

D. **Profit or Loss Problems** – Profit or loss problems ask you to compare the cost or value of a piece of property at an earlier point in time with its cost or value at a later point. Use the formula *Now = Then × Percentage*. Then represents the value or cost of the property at an earlier time; Now represents the value or cost at a later time. The percentage is 100% plus or minus the percentage of profit or loss.

1. **Profit or loss over several years** – Some profit or loss problems involve appreciation or depreciation that has accrued at an annual rate over a specified number of years. Solve this type of problem by applying the Then and Now formula one year at a time, repeating the process for the appropriate number of years.

E. **Capitalization Problems** – Capitalization problems involve the capitalization approach to value used in appraisal. Use the formula *Income = Value × Capitalization Rate*.

1. **Value** – An investment property's value, or the purchase price an investor should be willing to pay for the property in order to obtain a specified rate of return.

2. **Capitalization rate** – The specified rate of return (the percentage of return the investor wants). The desired rate of return varies according to many factors. A higher desired rate of return means a higher capitalization rate and a lower value for the property.

3. **Income** – The annual net income produced by the investment property.

4. **Deductions before applying formula** – In some problems, a vacancy factor and operating expenses must be deducted from gross income to arrive at the net income. *Effective gross income = gross income – vacancy factor.*

5. **Operating expense ratio** – A property's operating expense ratio (O.E.R.) is the percentage of gross income that is used to pay the annual operating expenses. The remainder is the annual net income.

Sample questions

An apartment building has eight units; each unit rents for $800 per month. It is also expected to earn $4,000 per year from laundry and vending machines. An appraiser estimates that the property typically operates with a 5% vacancy factor. What is the property's estimated annual effective gross income?

A. $10,080
B. $13,120
C. $76,760
D. $76,960

> D. Multiply the eight units in the building by the monthly rent to find the monthly income (8 x $800 = $6,400). Multiply that by 12 months per year, to find the annual income (12 x $6,400 = $76,800). Calculate what 5% of that amount is ($76,800 x .05 = $3,840), and subtract that figure from the annual income ($76,800 - $3,840 = $72,960). Add the $4,000 in additional revenue (which is not subject to the vacancy factor) to find the effective gross income ($72,960 + $4,000 = $76,960).

An owner sells a property, and the buyer is going to make a 20% downpayment. The lender requires the buyer to pay two discount points, which turn out to be $1,000. What was the purchase price?

A. $50,000
B. $62,500
C. $75,000
D. $200,000

> B. The purchase price was $62,500. This question is simply two separate percentage problems. First, find the loan amount. Two discount points is 2% of the loan amount, so divide the value of the discount points by 2% to determine that this was a $50,000 loan ($1,000 ÷ .02 = $50,000). The 20% downpayment means this is an 80% loan. Now you can use the loan amount and the loan-to-value ratio to find the purchase price. To calculate the purchase price, divide the loan amount by 80% ($50,000 ÷ .80 = $62,500).

The seller lists her property with XYZ Realty and agrees to pay a commission rate of 6%. The MLS provides that a listing brokerage will split commissions at a 50-50 rate with the selling brokerage. Suzy, a licensee for ABC Realty, finds a buyer and the property sells for $300,000. If Suzy is entitled to a 50/50 split with her brokerage, how much commission will she receive?

A. $2,250
B. $4,500
C. $9,000
D. $18,000

> B. The first step is to calculate how much the seller will owe XYZ Realty ($300,000 x .06 = $18,000). ABC Realty receives 50% of the commission ($18,000 x .5 = $9,000). And Suzy will receive 50% of ABC Realty's share ($9,000 x .5 = $4,500).

The maximum amount that a bank will lend to a borrower is twice the borrower's annual income. If a borrower's annual income is $76,200, and she wants to buy a house for $247,000, how large a downpayment will she need to come up with?

A. $47,300
B. $94,600
C. $170,800
D. She will be ineligible to purchase this house

> B. First, find the maximum amount the bank will lend by multiplying the borrower's income by two ($76,200 x 2 = $152,400). Subtract this amount from the house's cost to find the needed downpayment ($247,000 - $152,400 = $94,600).

A mortgage includes a prepayment penalty of 3% of the loan's principal balance at the time of payoff, if the owner pays off the entire principal before a specified date. Monthly amortized principal and interest payments are $1,484.40, with a 5% annual interest rate. The borrower's balance after making the January 1st payment was $44,731.15. On February 1st, he made the next payment as scheduled, and then after that, paid off the entire remaining balance. What would the prepayment penalty be?

A. $290.30
B. $1,257.20
C. $1,302.99
D. $1,319.37

> C. The first step is to calculate by how much the February 1st mortgage payment would reduce the principal balance. Start with the balance after the January payment and calculate how much annual interest the borrower would owe on that ($44,731.15 × .05 = $2,236.56 annual interest). Then divide that by 12, since this is a monthly payment ($2,236.56 ÷ 12 = $186.38 monthly interest). Subtract that interest from the total payment amount to find how much that payment will reduce the loan's principal ($1,484.40 – $186.38 = $1,298.02). Subtract that amount from the previous balance to find what the balance will be after making the February payment ($44,731.15 – $1,298.02 = $43,433.13). Multiply that balance by 3% to find the amount of the prepayment penalty ($43,433.13 × .03 = $1,302.99).

V. **Tax Assessment Problems** – Use the formula *Tax = Assessed Value × Tax Rate*.

   A. **Assessed Value** – The assessed value is a property's value for taxation purposes.

   B. **Tax Rate** – The tax rate may be stated in three different ways:

      1. **Percentage** – as a percentage of the assessed value,

      2. **Dollar amount** – as a dollar amount per hundred or per thousand dollars of assessed value, or

      3. **Mills** – as a specified number of mills per dollar of assessed value. A mill is one-tenth of one cent (.001). Ten mills equals one cent, and 100 mills equals 10 cents.

VI. Seller's Net Problems – In a seller's net problem, a seller wants to receive a specified net amount at closing, after paying the real estate agent's commission and other closing costs. You calculate how much the property must sell for if the seller is to receive the desired net.

   A. Steps – The usual approach is as follows:

      1. Add – Add the seller's desired net to the costs of the sale except for the real estate agent's commission.

      2. Subtract – Subtract the percent of the commission from 100% (for example, 100% – 6% = 94%).

      3. Divide – Divide the total from step one, by the total from step two. This will give the price at which the property must sell, for the seller to net the desired amount.

   B. Reverse Approach – You may see a problem that, rather than telling you a desired net and asking what the property should sell for, instead tells you what the property sold for and asks how much the seller netted. In this case, you would just go through the steps in reverse order: first, multiply the sales price by the commission percentage. Second, subtract the amount of the commission and the closing costs from the sales price to find the amount netted.

VII. Proration Problems – Proration is the allocation of an expense between two or more parties. In real estate closings, certain expenses are prorated based on the closing date.

   A. Solving Proration Problems – There are three steps in the proration process:

      1. Per diem – Calculate the per diem (daily) rate of the expense.

      2. Number of days – Determine the number of days for which one person is responsible for the expense.

      3. Apply formula – Multiply the per diem rate by the number of days to determine the share of the expense that one party is responsible for: *Share = Rate × Days*.

         a. Finding per diem of annual expense – To determine the per diem rate of an annual expense, divide the expense by 365 days. (Some problems will instruct you to divide by 360 days, to simplify the calculation.)

         b. Finding per diem of monthly expense – To determine the per diem rate of a monthly expense, divide the amount of the expense by the number of days in that particular month. (Some problems will instruct you to use 30-day months.)

B. **Property Taxes** – Property taxes are an annual expense. At closing, the taxes may or may not have been paid. If they've already been paid, the buyer will owe the seller a share of the taxes. If they haven't been paid, the seller will owe the buyer a share.

C. **Insurance Premiums** – A seller is entitled to a refund from the hazard insurance company for any prepaid insurance coverage extending beyond the closing date.

D. **Rent** – If the property being sold is rental property, the seller will owe the buyer a prorated share of any rent that has been paid in advance.

E. **Mortgage Interest** – Two different types of mortgage interest prorations are necessary in most transactions, one for the seller and one for the buyer.

   1. **Seller's interest** – The seller typically owes a final interest payment on the loan he is paying off.

   2. **Buyer's interest** – The buyer also owes some mortgage interest at closing. This is prepaid interest (interim interest) on the buyer's new loan. Prepaid interest covers the closing date through the last day of the month in which closing takes place.

Sample questions

The closing date is August 16. The property's fair market value is $180,000. In this community, property is assessed at 50% of its market value, and taxes are applied at 55 mills per dollar of assessed value. Using a 365-day calendar year and assuming the buyer is responsible for the closing day, what would the buyer's prorated share of the annual property taxes be?

A. $1,856.25
B. $1,871.28
C. $3,078.72
D. $3,743.01

  B. *This problem requires two steps: finding the annual property taxes, and then prorating them. Begin with the tax assessment problem. The assessed value is 50% of the market value ($180,000 × .5 = $90,000). The tax is calculated using mills, which are equivalent to one-tenth of a cent, so 55 mills equals 5.5 cents on the dollar ($90,000 × .055 = $4,950). Next, prorate the annual tax amount. First, find the per diem amount using a 365-day year ($4,950 ÷ 365 = $13.56). Calculate the number of days for which the buyer is responsible (16 in August, including the closing date, 30 in September, 31 in October, 30 in November, and 31 in December = 138 days). Multiply the number of days by the per diem rate to find the amount the buyer must pay at closing, to cover the remainder of the year's taxes ($13.56 × 138 = $1,871.28).*

A seller wants to net $60,000 from a transaction, but will have to pay off a mortgage and other fees, at a total cost of $181,800. The seller will also need to pay a 7% commission. What will the property need to sell for?

A. $241,800
B. $258,726
C. $260,000
D. $276,060

    C. *Start by adding the desired net and the other costs, including the mortgage ($60,000 + $181,800 = $241,800). Subtract the commission percentage from 100% (100% - 7% = 93%), and then divide the total costs by that percentage ($241,800 ÷ 0.93 = $260,000).*

Closing is set for August 1. The seller has already paid the property taxes for the year, totaling $6,000. How much of that amount is the buyer's responsibility?

A. $2,000
B. $2,500
C. $3,000
D. $3,500

    B. *Since the buyer is taking title on August 1, she's responsible for the property taxes for the remaining five months of the year (August, September, October, November, and December). Divide the annual taxes by 12 to find the monthly amount: $6,000 ÷ 12 = $500. Multiply that figure by 5 to determine the buyer's share of the taxes: $500 × 5 = $2,500.*

Chapter Quiz

1. A corn field is bisected by an access road, leaving two triangular lots with a depth of 900 feet and a frontage of 484 feet. If the land sells for $2,000 per acre, how much is each lot worth?

   A. $2,000
   B. $10,000
   C. $20,000
   D. $100,000

2. A rectangular lot measures 215 feet by 154 feet. If comparable land sells for $40,000 per acre, about how much is this lot likely to sell for?

   A. $20,000
   B. $30,000
   C. $40,000
   D. $50,000

3. A square parcel measures 1/8 of a mile by 1/8 of a mile. How many acres is this property?

   A. 10
   B. 20
   C. 40
   D. 80

4. A square parcel of farmland measures 1,320 feet from north to south. In the center of the parcel is eight acres of swampland that is not tillable. If the property sells for $2,000 per acre of tillable land, what is the selling price?

   A. $64,000
   B. $80,000
   C. $96,000
   D. $2,624,000

5. Rudiger purchases a home for $200,000, and receives an 80% loan from his bank. He has to pay three discount points to receive the loan. He is also responsible for a 1% origination fee and a $300 appraisal. The seller paid a 6% commission to the listing brokerage. What is the amount of the discount points that Rudiger paid?

   A. $4,800
   B. $6,000
   C. $6,400
   D. $7,500

6. Ajax Realty lists a property for a seller, at a commission rate of 8%. The multiple listing service provides that a listing brokerage will split commissions at a 50-50 rate. Baron Realty, a cooperating brokerage, finds a buyer for the property, at a price of $300,000. How much will the seller owe Ajax Realty at closing?

   A. $0
   B. $12,000
   C. $18,000
   D. $24,000

7. A metes and bounds description reads as follows: "Start at the intersection of Route 120 and Wells Lane. Proceed due south 1,815 feet, then due east 1,200 feet. Proceed due north 1,815 feet, then return west to point of beginning." How many acres is this property?

   A. 5
   B. 20
   C. 50
   D. 100

8. A living room needs to be re-carpeted. It measures 18 feet long by 15 feet wide. How many square yards of carpet will need to be purchased?

   A. 10
   B. 30
   C. 90
   D. 270

9. A 3,000 square foot retail property rents for $20 per square foot, plus 8% of gross sales. The building's tenant pays $120,000 rent in one year. What were that year's gross sales?

   A. $75,000
   B. $150,000
   C. $750,000
   D. $1,500,000

10. A ten-year-old home cost $120,000 to build and the land it's on cost $20,000. If depreciation has averaged 1.5% per year, what is the total amount of depreciation on the property?

    A. $1,800
    B. $2,100
    C. $18,000
    D. $21,000

11. A property produces a 12% rate of return. The property's net income is $10,500 per month. Using the capitalization method, what is the property's market value?

A. $875,000
B. $1,050,000
C. $1,512,000
D. $2,000,000

12. A property's net operating income is $12,000 per year. If an investor wants a 12% rate of return, how much is the property worth to him?

A. $1,440
B. $100,000
C. $144,000
D. $1,000,000

13. Bob's property has a fair market value of $190,000. It is in a county where properties are assessed at 50% of value, and the tax rate is $55 per $1,000 of assessed value. What's Bob's annual property tax?

A. $2,612.50
B. $5,225.00
C. $7,837.50
D. $10,450.00

14. Through careful management, a property manager increases an apartment building's monthly gross income of $3,000 by an additional $500 per month. Assuming a cap rate of 8%, what is the increase in the building's value?

A. $37,500
B. $43,750
C. $75,000
D. $525,000

15. A rural lot runs 500 feet east/west along its northern boundary, and 600 feet east/west along its southern boundary. Its eastern boundary runs 200 feet due north/south, while its western boundary runs 224 feet in a diagonal northeast/southwest direction. The cost of the land is $6 per square foot. What is the cost of this lot?

A. $600,000
B. $660,000
C. $672,000
D. $720,000

16. Art sold his house, which was not encumbered with a mortgage. Closing expenses were $5,264, and he paid a commission of 7% of the selling price. He received a check at closing for $372,316. What did the house sell for?

A. $398,000
B. $404,260
C. $406,000
D. $411,100

17. A property's real estate taxes are $250 per month, paid at the end of the year. The property is sold and the closing date is May 15. The seller's share of the taxes will be:

A. $750
B. $875
C. $1,000
D. $1,125

18. A borrower takes out an $88,000 loan at 6% interest. The monthly principal and interest payment, amortized over 30 years, is $585. He also makes a $12,000 downpayment. The borrower will need to pay one discount point to the lender. How much is the cost of one discount point?

A. $5.85
B. $88
C. $880
D. $1,000

19. A tenant has already paid his $1,200 rent for the month for a single-family property. The property's owner sells it to a new buyer, with closing occurring on the 15th of June. The parties decide the seller is entitled to rent for the closing date. On the settlement statement, the prorated rent will appear as a:

A. $600 debit for the buyer and a $600 credit for the seller
B. $600 debit for the seller and a $600 credit for the buyer
C. $1,200 credit for the buyer
D. $1,200 credit for the seller

20. Jamie's house is mostly rectangular, measuring 30 feet by 40 feet. There is an enclosed triangular foyer in front, measuring 4 feet across, 4 feet along the perpendicular side, and 5.7 feet along the diagonal side. In the back, there is a screened porch, which is 40 feet long and 5 feet deep. To the side, there is an attached garage, which measures 10 feet by 20 feet. What is the square footage of the living area?

    A. 1,200
    B. 1,208
    C. 1,408
    D. 1,608

Answer Key

1. B. One way to solve this problem would be to find the area of one of the triangular lots. Use the triangle area formula (900 feet × 484 feet × 0.5 = 217,800 square feet). Convert this to acreage (217,800 square feet ÷ 43,560 square feet per acre = 5 acres) and multiply by the cost per acre (5 acres × $2,000 = $10,000). Alternately, one could find the area of the entire corn field (900 feet × 484 feet = 435,600 square feet), convert it to acreage (435,600 square feet ÷ 43,560 square feet per acre = 10 acres), multiply by the cost (10 acres × $2,000 = $20,000), and divide by 2 to find the cost of one of the lots ($20,000 ÷ 2 = $10,000).

2. B. The first step is to find the square footage of the lot (215 feet × 154 feet = 33,110 square feet). Convert this to acreage (33,110 square feet ÷ 43,560 square feet per acre = 0.76 acres). $40,000 × 0.76 is $30,400, closest to $30,000.

3. A. One-eighth of a mile is equivalent to 660 feet (5,280 feet ÷ 8 = 660 feet). Multiply to find its square footage (660 feet × 660 feet = 435,600 square feet), and then divide to find the number of acres (435,600 square feet ÷ 43,560 square feet per acre = 10 acres).

4. A. First, multiply the property's boundaries to find its square footage (1,320 feet × 1,320 feet = 1,742,400 square feet). Convert it to acreage (1,742,400 square feet ÷ 43,560 square feet per acre = 40 acres), subtract the unusable portion (40 acres − 8 acres = 32 acres), and multiply by the price per acre (32 acres × $2,000 = $64,000).

5. A. To calculate the discount points, first find the loan amount ($200,000 x .8 = $160,000). Then multiply that by the percentage of the loan represented by the discount points ($160,000 x .03 = $4,800). Since the question only specified discount points, you would not include the origination fee in your calculations (and you certainly wouldn't need to know the cost of the appraisal or the commission).

6. D. Under the terms of the listing agreement, the seller will pay the listing firm (Ajax) 8% of the sales price ($300,000 × .08 = $24,000). Ajax will share half of that with Baron Realty.

7. C. It may help to sketch the property being described; once you do, you will notice that it is rectangular, and you can simply use the Area = Length × Width formula. Multiply the length and width to find that it is 2,178,000 square feet (1,815 ft. × 1,200 ft. = 2,178,000 sq. ft.). Convert this amount to acreage by dividing by 43,560 (2,178,000 ÷ 43,560 = 50 acres).

8. B. First, multiply the length and width to find the square footage (18 ft. × 15 ft. = 270 sq. ft.). Then, because there are 9 square feet in a square yard, divide by 9 to convert to square yards (270 ÷ 9 = 30 square yards).

9. C. First, calculate the year's rent, by multiplying the square footage by the rental rate (3,000 square feet × $20 per square ft. = $60,000). Next, subtract the amount attributable to the square footage from the total rent, to find the rent attributable to gross sales ($120,000 − $60,000 = $60,000). Finally, divide that portion of the rent by 8% to find the property's gross sales ($60,000 ÷ .08 = $750,000).

10. C. Only the building itself is depreciated, rather than the land, which cannot lose value due to depreciation. Multiply 1.5% by 10 years (since the question says "an average of" 1.5% per year, rather than saying it depreciated 1.5% each year), which is 15%. 15% of $120,000 is $18,000.

11. B. The first step is to determine the annual income ($10,500 per month × 12 = $126,000 per year). Divide that by the capitalization rate to find the property's value ($126,000 ÷ 0.12 = $1,050,000).

12. B. Use the capitalization formula to find the property's value ($12,000 income ÷ 0.12 rate of return = $100,000 value).

13. B. The first step in calculating a tax problem is to find its assessed value ($190,000 × 0.5 = $95,000). Divide the assessed value by $1,000 to find the number of increments ($95,000 ÷ $1,000 = 95) and then multiply by the tax rate to find the annual tax bill (95 × $55 = $5,225).

14. C. One way to solve the problem is to calculate the value before the increase ($3,000 x 12 = $36,000; $36,000 ÷ .08 = $450,000), calculate the value after the increase ($3,500 x 12 = $42,000; $42,000 ÷ .08 = $525,000), and then calculate the difference ($525,000 - $450,000 = $75,000). Another way would be simply to multiply $500 x 12 ($6,000) and then factor in the capitalization rate ($6,000 ÷ .08 = $75,000).

15. B. It's best to diagram this type of problem to solve it. Once you draw it, you would then break it down into a triangle at left and a rectangle at right. The rectangle at right is 500 feet in length and 200 feet in height (500 feet x 200 feet = 100,000 square feet). The triangle at left is 200 feet in height and 100 feet at its base (200 feet x 100 feet x 1/2 = 10,000 square feet); you can ignore the 224 foot diagonal side, which does not factor into your calculations. Add the two components together (100,000 square feet + 10,000 square feet = 110,000 square feet) and then multiply by the cost per square foot (110,000 square feet x $6 per square foot = $660,000) to find its price.

16. C. This is a seller's net problem. The first step is to add the costs of the sale to the seller's net (which in this case is the actual net, not a desired net). Add $5,264 to $372,316, which makes $377,580. Divide that by the commission rate subtracted from 100 (100% - 7% = 93%). $377,580 divided by 0.93 equals $406,000.

17. D. The seller is responsible for taxes for the first four and one-half months (January, February, March, April, and half of May). $250 × 4.5 = $1,125.

18. C. One discount point is the equivalent of one percent of the loan amount. Multiply the loan amount by 1% to find the cost of the discount point ($88,000 × .01 = $880).

19. B. The rent has already been paid to the seller, so the seller will need to give some of that rent to the buyer. Therefore, it will be a debit for the seller and a credit for the buyer. The seller's share is for the 1st through the 15th (15 days), and the buyer is entitled to a credit for the 16th through the 30th (also 15 days), so the seller owes the buyer half of the $1,200, or $600.

20. B. Keep in mind that a house's square footage is based on its outside dimensions, but excludes garages and porches. So, you would only need to calculate the area of the main part of the house (30 feet x 40 feet = 1,200 square feet) and the odd triangular foyer (4 feet x 4 feet x ½ = 8 square feet). Add the two together to find the square footage is 1,208 square feet.

Sample Exam 1

1. Buyers who are looking at a variety of properties should only be shown homes that:

    A. are listed by the agent's firm
    B. are located in neighborhoods where the residents are of a similar race as the buyers
    C. they are qualified to purchase, based on preapproval or qualification
    D. will result in the highest commission for their agent

2. A seller partially finances the buyer's purchase of her property. What should the seller do if she wants to give public notice of her interest in the property?

    A. Ask the buyer to give her a quitclaim deed
    B. Record the warranty deed
    C. Record the mortgage
    D. Secure the property by using a land contract

3. A real estate agent made a listing presentation to a property owner. The owner was impressed with the agent and signed a listing agreement. The owner told the agent that he was married, but his wife was in the hospital and could not sign the listing agreement. He asked the agent to proceed with the listing anyway, because they were in a hurry to sell the house. In these circumstances, the agent should:

    A. do as the seller asks; the agent can get the wife's signature later
    B. do as the seller asks, because dower rights give the husband the right to list the marital property
    C. refuse to take the listing, because the seller clearly has an ulterior motive for trying to sell the property while his wife is ill, and the agent should not get mixed up in a fraudulent transaction
    D. refuse to take the listing, but tell the seller that as soon as the wife signs the listing they can proceed with trying to find a buyer

4. The best description of steering is:

    A. recommending to residents of a neighborhood that they sell because persons of a particular race are increasingly moving into the area
    B. refusing to make loans in a neighborhood based on the race of the residents
    C. showing buyers of a particular race only properties in neighborhoods with many residents of that race
    D. telling a buyer of a particular race that a property has been sold when in fact it hasn't

5. A property manager usually:

    A. appeals tax assessments
    B. makes investment decisions regarding the property's income
    C. makes financing decisions
    D. oversees maintenance projects

6. The capitalized value of a property is $280,000, the capitalization rate is 10%, and the operating expenses are 76% of the annual gross income. What is the gross income?

    A. $110,544
    B. $116,667
    C. $121,503
    D. $128,888

7. A buyer would like protection against any unknown encumbrances on the property she plans to buy. The greatest protection would come from:

    A. a home inspection
    B. a survey
    C. an abstract of title
    D. title insurance

8. A real estate agent is working with buyers who are interested in a house in a new rural subdivision. She tells the buyers that the developer will pave the streets. However, she didn't verify this statement; she assumed that was the case, based on the developer's previous subdivisions. If the buyers rely on this statement and decide to buy the house, and the streets never get paved, who is potentially liable?

   A. The agent, for engaging in misrepresentation through an unverified statement
   B. The county, which is ultimately responsible for rural roads
   C. The developer, for not providing paving as expected
   D. Nobody, as this is a "let the buyer beware" situation

9. Marian needs to rent out her basement to make ends meet. She doesn't place any ads for a tenant or ask for any help from a real estate agent—she merely asks some of her friends if they know of any potential tenants. She carefully screens all the prospects, and decides to rent only to a religious, non-smoking, white female. On which basis is it illegal for her to discriminate?

   A. Race
   B. Gender
   C. Religion
   D. Smoking preference

10. A buyer and seller agree upon an option to purchase, with a 60-day option period. When should the parties agree upon the purchase price?

   A. Any point between the signing of the option agreement and closing
   B. At closing
   C. Before signing the option agreement
   D. When the buyer decides to exercise the option

11. A property is listed for $275,000. The buyers offer $265,000, and insist that the gourmet six-burner stove remain with the property. When the signed offer is presented to the sellers, the sellers accept the price, but want to take the stove with them. They cross out the item about the stove, sign the form, and return it to the buyers. Under these circumstances:

   A. there is now a valid contract that has been signed by all parties
   B. the offer has been invalidated and the buyers will need to begin looking for a new property
   C. the sellers can turn around and accept the original offer, if the buyers won't go along with giving up the stove
   D. the original offer is terminated, and the sellers have made a counteroffer

12. A property is listed for $400,000. The sellers owe $200,000 to the bank on the mortgage, and have agreed to pay a 6% commission. They will also owe $4,000 in other closing costs. If the property sells for full price, what will their net proceeds be?

   A. $172,000
   B. $184,000
   C. $193,600
   D. $200,000

13. A firm's managing broker requires agents to recommend a particular lender to buyers. However, the managing broker has a financial interest in this lender. What should an agent do about this?

   A. Avoid any recommendations of lenders to buyers
   B. Recommend only this lender, as per policy
   C. Recommend this lender after disclosing the broker's interest, and recommend other lenders as well
   D. Recommend whatever lender has the best rates

14. Buyer Bob and Seller Sam decide to wait until Sam's listing agreement with XYZ Real Estate Agency has expired, to avoid paying a commission. Does the firm (and, by extension, the individual listing agent) have any legal recourse?

   A. Yes, the listing agent can pursue criminal charges
   B. Yes, the listing agent can sue Bob under the listing agreement
   C. Yes, the listing agent can sue Sam under the listing agreement
   D. No, the listing agent has no further recourse

15. A legal action brought in court to compel a party to fulfill the terms of a contract because the land is unique and money damages would not adequately compensate the party victimized by a breach is called a/an:

   A. partition action
   B. suit for specific performance
   C. quiet title action
   D. injunction

16. A property sells for $100,000. The commission is 6%. The selling brokerage and listing brokerage split the commission 60/40. Each of the brokerages then splits its share of the commission evenly with its affiliated licensee. How much is the individual listing agent's share of the commission?

   A. $1,200
   B. $2,400
   C. $3,600
   D. $6,000

17. Darren and Martin are agents for a large brokerage firm. They decide that Darren will specialize in listing and selling houses on the north side of the river and Martin will specialize in listing and selling houses on the south side of the river. Such a practice is:

   A. illegal, because only designated brokers may agree to this kind of arrangement
   B. illegal, because both federal and state laws prohibit market allocation
   C. legal, because the agreement was to increase efficiency (and thus it did not restrict trade)
   D. legal, because the prohibition against market allocation does not apply to agents working for the same firm

18. In spite of Delia's objections, the city took a portion of her lot as part of a street widening project. Which of the following is true about eminent domain?

   A. The city can only take vacant land by eminent domain
   B. The city can only take private property for recreational purposes
   C. Delia's property was taken through the process of condemnation
   D. Delia won't be compensated for her lost property

19. A mortgage includes a prepayment penalty of 3% of the loan's principal balance at the time of payoff, if the owner pays off the entire principal before a specified date. Monthly amortized principal and interest payments are $1,484.40, with a 5% annual interest rate. The borrower's balance after making the January 1st payment was $44,731.15. On February 1st, he made the next payment as scheduled, and then after that, paid off the entire remaining balance. What would be prepayment penalty be?

   A. $290.30
   B. $1,257.20
   C. $1,302.99
   D. $1,319.37

20. The maximum amount that a bank will lend to a borrower is twice the borrower's annual income. If a borrower's annual income is $76,200, and she wants to buy a house for $247,000, how large a down-payment will she need to come up with?

    A. $47,300
    B. $94,600
    C. $170,800
    D. She will be ineligible to purchase this house

21. Which of the following would be subject to real property taxes?

    A. A house and the land it's on
    B. Cars and motorcycles
    C. Household furnishings
    D. Only the land, but not the improvements

22. A property is sold for $340,000. There is a remaining mortgage balance of $68,000, and other closing costs will be $6,400. The seller also must pay a brokerage fee of 6.5%. What will the seller net?

    A. $237,100
    B. $243,500
    C. $243,916
    D. $254,320

23. A real estate contract, in order to be valid, must include:

    A. a contingency
    B. a "time is of the essence" clause
    C. an option
    D. consideration

24. Tina is representing the buyers in a transaction; she described the property's boundaries to her clients without clarifying that she was not sure that the boundaries were exactly precise. The buyers, upon taking possession, built a fence along the boundaries that she described, but the neighbors then filed suit because the fence didn't follow the actual boundaries and encroached on their land. Can Tina be held liable for misrepresentation?

    A. Yes, because any offer must include a photocopied legal description of the property
    B. Yes, because she reasonably knew that the described boundaries might not have been correct
    C. No, because the description was not in writing
    D. No, because the buyers were duty-bound to perform their own survey

25. A seller asks an agent to list her property "as is." After signing the listing agreement and completing the disclosure statement, she also orders an inspection that finds black mold behind some insulation in the attic. The seller tells the agent about the inspection results, but neither the seller nor the agent gets around to telling the buyer. Can the buyer sue if he finds the mold at a later date?

    A. No, because it was an "as is" sale
    B. No, because the buyer is obligated to perform his own inspection
    C. No, because mold is not considered a latent defect
    D. Yes, because the seller and agent did not disclose the mold

26. An investor bought four adjacent lots for $88,000 each, and then combined them and divided them into five lots of equal size. These five lots were then sold for $72,000 each. What is the investor's percentage of gross profit?

    A. 2.27%
    B. 18.18%
    C. 34.55%
    D. 97.78%

27. Which of the following would have the greatest negative effect on a residential subdivision property's value?

A. The home's electrical system needs to be updated

B. The improvements are more than 30 years old

C. The property is located next to a busy freeway

D. The property is in a subdivision of very similar-looking houses

28. Erin entered into a lease that begins on February 1, and is set to end on January 31 three years later. This leasehold is a/an:

A. estate for years

B. tenancy at sufferance

C. periodic tenancy

D. estate from year to year

29. A real estate agent shows a listing to two different buyers. One buyer decides in the early morning to make an offer on the property for less than the listed price. The agent writes up the offer and plans to meet with the seller later in the day. The other buyer then contacts the agent and says that she'd like to make a full price offer. What should the agent do?

A. Meet with the sellers but present only the first offer, and then present the second offer only if the first offer is rejected

B. Present both offers to the seller at the same time

C. Tell the second buyer that her offer is invalid because there is already an offer on the property

D. Tell the second buyer that he can only present the first offer to the seller, but he'll present her offer if the first one is rejected

30. A real estate agent completed a listing agreement form, which the sellers signed. At what point should the agent give the sellers a copy of the form?

A. Immediately after they sign the listing form

B. Only after a buyer has made an offer

C. Once the listing has been entered into the local MLS database

D. When the sellers finish filling out the seller disclosure statement

31. Two parties enter into an option agreement, scheduled to end in December. However, in October the optionee decides he doesn't want to buy the property. What should the parties do in order to terminate the option?

A. Complete a formal statement of novation

B. Exercise the option's contingency clause

C. File an interpleader action so a court can void the contract

D. Nothing; the option will expire automatically

32. A prospective tenant asks a licensee to show him only properties that do not allow children. How should the licensee respond?

A. Say that only bona fide retirement communities may exclude children

B. Say that the law requires that all available properties must be shown

C. Say that to do so would be steering, and therefore illegal

D. Show properties that are billed as "adults only"

33. Under normal circumstances, a real estate agent may do which of the following on behalf of a principal?

A. Receive financial benefits from a sale without the principal's knowledge

B. Sign a contract on behalf of the principal

C. Submit all written offers

D. Withhold disclosure of known defects to protect the principal's interests

34. A property produces a 12% rate of return. The property's net income is $10,500 per month. Using the capitalization method, what is the property's market value?

A. $875,000

B. $1,050,000

C. $1,512,000

D. $2,000,000

35. Of the following types of contracts, which one is a unilateral contract?

A. Escrow instructions
B. Exclusive right-to-sell listing
C. Lease
D. Option

36. A property sold for $410,000. The seller has a mortgage outstanding, with a balance of $170,000 that will need to be paid off. The seller owes his real estate agent a 6% commission. The seller also agreed to pay 3% in discount points as a buydown, to help the buyer receive a loan with a 95% LTV. Finally, the seller must pay another $8,000 in closing costs. After all costs are paid, how much will the seller net?

A. $195,715
B. $195,820
C. $200,920
D. $208,939

37. As a result of Federal Reserve action, interest rates for residential loans go down. Which of the following is most likely to occur as a result?

A. Fewer buyers will qualify for loans
B. There will be a decrease in sale prices for homes
C. There will be an increase in sale prices for homes
D. There will be more homes for sale

38. A seller tells her agent that there have been leaks in a bathroom wall from some faulty plumbing, but that the leaks were repaired and that there haven't been any other problems with those pipes. The seller tells the agent not to disclose this information to the buyers, since the problem has been fixed. The agent should:

A. say nothing, since he owes the duty of loyalty to the seller
B. say nothing about the leak, even if asked
C. tell the buyers about the leak, but emphasize that the leak was a minor issue
D. tell the buyers about the leak and that the buyers are entitled to request an inspection

39. Agent Ralph represents the sellers in a transaction. At the time he takes the listing, which of the following should he disclose to the sellers?

A. Current market conditions
B. Neighborhood's racial demographics
C. Presence of asbestos in a neighboring house
D. Presence of sex offender in the neighborhood

40. Carrie owns an apartment building and is discussing marketing strategy with her property manager, Isabel. Isabel suggests that Carrie advertise in the local weekly alternative newspaper, but Carrie refuses to, because it's published by a former business partner with whom she's fallen out. Isabel argues that she's had great results advertising other properties in this publication, but Carrie still refuses. What should Isabel do?

A. Advertise in it, because the property manager is an independent contractor and has authority to make low-level administrative decisions
B. Advertise in it, to avoid potential discrimination claims
C. Not advertise in it, because the property manager is an agent who must obey a principal's instructions
D. Not advertise in it, because the property manager, as a special agent, does not have authority to make such decisions

41. Which of the following statements by a seller's agent to a buyer would be a violation of the agent's fiduciary duties toward his principal?

A. The house has been on the market for four months
B. The owner is eager to sell and willing to accept an offer lower than the listing price
C. The roof has leaked in especially heavy rains in recent years
D. Your earnest money deposit will be returned to you if you aren't able to obtain financing

42. Which of the following persons could be eligible to receive a VA loan?

   A. A veteran or a deceased veteran's children
   B. A veteran or a deceased veteran's children or unremarried spouse
   C. A veteran or a deceased veteran's unremarried surviving spouse
   D. Only a veteran him or herself

43. Cho is representing a buyer who decides to purchase a home listed by another agent who works for the same real estate firm as Cho. What type of an agency has been created?

   A. Dual
   B. Implied
   C. Non-agency
   D. Universal

44. Of the following, which would have the greatest effect on the supply of real estate in a particular market?

   A. Demographic change
   B. Employment rates
   C. Local amenities
   D. Size of labor force

45. A property owner has riparian rights. This suggests that her property is next to:

   A. a river or stream
   B. a road or street
   C. agricultural property
   D. oil or mineral deposits

46. A neighbor's fence mistakenly extends onto a property. This would be considered a/an:

   A. easement
   B. encroachment
   C. encumbrance
   D. license

47. A one-story house had original dimensions of 60' by 30'. However, a new addition, measuring 24' by 20', was recently added by the owners. The house's total square footage is now:

   A. 1,320
   B. 1,800
   C. 2,280
   D. 5,040

48. A buyer makes an offer that's accompanied by a deposit. The deposit is sometimes called:

   A. escrow
   B. option money
   C. referral fee
   D. earnest money

49. One tax advantage of investing in real estate is:

   A. high liquidity
   B. low risk
   C. homestead protection
   D. sheltering of income

50. A mortgage company charges three points on a $250,000 loan. How much is the charge?

   A. $750
   B. $2,250
   C. $7,500
   D. $22,500

51. A tenant farmer had a heart attack, and he had to terminate his lease and retire. However, his last crop was still growing in the field and he wanted the right to come back and harvest it when it was ripe. The crops are considered to be:

   A. emblements, which belong to the tenant farmer
   B. fixtures, which belong to the property owner
   C. real property, which belongs to the property owner
   D. trade fixtures, which belong to the farmer

52. What principle underlies competitive market analysis?

   A. A property's highest and best use is the most profitable use it can legally be used for
   B. A property's selling price can be estimated using selling prices of comparable properties
   C. Competition within the marketplace leads to lower interest rates
   D. Market value can only be determined precisely through an appraisal

53. A homeowner has an unpaid hospital bill for $20,000. The hospital files suit and wins a judgment for the full amount. Is the homeowner's home (which he owns free and clear) at risk?
    A. No, because the debt must be at least $25,000 to force a sale
    B. No, because the debt must exceed the value of the homestead
    C. Yes, but he may be partly or fully protected by state homestead laws
    D. Yes, a court may always force a sale to fulfill a judgment

54. The result of an unreleased lien is a/an:
    A. easement
    B. cloud on the title
    C. condemnation action by the city
    D. lis pendens

55. The listing agreement states that a property is 5.1 acres. The purchase and sale agreement states that it's 5.12 acres. The mortgage notes that the property is 5.22 acres, while the deed states that the lot's size is 5.21 acres. If there is a dispute, which of the documents will take precedence?
    A. Deed
    B. Listing agreement
    C. Mortgage
    D. Purchase and sale agreement

56. Which of the following entities would participate in the primary market for mortgage lending?
    A. Commercial bank
    B. Federal Home Loan Mortgage Corporation
    C. Federal Housing Administration
    D. Federal National Mortgage Association

57. Price fixing (including setting commission rates in a community) is prohibited by the:
    A. state Usury Act
    B. federal Regulation Z
    C. Sherman Antitrust Act and state antitrust laws
    D. federal Real Estate Settlement Procedures Act

58. A borrower obtains a home equity loan on a property he already owns. The Truth in Lending Act allows the borrower to rescind the loan transaction within:
    A. three days after signing the agreement or receiving the disclosure statement
    B. three days after receiving the funds
    C. one week after signing the agreement or receiving the disclosure statement
    D. one week after receiving the funds

59. When performing a competitive market analysis, a real estate agent should:
    A. disregard current and expired listings
    B. consider the land and improvements separately
    C. pick comparables similar in age and quality to the subject property
    D. use the gross rent multiplier method

60. A federal law requires lenders to give the booklet "Shopping for Your Home Loan" to all prospective borrowers within three business days of loan application. What law is this?
    A. Regulation Z
    B. Home Loan Disclosure Act
    C. RESPA
    D. Truth in Lending Act

61. Which of the following is true about surveys?
    A. They determine placement of improvements on a property
    B. They identify setback lines from property boundaries
    C. They protect against easements by prescription
    D. They reveal encroachments not of public record

62. A property management agreement must contain which of the following?
    A. A salary for the property manager
    B. What percentage of the property's net income will be used as the manager's commission
    C. Marketing plans
    D. The property manager's scope of authority

63. A test that a court might apply to determine whether an item is a fixture or personal property is:

   A. age
   B. expense
   C. size
   D. use

64. Marla and Jerry bought property together. They set it up so that the following would happen: if Marla died, Jerry would own the entire property, and if Jerry died, Marla would own the entire property. They own the property in which manner?

   A. Joint tenancy
   B. Severalty
   C. Tenancy in common
   D. An estate for years

65. A buyer is about to purchase a vacant lot in a new subdivision. The development plans for the subdivision state that all lots must be a minimum size of one acre. If the buyer goes through with the purchase, his deed would be subject to a/an:

   A. easement
   B. encroachment
   C. lien
   D. restriction

66. Sara is interested in buying a home that is located next to a creek. Sara's agent should advise her to check whether:

   A. a death has ever occurred on the property
   B. the property has asbestos insulation
   C. the property is located in a flood plain
   D. the property is subject to radon

67. An investor would like to invest in real estate, but without being involved in management or subjecting himself to any personal liability. He should invest in a:

   A. general partnership
   B. joint venture
   C. limited partnership
   D. sole proprietorship

68. Which of the following describes a violation of the Americans with Disabilities Act?

   A. A recently built one-story apartment complex with doorways too narrow for wheelchair users
   B. A rental house that does not have a wheelchair ramp at its entrance
   C. A shopping center without wheelchair-accessible restrooms
   D. An older 40-unit apartment building without elevators

69. What is a final mortgage payment that is larger than all of the other payments called?

   A. Advanced
   B. Amortized
   C. Balloon
   D. Expanded

70. One of the economic characteristics of real estate is:

   A. immobility
   B. location
   C. scarcity
   D. topography

71. A metes and bounds description reads as follows: "Start at the intersection of Route 120 and Wells Lane. Proceed due south 1,815 feet, then due east 1,200 feet. Proceed due north 1,815 feet, then return west to point of beginning." How many acres is this property?

   A. 5
   B. 20
   C. 50
   D. 100

72. Milo is filing his federal income tax return. He can deduct:

   A. capital improvements he's made to his home
   B. the interest paid on his mortgage
   C. the principal paid on his mortgage
   D. maintenance expenses for his home

73. The deed restrictions in a subdivision prohibit homeowners from building fences. However, the city where the subdivision is located permits the construction of fences. Which of the following is true?

   A. Deed restrictions cannot address matters such as fence construction

   B. The city's ordinances would take precedence, because it is a governmental entity

   C. The deed restrictions would take precedence, because they are more restrictive

   D. The deed restrictions would be found unenforceable as against public policy

74. A contract gives a person the right to purchase property for a particular price within a certain timeframe. This contract is a/an:

   A. land contract

   B. lien agreement

   C. sale-leaseback

   D. option

75. A loan's interest is best defined as:

   A. a charge paid by a borrower in exchange for use of the lender's money

   B. a penalty assessed against a borrower's debt

   C. a surcharge that increases a lender's yield

   D. compensation for the lender's potential loss

76. Amortization is defined as:

   A. declaring an entire debt due in the event of default

   B. mutual withdrawal from a contract

   C. paying both principal and interest on a loan on an installment basis

   D. use of secondary financing to complete the purchase of real estate

77. A seller asks an appraiser to help determine a realistic listing price for her single-family, owner-occupied house. Which approach to value would the appraiser rely on when making this decision?

   A. Cost approach

   B. Gross rent multiplier method

   C. Income approach

   D. Market data approach

78. To be valid, a listing agreement may be signed by:

   A. an attorney in fact

   B. the buyer

   C. the designated broker only, with the owner's authorization via telephone

   D. the licensee only

79. The best description of the boundary lines for a property found in a subdivision would be found on:

   A. a plat map

   B. the deed

   C. the mortgage

   D. the purchase and sale agreement

80. A seller complains that the seller's agent is showing other properties to buyers that compete with the seller's property. Which of the following is true?

   A. Seller's agent is breaching the duty of loyalty to seller

   B. Seller's agent is not breaching the duty of loyalty

   C. Seller's agent has created a conflict of interest

   D. Seller's agent may do so, but only with the seller's express permission

81. Which of the following will terminate a lease?

   A. Lis pendens

   B. Mutual agreement

   C. Revocation

   D. Special assessment

82. The process of acquiring title to property through open, notorious, hostile, and continuous use is known as:

   A. adverse possession

   B. condemnation

   C. dedication

   D. prior affiliation

83. A property has lost value because its maintenance and upkeep have been neglected. This would be an example of:

   A. external obsolescence

   B. functional obsolescence

   C. internal obsolescence

   D. physical deterioration

84. Sheila obtained a home loan from a commercial lender, and paid for a mortgagee's title policy. Who would this policy protect?

    A. Sheila (the buyer)
    B. Only the lender
    C. Both Sheila and the lender
    D. The seller

85. A real estate agent is helping a young couple buy a home. The husband's sister will be living with them, and the couple would like to take title so that if either the husband or wife died, the remaining spouse and the sister would own the home together. The agent should:

    A. tell them to consult an attorney
    B. refer them to another agent who specializes in titles
    C. suggest they take title as joint tenants
    D. suggest they take title as tenants in common

86. Which of the following actions would most likely create the largest increase in the value of a property?

    A. Installing a second bathroom in a house with four bedrooms and only one bath
    B. Putting a swimming pool in the yard of a small house
    C. Replacing an obsolete, inefficient furnace
    D. Repairing a leaking basement

87. In what order would these steps be performed when using the income approach to value?

    1. Apply the cap rate to the net income.
    2. Estimate the potential gross income.
    3. Determine the net operating income.
    4. Calculate the effective gross income.
    A. 3, 1, 4, 2
    B. 1, 3, 2, 4
    C. 2, 4, 3, 1
    D. 2, 3, 1, 4

88. Under Title VIII of the Civil Rights Act of 1968, certain transactions are exempt. Which one of the situations below would be exempted and not a violation of the act?

    A. A church-owned apartment complex where language in the lease restricts tenancy to members of a specific national origin
    B. Members of a certain ethnic group are denied lodging in facilities operated by a private club for commercial purposes
    C. An unlisted home that is for sale by owner, where the only advertising is a sign in front of the property that reads simply "For Sale" and the owner owns only one other home
    D. An absentee owner who rents units in a four-plex without the help of a real estate agent

89. Allen begins providing construction services on May 2 and records a construction lien on May 5. Bart begins providing services on May 3 and records a construction lien on May 4. On May 10, a judgment lien against the property is recorded. The property's owner also receives notice on May 10 that he is in arrears on his property tax payments. Which lien has lien priority?

    A. Allen's lien
    B. Bart's lien
    C. Judgment lien
    D. Tax lien

90. Which of the following is true about a building designated a historical landmark?

    A. All lead paint must be removed immediately
    B. It may not be willfully destroyed without a permit
    C. It may only be sold to family members
    D. It must comply with all local ordinances

91. An apartment building was built in 1960. An apartment is being rented to a couple with no children. Which of the following is true?

    A. The rules on lead-based paint don't apply unless the tenants have children
    B. The rules on lead-based paint don't apply to tenants, only purchasers
    C. The tenants must receive a ten-day window in order to test for lead-based paint
    D. The tenants should sign the lead-based paint disclosure and receive a pamphlet on lead-based paint

92. A buyer's agent has repeatedly seen sales collapse at the last minute because the buyers weren't able to obtain financing. How could he best limit this in the future?

    A. Qualify all prospects himself
    B. Refer buyers to a specific lender
    C. Require prospects to be approved first
    D. Show lower-priced properties

93. A property manager of a ten-unit building shows an apartment to a woman who uses a wheelchair. The woman says that she would need to make some modifications, such as adding grab bars in the shower and removing some carpeting in the bedroom. The landlord:

    A. can refuse to rent to the tenant because of the tenant's proposals
    B. must allow the tenant to make the modifications at her own expense, but can require her to restore the property at the end of the lease
    C. must allow the tenant to make the modifications at her own expense, and cannot require the tenant to restore the property at the end of the lease
    D. must make the modifications and pay for the expenses himself

94. A warehouse is listed at 60 feet long by 90 feet wide, with 15-foot ceilings. The building rents for five cents per cubic foot per month. What is the amount of the monthly rental payment?

    A. $270
    B. $2,700
    C. $4,050
    D. $405,000

95. Chin, a home seller, is talking to his real estate agent. He mentions that he rents the backup generator; it doesn't belong to him. The generator would be considered:

    A. a fixture
    B. a natural attachment
    C. a trade fixture
    D. personal property

96. Carl is housebound and never goes outside. Neighbor Salvador plants a vegetable garden on a corner of Carl's property that is not visible from the main house. After the required period of time, Salvador claims a prescriptive easement over this portion of Carl's land. This easement is:

    A. not valid, because Salvador had a duty to inform Carl of his intended use
    B. not valid, because Carl didn't know of the use and had no chance to formally object
    C. valid, because Salvador's vegetable garden is a productive use of the land
    D. valid, because the use was open, and Carl's knowledge of the use isn't considered

97. To be enforceable, a contract for the sale of real estate must be in writing and signed by the parties. This is true because of which law?

    A. Real Estate License Law
    B. Uniform Commercial Code
    C. Real Estate Settlement Procedures Act
    D. Statute of Frauds

98. A mortgage that uses both real and personal property to secure the borrower's debt is a:

    A. reverse equity mortgage
    B. budget mortgage
    C. package mortgage
    D. deed of trust

99. When a borrower makes payments on a fully amortized loan, her debt service payments will cover:

    A. only principal on the loan
    B. only interest on the loan
    C. both principal and interest on the loan
    D. principal, interest, taxes, and insurance

100. An appraiser is trying to estimate depreciation when valuing an older residential rental property, but is finding it difficult because no comparables have sold recently. However, the appraiser can find sufficient data on rental rates in the same market, and a capitalization rate can be supported. Which approach to value should the appraiser use?

   A. Cost
   B. Income
   C. Market data
   D. Sales comparison

101. The term "familial status" in the federal Fair Housing Act refers to the presence of:

   A. adult children of tenants living on the property
   B. children under the age of 18 living on the property
   C. disabled persons living on the property
   D. unmarried persons living on the property

102. A type of lease that allows the lessor to share in the increasing sales generated by a retail property is a/an:

   A. percentage lease
   B. graduated lease
   C. index lease
   D. net lease

103. Special assessments levied against a property for local improvements, such as streetlights and sidewalks, are computed on the basis of:

   A. the market value of the property
   B. the benefit the property receives from the improvements
   C. a recent appraisal of the property
   D. the square footage of the land

104. Under which of the following circumstances would a listing be terminated?

   A. Real estate agent who took the listing dies
   B. Seller dies
   C. Property is rezoned after listing is signed
   D. Listing agent goes to work for another firm

105. A property's net operating income is $12,000 per year. If an investor wants a 12% rate of return, how much is the property worth to him?

   A. $1,440
   B. $100,000
   C. $144,000
   D. $1,000,000

106. J is selling real estate without a license. J is guilty of a:

   A. misdemeanor
   B. gross misdemeanor
   C. second degree felony
   D. first degree felony

107. The pamphlet on agency law:

   A. must be given to parties before a written agreement is signed
   B. must be given to the seller before completing the Seller Disclosure Form
   C. must be available at open houses
   D. is not relevant in commercial transactions

108. T represents J, a buyer. A week after J purchases a home, he decides to resell it. What role can T play in the resale transaction?

   A. T could act as dual agent for the two parties, or represent either of them
   B. T can only represent J
   C. T can only represent a prospective buyer
   D. T must wait 90 days before representing either party to the new transaction

109. A buyer discovered, after purchasing a property, that there was major foundation damage that would cost $13,500 to repair. It was later discovered that the agent representing the seller knew of this damage yet failed to disclose it to the buyer. The agent could be subject to:

   A. a fine of up to $5,000
   B. a fine of up to $10,000
   C. a fine of up to $13,500
   D. prosecution for conversion

110. If a designated broker wishes to terminate an affiliated licensee, or an affiliated licensee wants to terminate employment with a brokerage, which of the following statements is true?
    A. Either party may act unilaterally to end the relationship
    B. An affiliated licensee may terminate only after she pays all debts incurred to the brokerage
    C. A designated broker may terminate an affiliated licensee only if there is good cause for termination
    D. Only the affiliated licensee can terminate employment

111. A brokerage manages a property. The property management records must be kept in:
    A. a location where the firm is licensed to have an office
    B. the property being managed
    C. the firm's personal files
    D. the firm's safe deposit box

112. A real estate licensee would enter into a buyer agency relationship when she:
    A. agrees to show the buyer her listings
    B. agrees to show the buyer another agent's listings
    C. signs a subagency agreement with the seller
    D. None of the above

113. If any criminal charge is filed against a licensee, he:
    A. must report this to the Department of Licensing within 20 days
    B. must report this to the Department of Licensing only if a jail sentence is imposed
    C. must ask the prosecutor to report the charges to the Department of Licensing
    D. is subject to immediate license suspension

114. A broker can serve as a closing agent for a fee in the state of Washington, if the:
    A. broker is a licensed escrow officer
    B. fee is reasonable
    C. buyer and seller agree
    D. broker discloses the fact to all parties

115. Who is responsible for the earnest money deposit?
    A. The listing firm
    B. The selling firm
    C. The mortgage company
    D. The firm to which the check is made payable

116. Who issues rules and regulations that govern the activities of real estate licensees?
    A. Director
    B. Governor
    C. Real Estate Commission
    D. Real Estate Program Manager

117. Which of the following is an example of commingling?
    A. Placing a buyer's deposit in a trust account
    B. Depositing rent from a commercial rental account in a trust account
    C. Depositing an employee's paycheck in a trust account
    D. Paying the firm's commission directly from a trust account

118. Real estate license fees are put into the:
    A. Director's personal account
    B. Real Estate Commission Account
    C. Real Estate Education Fund
    D. Washington Association of Realtors trust account

119. ABC, a brokerage firm, is entitled to a commission of $10,000 from a client. The commission will come out of its trust account for that client. ABC has an advertising bill in the amount of $10,500. The designated broker deposits $500 of the firm's money into the trust account and then writes a check for $10,500 out of the trust account to the advertiser. Which of the following is TRUE?

A. ABC is subject to disciplinary action for commingling

B. This is permissible, since ABC was entitled to the money for the commission

C. This is lawful, but confusing for the advertiser, who receives a trust fund check

D. As long as ABC kept accurate records, its actions were legal

120. An affiliated licensee owns a wholly owned S corporation, A Realty. He instructs an escrow agent to issue a commission check directly to A Realty. How has he violated the real estate license law?

A. A third party can't give instructions to an escrow agent

B. Commissions can be paid to licensees only via their firm

C. The licensee didn't first inform the principals

D. The licensee may charge for escrow services only if he is also a licensed escrow agent

121. A 30 clock-hour course must be completed to activate a license that has been inactive for more than:

A. six months
B. one year
C. two years
D. three years

122. All advertising placed by a real estate licensee (except ads for a licensee's own property) must:

A. meet the requirements for a blind ad
B. be paid for with trust funds
C. include the brokerage's name, as it appears on its license
D. include the Washington Fair Housing logo

123. Q makes a full-time living selling real estate, even though Q does not have a real estate license. Q's activities are legal if Q:

A. sells his own property
B. sells raw land only
C. is an employee of a developer
D. is a salaried employee of a real estate brokerage firm

124. When a licensee appeals the Director's disciplinary decision to the superior court, which of the following is true?

A. The sanctions imposed by the Director remain in effect throughout the appeals process

B. The sanctions imposed by the Director are stayed until the appeals process is complete

C. The results of the Director's disciplinary hearing are set aside

D. The licensee has no right of appeal

125. Which of the following is an absolute requirement of a selling agent in every real estate transaction?

A. The agent must disclose that he is the agent for the buyer

B. The agent must disclose that he is the agent for the seller

C. The agent must conduct himself in accordance with the agency disclosure made

D. The agent must disclose that his fiduciary responsibilities rest with the party that is paying the commission

126. The selling agent must NOT accept a promissory note as an earnest money deposit:

A. unless the agent knows that the buyer has an excellent credit history

B. unless the purchase and sale agreement discloses that the deposit is a note

C. unless the seller agreed during negotiation discussion to accept a promissory note

D. under any circumstances

127. S's license is temporarily suspended by the Director for a violation of the license law. S is also fined $500. The money collected as a result of the fine is:

    A. placed in the state's general fund
    B. used to support existing auditing and investigation services
    C. deposited in the real estate education account, to be used solely for education for the benefit of licensees
    D. used to compensate victims of real estate fraud

128. M tells her next-door neighbor, P, that she will pay him a commission if he can help sell her home. P, an unemployed bartender, locates a buyer and a sale results. M changes her mind and refuses to pay P his promised commission. Which of the following is TRUE?

    A. P is entitled to a commission if it is called a finder's fee
    B. P is entitled to a commission, as long as he did nothing that would require a license
    C. P is not entitled to a commission, because he is unlicensed
    D. P is not entitled to a commission, because M is unlicensed

129. M passes her real estate license examination on August 16. Three months later she accepts employment from ABC Realty. No later than two years following the activation of her license, she must at a minimum:

    A. pay the stipulated renewal fee
    B. complete a 30 clock-hour advanced real estate practices course, a 30 clock-hour law course, plus an additional 30 hours of continuing education, and pay the stipulated renewal fee
    C. take a real estate law course and pay the stipulated renewal fee
    D. apply for the real estate managing broker's license examination

130. Appointments to the Real Estate Commission are made by:

    A. general election
    B. the Director of the Department of Licensing
    C. the Governor
    D. the state legislature

131. A brokerage firm's trust accounts must be opened:

    A. in the firm's name, and must be designated as trust accounts
    B. with the designated broker listed as the beneficiary of the trust
    C. in a recognized financial institution in the same county as the firm's office
    D. with signature cards for all trust beneficiaries

132. A quarterly summary statement given by a property manager to her client would contain all of the following, EXCEPT:

    A. balance carried forward from last statement
    B. rent receipts
    C. itemized expenditures
    D. a recent appraisal of the property

133. Any person employed, either directly or indirectly, by a real estate brokerage—or any person who represents a real estate brokerage—in any capacity that requires a real estate license, is a/an:

    A. associate licensee
    B. broker
    C. business opportunities broker
    D. designated broker

134. It is not necessary to complete 30 hours of continuing education in order to renew a/an:

    A. active license
    B. broker's license
    C. inactive license
    D. managing broker's license

135. A licensee, with permission from his designated broker, sets up his own subsection S corporation, which he calls M Realty. He then rents a billboard and advertises a listing on it, using only the M Realty name. Is this legal?

    A. No, because ads must give the name of the firm
    B. No, because the firm must be the one that rents the billboard
    C. Yes, because he had the designated broker's consent
    D. Yes, because he used the exact corporation name that was registered with the Secretary of State

136. In Washington, a person licensed to act on behalf of a real estate brokerage is called a/an:

    A. independent licensee
    B. affiliated licensee
    C. associate licensee
    D. designated licensee

137. When a licensee is terminated, the date of termination is the:

    A. postmark date or the date the license is hand-delivered to the Department of Licensing
    B. moment the termination is understood and agreed upon by both the designated broker and the affiliate
    C. date the termination notice is tendered by either the designated broker or the agent
    D. date the terminated license is received by the Department of Licensing

138. A real estate agent sold a home for $275,000. Prior to closing, the agent's license was revoked on grounds of moral turpitude. With respect to his eligibility for the commission, which of the following statements is true?

    A. He is eligible for the commission because he was duly licensed when the sale was made
    B. He is eligible for the commission because he is technically licensed until all appeals have been exhausted
    C. He is not eligible for a commission because he was not licensed at the time the commission was paid
    D. He is not eligible for a commission because a license revocation automatically nullifies any right to commissions that are yet unpaid

139. In a disciplinary action, the Director of the Department of Licensing can do any of the following, EXCEPT:

    A. award damages to individuals defrauded by real estate licensees
    B. revoke a license
    C. deny a license
    D. refer criminal violations to the prosecuting attorney in the county where the offense was committed

140. Q falls behind on his child support payments. The matter is forwarded to the Director of the Department of Licensing. What action is available to the Director? She can:

    A. suspend Q's license
    B. revoke Q's license
    C. fine Q up to $5,000
    D. issue a cease and desist order

317

Answer Key

1. **C** It is a waste of time and a source of frustration to show properties to buyers that they will not be able to afford. As a result, it's important to make sure buyers are preapproved or prequalified before showing properties.

2. **C** The seller would want to record the mortgage, to give notice to the world of her financial interest in the property. The buyer, of course, will want to record the deed, to give notice of his ownership interest.

3. **D** All of the owners of a property should sign the listing agreement. Even if the spouse of an owner doesn't have any ownership interest, he or she should sign the listing to avoid any doubt as to the agent's authority.

4. **C** Steering involves channeling buyers or tenants of a particular protected class either toward or away from a neighborhood based on the presence or absence of that protected class.

5. **D** It would depend on the scope of the authority given to the property manager in the management agreement, but investment decisions are not commonly made by property managers. Property managers are usually concerned with the building's maintenance, and may arrange with contractors to provide needed services.

6. **B** Multiply the property value by the capitalization rate to get the net income ($280,000 × 10% = $28,000). If the operating expenses are 76% of the gross income, then the net income ($28,000) is the remaining 24% of the gross. Divide $28,000 by 24% to get the gross income ($28,000 ÷ 24% = $116,667).

7. **D** Title insurance offers protection against latent or undiscovered defects in the title. Buyers almost always protect their interests with a title insurance policy.

8. **A** A licensee owes all parties the duty of acting honestly and in good faith. Even an unintentional misrepresentation can be constructive fraud, so the buyers could sue for damages.

9. **A** Marian falls under the "Mrs. Murphy" exemption to the federal Fair Housing Act, but there is no such exemption from the Civil Rights Act of 1866, which prohibits discrimination based on race.

10. **C** An option agreement should contain all of the details that a purchase and sale agreement would contain. Once the option is exercised, the option agreement serves as the sale contract.

11. **D** Even though the sellers accepted the price change, they still changed the terms of the offer by altering the part about the stove. This had the effect of terminating the offer and creating a counteroffer. The sellers, in essence, become the new offerors.

12. **A** First, calculate the amount of the commission ($400,000 × .06 = $24,000). Subtract the outstanding mortgage balance, commission, and other costs from the selling price ($400,000 − $200,000 − $24,000 − $4,000 = $172,000).

13. **C** It is best for a real estate agent to recommend multiple lenders, so that a buyer can shop around for the best rates (and consider other factors, like quality of services provided). If the licensee or the firm has a financial relationship to the lender, that business relationship should be disclosed.

14. D If a listing agreement does not include an extender clause (a safety clause), the listing agent has no recourse against a buyer and seller who avoid paying a commission by waiting to close until after the listing has expired. For this reason, most listing agreement forms have an extender clause. (Note: this question doesn't involve the license law, so it's a national question and not about Washington law or practice. While the question might be considered tricky, if you face a question like this on the state exam you should assume there is no extender clause since the question doesn't mention one.)

15. B The legal premise that no two properties are alike is the basis for a suit for specific performance, which asks the court to order someone who has breached to actually perform the contract as agreed (deliver the deed to the buyer), rather than simply pay money damages.

16. A The total commission amount is $6,000 ($100,000 × .06 = $6,000). If the brokerages split it 60/40, the selling brokerage will receive $3,600 ($6,000 × .6 = $3,600) and the listing brokerage will receive $2,400 ($6,000 × .4 = $2,400). The individual listing agent's share will be $1,200 ($2,400 ÷ 2 = $1,200).

17. D If Darren and Martin worked for competing brokerage firms, this would be market allocation, and a violation of the Sherman Act. However, because they work for the same firm, they are technically not in competition with each other and their actions are legal.

18. C Eminent domain is the constitutional power to take private property for a public use. Condemnation is the process by which the property is taken.

19. C The first step is to calculate by how much the February 1st mortgage payment would reduce the principal balance. Start with the balance after the January payment and calculate how much annual interest the borrower would owe on that ($44,731.15 × .05 = $2,236.56 annual interest). Then divide that by 12, since this is a monthly payment ($2,236.56 ÷ 12 = $186.38 monthly interest). Subtract that interest from the total payment amount to find how much that payment will reduce the loan's principal ($1,484.40 − $186.38 = $1,298.02); this is important—otherwise, you are calculating the penalty on interest that hasn't accrued yet (interest on a real estate loan isn't due till the end of a payment period). Subtract that amount from the previous balance to find what the balance will be after making the February payment ($44,731.15 − $1,298.02 = $43,433.13). Multiply that balance by 3% to find the amount of the prepayment penalty ($43,433.13 × .03 = $1,302.99). [Note: alternatively, the interest rate itself may be divided by 12 and the result multiplied by the balance after the January payment and then proceed from there.]

20. B First, find the maximum amount the bank will lend by multiplying the borrower's income by two ($76,200 × 2 = $152,400). Subtract this amount from the house's cost to find the needed downpayment ($247,000 − $152,400 = $94,600).

21. A Real property taxes are assessed on the entire value of the property, taking into account both the value of the land and the improvements.

22. B This is a seller's net problem, except backwards, starting with the sales price. Start by finding the amount of the commission ($340,000 × 0.065 = $22,100) and then subtract the commission from the price paid ($340,000 − $22,100 = $317,900). Subtract the other costs that must be paid to find the seller's net ($317,900 − $74,400 = $243,500).

23. D Any contract, whether for real estate or anything else, must include consideration as one of the four basic elements.

24. B An agent's duty of honesty and good faith requires her to avoid inaccuracies in statements to all parties to a transaction. This includes even unintentional misrepresentation, which could be considered constructive fraud.

25. D Both the agent and the seller are obligated to disclose all known latent defects to prospective buyers. Mold behind some insulation, not easily discoverable upon a simple visual inspection by the buyer, would be a latent defect.

26. A First, calculate the investor's original investment ($88,000 × 4 = $352,000). Calculate the amount he grossed from the sale of the lots ($72,000 × 5 = $360,000). Use the Now and Then formula to find the percentage of profit ($360,000 ÷ $352,000 = 1.0227, of which 2.27% is gross profit). (Alternatively, you could find the difference between the purchase and sale prices ($360,000 − $352,000 = $8,000) and divide that by the cost of the initial investment ($8,000 ÷ $352,000 = 0.0227).)

27. C External obsolescence, such as that caused by a freeway being located near a house, often has the greatest effect on a property's value.

28. A An estate for years begins on a certain date and ends on a certain date.

29. B A real estate agent has the duty to present all written communications to and from all parties in a timely manner. Failing to inform a party of any offer would be a breach of this duty. This is the law no matter who the agent is representing.

30. A Real estate agents should give copies of documents to all parties, as soon as possible after they sign.

31. D An optionee must take an affirmative step to exercise an option, by giving written notice of acceptance to the optionor. If the optionee does not do so by the end of the option period, the option automatically expires.

32. A The Fair Housing Act forbids "adults only" apartment complexes. There is, however, an exemption for properties that qualify as "housing for older persons," such as those intended for and solely occupied by persons 62 or older.

33. C One of an agent's duties to his principal (and to all parties) is to present all written communication, including offers. The other options are not permissible.

34. B The first step is to determine the annual income ($10,500 per month × 12 = $126,000 per year). Divide that by the capitalization rate to find the property's value ($126,000 ÷ 0.12 = $1,050,000).

35. D An option is a unilateral contract; in other words, only one party is obligated to act. Exercising the option creates a bilateral purchase and sale contract.

36. A First, calculate the commission amount ($410,000 × .06 = $24,600). Next, calculate the amount remaining after the mortgage balance is deducted (the property's equity) ($410,000 − $170,000 = $240,000). Subtract the commission amount from the property's equity ($240,000 − $24,600 = $215,400). Calculate the buydown amount ($410,000 × .95 × .03 = $11,685) and subtract that ($215,400 − $11,685 = $203,715). Finally, subtract the other closing costs ($203,715 − $8,000 = $195,715).

37. C Home sales prices are likely to go up in the event of lower interest rates. Lower interest rates will enable more buyers to get more house for their money, motivating more buyers and increasing demand, which will in turn drive up sales prices.

38. D The agent and seller should disclose the previous leaking. Buyers should also be informed of their right to request an inspection.

39. A When taking a listing, a seller's agent should disclose current market conditions to the sellers while discussing an appropriate listing price. (Note that the other options involve disclosures that might be made to prospective buyers, not to the sellers. And even if the question concerned disclosures to buyers, none of the other options is information that would have to be disclosed.)

40. C A property manager, as an agent, is bound by the duty of loyalty to follow the lawful instructions of a principal, in this case the property's owner.

41. B A licensee should not disclose confidential information about the principal, unless the principal has given permission to reveal that particular piece of information. For a seller, confidential information would include details about the seller's negotiating position.

42. C A veteran's surviving spouse may be eligible for a VA loan if he or she has not remarried, and the veteran was killed in action or died of service-related injuries.

43. A A dual agency exists when the same agent represents both the buyer and the seller in a transaction. When the same brokerage firm represents both parties (an in-house transaction), the firm and the designated broker are dual agents, even though each party is represented by a different broker working for the firm.

44. D The size of the labor force has the greatest influence on supply and demand for real estate. The size of the labor force determines how many people are able to afford to purchase homes within the local market.

45. A Riparian rights allow property owners who have flowing water, such as a river or stream, next to or across their property to take reasonable amounts of water for use on the property.

46. B A physical object that is on someone else's property is an encroachment. It is not an encumbrance, because the encroacher doesn't hold a right or interest in the other property.

47. C The original part of the house measures 1,800 square feet (60 × 30 = 1,800). The new addition is 480 square feet (24 × 20 = 480). Add the two together, for a total of 2,280 square feet (1,800 + 480 = 2,280).

48. D An earnest money deposit is usually given by a buyer to a seller along with the offer to purchase, as an indication of the buyer's good faith.

49. D Real estate investment is often thought of as a "tax shelter" because it serves to partially shelter investors from income tax liability.

50. C A point equals one percent of the loan amount. Three percent of $250,000 is $7,500 ($250,000 × 0.03 = $7,500).

51. A The doctrine of emblements applies to crops planted by tenant farmers. If a tenancy is terminated through no fault of the tenant before crops are ready to harvest, the tenant may re-enter the land and harvest the first crop after the tenancy ends.

52. B Competitive market analysis is a process similar to the sales comparison approach to appraisal, where a real estate agent uses the sales prices of similar properties to estimate what a property might sell for.

53. C Homestead laws are state-level laws that give limited protection against foreclosure over judgment liens. Generally, foreclosure is not allowed unless the net value of the property exceeds the homestead exemption amount.

54. B A cloud on the title is any claim, encumbrance, or apparent defect that makes the title to property unmarketable. A quitclaim deed is most often used to remove a cloud on title.

55. A Various documents make up an agreement to transfer property from a seller to a buyer (the mortgage and listing agreements are not really part of that transfer, however). Two rules apply here. First, when the documents making up a contract conflict, the one signed last usually controls. Also, deeds tend to control over purchase and sale agreements.

56. A Commercial banks, savings and loans, mortgage companies, and other entities that make loans to consumers are all part of the primary mortgage market. The Federal Home Loan Mortgage Corporation (Freddie Mac) and Federal National Mortgage Association (Fannie Mae) are part of the secondary market instead.

57. C The Sherman Antitrust Act and state antitrust laws prohibit price fixing, group boycotts, market allocation, and tie-in arrangements.

58. A The Truth in Lending Act gives home equity loan borrowers the right of rescission for three days after the loan agreement has been signed, the disclosure statement has been received, or the notice of the right of rescission has been received, whichever occurs last.

59. C A competitive market analysis should be based on comparables that are as similar as possible to the subject property in size, age, quality, and location. A CMA can also include current or expired listings, as well as recently sold properties.

60. C RESPA requires, among other things, that all lenders give prospective borrowers a copy of the booklet about settlement procedures, entitled "Shopping for Your Home Loan."

61. D A survey may reveal matters that are not part of the public record that would only be discovered through a personal inspection, such as encroachments. That is why a survey is often performed as part of obtaining an extended coverage title insurance policy. While there are arguments for other answers to this question, this course and the state exam basically concern buying and selling homes; from that perspective, the most common reason for a survey is to check for encroachments.

62. D Any property management agreement should include the scope of the manager's authority, such as whether he can collect and disburse funds. It should also discuss the manager's compensation, but the compensation need not take the form of salary; it could be by commission, for example.

63. D A court might inquire into the item's use, for instance, to decide whether it is specifically adapted to the property, or what the intention of the annexor was. Age, cost, and size of the item are not at issue.

64. A In a joint tenancy, each joint tenant has the right of survivorship. Upon the death of a joint tenant, her interest passes automatically to the other joint tenant.

65. D A limitation on the use of the land, such as a minimum lot size requirement that would prohibit partitioning the lot, would be considered a deed restriction. It is not an easement, as it does not benefit another property or person, and it is not a lien, as it is not a financial interest secured by the property.

66. C For properties that are located on or near a body of water, it is advisable to check whether the property is in a flood plain. It may affect the buyer's decision, and it should also factor into the decision whether to purchase flood insurance.

67. C In a limited partnership, the limited partners are not personally liable for the partnership's debts and obligations. Limited partners are commonly passive investors who aren't directly involved in managing the business.

68. C The Americans with Disabilities Act requires public accommodations to be accessible to the disabled. This would include a shopping center, as it is open to the public and affects commerce. The ADA does not apply to residential properties (although the Fair Housing Act does impose some restrictions on new apartment construction).

69. C A balloon payment is required if, at the end of a loan term, the borrower has not paid off the loan balance. Usually the payment will be much larger than any of the mortgage's regular payments.

70. C The four elements of value, for anything at all with value, are: demand, scarcity, transferability, and utility.

71. C It may help to sketch the property being described; once you do, you will notice that it is rectangular, and you can simply use the Area = Length × Width formula. Multiply the length and width to find that it is 2,178,000 square feet (1,815 ft. × 1,200 ft. = 2,178,000 sq. ft.). Convert this amount to acreage by dividing by 43,560 (2,178,000 ÷ 43,560 = 50 acres). (43,560 is the number of square feet in an acre.)

72. B Interest paid on a mortgage or deed of trust is deductible. Principal payments (also known as debt service) are not. Capital improvements can be factored into the property's adjusted basis when the property is sold, but are not deducted from a taxpayer's annual income.

73. C When deed restrictions and zoning regulations are in conflict, whichever is more restrictive will apply. In this case, the deed restriction is more restrictive (it prohibits fences, while the municipal ordinance allows them), so it takes precedence.

74. D An option is an agreement that gives one party the right to buy or lease property at a set price within a set period of time.

75. A Interest is charged to a borrower as compensation for the lender, in exchange for the lender allowing the borrower to borrow money.

76. C An amortized loan includes payments for both principal and interest. A fully amortized loan will be entirely repaid at the end of the loan term, with the monthly payment remaining the same throughout.

77. D The market data approach, or sales comparison approach, is most commonly used when estimating the value of a single-family residence.

78. A A listing agreement needs to be signed both by the listing agent, on the listing firm's behalf, and by the seller. An attorney in fact, someone the seller has appointed in a power of attorney and granted the authority to convey the property, may sign the listing agreement on the seller's behalf.

79. A Subdivided property is usually described in deeds and purchase and sale agreements by reference to a map of the subdivision and a particular lot. The map, known as a plat map, describes the boundaries of the lot and is prepared by a surveyor.

80. B A seller's agent has a duty of loyalty to the seller. However, a real estate licensee will most likely have other clients as well, so even if a dual agency doesn't exist, the duty of loyalty to one client must still be balanced against the need to work for the best interests of other clients as well.

81. B One easy way to terminate a lease is by the mutual agreement of landlord and tenant, known as a surrender. A lease may also terminate because of a breach of the covenant of quiet enjoyment, a breach of the warranty of habitability, failure to pay rent, illegal use, destruction of the premises, or condemnation.

82. A Adverse possession allows a person who has put an otherwise unused property to productive use for a required number of years to obtain title.

83. D A loss in value due to wear and tear or other damage is called physical deterioration.

84. B The mortgagee is the lender, and the mortgagee's title insurance policy (extended coverage policy) protects the mortgagee (the lender).

85. A A real estate agent should never give advice on matters in a transaction that are beyond the agent's expertise. For issues such as how to take title, a lawyer should be involved.

86. A Installing a second bathroom in a house with four bedrooms and only one bathroom would rectify a serious case of functional obsolescence. An owner who adds a swimming pool to a lower-end house is not likely to recoup the costs of the addition, and the other options are maintenance issues more oriented toward preserving, not increasing, the property's value.

87. C When one performs the income approach to value, the steps are to estimate potential gross income, calculate effective gross income, determine net operating income, and then apply the cap rate to the net income. (Note that selecting and applying the cap rate may be viewed either as one step or two separate steps.)

88. C The Federal Fair Housing Act (Title VIII of the Civil Rights Act of 1968) does not apply to the sale or rental of a single-family home by its owner, provided that the owner doesn't own more than three such homes, no real estate agent is used, and no discriminatory advertising is used.

89. D Property tax liens take priority over other liens, including construction liens. Allen's lien still takes priority over Bart's lien, as construction liens take priority based on the date of the start of construction, but the tax lien takes priority over both. Property tax liens get recorded automatically when levied.

90. B Historical preservation ordinances may protect existing buildings of historical value, and prohibit their destruction or modification without approval from an appropriate local authority.

91. D A landlord must disclose the location of any known lead-based paint, provide a copy of any report concerning lead-based paint if the property has been inspected, and give tenants a copy of the lead-based paint pamphlet. Tenants do not receive the ten-day period in which to have the home tested for lead-based paint that buyers do.

92. C Getting preapproved for a loan before beginning the house hunting process is now standard procedure; this way, the buyer knows in advance the maximum amount he can count on from the bank.

93. B The Fair Housing Act says that a disabled tenant may make reasonable modifications to a leased property at her own expense. The tenant can be required to restore the premises at the end of the tenancy.

94. C First, calculate the building's volume (60 × 90 × 15 = 81,000 cubic feet). Multiply that by the monthly rent rate to find the amount of the monthly payment (81,000 × $0.05 = $4,050).

95. D The generator is the personal property of the company that owns it. While it might remain on the property after possession of the property changes hands, it still belongs to the rental company and they could reclaim it according to the terms of their contract.

96. D A prescriptive easement requires a use that is open and notorious, meaning that it should be reasonably apparent to the landowner. Someone establishing an easement by prescription is not expected to find out whether the true owner is living on the property, what his limitations are, or whether he is actually aware of the prescriptive use. The rule only requires actions that would be enough to put the typical owner on notice that his property interest is threatened.

97. D The statute of frauds requires certain contracts, including virtually all real estate contracts, to be in writing.

98. C A package mortgage includes both real and personal property as collateral.

99. C A fully amortized loan is repaid through regular payments that include both a portion of the principal and interest. The final payment will pay off the principal balance, leaving no need for a balloon payment. (Most home purchase loans are budget mortgages, which include taxes and insurance in each payment, but this is not a characteristic of all fully amortized loans. Note also that the question refers to debt service payments only.)

100. B If comparable sales aren't available and the accrued depreciation is difficult to estimate (which is generally true for older properties), but the data necessary to use the income approach are available, then it's appropriate to use the income approach.

101. B Discrimination based on familial status refers to discrimination against someone because a child (a person under 18 years old) is or will be living on the property. In addition to parents, this rule protects legal guardians, pregnant women, and people in the process of obtaining custody of a child.

102. A Percentage leases are frequently used in shopping centers and with other retail properties. They enable the landlord to share in the tenant's profits as part of the rent.

103. B As a rule, special assessments are allocated according to the benefits each property receives, instead of the market value of the property. Thus a special assessment is not an ad valorem tax. Sometimes the allocation is based on the front footage of the lot, if the assessment is levied to pay for storm drains, curbs, and gutters.

104. B According to agency law, if either the principal (in this case the seller) or the agent dies, the agency is terminated. However, the "agent" in an agency relationship is the real estate firm, not the individual who took the listing, so the listing is still in effect even if the individual real estate agent dies or moves to another firm.

105. B Use the capitalization formula (Income ÷ Capitalization Rate = Value) to find the property's value: $12,000 net income ÷ 0.12 rate of return = $100,000 value.

106. B Selling real estate without a license is a gross misdemeanor, which in terms of seriousness is somewhere between a misdemeanor and a felony.

107. A Each party must receive the agency law pamphlet before either party signs an agency agreement, signs an offer, consents to a dual agency, or waives any agency rights, whichever of these events comes first.

108. A In the new transaction, T may represent the buyer, the seller, or, if he makes the proper disclosures, he may represent both parties as a dual agent. If representing the new buyer, T would not be able to disclose to the buyer any confidential information previously learned about J.

109. A   Licensees may be fined up to $5,000 per violation of the license law, regardless of the amount of actual damages caused by the licensees' actions. Of course, the licensee may still be subject to civil liability for part or all of the $13,500 in actual damages, but the buyer would need to file a lawsuit to recover that amount. Conversion is not involved here.

110. A   Either a designated broker or an affiliated licensee may act unilaterally in order to terminate their employment relationship.

111. A   All property management records must be kept at a location where the firm is licensed to have an office, which can be either a main office or branch office.

112. B   In Washington, a buyer agency relationship is formed as soon as a licensee agrees to perform real estate brokerage services for a buyer. However, there's an exception to this rule: if the licensee already has an agreement to represent someone else, then no buyer agency is automatically created. The listing agent would have to do something more substantial than what's described in answer A to create a dual agency, such as counseling the buyer on how much to offer.

113. A   Any and all criminal charges must be reported to the Department of Licensing within 20 days after the licensee receives notice of the action.

114. A   A broker who is not a licensed escrow officer can act as closing agent for any transaction in which she is the broker of record, but she cannot collect a fee, other than her normal commission. However, if the broker is also a licensed escrow officer, she may collect a fee for acting as a closing agent.

115. D   The firm or individual to whom the check is made payable has a responsibility to see that the money is deposited in a trust account on behalf of the buyer; this is usually the selling firm.

116. A   The Director, with the advice and approval of the Real Estate Commission, issues rules and regulations to govern the activities and practices of real estate licensees.

117. C   Depositing an employee's paycheck in a trust account is commingling: mixing non-trust funds with trust funds. (The commission payable to the brokerage can be transferred from the trust account to the firm's general account. The designated broker cannot pay individual commissions out of the trust account, however.)

118. B   Real estate license fees (application fees, renewal fees, etc.) are placed in the Real Estate Commission Account in the state treasury.

119. A   It is never permissible to mix trust funds and personal funds together. The designated broker should have transferred the commission into the firm's business account first, and then paid the advertising bill from the business account.

120. B   A licensee may be paid a commission only by the real estate firm he is affiliated with. Affiliated licensees are not designated brokers; they work for a firm. "A Realty" cannot be a brokerage because no designated broker has a controlling interest in the entity. An affiliated licensee cannot receive compensation directly from a client or customer, or from another licensee, another real estate firm, or another business entity.

121. D   To activate a license that has been inactive for more than three years, the licensee must complete a 30 clock-hour course.

122. C   All advertising placed by a real estate licensee must include the brokerage firm's name, as it appears on its license. (There is an exception if the licensee is advertising her own property—then only the fact that the seller is licensed must be noted.)

123. A   Anyone acting as a principal (in this case the seller) can buy and sell without a license. It is when you are acting on behalf of someone else that you need a license.

124. A   Whatever disciplinary measure was imposed by the Director remains in effect throughout the appeals process.

125. C   The agent's conduct must be consistent with the agency disclosure made. This means that whoever he claims to be representing must be the person he actually represents. The "selling agent" might be the buyer's agent, or might be a dual agent, so only answer C is always true.

126. B   When preparing the buyer's offer to purchase, the selling agent must disclose on the purchase and sale agreement form that the deposit is in the form of a promissory note (or any other form that is not the equivalent of cash). The seller can then take this into account in deciding whether or not to accept the buyer's offer.

127. C   Fines are deposited in the education account and used for the education of licensees.

128. C   P is unlicensed and cannot collect a commission for real estate services. Option B is incorrect because collecting a commission requires a license.

129. B   She must complete 30 hours in advanced real estate practices, 30 hours in real estate law, and 30 hours in elective courses, and she must pay the fee.

130. C   The real estate commissioners are appointed by the Governor.

131. A   A trust account must be opened in the firm's name (as trustee) and must also be designated as a trust account. The depository institution must be in Washington State.

132. D   The property manager would presumably want to share with the owner the conclusions of a recent appraisal, but it wouldn't be done in the summary statement. A summary statement is a brief report showing the property's financial status over a certain period of time.

133. B   This is the definition of a real estate broker.

134. C   The renewal fee must be paid every two years, but as long as the license remains inactive, there is no education requirement. However, after three years of inactive status, reactivating the license--as opposed to renewing it--does require a 30-hour course.

135. A   Under Washington's real estate license law, every advertisement placed by a licensee on behalf of others must contain the name of the real estate firm as licensed. This is true even if a licensee conducts his own operations under a separately named business entity.

136. B   A person licensed to act on behalf of a real estate brokerage is called an affiliated licensee.

137. A   The termination date is the postmark date or the date the license is hand-delivered to the Department of Licensing.

138. A   The commission is earned when the sale is made, not when it is paid (at closing). The agent's license was revoked after the sale was made, so the agent was eligible for a commission when the services were provided and is still entitled to collect it.

139. A   The Director cannot award damages to victims of real estate fraud. Many states have what is called a "recovery fund" from which victims of real estate fraud can recover at least part of their losses. Washington doesn't have such a remedy for the consumer, however.

140. A   The Director can suspend Q's license until satisfactory arrangements are made to correct the delinquency.

Sample Exam 2

1. An investor wants to invest $250,000 in the development of a shopping mall by taking out a loan secured by a residential property that he owns. Will the Truth in Lending Act apply to this transaction?

   A. Yes, because the loan is for less than $500,000
   B. Yes, because the loan is secured by residential property
   C. No, because the loan is for more than $53,000
   D. No, because this is a commercial transaction

2. A seller accepts an offer, but then a second buyer makes an offer on the same property for a higher purchase price. A licensee should tell the second offeror that:

   A. she will encourage the seller to breach the contract and accept the second offer
   B. she will present the second offer as well and the seller will consider it
   C. the second offer can be presented, but only as a backup offer
   D. the second offer cannot be presented as the property is already under contract

3. Tyler asks a real estate agent to list his house for sale. Tyler is moving to another house within the same neighborhood, and tells his agent that in order to preserve the character of the neighborhood, he does not want the property shown to non-white buyers. Which of the following should the agent do?

   A. Comply with Tyler's wishes because of the fiduciary duty of loyalty
   B. Enter into a listing agreement that contains Tyler's terms, but still show the property to any interested buyer
   C. Refuse to accept the listing because it violates federal antidiscrimination laws
   D. Tell Tyler that the listing cannot contain such instructions, but Tyler may still refuse to sell to buyers based on their race

4. An agent is ready to list a farm that was previously owned by a deceased woman with four adult children. Two of the children asked the agent to take the listing. Before taking the listing, the agent should:

   A. insist that all four children sign quit-claim deeds
   B. check the public records to see who owns the property
   C. have the two children sign a lien release
   D. examine the deceased woman's will

5. After a purchase agreement has been signed, but before the transaction closes, the buyer attempts to have the contract voided. It is likely he will be able to prove that, because of bipolar disorder, he was mentally incompetent at the time the contract was signed. Is the contract still valid?

   A. Yes, because mental illness does not factor into questions of contractual capacity
   B. Yes, because the deed has already been placed into escrow
   C. No, because buyers are entitled to rescind contracts before closing
   D. No, because his temporary incapacity allows him to rescind the contract

6. The owner of a lot that is 99' by 110' would like to sell it. Similar properties sell for $180,000 per acre. What is the likely selling price for this property?

   A. $45,000
   B. $54,450
   C. $60,000
   D. $90,000

7. One side of a section (in a government survey) is how many feet long?

   A. 100
   B. 2,640
   C. 5,280
   D. 43,560

8. Victoria receives an offer from Lloyd for her property. The offer is for $225,000, and she receives it on Friday morning. On Saturday, she counters by changing the purchase price to $235,000. The counteroffer states that Lloyd has 48 hours to accept the offer. On Sunday, Lloyd rejects the counteroffer. Victoria immediately accepts Lloyd's original offer. Under these circumstances, the agreement is:

A. valid, because Victoria accepted all the terms of Lloyd's original offer

B. valid, because Victoria accepted a written, valid offer

C. not valid, because Victoria did not accept the offer within a reasonable period of time

D. not valid, because Victoria terminated Lloyd's original offer when she made the counteroffer

9. An apartment rents for $1,000 per month. At move-in, a security deposit equal to one month's rent is due. In addition, if the tenant owns a cat or dog, a pet deposit of one-quarter of a month's rent is required. How large a deposit (the term "deposit" refers to refundable money, not rent) would a tenant with a dog need to make?

A. $750
B. $1,000
C. $1,250
D. $2,250

10. Which of the following loans would result in the borrower paying the least interest over the life of the loan term?

A. 15-year loan at 10% interest
B. 15-year loan at 11% interest
C. 20-year loan at 10% interest
D. 20-year loan at 11% interest

11. There are several environmental issues that would be likely to lead to a property being declared a toxic waste site. Which of the following is one of those issues?

A. A methamphetamine lab
B. Lead-based paint that is not chipped or damaged in any way
C. Mildew found in the kitchen sink
D. Low levels of radon gas

12. A seller has entered into a listing agreement with an expiration date of April 30. Under which of these circumstances would the listing NOT terminate on the date mentioned in the answer option?

A. The house burns down on April 25
B. The licensee who took the listing is legally declared incompetent on April 26
C. The seller revokes the listing on April 27
D. The property has still not sold on April 30

13. Which of the following statements about prepayment penalties is true?

A. Both the FHA and VA loan programs impose prepayment penalties
B. FHA loans include prepayment penalties, but VA loans do not
C. VA loans include prepayment penalties, but FHA loans do not
D. Neither the FHA nor VA loan programs allow prepayment penalties

14. Chris, a real estate agent, met with Zach, a property owner, to discuss listing the property. Zach told Chris that he was illiterate and that he needed Chris to read the listing agreement to him. Chris did so, plus he spent a long time explaining the various terms and answering Zach's questions. Zach agreed to everything, and signed the agreement with an "X." The listing agreement is:

A. valid, as long as Zach gets his attorney to verify what Chris told him

B. valid, because Zach fully understood the terms of the contract (he was illiterate, not incompetent)

C. invalid, because an illiterate person is not mentally competent

D. invalid, because Chris was guilty of the unauthorized practice of law when he discussed the terms of the listing agreement with Zach

15. A buyer is considering purchasing a video store in a standalone building in a strip mall. The building has steps in front, without a ramp, and no handicapped parking spots in front. The buyer's agent should tell the buyer that:

A. it would be prohibitively expensive to bring the property into compliance with the ADA

B. the property complies with all federal antidiscrimination laws

C. the property probably does not comply with the Americans with Disabilities Act

D. the property does not comply with the Fair Housing Act

16. Shelly takes out a new mortgage on her house, paying off her old mortgage with part of the proceeds. The new mortgage has a rate several percentage points lower than the old mortgage. This is called:

A. alienation

B. refinancing

C. a home equity line of credit

D. a reverse equity mortgage

17. Of the following, which is the best definition of a fee simple estate?

A. Title and ownership without limitations

B. An estate for years

C. A leasehold interest in property that is supported by consideration

D. The greatest interest one can own in land

18. A property owner dies without a will or any known heirs. The property passes to the state, under its:

A. escheat power

B. police power

C. power of eminent domain

D. taxation power

19. A deed restriction is used to:

A. control future uses of the property

B. limit housing costs in a subdivision

C. prevent housing from being encumbered

D. require the use of high-quality building materials and construction techniques

20. Teresa gives her little brother, Mark, a life estate pur autre vie. Which of the following is true?

A. Teresa is the life tenant

B. Mark is both the life tenant and the measuring life

C. Mark is the life tenant, but the measuring life is someone else

D. Mark will have title to the property for as long as he lives

21. How would a limited partner's role in a limited partnership be best described?

A. Ability to appoint corporate officers

B. Anonymity but subject to double taxation

C. Authority over decision-making process and personal liability for company debts

D. Limited personal liability

22. A homeowner bought his home for $150,000. Ten years later, he refinanced his mortgage and borrowed $100,000. Which of the following is true for this type of property?

A. Interest on the difference between the original loan amount and the refinanced amount is not deductible

B. Interest on only half of the difference between the original amount and refinanced amount is deductible

C. Interest on loans such as this one for the purchase or refinance of a principal residence is deductible

D. Interest deductibility will depend on the borrower's tax bracket

23. The full cost of which of the following could be an income tax deduction for an investment property owner?

A. Adding a swimming pool

B. Installing a new HVAC system

C. Prepaying additional principal on the mortgage

D. Repainting the building

24. A parcel occupies the NW 1/4 of the SE 1/4, and the S 1/2 of the SW 1/4 of the NE 1/4 of Section 4. How many acres is this parcel?
    A. 40
    B. 60
    C. 80
    D. 100

25. A licensee locates what seems like a ready, willing, and able buyer. However, the deal falls through at closing because the buyer can't obtain necessary financing. At the same time, though, the seller turns out to be unable to provide marketable title. Does the seller still owe a commission to the listing agent in this case?
    A. No, because the sale didn't close
    B. No, because there was no ready, willing, and able buyer
    C. Yes, because the licensee saw the transaction through to the closing date
    D. Yes, because the seller has an absolute duty to provide marketable title at closing

26. With the closing date fast approaching, the buyer's real estate agent learns that the seller's sister may have an ownership interest in the property. The parties have already signed the purchase and sale agreement. The buyer's agent should:
    A. ask the listing agent to suggest that the seller see a lawyer about obtaining a quitclaim deed from the sister
    B. ask the buyer to sue the seller for specific performance
    C. inform both buyer and seller that the transaction is void
    D. postpone the closing date

27. A buyer was considering purchasing a property sight unseen through a foreclosure auction. A friend warned him, "Caveat emptor." This expression means:
    A. Let the buyer beware
    B. Let the lender beware
    C. Neither a borrower nor a lender be
    D. Time flies

28. An elderly woman gives a power of attorney to her son to manage all of her affairs. What sort of agent is he?
    A. Ostensible agent
    B. Special agent
    C. Universal agent
    D. Unlimited agent

29. The document that would enable a listing licensee to sign a sales contract in the owner's absence would be known as a:
    A. covenant of right to convey
    B. habendum clause
    C. power of attorney
    D. power of sale

30. Agent Marcus is showing a property that was built in the early 1970s. The buyer asks about the presence of lead-based paint in the house. What should the agent say?
    A. Any lead-based paint has been painted over, and is no longer a problem that should concern the buyer
    B. Federal law requires sellers of houses built before 1978 to make disclosures concerning lead-based paint, and the buyer may request an inspection
    C. Federal law requires sellers of houses built after 1978 to make disclosures concerning lead-based paint, but the buyer may still request an inspection
    D. The buyer could request an inspection, although no law regulates this

31. A commercial building is valued at $1,600,000 if its annual net income is capitalized at a rate of 20%. If the operating expenses total 40% of the gross income, what is the approximate annual gross income?
    A. $128,000
    B. $192,000
    C. $533,333.33
    D. $800,000

32. To avoid tenant problems, a landlord is best off using a standardized lease form that includes:
    A. a copy of the Uniform Landlord Tenant Act
    B. a warranty of quiet enjoyment
    C. a tenancy at will provision
    D. specific rules and regulations

33. Which of the following items would a homeowner generally be able to deduct on her income taxes?

    A. Depreciation
    B. Maintenance expenses
    C. Points paid on the mortgage
    D. The downpayment at the time of purchase

34. Jack receives a life estate in a property, for the life of Larry. When Larry dies, the property passes to Mary, rather than to the grantor or the grantor's heirs. This is a:

    A. life estate pur autre vie, in remainder
    B. life estate pur autre vie, in reversion
    C. standard life estate, in remainder
    D. standard life estate, in reversion

35. When part of the land is removed, but generally the boundaries of a property stay the same, it is known as:

    A. accretion
    B. adverse possession
    C. avulsion
    D. partition

36. When homes in a new development are sold, a $2,000 fee is charged to the buyers. This fee covers the homeowners association dues for the first year. HOA dues for each subsequent year are $1,000. In the development's first year, ten homes are sold. Ten more are sold the second year. Assuming that the HOA's account had no disbursements or expenses (and ignoring any possible contributions from the developer), what is the balance of the account after two years?

    A. $30,000
    B. $40,000
    C. $50,000
    D. $60,000

37. Which of the following situations would cause prices for residential real estate to go up in a particular area?

    A. A large new factory that will employ thousands
    B. Interest rates are going up
    C. There is a large supply of recently built homes on the market
    D. Zoning change to allow an assisted living facility for seniors

38. A new subdivision is built in a rural area, outside urban growth boundaries. It is set up so that houses are situated on small lots, with most of the subdivision's land taken up by green space that is held by all owners in common. This is an example of:

    A. condominiums
    B. rural cluster development
    C. spot zoning
    D. townhouses

39. A landlord enters an apartment to make sure everything is in working order without providing any advance notice. Is the landlord correct to do so?

    A. Yes, a landlord always has the right to enter a tenant's apartment
    B. Yes, a landlord may offer his potential liability for the tenant's safety as an affirmative defense
    C. No, the landlord would breach the covenant of quiet enjoyment
    D. No, the landlord would breach the warranty of habitability

40. How many square feet are in a square yard?

    A. 3
    B. 9
    C. 27
    D. 81

41. Property management for residential property is different from property management for commercial property, in that a manager would be more concerned about:

    A. a written lease for a residential tenant than for a commercial tenant
    B. future space needs of a commercial tenant than of a residential tenant
    C. the credit rating of a commercial tenant than of a residential tenant
    D. the security deposit of a commercial tenant than of a residential tenant

42. Which of the following actions by a developer would require a zoning variance or a rezone, because it would result in a more intensive use of the land?

A. Deed restriction prohibiting further subdivision of individual lots

B. Deed restriction prohibiting painting houses non-earth-tone colors

C. Fewer outbuildings placed on each lot than allowed by law

D. Increase in number of lots per acre

43. A square parcel measures 1/8 of a mile by 1/8 of a mile. How many acres is this property?

A. 10
B. 20
C. 40
D. 80

44. Special, general, and universal agency all:

A. create a long-lasting relationship over multiple transactions

B. give the agent authority to act on the principal's behalf in all financial matters

C. originate with the principal

D. terminate with the end of a particular transaction

45. A 17-year-old purchased a house. He moved in, lived in it for a year, and then decided he didn't want the responsibility of owning a home. He refused to honor the contract. In this case the contract:

A. is valid; the buyer must abide by its terms

B. is voidable; the buyer can choose whether or not to carry out its terms

C. was voidable when signed; however, the buyer probably ratified it by living in the house

D. is void; it was missing an essential contract element

46. A store owner would like to sell common stock in her business (a chain of stores) to investors. She asks an inexperienced licensee for help. The licensee should:

A. ask her managing broker which listing agreement to use

B. disclose her licensed status on the stock certificates

C. hire an attorney to draft the listing agreement

D. refer the client to a securities dealer

47. A homeless shelter, which contains a number of units for different families, is owned by a religious group. The religious group's leaders instruct the shelter's manager to limit occupancy only to individuals who are of their faith. This would be permissible under which of the following circumstances?

A. Under any circumstances, because shelters are not subject to the Federal Fair Housing Act

B. Membership in the religious organization is not restricted on the basis of race, color, or national origin

C. The shelter contains ten or fewer units

D. The shelter contains four or fewer units

48. There's a strip of land that lies between two neighbors. One neighbor mistakenly believes the land is his, and he consistently cares for it by mowing it, fertilizing it, etc. At one point, he encloses the property with a chain link fence. After enough time passes, he might be able to obtain title to this strip of land by:

A. escheat
B. prescribed use
C. eminent domain
D. adverse possession

49. The owner of a small store leased a retail space and the tenant installed his own shelving by bolting it to the walls. At the end of his lease, he wanted to take the shelving with him to his new location. Which of the following is true?

A. The shelves are fixtures, and must be removed by the tenant

B. The shelves are fixtures, and must remain as part of the building

C. The shelves are trade fixtures, and may be removed by the tenant

D. The shelves are trade fixtures, and must remain as part of the building

50. A buyer's earnest money deposit can be kept by a seller in the event of a buyer's default only if the:

A. seller breaches the contract

B. seller can prove that she has suffered a financial loss

C. purchase and sale agreement includes a forfeiture clause for liquidated damages

D. purchase and sale agreement provides for specific performance

51. Theo takes an exclusive right to sell listing in early September, while working as a licensee for West Side Realty. In mid-October, he quits his job, surrenders his license, and moves out of state. What happens to Theo's listing?

    A. It is converted to an open listing
    B. It continues to be a valid exclusive listing with West Side Realty
    C. It will be reassigned to another brokerage firm in the same multiple listing service
    D. The agency relationship automatically terminates

52. A buyer received a general warranty deed when she took title to a property. The seller's cousin showed up several months later and claimed an ownership interest in the property. The buyer would be protected against this claim by the general warranty deed's:

    A. covenant against encumbrances
    B. covenant of hostile enjoyment
    C. covenant of seisin
    D. covenant of freehold warranty

53. Max would like to know if there's an encroachment on his boundary line. He should:

    A. examine the legal description
    B. order an appraisal
    C. order a survey
    D. do a title search

54. XYZ Realty has the exclusive right to represent a new subdivision. An agent working for the subdivision office, and named on the listing agreement, shows a property to the Meyers, who are not working with their own agent. When the Meyers decide to buy, they have XYZ's agent provide basic help in filling out an offer form. Which of the following is true?

    A. The agent owes the buyers the duty of loyalty
    B. The buyers are not represented by an agent
    C. The buyers are represented by this agent
    D. This has created a dual agency

55. A buyer would like to start out with a significant amount of equity invested in his house, so that he can reborrow against the equity if necessary. When structuring a loan, what should the buyer's highest priority be?

    A. Largest downpayment possible
    B. Longest loan term possible
    C. Lowest interest rate possible
    D. Smallest downpayment possible

56. What information does an appraiser need in order to calculate a capitalization rate?

    A. Price and gross income
    B. Price and net income
    C. Value and gross income
    D. Value and net income

57. A buyer asks the buyer's agent to write an offer on terms that don't match the listing agreement. The buyer's agent refuses to write the offer and then, in writing, unilaterally terminates the agency relationship with the buyer. Which is true?

    A. Buyer's agent will be subject to disciplinary action
    B. Buyer's agent is permitted to unilaterally terminate the agency relationship
    C. Buyer's agent is allowed to terminate the agency, but must write the offer before terminating
    D. Buyer's agent is not permitted to write such an offer

58. Paul would like to make an offer on a house right away, but he doesn't have the cash available for an earnest money deposit yet. He is, however, expecting a large commission check from his sales job within several weeks, so he offers the seller a promissory note for $10,000 as the earnest money deposit. He will also be seeking conventional financing to pay for the rest of the home's price. Will the promissory note be tied to the buyer's mortgage?

    A. Yes, the institutional lender will require both promissory notes to be collateralized
    B. Yes, the promissory note is not valid unless it has been collateralized
    C. No, the promissory note is a promise to pay a debt and is a contract on its own
    D. Not relevant; a promissory note may never be used as earnest money

59. Jean has operated a store on a busy corner in a suburban area. The city decides to rezone the area from commercial to residential use. Which of the following is true?

    A. Jean is prohibited from operating the store and must stop doing business
    B. Jean must sell the store to residential buyers
    C. Jean must try to obtain a variance
    D. Jean now has a nonconforming use

60. The purchase and sale agreement required the seller to order a pest inspection. The inspector found an infestation, and remedial action was required. Which party was responsible for paying to fix the problem?

    A. Only the buyer
    B. The brokerage
    C. The buyer and seller were required to split the cost
    D. Whichever party agreed to pay for the expense in the purchase and sale agreement

61. When is an enforceable purchase and sale agreement formed?

    A. When the buyer knows of the seller's written acceptance of the offer
    B. When the seller has orally informed the buyer of her acceptance
    C. When the seller has received the earnest money
    D. When the transaction has closed

62. A real estate firm handles property management for a number of property owners. Rather than use one standard form, though, each lease must be separately drafted, based on individual negotiations. Which of the following statements is true?

    A. A lease agreement can be prepared by anyone
    B. An attorney must be engaged to draft each contract
    C. Any licensed real estate agent can draft these leases
    D. A real estate firm can draft the leases if both parties agree in writing

63. Maria offered to purchase Alexander's house for $135,000. After talking it over with his agent, Alexander signed the offer and returned it to Maria. At this point, what type of title does Maria have to the house?

    A. Legal
    B. Indivisible
    C. Equitable
    D. Chattel

64. A licensee represents the seller in a transaction. Which of the following fiduciary duties does she owe to the buyer?

    A. Confidentiality
    B. Honesty
    C. Loyalty
    D. Recommend expert advice

65. The comparable has a two-car garage and the subject property only has a one-car garage. The appraiser estimates that space for a second car contributes about $800 to the value of a home. To take this into account, the appraiser will:

    A. add $800 to the sales price of the subject property
    B. add $800 to the sales price of the comparable property
    C. subtract $800 from the sales price of the comparable property
    D. subtract $800 from the sales price of the subject property

66. A movie theater was built ten years ago. If the neighborhood is now zoned entirely residential, the movie theater:

    A. will have to be torn down
    B. must be remodeled to better conform to the neighborhood's intended use
    C. will be allowed to continue if the owner obtains a conditional use permit
    D. will be allowed to continue since it was built before the new zoning law went into effect

67. A builder plans to construct a single-family home on spec, which he will then sell himself. He needs to borrow $60,000 to do so, and he approaches the local bank for a construction loan. Is this loan subject to Truth in Lending Act disclosure laws?

   A. No, because no disclosure is required for business loans
   B. No, because TILA applies to loans of $54,600 or less
   C. Yes, because the loan concerns a single-family residence
   D. Yes, because TILA applies to loans of $51,800 or more

68. The primary purpose of the Real Estate Settlement Procedures Act is to:

   A. ensure that the seller receives the purchase price, the buyer receives clear title to the property, and the lender's security interest in the property is perfected
   B. require lenders to disclose the complete cost of credit to consumer loan applicants
   C. promote uniformity and accuracy in the closing process by requiring closing agents to be state-certified
   D. provide borrowers with information about their closing costs and to eliminate kickbacks and referral fees

69. A property owner would like to use a tax-deferred exchange. The owner's property would qualify if it was:

   A. a principal residence
   B. financed over a 30-year loan term
   C. owner-occupied
   D. used in a business or trade

70. A woman owns a large house in a subdivision that is zoned strictly residential. She would like to operate a preschool out of her house. She should seek to obtain a/an:

   A. HOA release
   B. conditional use permit
   C. nonconforming use
   D. variance

71. ABC Realty signed a property management agreement to manage property for XYZ Apartment Rentals. Do they have an agency agreement and, if so, what kind of agency authority has been created?

   A. No; to create an agency relationship, they would have to sign a listing agreement
   B. No; XYZ has only hired ABC Realty to manage the properties, not to be its agent
   C. Yes; ABC has been hired by XYZ to be a special agent
   D. Yes; ABC has been hired by XYZ to be a general agent

72. Prices in a local market are trending downward. A seller found that she had to lower the price of her house by $25,000 over the course of six months before she could find a buyer. Upset over selling at a loss, she informs her listing agent that she is going to lower the commission rate that she pays. Can she do this?

   A. Yes, a loss by the seller must be shared by the listing agent
   B. Yes, since commission rates are negotiated and can be changed at any time
   C. No, commission rates are established by the local multiple listing service and cannot be changed
   D. No, the commission rate, once established in the listing agreement contract, cannot be changed unless both parties agree

73. W, age 17, enters into an installment contract to purchase a five-year-old car from S, an adult. From a legal point of view, the contract is:

   A. void
   B. voidable by W only
   C. voidable by S only
   D. voidable by either S or W

74. Sarita bought a home. She had poor credit, so the owner agreed to finance the purchase. The parties agreed to a 20-year loan term. Sarita took title to the property, and the seller held a lien against the property. What type of financing instrument was used?
   A. Option to buy
   B. Land contract
   C. Purchase money mortgage
   D. Open mortgage

75. Monica has been preapproved for a loan of up to $250,000 to buy her first house. She has good credit, and plans to make a downpayment of at least 20%. Which type of loan is she most likely to use?
   A. Blanket mortgage
   B. Conventional loan
   C. Swing loan
   D. Wraparound mortgage

76. A former mansion has been divided into three apartments. The best approach to finding the property's value is:
   A. cost
   B. income
   C. reconciliation
   D. sales comparison

77. An appraiser makes projections about how the population of a metropolitan area will grow and how much residents' income will increase, using data about both basic and non-basic industries. This is known as:
   A. anticipation
   B. economic-base analysis
   C. economic-life analysis
   D. highest and best use

78. A property manager is replacing the filters on the building's air conditioning units, which must be done quarterly. Which kind of maintenance is this?
   A. Corrective
   B. Deferred
   C. Housekeeping
   D. Preventive

79. The owner of a vacant lot along a commercial street would like to develop a strip mall, but needs more space. The lot that he owns is 39,375 square feet and is 175 feet deep. He would like to purchase the lot next to it as well, which is also 175 feet deep, but only 21,875 square feet. If he does buy the additional lot, what would the front footage of the combined lot be?
   A. 175 feet
   B. 225 feet
   C. 350 feet
   D. 450 feet

80. It is legal for a property manager to:
   A. collect a larger security deposit from tenants with a service animal
   B. obtain employment information to determine if a tenant can afford the rent
   C. refuse to rent to families with children
   D. refuse to allow a disabled tenant to install grab bars in the bathroom

81. Ryan needs to replace his roof; not having the cash available, he decides to borrow several thousand dollars through a home equity line of credit, which is a:
   A. fully amortized fixed-term loan
   B. loan financing the purchase of both real and personal property
   C. loan with smaller payments at first and larger payments later
   D. secured loan

82. Which of the following is an example of functional obsolescence?
   A. Boards need to be replaced on deck
   B. House downwind from paper mill
   C. Only bathroom can be accessed only through bedroom
   D. Worn-out carpet in hallway

83. A seller wants to net $60,000 from a transaction, but will have to pay off a mortgage and other fees, at a total cost of $181,800. The seller will also need to pay a 7% commission. What will the property need to sell for?
   A. $241,800
   B. $258,726
   C. $260,000
   D. $276,060

338

84. A tenant has already paid his $1,200 rent for the month for a single-family property. The property's owner sells it to a new buyer, with closing occurring on the 15th of June. The parties decide the seller is entitled to rent for the closing date. On the settlement statement, the prorated rent will appear as a:

    A. $600 debit for the buyer and a $600 credit for the seller
    B. $600 debit for the seller and a $600 credit for the buyer
    C. $1,200 credit for the buyer
    D. $1,200 credit for the seller

85. Closing is set for August 1. The seller has already paid the property taxes for the year, totaling $6,000. How much of that amount is the buyer's responsibility?

    A. $2,000
    B. $2,500
    C. $3,000
    D. $3,500

86. The IRS issues rules that determine when a real estate agent is an employee and when he is an independent contractor. Which of the following statements on that topic is FALSE?

    A. The brokerage may allow an independent contractor to place her own ads but the ads must conform with the firm's advertising rules
    B. The brokerage may require an independent contractor to have a cell phone
    C. The brokerage will take taxes from an employee's paycheck
    D. The brokerage will tell an employee when to work certain hours

87. Mineral rights associated with real property are always:

    A. conveyed along with the surface rights to the property
    B. separable and divisible
    C. sold separately from the property
    D. an interest in personal property

88. John, Kevin, and Lyle own a property as tenants in common, but only Kevin and Lyle live on the property. John would like to sell the property for redevelopment, but Kevin and Lyle refuse. What is John's best option?

    A. Charge Kevin and Lyle rent
    B. Create a trust to manage the property
    C. Evict Kevin and Lyle
    D. Obtain a court order to sell the property

89. A purchase and sale agreement is for $150,000, with 80% financing, closing in 30 days with possession at closing, and a rent provision for possession after closing. This is an example of a/an:

    A. acceptance
    B. contract with contingencies
    C. counteroffer
    D. unilateral contract

90. While preparing a competitive market analysis, an agent finds four comparables to choose from. Comparable 1 sold for $180,000 13 months ago under normal conditions. Comparable 2 sold for $190,000 14 months ago under normal conditions. Comparable 3 sold for $175,000 10 months ago as a foreclosure. Comparable 4 sold for $180,000 16 months ago as a foreclosure. The agent should use:

    A. the oldest two
    B. the newest two
    C. all four
    D. None, because they are all older than nine months

91. An investor rents a property to a tenant. For tax purposes, depreciation on this property is based on:

    A. market value, plus capital improvements, minus land value
    B. market value, plus rental income, minus land value
    C. price, plus capital improvements, minus land value
    D. price, plus rental income, minus land value

92. A buyers' purchase and sale agreement contained a financing contingency. The buyers applied for a loan with a local lender, who verbally informed them that their loan application was denied. The buyers' agent should:

A. ask the sellers to provide a purchase money loan instead
B. have the sellers extend the contingency deadline
C. tell the buyers about their right to receive the denial in writing
D. terminate the agency relationship

93. An apartment building is right where a new city park is going to be built. The city condemns it. Can the city terminate the leases of the building's tenants?

A. No; this is a violation of the federal Fair Housing Act
B. No; if the government forces a landlord to breach a contract with a tenant, it is violating the Landlord-Tenant Act
C. Yes, if notice is provided to the tenants, and they receive relocation assistance
D. Yes, if the tenants receive just compensation from the city

94. An offer is dated June 4. The offer is accepted on June 7. The buyers are approved for a loan and satisfy the financing contingency on June 9. The transaction closes on June 28. The date of the contract is:

A. June 4
B. June 7
C. June 9
D. June 28

95. A couple with children would like to buy a house that was built in 1950. The home was recently remodeled, with completely new paint and plumbing. In this situation, what does the agent always have to do?

A. Ensure that the paint used during the remodel is lead-free
B. Make sure the buyers receive a pamphlet on lead-based paint
C. Provide them with a copy of a recent lead inspection report
D. Nothing; the house was remodeled so lead-based paint rules don't apply

96. A residential property manager should inform prospective tenants about:

A. a neighbor who is an alcoholic
B. the planned removal of a swimming pool
C. the property's appraised value
D. the racial composition of the tenants

97. A rural lot runs 500 feet east/west along its northern boundary, and 600 feet east/west along its southern boundary. Its eastern boundary runs 200 feet due north/south, while its western boundary runs 224 feet in a diagonal northeast/southwest direction. The cost of the land is $6 per square foot. What is the cost of this lot?

A. $600,000
B. $660,000
C. $672,000
D. $720,000

98. Rudiger purchases a home for $200,000, and receives an 80% loan from his bank. He has to pay three discount points to receive the loan. He is also responsible for a 1% origination fee and a $300 appraisal. The seller paid a 6% commission to the listing brokerage. What is the amount of the discount points that he paid?

A. $4,800
B. $6,000
C. $6,400
D. $7,500

99. A buyer purchases a rental home that is fully furnished. The document used to transfer title to the furniture is a:

A. quitclaim deed
B. bill of sale
C. special warranty deed
D. general warranty deed

100. Ben receives a life estate in a property, with his nephew Will designated as the remainderman. When Ben dies, what kind of interest does Will receive?

A. Fee simple estate
B. Life estate
C. Remainder interest
D. Reversionary interest

101. In a bilateral contract:
    A. a duty will be performed by one party only
    B. one party can restrict the performance of another party
    C. two parties have exchanged promises, and both parties are obligated to perform
    D. all parties have fully performed their duties

102. Gerald engages a licensee to list his property and find a buyer for it. In this context, the licensee is acting as a:
    A. general agent
    B. power of attorney
    C. property manager
    D. special agent

103. A mortgage often includes a clause requiring the lender's consent before another borrower may assume the mortgage. This clause is called a/an:
    A. power of sale clause
    B. subordination clause
    C. defeasance clause
    D. alienation clause (due-on-sale clause)

104. A small house is situated on a large lot in a mixed-use neighborhood. The city decides that the area will, in the future, be zoned commercial. What will most likely happen to the property's value?
    A. It will decrease, because of fears of new businesses being built nearby
    B. It will increase, in anticipation of the changing uses
    C. No effect, since the house is a non-conforming use
    D. No effect, until the change actually occurs

105. The Real Estate Settlement Procedures Act (RESPA) applies to:
    A. contracts for deed
    B. seller-financed transactions
    C. commercial and residential mortgages
    D. residential first mortgages

106. The Director of the Department of Licensing has the authority to take which of the following disciplinary actions against a licensee?
    A. Prosecute for criminal offense in superior court
    B. Fine up to $10,000 per offense
    C. Suspend a license
    D. Bar future licensing opportunities in this state, or in any other state with comparable licensing requirements

107. If B fails to renew his license by the expiration date:
    A. it is automatically canceled, and B must requalify for the license
    B. B can renew the license within a year by paying a renewal fee and a late fee
    C. B is subject to disciplinary action
    D. B's license becomes inactive for six months

108. A company that is organized as an LLC wants to represent clients in real estate transactions. Who must be licensed?
    A. The company only
    B. A partner with at least a 10% ownership interest
    C. All directors, officers, or co-partners
    D. The company and a person with control over operational and financial decisions

109. Who needs to submit continuing education credits with each license renewal?
    A. Active brokers only
    B. Active managing brokers only
    C. All active licensees
    D. All active and inactive licensees

110. An affiliated licensee requests that her designated broker release her license and her listings so that she can open her own brokerage. The designated broker must surrender the license:
    A. immediately
    B. together with the listings immediately
    C. within ten days
    D. once the listings have sold or expired

111. A licensee has obtained the signatures of the buyer and seller on a sales contract. Failure to do which of the following could result in disciplinary action by the Director?

A. Accurately determine the settlement costs of the buyer

B. Provide a copy of the sales contract to the buyer and the seller when they signed it

C. Accurately determine the settlement costs of the seller

D. Provide a good faith estimate of the value of the property before the contract is signed

112. S's real estate license is inactive. This is because:

A. her application has not yet been received by the Department of Licensing

B. she has not gotten a listing in over six months

C. her license has been delivered to the Director of the Department of Licensing

D. she failed to renew her license before the expiration date

113. Real estate transaction records should be kept for a minimum of:

A. one year

B. two years

C. three years

D. four years

114. A real estate broker is:

A. an affiliated licensee

B. a designated broker

C. authorized to receive a commission directly from a client

D. an associate licensee

115. A licensee manages a property for one of her friends for a fee of $70 per month. Which of the following is true?

A. A written agreement is required between the licensee and the property owner

B. A written agreement is required between the licensee's firm and the property owner

C. No written agreement is required because the fee is so low

D. No written agreement is required because the licensee and property owner are friends

116. According to Washington license law, a licensee who is acting as a property manager must give the owner a summary statement for all of the following, except:

A. rent receipts

B. property condition

C. outstanding balances

D. owner's contributions

117. A person who represents a real estate brokerage in selling, listing, renting, leasing, or exchanging real property, and who is managed by a designated or managing broker, is a/an:

A. incorporated associate broker

B. land development representative

C. associate licensee

D. real estate broker

118. If a licensee is sued based on her real estate activities, the licensee must notify the Real Estate Program Manager:

A. if the judge determines the case to be serious enough to warrant disclosure

B. within 20 days of any settlement conference

C. within 20 days of a court order, verdict, or judgment against the licensee

D. at the conclusion of the case, unless the licensee intends to appeal

119. A licensee who knows that there's an encroachment on the seller's property is discussing the property with a buyer. Which of the following statements is true?

A. It is illegal for the seller to sell the property with an encroachment

B. The licensee should mention the encroachment and tell the buyer to consult an attorney before making an offer on the property

C. The licensee should not reveal the encroachment because to do so would harm the seller

D. The licensee should withdraw from the listing, claiming a conflict of interest

120. In place of three years of actual full-time real estate sales experience, a managing broker license applicant can qualify to take the managing broker's examination with:

    A. six months of experience as a real estate attorney
    B. five years of experience as a commercial insurance agent
    C. two years of experience as a resident apartment manager
    D. five years of experience as a mortgage loan broker

121. After a disciplinary hearing, if the Director imposes sanctions, the licensee may appeal the Director's order within:

    A. six months, by filing an appeal with the court of appeals
    B. 30 days, by filing an appeal with the superior court
    C. two months, by filing an appeal with the superior court
    D. 30 days, by filing an appeal with an appellate administrative judge

122. How many years of experience in real estate is required for appointment as a real estate commissioner?

    A. Two
    B. Three
    C. Four
    D. Five

123. All of the following places are appropriate for the display of a license EXCEPT:

    A. on a designated broker's office wall
    B. in the front window of a brokerage office
    C. above a filing cabinet in a brokerage office
    D. in the licensee's personnel file in the designated broker's office

124. A licensee hires another licensee, who works for the same firm, to be an assistant for negotiating and selling properties. The supervising licensee, in this relationship, must:

    A. be a managing broker
    B. be a member of the team
    C. have a controlling interest in the firm
    D. take a 30 clock-hour course on supervision

125. Unlicensed staff members in a real estate office can do which of the following without obtaining a real estate license?

    A. Discuss listings over the phone
    B. Show properties to interested parties
    C. Host open houses provided they don't discuss terms of sale
    D. Anything that is not covered by Washington real estate license law

126. A licensee's unlicensed assistant has failed to complete the paperwork for the last ten closings. Under the Uniform Regulation of Business and Professions Act, the licensee may be subject to disciplinary action on what grounds?

    A. Aiding or abetting an unlicensed person to perform real estate activities that require a license
    B. Failure to supervise staff adequately
    C. Failure to follow proper document handling procedures
    D. Being party to a concealment in conduct of real estate activities

127. When making the required agency disclosure, a licensee must always:

    A. conduct herself in conformity with the agency disclosure she has made
    B. explain that she is the agent for the seller
    C. avoid dual agency situations, because they are illegal
    D. explain that she is the agent of the party who is responsible for paying the commission

128. Where should an amendment to a purchase and sale agreement be filed?

    A. Alphabetically, under the buyer's name
    B. Alphabetically, under the seller's name
    C. In the designated broker's trust account ledgers
    D. In the appropriate transaction file

129. Clarence Johnson is the listing designated broker and Alison Takahashi is the selling designated broker. Broker Samantha, who works for Alison, procured the sale of the property. Who writes the check to Samantha for her commission?

    A. Alison
    B. Clarence
    C. Buyer
    D. Seller

130. A brokerage is under investigation by the Department of Licensing. The designated broker is responsible for all of the following EXCEPT:

    A. responding to a subpoena where the designated broker's name isn't listed
    B. allowing open access by investigators to the firm's office
    C. providing a written statement to investigators if requested
    D. maintaining records for the transactions in which the firm was involved

131. Client trust funds must be placed in an interest-bearing trust account in all of the following cases EXCEPT:

    A. when a buyer makes an earnest money deposit in the amount of $1,000
    B. when a buyer makes an earnest money deposit in the amount of $5,500
    C. for property management accounts
    D. for commercial real estate trust accounts

132. A real estate broker represents the seller in a transaction involving an investment property. Several months later, the new owner asks the broker if he would act as property manager for that property. The broker may take this position:

    A. only if his designated broker allows it
    B. only if the broker and the buyer are not related
    C. only if the broker does not work for compensation
    D. only if the broker works for a third party rather than the buyer

133. When a broker attempts to renew his license, he intentionally lists a 3-hour course twice in order to reach 30 hours. The Director can:

    A. grant a 45-day interim license until the course is completed
    B. suspend the license and charge him with misrepresentation in obtaining or reinstating a license
    C. audit the school administrator
    D. refer the case to the Attorney General for prosecution

134. A real estate agent from Oregon is involved in a commercial property transaction in Washington. The agent from Oregon must do all of the following EXCEPT:

    A. associate with a Washington brokerage
    B. provide a copy of the out-of-state real estate license to the Washington firm
    C. deposit all records in the transaction with the firm in Washington
    D. register with the Department of Licensing at least 20 days before engaging in brokerage activities

135. A Washington real estate licensee's license has expired because he did not pay his license fee as required. His license can be reinstated if he:

    A. completes an additional 30 hours of continuing education electives
    B. obtains special permission from the Director of the Department of Licensing
    C. pays back renewal fees, plus penalties
    D. retakes the real estate examination

136. A Washington real estate broker takes a listing for a waterfront bungalow while working for Firm A. However, before a purchase agreement is signed, she terminates her affiliation and begins working for Firm B. Which of the following statements is true?

    A. The listing belongs to Firm A, but Firm A will still owe a commission to the original broker
    B. The listing belongs to the firm, and will remain with Firm A
    C. The listing belongs to the licensee, and will go with her to Firm B
    D. The listing is canceled automatically, and the seller must re-list with the broker

137. The cost of an appeal from a final decision made by the Director of the Department of Licensing in an adjudicative proceeding is paid by the:

    A. appellant
    B. appellant's real estate brokerage
    C. Real Estate Commission
    D. state Attorney General

138. Unless the purchase agreement or other contract states differently, an earnest money check given to a real estate licensee shall be made out to the:

    A. licensee's firm, as licensed
    B. closing or escrow agent
    C. seller
    D. appropriate multiple listing association

139. If a real estate agent is sending out emails offering his services, the federal CAN-SPAM Act requires the agent to:

    A. avoid emailing persons on the "do not call" list
    B. include the brokerage firm's name as licensed
    C. make sure that a licensee, not an unlicensed person, was responsible for the content
    D. tell recipients how to opt out of receiving future emails

140. To be entitled to sue for a commission, a person must be able to prove that at the time the real estate activities were performed, she:

    A. was licensed
    B. had passed the real estate exam
    C. had at least a verbal promise of compensation
    D. was under the supervision of a mentor

Answer Key

1. D The Truth in Lending Act covers consumer loans—loans used for personal, family, or household purposes. If the borrower will use the proceeds to invest in a commercial purpose, TILA does not apply, even if the loan is secured by owner-occupied residential property. (By contrast, if the proceeds of a loan against real property are used to send a child to college, for example, then TILA would apply.)

2. C Offers may continue to be presented after a seller has accepted an offer, but such an offer should be made contingent on the first sale's failure to close. Such an offer is known as a backup offer.

3. C The real estate agent should decline the listing, as what Tyler has proposed will violate antidiscrimination laws.

4. B The agent can check with the county recorder's office to determine who owns the property. The agent will want all owners of the property, not just the two children who contacted her, to sign the listing agreement.

5. D A contract signed by a person who was temporarily incompetent at the time may be voidable, if the person takes action within a reasonable period of time after regaining competency.

6. A First, find the square footage of the lot (99 feet × 110 feet = 10,890 square feet). Convert that to acreage (10,890 square feet ÷ 43,560 square feet per acre = 0.25, or one-quarter of an acre). Multiply that by the price per acre to find the selling price ($180,000 × 0.25 = $45,000).

7. C A section is one square mile, with each side being one mile long. One mile equals 5,280 feet.

8. D A counteroffer serves to terminate an offer. Once an offer has been rejected, it cannot be accepted. At this point, though, Victoria may simply make a new offer to sell the property to Lloyd for $225,000, and hope that he hasn't changed his mind.

9. C Calculate the size of the pet deposit by determining what one-quarter of a month's rent is ($1,000 × 0.25 = $250). Add that to the ordinary security deposit to find the total amount ($1,000 + $250 = $1,250).

10. A The shorter the loan term is, the less interest a borrower will pay. A shorter loan may not always be the best option for a borrower, though, as a shorter loan for the same loan amount will mean higher payments and may limit what properties the borrower can afford.

11. A Manufacture of illegal drugs, such as methamphetamine, can leave behind toxic residues that are difficult to clean up.

12. B It wouldn't matter, for the purposes of agency law, whether the individual licensee who took the listing becomes incompetent or not. The situation in B is the only one in which the listing does not terminate on the date mentioned in the answer option. So only B is correct. The listing agreement is between the seller and the brokerage firm, not an individual. Agency relationships can terminate because of seller revocation, expiration of term, or destruction of the subject property.

13. D Prepayment penalties are not allowed by either the FHA or VA loan programs. Borrowers are allowed to prepay part or all of their loans at their own discretion.

14. B As long as an illiterate person understands the terms of the contract, he can give his consent to it.

15. C A retail store open to the public would be a public accommodation, subject to the Americans with Disabilities Act. The building's owner would need to remove architectural barriers to persons with disabilities, for instance by building a wheelchair ramp.

16. B Refinancing involves taking out an entirely new mortgage loan to replace an existing one. It often is done when mortgage interest rates drop, allowing borrowers to have lower payments.

17. D A fee simple estate is the highest and most complete form of land ownership. A fee simple estate may still be subject to other limitations, like liens or encumbrances.

18. A The state's power of escheat means that property with no known owner, such as cases where an owner dies intestate and with no heirs, passes to the state.

19. A Deed restrictions are limitations on what property owners can and cannot do. Since these restrictions run with the land, they limit the ways future owners may use the property.

20. C In a life estate pur autre vie ("for another life"), the measuring life is someone other than the life tenant.

21. D The main advantage of the limited partnership arrangement, for a limited partner, is that liability for the entity's debts is limited.

22. C For a principal residence, interest on a purchase or refinance loan is fully deductible. Interest on a home equity loan of up to $100,000 is also deductible, regardless of the size of the purchase loan, and regardless of the taxpayer's income.

23. D Repairs to keep an investment property in ordinary operating condition are deductible in the year they are performed. This would include repainting. Adding a pool or installing a new furnace would be considered capital expenditures, which have tax advantages too but are not deductible in the year they are made (although capital expenditures may be gradually deducted over a set number of years in the form of depreciation deductions).

24. B A section is 640 acres, so a quarter-section is 160 acres (640 ÷ 4 = 160) and a quarter-quarter section, like the NW 1/4 of the SE 1/4, is 40 acres (160 ÷ 4 = 40). Half of a quarter-quarter section, like the S 1/2 of the SW 1/4 of the NE 1/4, is 20 acres (40 ÷ 2 = 20). Add the two parts together to find the parcel is 60 acres (40 + 20 = 60).

25. B The most important rule in determining whether a seller is obligated to pay a commission is whether a ready, willing, and able buyer was found during the listing period. This would take precedence over the seller's failure to provide marketable title. A buyer who does not have the financial ability to complete the purchase does not qualify as "able."

26. A The agent's best bet is to suggest that the sellers get legal advice about obtaining a quitclaim deed from the relative who may have a claim. The agent should not presume that the transaction will have to be scrapped. Only the parties, not the escrow agent or a real estate licensee, can change the closing date.

27. A "Caveat emptor" is a Latin phrase meaning "let the buyer beware," suggesting that the duty of investigating a potential purchase ultimately falls on the buyer. While this phrase is generally applicable to most transactions, laws regarding real estate transactions limit this somewhat. For instance, sellers must, in most cases, disclose latent defects to buyers.

28. C The description of the power of attorney doesn't mention any limitations; therefore, the document gives the son universal agency authority.

29. C A power of attorney is a document that appoints a person to act on another person's behalf. The person who receives that authority is an attorney in fact.

30. B The Residential Lead-Based Paint Reduction Act requires sellers of houses built before 1978 to disclose the location of any known lead-based paint. The buyer must be offered at least a ten-day window in which the house may be tested for lead-based paint.

31. C First, calculate the annual net income, using the capitalization formula ($1,600,000 x .2 = $320,000). Now you need to use the percentage formula to calculate the gross income, but don't use the percentage of the gross income that is taken up by the operating expenses (which is .4); instead, you will want to use the percentage of the gross income that is not taken up by the operating expenses (which is 1 - .4, or .6). Calculate the gross income ($320,000 ÷ .6 = $533,333.33). You can double-check your math by calculating what is 40% of the gross income ($533,333.33 x .4 = $213,333.33), and subtracting that amount (which represents the operating expenses) from the gross income to verify the net income ($533,333.33 - $213,333.33 = $320,000).

32. D Including the rules that govern the tenancy in the lease itself helps prevent disputes between landlord and tenant.

33. C Points paid in connection with a mortgage loan on one's home are considered by the IRS to be prepaid interest, and therefore are deductible on a homeowner's income taxes just as mortgage interest is.

34. A A life estate pur autre vie is based on a measuring life that's someone other than the life tenant. An estate in remainder is one that passes to a third party at the end of the measuring life, rather than to the grantor or the grantor's heirs. Note that if the grantor will get the estate at the end of the measuring life, it's called a reversion because the property is reverting (returning) to the original owner.

35. C Avulsion is a form of accession, which is involuntary alienation of property due to natural causes. In the case of avulsion, an owner may lose title to land that has been torn away by flowing water and deposited elsewhere.

36. C To solve this problem, first calculate how much money is deposited in the first year. There are ten properties sold, and $2,000 is charged for each one (10 × $2,000 = $20,000). In the second year, ten additional properties are sold (10 × $2,000 = $20,000). The first ten properties each owe an additional $1,000 in the second year, though (10 × $1,000 = $10,000). Add $20,000, $20,000, and $10,000 to find a total of $50,000.

37. A If a new large employer arrives in the area, that will increase the population seeking to buy homes. The increased demand will cause prices to go up. Higher interest rates, on the other hand, will lower demand and thus lower prices, while an oversupply of houses will also lower prices.

38. B Rural cluster development is a zoning practice that allows subdivisions in rural zoning districts to be made up of small lots and reserved green space, in order to conserve rural open space.

39. C A tenant is guaranteed quiet enjoyment, which is freedom of possession without being disturbed by others, including the landlord. A landlord may enter the premises, but only by giving notice within the period required by law. (However, no notice is required for a landlord to enter in an emergency, such as fire or flooding.)

40. B There are nine square feet in a square yard (3 feet per yard × 3 feet per yard = 9 square feet).

41. B A commercial tenant may need to expand into remodeled adjacent units, if its operations grow, so a property manager will want to consider that possibility when helping a commercial tenant find the right space. However, this is not usually a concern for residential tenants. By contrast, a written lease, a security deposit, and a check of credit scores are all common in both commercial and residential leases.

42. D An increased number of lots per acre would be a more intensive use than before. If it exceeds the maximum number of lots per acre allowed under zoning laws, it would require either a variance or a rezone.

43. A One-eighth of a mile is equivalent to 660 feet (5,280 feet ÷ 8 = 660 feet). Multiply to find its square footage (660 feet × 660 feet = 435,600 square feet), and then divide to find the number of acres (435,600 square feet ÷ 43,560 square feet per acre = 10 acres).

44. C Special, general, and universal agency have varying lengths, and give the agent varying levels of authority. The common thread is that they all are created when a principal delegates to an agent the right to perform certain actions on his behalf.

45. C A contract entered into by a minor is voidable, which means it can be rescinded by the minor. However, if the buyer does not act promptly, the contract may be deemed to have been ratified.

46. D A real estate licensee would not be involved in a sale of stock in a company that does not also involve the sale of real property. A licensed securities dealer would need to be involved instead.

47. B In dealing with its own property in non-commercial transactions, a religious organization may limit occupancy to its members, provided that membership isn't restricted on the basis of race, color, or national origin.

48. D Adverse possession allows a person who has occupied land in a manner that is actual, open and notorious, hostile, exclusive, and continuous and uninterrupted, to take title to the property after a specified period of time.

49. C Items installed by a commercial tenant involved in a trade or business are a special category of fixtures, known as trade fixtures. The tenant may remove trade fixtures, even if permanently attached to the property, as long as the property is restored to its original condition (or the landlord is compensated for any damage).

50. C Liquidated damages are only available as a remedy for breach of contract if the contract contains a liquidated damages provision. Most purchase and sale agreements provide that the earnest money will be treated as liquidated damages if the buyer (not the seller) breaches the contract. The seller is allowed to keep the buyer's deposit, and generally is not required to prove that she has suffered a loss as a result of the buyer's breach.

51. B A listing belongs to a brokerage firm, not to an individual licensee. It is a contract between a seller and a firm, so it would remain in place even if the seller's particular agent left the firm.

52. C The covenant of seisin protects the buyer in this case, in that it promises that the grantor actually owns the property interest being transferred to the grantee. The covenant of warranty might also apply, but that's not an answer choice; there is no such thing as a covenant of freehold warranty.

53. C The best way to ascertain if a physical object encroaches on a boundary line would be through a survey.

54. B Generally, providing any brokerage services creates an agency. However, there's an important exception to this rule: if the agent is already representing another party under a written agreement (usually, a listing agreement), then providing minimal services does not create an agency. In this question, the buyers would be proceeding without representation. Most listing agents would strongly encourage the buyers to find representation rather than merely helping them with their offer.

55. A Equity refers to the difference between the property's value and the loans against the property. Therefore, the larger the downpayment the buyer makes, the more equity in the property he will have initially.

56. D In order to calculate a property's value, an appraiser using the income approach would need to know the property's net income and capitalization rate. So, conversely, if the appraiser wanted to find the capitalization rate, he would need to know the property's value and net income.

57. B An agent may unilaterally renounce an agency relationship. (Termination of the agency may involve a breach of contract; if so, the agent could be liable to the principal for damages resulting from the breach.)

58. C It is acceptable, though not always wise, to use a promissory note in place of earnest money. A promissory note is a complete contract and never needs to be tied to a mortgage or deed of trust, although institutional loans will always be collateralized with a mortgage or deed of trust.

59. D Certain established uses that were lawful before a rezone may be permitted to continue to operate. These uses, such as Jean's store, are known as nonconforming uses.

60. D If a purchase and sale agreement is contingent on the results of an inspection, the parties also should specify in the contract how repairs will be handled.

61. A Formation of a contract occurs when the offeree communicates acceptance to the offeror in an acceptable method and within the proper time period. For a real estate contract to be enforceable, the agreement must be in writing.

62. B Only an attorney may draft a contract for someone else; for a real estate agent to do so would be the unauthorized practice of law. The agent may fill out pre-printed forms, but not draft new contract language.

63. C A buyer receives equitable title to the property once the sales contract has been signed.

64. B One of the duties owed to all parties, whether a principal or not, is the duty of honesty and good faith. Confidentiality, loyalty, and seeking expert advice are duties owed only to a principal.

65. C Since the comparable has a feature the subject property lacks, the appraiser will subtract the value of that feature ($800) from the sales price of the comparable property. The resulting figure will suggest what the comparable might have been worth if it, like the subject property, only had a one-car garage. (Note that the sales price of the subject property is not an appropriate consideration in appraising its market value.)

66. D The movie theater is an example of a nonconforming use, which predates a zoning change. Nonconforming uses are generally allowed to continue, although they may not be enlarged, or resumed if they are stopped.

67. A The Truth In Lending Act applies to consumer loans (those made for personal, family, or household purposes); it would not apply to a business loan, even if it will be used to construct a single-family residence.

68. D RESPA is a federal law that requires certain information about closing costs to be disclosed to loan applicants, and also prohibits kickbacks and referral fees that unnecessarily increase the cost of settlement.

69. D Tax-deferred (also called tax-free) exchanges may be used for unimproved investment property, income-producing property, or property used in a trade or business. Principal residences and personal use properties are not eligible.

70. B A conditional use permit will allow certain beneficial uses (like schools and churches) to operate in residential neighborhoods despite zoning laws.

71. D A property management agreement creates a general agency relationship, in which the agent (ABC Realty) is authorized to handle all of the principal's (XYZ Apartment Rentals) affairs in one or more specified areas.

72. D A change to the commission rate could be made by both parties, as the listing agreement is a contract that could be amended. However, once the contract exists, it is not something that can be changed unilaterally by one dissatisfied party.

73. B The contract is voidable by the minor, but not by the other party.

74. C A purchase money mortgage is one given by the buyer to the seller to secure credit extended by the seller. (Since the question mentions a loan and also that the buyer took title, the parties' arrangement could not be a land contract.)

75. B A conventional loan is typically used for purchase of a first home. While conventional loans can have downpayments smaller than 20%, no private mortgage insurance is required if the buyer puts down 20% or more.

76. B The income approach is appropriate for properties that are oriented toward generating income for the property's owner. That would be true even if the property originally was intended as a single-family residence.

77. B Economic-base analysis looks at economic activity in both basic industries (those that drive a local economy) and non-basic industries (those that support the basic industries), in order to predict employment and other economic trends.

78. D Preventive maintenance is all maintenance that is done on a routine basis to help preserve the physical integrity of the property. The goal is to prevent development of problems that would require corrective maintenance instead.

79. C There are two ways to solve this. One way would be to add the square footage of the two lots (39,375 + 21,875 = 61,250) and then, since both lots have the same depth, divide the square footage by the depth (61,250 square feet ÷ 175 feet = 350 feet). The other way would be to calculate the frontage of the first lot (39,375 ÷ 175 = 225), calculate the frontage of the second lot (21,875 ÷ 175 = 125), and add the two frontages together (225 feet + 125 feet = 350 feet). Either way, it's a good idea to sketch the dimensions before attempting to solve.

80. B Property managers may take steps to determine whether or not a tenant is able to afford the rent, such as requesting employment and credit information. Antidiscrimination law makes it illegal to charge a disabled person a security deposit for her service animal. Note that the disabled tenant is liable for any damage the animal actually causes, however.

81. D A home equity line of credit is a revolving credit account rather than a loan with a fixed term and amount. Unlike a credit card, though, it is secured by the borrower's real property.

82. C A design flaw, such as a bathroom that is accessible only through a bedroom, is functional obsolescence. Items that need to be replaced because of wear and tear are physical deterioration, while problems outside the property's boundaries (such as a nearby factory) are external obsolescence.

83. C Start by adding the desired net and the other costs, including the mortgage ($60,000 + $181,800 = $241,800). Subtract the commission percentage from 100% (100% − 7% = 93%), and then divide the total costs by that percentage ($241,800 ÷ 0.93 = $260,000).

84. B The rent has already been paid to the seller, so the seller will need to give some of that rent to the buyer. Therefore, it will be a debit for the seller and a credit for the buyer. The seller's share is for the 1st through the 15th (15 days), and the buyer is entitled to a credit for the 16th through the 30th (also 15 days), so the seller owes the buyer half of the $1,200, or $600.

85. B Since the buyer is taking title on August 1, she's responsible for the property taxes for the remaining five months of the year (August, September, October, November, and December). Divide the annual taxes by 12 to find the monthly amount: $6,000 ÷ 12 = $500. Multiply that figure by 5 to determine the buyer's share of the taxes: $500 × 5 = $2,500.

86. B One of the key differences between employees and independent contractors is the level of supervision; an independent contractor uses his judgment how to perform a task, while an employee receives specific instructions on how to accomplish each task. An instruction to carry a cell phone would be the hallmark of an employer/employee relationship. (Practically speaking, virtually all real estate agents do carry cell phones, but because it makes their job easier and not because they are instructed to do so.)

87. B Mineral rights may be sold separately from the land. However, they are appurtenant to the land and will be conveyed with the land unless there is an agreement otherwise.

88. D A partition suit can be used when co-owners cannot agree on how to divide a property. If there isn't a feasible way to physically divide the property, the court may order the property to be sold and the proceeds to be divided between the co-owners.

89. B The contract includes 80% financing as one of its conditions, so this is a contract with contingencies: a financing contingency, to be specific. A purchase and sale agreement is a bilateral contract, not a unilateral contract.

90. D The general rule for choosing comparables is that the sale should have occurred within six months. A sale older than six months is allowable if necessary and if adjustments for inflation are made, but sales older than one year generally can't be used. In addition, only comparables that sold under normal conditions should be used, which would rule out foreclosed properties. Comparables 1 and 2 are too old, Comparable 3 is a foreclosure, and Comparable 4 is both, so none of them can be used. The agent should instead cast a wider net for comparables, even if that means using houses that need more adjustments for features or are located farther away.

91. C Adjusted basis is calculated by starting with initial basis (the cost of obtaining the property), adding capital expenditures, and then subtracting depreciation deductions. The value of the land must also be subtracted from what is depreciable; land does not wear out, so depreciation doesn't apply.

92. C Under the Fair Credit Reporting Act, when a lender takes an adverse action on the basis of a credit report, the applicant or borrower must receive written notice of that action. The consumer should also be notified of which consumer reporting agency provided that information, so that the consumer can verify and, if necessary, contest that information.

93. D In a condemnation proceeding, anyone with an interest in the condemned property is entitled to just compensation, including tenants as well as owners. Many leases contain a "condemnation clause" that discusses how any condemnation award will be allocated between landlord and tenant.

94. B The date on which acceptance occurs is considered to be the date of the contract. In this case, that would be June 7.

95. B A seller of a house built before 1978 must always give buyers a copy of a pamphlet on lead-based paint prepared by the Environmental Protection Agency. If (but only if) the property has been inspected for lead-based paint, the seller must also give a copy of the inspection report. The agent must make sure that the seller takes these steps.

96. B A property manager should inform tenants about the property's amenities; however, he shouldn't misrepresent the amenities (for instance, if a pool were about to be removed, he would want to let a prospective tenant know that before the tenant signs the lease). Antidiscrimination laws would prohibit a manager from letting a prospective tenant know about an alcoholic resident (which would be discrimination on the basis of disability) or the race of the other tenants, and while he could legally tell the prospective tenant about the property's appraised value, that's likely to be of little interest to a tenant.

97. B It's best to diagram this type of problem to solve it. Once you draw it, you would then break it down into a triangle at left and a rectangle at right. The rectangle at right is 500 feet in length and 200 feet in height (500 feet × 200 feet = 100,000 square feet). The triangle on the left side is 200 feet in height and 100 feet at its base (200 feet x 100 feet × 1/2 = 10,000 square feet); you can ignore the 224 foot diagonal side, which does not factor into your calculations (remember, the formula for a triangle's area is 1/2 × Base × Height. The hypotenuse or diagonal is not part of the equation). Add the two components together (100,000 square feet + 10,000 square feet = 110,000 square feet) and then multiply by the cost per square foot (110,000 square feet × $6 per square foot = $660,000) to find its price.

98. A To calculate the discount points, first find the loan amount ($200,000 × .8 = $160,000). Then multiply that by the percentage of the loan represented by the discount points ($160,000 × .03 = $4,800). Since the question only specified discount points, you would not include the origination fee in your calculations (and you certainly wouldn't need to know the cost of the appraisal or the commission).

99. B Deeds transfer title to real estate; a bill of sale is generally needed to transfer title to personal property.

100. A The interest that passes to a designated person upon the death of the life tenant (or other measuring life) is a fee simple estate. Will has a remainder interest only up until the moment Ben dies. Once Ben is dead, Will's interest immediately becomes a fee simple interest.

101. C In a bilateral contract, two parties have exchanged promises and both parties are obligated to perform.

102. D When a licensee represents a seller in a single transaction, and is authorized to perform typical duties associated with listing a property, she acts as a special agent.

103. D   An alienation clause (or due-on-sale clause) prevents assumption without the lender's consent by stipulating that the loan balance is due and payable in full if the property is sold.

104. B   Under the principle of anticipation, a property's value is based on expectations of what will happen to the property in the future. Generally commercial land is worth more than residential land. A small house on a large lot would be viewed as a tear down.

105. D   RESPA applies to mortgages secured by a dwelling with up to four units. It does not apply to commercial transactions or seller financing. (A contract for deed, which is the same thing as a land contract, can only be used in a seller-financed transaction.)

106. C   The Director can suspend the licensee's license.

107. B   A licensee can renew his license within one year after the expiration date by paying the renewal fee and a late penalty.

108. D   The company itself must obtain a real estate license, and the company's designated broker must hold a managing broker's license. The designated broker (typically a member in an LLC) must have the ability to control the company's operational and financial decisions. (In addition, all other members of the firm acting as affiliated licensees must be individually licensed.)

109. C   Both brokers and managing brokers must take continuing education courses, so long as they are actively licensed. Inactive licensees do not need to comply with the continuing education requirement, although a 30-hour class is required in order to reactivate a license that has been inactive for more than three years.

110. A   The brokerage must release the affiliated licensee's license at once, and without any conditions attached.

111. B   A copy of the sales contract must be given to any principal who signs it at the time she signs it.

112. C   Any time a license is surrendered to the Director of the Department of Licensing, it becomes inactive.

113. C   Transaction records should be kept for at least three years after the transaction closes.

114. A   A real estate broker is considered the brokerage firm's affiliated licensee.

115. B   Regardless of the amount of the fees involved, there must be a written property management agreement between the owner and the real estate firm. The property manager represents the firm, so the agreement is between the owner and firm (as opposed to between the owner and property manager).

116. B   A summary statement is a brief report showing the property's financial status over a certain period of time, such as one month or one quarter. It would not include a report on the managed property's physical condition.

117. D   The question describes a real estate broker as defined in the license law.

118. C   If a licensee is sued in connection with real estate activities (or other business activities), she must inform the Real Estate Program Manager within 20 days after receiving notice of any court order, verdict, or judgment against the licensee. This is true whether or not the licensee intends to appeal the decision.

119. B   The encroachment must be revealed to the purchaser, and its implications should only be explained by an attorney.

120. D   Examples of real estate-related experience that will qualify include five years of experience in escrow, mortgage finance, appraising, property management, land development, investment, etc.

121. B A licensee may appeal the Director's order within 30 days after the date the order was issued, by filing an appeal with the superior court.

122. D The commissioners are required to have at least five years of experience; they are usually managing brokers.

123. D State law requires that all licenses must be displayed "prominently" in the brokerage office. A license in a file cabinet isn't prominently displayed.

124. A A managing broker's license authorizes a licensee to manage other licensees. This applies even in the "team" context, not just to the management of branch offices.

125. D They may do anything that is not covered by Washington real estate license law; for instance, placing lockboxes on listed properties or providing accounting services for the employing brokerage firm.

126. B A licensee has the duty, under URBPA, to adequately supervise or oversee staff, whether employees or independent contractors. Failure to do so is grounds for disciplinary action.

127. A The licensee's conduct must be in accord with the agency disclosure.

128. D Copies of the purchase and sale agreement and any amendments belong in the transaction file.

129. A A licensee may receive compensation only directly from her designated broker. A licensee cannot receive compensation from a seller, or from another designated broker.

130. A A designated broker would not need to respond to a subpoena if he is not specifically named.

131. C Property management trust accounts don't have to be interest-bearing, nor are they subject to the pooled interest-bearing account requirements that apply to other real estate trust funds.

132. A A broker represents his brokerage firm, and cannot act without the designated (or managing) broker's knowledge and permission.

133. B It is a violation of the license law, and grounds for disciplinary action, for a licensee to engage in misrepresentation or concealment of a material fact when obtaining or reinstating a license.

134. D An out-of-state licensee may handle commercial real estate transactions in Washington without a Washington license if she works in cooperation with a brokerage in Washington. The Washington firm must have custody of the out-of-state broker's records concerning the in-state transaction, and it must be given a copy of the out-of-state broker's license. Out-of-state licensees aren't required to register with the Department of Licensing.

135. C A license that hasn't been properly renewed will expire. It can be reinstated within one year of the expiration, if the licensee pays a penalty and any back fees.

136. B Listing agreements are the property of a firm, not a licensee. If a licensee leaves a firm mid-transaction, the listing still will belong to the firm and will not follow the licensee to a new firm. Whether the firm owes a commission to the licensee is a matter of the licensee's employment agreement with the firm, not of law.

137. A A licensee appealing the outcome of a disciplinary hearing must post a $1,000 appeal bond to cover court costs, in case the superior court judge decides against the licensee. Even if the licensee wins the appeal, the licensee will still be responsible for the cost of a transcript of the hearing.

138. A The question and answer correctly state the law; however, it is common practice for the buyer to name an escrow agent in the offer and make out the check to that person.

139. D   The CAN-SPAM Act is a federal law that places limits on unsolicited emails. One requirement is that an email must give information on how recipients can avoid receiving further emails.

140. A   A person must have been validly licensed at the time she engaged in the real estate activities for which a commission is claimed.

Sample Exam 3

1. An easement for ingress and egress that is created by a court of law where it is reasonably necessary for the enjoyment of the property is an easement:
   A. appurtenant
   B. by necessity
   C. by prescription
   D. in gross

2. What kind of property could a buyer purchase with a FHA 203(b) loan?
   A. Apartment building
   B. Commercial property
   C. Farm occupied by a tenant
   D. Four-unit dwelling where the buyer will occupy one of the units

3. Maria buys a home in a subdivision that is subject to restrictive covenants. The city Maria lives in allows fences, but the subdivision's restrictive covenants don't. Of the following, which is true?
   A. Restrictive covenants only limit lot size; they don't limit fencing
   B. The city is a government entity, so its rules take precedence over private restrictions
   C. The deed's restrictive covenants take precedence over the city because they are more restrictive
   D. Maria owns the property, so she has a legal right to build a fence regardless of the deed's restrictions

4. Which of the following people might bring a suit for specific performance?
   A. A buyer in a real estate transaction in which the seller backed out one day before closing
   B. A homeowner unhappy about a neighbor who painted her house purple in violation of the subdivision CC&Rs
   C. A real estate broker who didn't receive the commission she was promised
   D. A seller who was overcharged during escrow

5. After listing a property for sale, a licensee learns that the property was used as a beer hall during Prohibition, for illegal drug sales in 2003, and as a homeless shelter in 2009. What is the licensee's duty regarding property disclosures?
   A. All of these uses must be disclosed
   B. Only the most recent use must be disclosed
   C. The drug sales must be disclosed
   D. None of these uses must be disclosed

6. Which of the following methods would be most appropriate for valuing a recently built, single-family home?
   A. Replacement cost and income approach
   B. Income approach and cost approach
   C. Market analysis and replacement cost
   D. Income approach and cap rate

7. A seller and a brokerage firm sign an exclusive listing agreement. The listing is set to expire in three months, but after a few weeks, the seller decides she doesn't want to sell at all. Which is true?
   A. The listing can only be terminated with the mutual consent of both seller and brokerage
   B. The seller can revoke the listing and will not owe anything to the brokerage
   C. The seller can revoke the listing but may be liable to the brokerage for damages
   D. The seller can revoke the listing but can't list the property with any competing firm for three months

8. A tenant signs a one-year lease. Four months later the owner sells the property to a third party, who wants to move in immediately. Which of the following is correct?

   A. The new owner takes ownership subject to the lease and must wait until the lease ends to move in
   B. The landlord (the previous owner) can force the tenant to move out as a matter of law
   C. The new owner holds title and can force the tenant to move out
   D. The lease automatically terminates whenever the property is sold

9. A ten-year-old home cost $120,000 to build and the land it's on cost $20,000. If an appraiser finds that depreciation has averaged 1.5% per year, what is the total amount of depreciation on the property?

   A. $1,800
   B. $2,100
   C. $18,000
   D. $21,000

10. An easement appurtenant is one that:

    A. can only be created by prescription
    B. is of more benefit to the servient tenant than the dominant tenant
    C. is given to a commercial tenant
    D. runs with the land

11. X and Y execute a properly drawn up option agreement for X to purchase Y's commercial property. X gives $5 in consideration. The option is:

    A. unenforceable
    B. valid
    C. void
    D. voidable

12. Once a lender issues a veteran a VA-guaranteed loan, the veteran:

    A. can never receive another VA loan
    B. cannot prepay the principal on the loan
    C. immediately becomes liable for the guaranteed amount
    D. must purchase private mortgage insurance

13. For how long is a deed restriction valid?

    A. Potentially forever
    B. Only as to the first purchaser of the property
    C. Only if the restriction is a covenant, not a condition
    D. Until a subsequent buyer and seller agree to release it

14. Which of the following is true regarding a sublease?

    A. The lessee is no longer liable to the lessor
    B. The lessee is still liable to the lessor if the sublessee defaults on the rent
    C. The sublessee is liable to the lessor during the sublease period
    D. The sublessee takes possession for the entire remainder of the rental period

15. A quitclaim deed conveys:

    A. unencumbered title
    B. the grantor's interest in a given property, if any
    C. an estate for years
    D. fee simple title, including a covenant of quiet enjoyment

16. Josephine, a real estate agent, is showing a house to a buyer. The buyer loves the house, but wants certain appliances and pieces of furniture to stay with the house. Josephine should advise the buyer:

    A. to make an offer that includes the appliances and furniture (which would be reflected in a higher purchase price)
    B. that the furniture and appliances are fixtures and will automatically transfer to the buyer along with the house
    C. that it's illegal to say anything about the appliances and furniture in an offer for real property
    D. to refuse to make an offer unless the seller agrees to throw in the appliances and furniture for free

17. A property manager decides to offer some additional services beyond what is specified in the property management agreement. She may do so after:

   A. giving the tenants 30 days' notice
   B. obtaining written authorization from the owner
   C. providing notice to the Department of Licensing
   D. the management agreement is amended in a writing signed by the owner and designated broker

18. A mortgage, and the associated mortgage note, are both examples of:

   A. contracts
   B. deeds
   C. non-negotiable instruments
   D. option agreements

19. John leases a commercial property. In the lease, he agrees to pay part of the utilities and taxes, as well as a fixed monthly rent amount. This is a:

   A. net lease
   B. percentage lease
   C. ground lease
   D. graduated lease

20. Jerry offered to buy some vacant land for $500,000. There were no contingencies in his offer, and it was accepted by the seller. Jerry was planning on building a shopping center on the property, but didn't mention this to the seller or his real estate agent. A few days before closing, Jerry learned that his financing for the shopping center had fallen through. The contract is:

   A. void
   B. voidable
   C. unenforceable
   D. valid

21. A real estate agent takes a listing for a mobile home. He may do this without any additional license if:

   A. the mobile home contains a minimum of 1,500 square feet
   B. he holds a real estate securities license
   C. the listing agreement is clearly identified as a personal property listing
   D. the listing includes the land on which the mobile home rests

22. A home is listed for $200,000. A prospective buyer tells the listing agent that she may make an offer for $190,000. The listing agent tells her that the seller won't accept anything under $195,000. The buyer offers $195,000 and the seller accepts. Which is correct?

   A. The listing agent violated her fiduciary duty to the seller by engaging in self-dealing
   B. The listing agent violated her fiduciary duty to the seller by telling the buyer how low the seller would go
   C. The listing agent did not violate her fiduciary duty to the seller because that is not information that the seller would expect to remain confidential
   D. The listing agent fulfilled her fiduciary duty to the seller by facilitating a successful offer and acceptance

23. The owner of property located along a stream or river may have which type of water right?

   A. Alluvion
   B. Riparian
   C. Appropriation
   D. Littoral

24. A property's real estate taxes are $250 per month, paid at the end of the year. The property is sold and the closing date is May 15. Which of the following options is closest to what the seller's share of the taxes would be?

   A. $750
   B. $875
   C. $1,000
   D. $1,125

25. An optionee's rights can be assigned under all of the following circumstances, except when the:

   A. option money is $10 or less
   B. option money is in the form of a promissory note
   C. optionor has died
   D. optionee has died

26. An Asian-American buyer asks to be shown homes that are located in neighborhoods that he knows are primarily Asian. If a real estate agent complies with his wishes, this is:

    A. illegal, as it is blockbusting
    B. illegal, as it is steering
    C. legal, as it is done at the buyer's request
    D. legal, as the Fair Housing Act has an exception for single-family homes

27. Five people buy an investment property. They take title so that they each have equal ownership shares, and so that if one of them dies, his share will pass to his heirs. How did they take title?

    A. Community property
    B. Joint tenancy
    C. Tenancy in common
    D. Term tenancy

28. A buyer who records a deed is giving:

    A. constructive notice
    B. actual notice
    C. pending notice
    D. statutory notice

29. An older retail building has narrow hallways and window air conditioning units rather than central AC. These would be examples of:

    A. economic obsolescence
    B. external obsolescence
    C. functional obsolescence
    D. physical deterioration

30. Maya and Andrew are real estate agents who work for competing brokerages. They don't like a new discount broker and decide together not to show any of the new broker's listings. This is a violation of the Sherman Act because it's:

    A. a group boycott
    B. a tie-in arrangement
    C. market allocation
    D. price fixing

31. If the mortgage amount is $80,000 and the borrower paid $4,800 in discount points, how many discount points were charged?

    A. 4
    B. 5
    C. 6
    D. 8

32. Most conventional loans contain an alienation clause which prohibits:

    A. the sale of the property
    B. prepayment of the loan
    C. the loan from being assumed
    D. increases or decreases in the loan's interest rate

33. A corporation takes title to real property through a/an:

    A. estate in severalty
    B. joint tenancy
    C. tenancy at will
    D. A corporation may not take title

34. Siobhan listed her property with ABC Realty. She asks her agent, Robert, to draft deed covenants that will prevent a buyer from subdividing the land in the future. She'd also like the agent to create a trust from the sale, to benefit her disabled sister. Robert's reply should be:

    A. I can draft the trust, but an attorney will need to draft the covenants
    B. I can draft both of these documents
    C. I can draft the covenants, but an attorney will need to draft the trust
    D. I can't help you with either of these things; you'll need to contact an attorney

35. A seller lists his house and sells it "as is" to a buyer. Shortly after the sale closes, the buyer finds a large hole in the ground next to the house. The hole, which has caused significant damage to the foundation, was almost certainly intentionally concealed with leaves and branches. Which of the following is correct?

    A. Only the licensee is liable
    B. Only the seller is liable
    C. Both the seller and the licensee may be liable
    D. Neither is liable, because the house was sold "as is"

36. A tenant farmer has occupied a farm on which she has grown crops for several years. The landowner sells the farm to someone else who immediately gives the tenant notice to vacate. The timing of the notice will mean the crops currently in the ground will not be ready for harvest before the end of her lease. Who do the first crops belong to?

    A. The tenant
    B. The former owner
    C. The new owner
    D. The tenant and the new owner

37. The seller tells the buyer's agent that the home has never had flooding issues, but when touring the home, the buyer's agent notices a sump pump in the basement. The buyer's agent should:

    A. say nothing because the seller said there was no flooding
    B. advise the buyer that the sump pump may be a sign of flooding and that she should inquire into whether flooding is an issue
    C. contact the seller directly to ask about the sump pump/flooding
    D. instruct the buyer to stop considering the property

38. Sally lists her property for sale with Broker Al. Al learns that the property is about to be rezoned to a higher use. He tells Sally he would like to purchase the property himself. She agrees, and the sale closes. Six months later, Al resells the property for a significant profit. This is legal:

    A. as long as before Sally agreed to the sale, Al informed her of the upcoming zoning change and what it would mean for the property's value
    B. as long as he disclosed to Sally the profit he made off the resale, after his sale closed
    C. only if Al shares his profits with Sally
    D. under no circumstances

39. Sonya buys a parcel of land and pays taxes on it for five years. After she builds a home on it, the taxes she'll pay are:

    A. special assessments
    B. ad valorem taxes
    C. estate taxes
    D. excise taxes

40. What would cause a judgment lien to be imposed on a landowner's property?

    A. Foreclosure
    B. Lawsuit
    C. Unpaid construction project
    D. Unpaid property taxes

41. By what right would a railroad company acquire private land necessary for a new railway line?

    A. Partition action
    B. Eminent domain
    C. Suit in federal court
    D. Condemnation

42. On a settlement statement, the seller's net proceeds are calculated by:

    A. subtracting closing costs from the purchase price
    B. subtracting the buyer's credits from the seller's credits
    C. subtracting the seller's debits from the buyer's debits
    D. subtracting the seller's debits from the seller's credits

43. A buyer and seller were inspecting a property, prior to the buyer making an offer. The property was occupied by a tenant at the time of inspection. The seller told the buyer that the garden furniture would be included in the sale. However, the buyer discovers upon possession that the garden furniture belonged to the tenant, not the seller. Is the buyer entitled to the garden furniture?

    A. No, because the garden furniture was the tenant's real property
    B. No, because the seller didn't have the right to include the tenant's personal property in the deal
    C. Yes, because garden furniture is a fixture included with the sale of real property
    D. Yes, because the buyer relied on the seller's representation

44. A minor purchases a home right before he turns 18. Immediately after he reaches the age of majority, he contacts the seller and rescinds the contract, demanding his money back. Which is true?

   A. This is possible if the home was purchased with a mortgage, because of the right of rescission under Regulation Z
   B. This is possible because he is doing so within a reasonable amount of time after having reached the age of majority
   C. This isn't possible because buyers are subject to caveat emptor
   D. This isn't possible because a buyer can't rescind a voidable contract after closing

45. Mortgage interest rates are primarily influenced by the:

   A. assessed value of the property
   B. condition of the money market
   C. credit history of the borrower
   D. value of similar mortgaged properties in the area

46. For income tax purposes, a homeowner can deduct:

   A. property taxes
   B. principal payments on a mortgage
   C. capital expenditures
   D. the adjusted basis

47. Mark and Kim's two-year lease on their apartment expires. Unhappy that the couple doesn't plan to renew the lease, the property manager charges them one month's rent for failure to give notice. If the lease says nothing about this issue, in this case:

   A. no notice is required and no additional fee must be paid
   B. Mark and Kim owe one month's additional rent
   C. Mark and Kim owe one month's additional rent plus a nonrenewal fee
   D. Mark and Kim will lose the full amount of their security deposit

48. A seller finds that he cannot provide marketable title because of a cloud on the title. To clear the title, he must file a/an:

   A. adverse possession claim
   B. quiet title action
   C. quitclaim deed
   D. partition suit

49. A minority buyer with a disabled daughter makes a full-price offer on a property. The home doesn't have any grab bars in the bathroom and the front door isn't wide enough for a wheelchair. The seller informs the buyer's agent that the property wouldn't be suitable for the daughter, so he is going to refuse the offer. The buyer's agent should:

   A. explain the situation to the buyer, and advise her to consult an attorney and/ or file a complaint with HUD
   B. instruct the seller to make those modifications at his own expense
   C. not say anything to the buyer about the circumstances, but help her find a more suitable property
   D. not say anything to the buyer, since a seller can choose who to sell his home to

50. A buyer would be protected from risk of loss due to a failed heating system through:

   A. an agency disclosure statement
   B. a home protection plan
   C. mortgage insurance
   D. title insurance

51. Which is true regarding a standard 203(b) FHA loan?

   A. An FHA appraisal is required
   B. No downpayment is required
   C. Secondary financing from an institutional lender may be used for the downpayment
   D. The maximum loan term is 20 years

52. After the sale of a property in a 1031 exchange, the seller must close on the new property within:

   A. 10 days
   B. 30 days
   C. 45 days
   D. 180 days

53. A borrower defaults on a mortgage. What does the acceleration clause in the mortgage allow the lender to do?

   A. Compel the borrower to sell the property and repay the debt
   B. Demand immediate payment of the entire loan balance
   C. Prevent the borrower from selling the property
   D. Report the borrower to a collection agency

54. Cluster zoning, which allows smaller lot sizes and reduced frontages, is suitable if a development:

   A. includes both commercial and residential uses
   B. still has a density ratio consistent with the general plan
   C. abuts a wetland or other sensitive site
   D. abuts state- or city-owned land

55. Mark is selling his property, which has an unfinished basement. He gets a full-price offer from Susan, but the offer requires Mark to finish the basement prior to closing. Do Mark and Susan have a binding contract?

   A. Yes, because both parties have made offers to each other
   B. Yes, because Susan made a full-price offer
   C. No, because a valid offer must be written and recorded
   D. No, because Mark has not accepted Susan's offer

56. A broker would need to have a securities license to participate in:

   A. a sale of both real and personal property
   B. a sale of a commercial building that is showing a profit
   C. a transaction involving an investment contract
   D. listing a property owned by a corporation

57. Buyer Perry would like to assume Seller Joan's loan with ABC Mortgage Company, in a way that would mean no further liability for Joan. To accomplish this, Perry and Joan should use a/an:

   A. acknowledgment of the agreement from ABC Mortgage
   B. purchase contract signed by the buyer and seller
   C. release of liability signed by ABC Mortgage
   D. release of liability signed by Joan

58. The manager of a 6-story, 18-unit apartment building, carefully screens tenant applications to make sure that tenants who use wheelchairs are assigned to the first floor. This:

   A. is allowed if there's no elevator to the upper floors
   B. is an example of a property manager making reasonable accommodations
   C. violates the Fair Housing Act
   D. violates the Civil Rights Act of 1866

59. An owner-occupied property qualifies for its state's homestead exemption from property taxes. Shortly after closing, the new assessed value of the property is issued, and the property tax amount increases significantly. The selling agent is obligated to:

   A. contact the closing agent and ask for details on the assessment
   B. contest the increased assessed value with local authorities
   C. do nothing
   D. tell the buyer that the tax amount has increased

60. A 3,000 square foot retail property rents annually for $20 per square foot, plus 8% of the tenant's gross sales. The building's tenant pays $120,000 rent in one year. What were that year's gross sales?

   A. $75,000
   B. $150,000
   C. $750,000
   D. $1,500,000

61. A commercial tenant leases retail space for $1,500 per month. A few months later, the owner of the complex adds new counters and increases the rent to $1,750 per month. At the end of the lease term, the commercial tenant:
    A. cannot take the counters with her, because the owner installed them
    B. can take the counters with her if she reimburses the owner for the fair market value of the counters
    C. can take the counters with her if she reimburses the owner for any damage caused by removal
    D. can take the counters with her without any charge

62. A veteran's guaranty benefits may be restored by a:
    A. simple loan assumption
    B. substitution of eligibility/entitlement by another veteran assuming the loan
    C. wraparound mortgage
    D. refinance to a lower rate

63. Three friends own an old lakefront house together. One friend found a developer who would like to buy and redevelop the property, but the other two friends don't agree. What can the friend who'd like to sell do?
    A. File a partition suit in the hope that the court will order the sale of the property and division of the proceeds
    B. Request a court order for the eviction of the friends
    C. Sell his interest in the property, but let the friends continue to live there as tenants
    D. Unilaterally sell the property to the developer, and divide the proceeds with his friends

64. A borrower takes out an $88,000 loan at 6% interest. The monthly principal and interest payment, amortized over 30 years, is $585. He also makes a $12,000 downpayment. The borrower will need to pay one discount point to the lender. How much is the cost of one discount point?
    A. $5.85
    B. $88
    C. $880
    D. $1,000

65. A real estate agent lists Harold's home, which he owns as a life estate. Harold's children hold the remainder interest. Which of the following is true?
    A. Anyone who buys Harold's life estate receives only the interest held by Harold
    B. Harold's children need to sign the listing agreement
    C. The buyer will automatically receive a fee simple absolute interest
    D. Since a life estate cannot be sold, the listing is invalid

66. A seller tells a prospective buyer that the attic's insulation is 16 inches thick. The seller's agent, however, observes that the insulation is only six inches thick. The seller's agent should:
    A. say nothing, but advise the buyer to get an inspection
    B. say nothing because of the duty of loyalty to the seller
    C. say nothing because this does not rise to the level of material fact
    D. tell the prospective buyer that there is six inches of insulation

67. Once a contract for deed is signed by the parties, the buyer immediately receives:
    A. a life estate
    B. legal title
    C. equitable title
    D. the right to lease the property

68. The entity that determines the maximum number of people who may legally live in a rental unit is the:
    A. Department of Housing and Urban Development
    B. state government
    C. local health department and zoning authority
    D. property owner

69. Of the following factors, which one is the most significant in influencing value?
    A. Building materials
    B. Annual property tax bill
    C. Location
    D. Style of building

70. Which law prohibits discrimination in real estate transactions based on race, with no exceptions?

    A. Civil Rights Act of 1866
    B. Civil Rights Act of 1964
    C. Civil Rights Act of 1968
    D. Fair Housing Act

71. If a buyer wants to protect herself against unrecorded encumbrances, she should:

    A. assume the seller's standard policy of title insurance
    B. order a survey
    C. request a title insurance policy that has the fewest exceptions
    D. have her attorney prepare an abstract of title

72. A licensee hears that a religious group will be opening a commune in a neighborhood. He begins contacting neighbors and telling them about this, encouraging them to list their properties with him before property values decline. This would be:

    A. blockbusting
    B. redlining
    C. steering
    D. legal

73. A rectangular lot measures 215 feet by 154 feet. If comparable land sells for $40,000 per acre, how much is this lot likely to sell for?

    A. $20,000
    B. $30,000
    C. $40,000
    D. $50,000

74. A three-year lease ends. The tenant is allowed by the landlord to stay on and to continue to pay rent, on a month-to-month basis. This would be a:

    A. estate for years
    B. periodic tenancy
    C. term tenancy
    D. tenancy at sufferance

75. Branches from a neighbor's apple tree hang over the fence and overripe fruit falls into a homeowner's yard. This is an example of a/an:

    A. easement in gross
    B. emblement
    C. encroachment
    D. lien

76. The purpose of a building code is to:

    A. support zoning objectives
    B. acquire land for public use
    C. establish lot size and setback requirements
    D. provide minimum standards for construction

77. A local bank refuses to make residential loans in a particular section of town, because of the ethnic background of its residents. This is a discriminatory practice called:

    A. blockbusting
    B. redlining
    C. steering
    D. collusion

78. A square parcel of farmland measures 1,320 feet from north to south. In the center of the parcel is eight acres of swampland that is not tillable. If the property sells for $2,000 per acre of tillable land, what is the selling price?

    A. $64,000
    B. $80,000
    C. $96,000
    D. $2,624,000

79. The property description in a deed reads: "Starting at the old stone well, then going south 120 feet, west 400 feet, north 80 feet, and east 210 feet." This description is:

    A. invalid, because it doesn't return to the point of beginning
    B. invalid, because it uses a point of beginning that is man-made
    C. valid, because it returns to the point of beginning
    D. valid, because all descriptions must start with a man-made point of beginning

80. A property investor sells his 100-acre rural parcel of land with the restriction that the buyer may not divide the land into parcels smaller than one acre each. This restriction is:

    A. invalid; this restriction violates the rule against perpetuities
    B. invalid; one cannot put private restrictions on rural land
    C. valid; restrictions are always valid on agricultural land
    D. valid; this restriction doesn't violate public policy

81. An appraiser is valuing a commercial property that contains a restaurant run by the property owner. Which method of valuation would be most appropriate?
    A. Cost
    B. Income
    C. Market data
    D. Sales comparison

82. A landowner is negotiating the lease of his land to a developer who wants to build a mall there. They should use a:
    A. gross lease
    B. ground lease
    C. net lease
    D. percentage lease

83. A buyer and seller sign a contract for deed. Two weeks later, the buyer is declared mentally incompetent. The buyer's guardian contacts the seller and says that he can continue to make the buyer's payments as agreed. Which of the following is true?
    A. The buyer can disaffirm the contract within a reasonable period of time
    B. The buyer can finish out the contract as the buyer's guardian has proposed
    C. The seller can agree to receive payments from the guardian and if the payments become unreliable, the seller can then cancel the contract
    D. The contract is automatically voided because of the buyer's incapacity, regardless of what the guardian says

84. A licensee takes a listing for a house that is owned by a married couple. The husband is working overseas in the Middle East for the next two years. The wife can sign the listing agreement for her husband:
    A. as long as he has given her a power of attorney
    B. as long as he is overseas for work purposes and not for pleasure
    C. if they were originally married in a state that does not follow the law of community property
    D. under any circumstances

85. The purchase and sale agreement has been signed and the seller has completed the seller disclosure form. A windstorm damages the property. The seller's agent is obligated to:
    A. contact the buyer's agent and inform him
    B. amend the seller disclosure form
    C. terminate the purchase and sale agreement
    D. subtract the cost of repairing the damage from the purchase price

86. The requirements of the Truth in Lending Act would apply to a:
    A. construction loan used by a builder to build a model home
    B. loan for the purchase of a mobile home and lot for use as a principal residence
    C. loan to purchase an airplane
    D. loan to plant soybean and corn crops

87. A real estate licensee is performing a competitive market analysis. He locates a comparable property that is slightly older than the subject property. The age of the comparable makes it worth $2,000 less. The comparable has a small porch worth $1,000 that the subject property lacks. If the comparable sold for $269,500 recently, what is the estimated value of the subject property?
    A. $266,500
    B. $268,500
    C. $270,500
    D. $272,500

88. Which of the following situations would be exempt under the Fair Housing Act?
    A. A religious organization refuses to allow people of a particular national origin to spend the night in its temporary crisis housing
    B. An elderly homeowner who rents out a room in her house asks that no people of a particular national origin apply, in her classified ad
    C. The owner of a fourplex lives in one unit and refuses to rent the other three units to students because of their national origin
    D. The owner of a house refuses to sell the property to buyers because of their national origin, after his real estate agent confirms that is allowed

89. Jamie's house is mostly rectangular, measuring 30 feet by 40 feet. There is also an enclosed triangular foyer (a fully walled-in entry area) in front, measuring four feet across, four feet along the perpendicular side, and 5.7 feet along the diagonal side. In the back, there is a screened porch, which is 40 feet long and 5 feet deep. To the side, there is an attached garage, which measures 10 feet by 20 feet. What is the square footage of the living area?

   A. 1,200
   B. 1,208
   C. 1,408
   D. 1,608

90. An assigned parking space in a lot at a condominium development would be considered a/an:

   A. common element
   B. easement
   C. limited common element
   D. private restriction

91. Sam takes possession of an unused farm and begins growing crops. He sends the farm's owner a letter describing his actions. Can Sam ever become owner of the farm?

   A. Yes, because he is putting the land to productive use
   B. Yes, as long as he maintains possession
   C. No, because adverse possession requires that the true owner be unaware of the possession
   D. No, because his possession is not hostile to the owner's interest

92. Jones and Smith live across the street from each other in a subdivision that has deed restrictions prohibiting the keeping of large animals as pets. Jones realizes that Smith is keeping a pet Shetland pony in the backyard. Jones can:

   A. enforce the deed restriction against Smith via lawsuit
   B. do nothing, because Smith's ownership rights take precedence over deed restrictions
   C. do nothing, because only a next-door neighbor can enforce such a deed restriction against Smith
   D. notify the local zoning authority, who will investigate

93. A contract signed by a person who was intoxicated at the time of the signature would be:

   A. valid
   B. void
   C. voidable by the intoxicated party
   D. voidable by the other non-intoxicated party

94. The seller lists her property with XYZ Realty and agrees to pay a commission rate of 6%. The MLS provides that a listing brokerage will split commissions at a 50-50 rate with the selling brokerage. Suzy, a licensee for ABC Realty, finds a buyer and the property sells for $300,000. If Suzy is entitled to a 50/50 split with her brokerage, how much commission will she receive?

   A. $2,250
   B. $4,500
   C. $9,000
   D. $18,000

95. A developer wants a construction loan to build 20 homes. The lender requires a take-out commitment. This means the developer needs:

   A. a clause that allows individual lots to be released from the blanket lien when they are sold to purchasers
   B. a new mortgage that wraps around an existing first mortgage
   C. a permanent lender who will provide financing once construction is completed
   D. an interim contract guaranteeing that the property will be finished by certain date

96. A licensee who is taking a listing on a property finds a number of problems that need to be fixed, such as several leaking faucets and faulty electrical outlets. This would be an example of:

   A. economic obsolescence
   B. external obsolescence
   C. functional obsolescence
   D. curable depreciation

97. Which of the following is true concerning federal fair housing laws?

A. Enforcement may be brought about by filing a complaint with the Dept. of Housing and Urban Development
B. Parts of these laws were overturned by the Supreme Court in the case of Jones v. Alfred H. Mayer Co.
C. They only apply to racial discrimination
D. They preempt state-level antidiscrimination laws

98. An apartment building has eight units; each unit rents for $800 per month. The property can also be expected to earn $4,000 per year from laundry and vending machines. An appraiser estimates that the property typically operates with a 5% vacancy factor. What is the property's estimated annual effective gross income?

A. $10,080
B. $13,120
C. $76,760
D. $76,960

99. When determining the value of a vacant lot, an appraiser will typically use the:

A. cost approach
B. income approach
C. sales comparison approach
D. summation approach

100. John wants to rent a heated garage and is willing to pay a flat rate of $100 per month. Which type of lease would this be?

A. Gross lease
B. Ground lease
C. Net lease
D. Percentage lease

101. In an option:

A. no consideration is required
B. the seller is the optionee and the buyer is the optionor
C. the seller must apply the option money to the purchase price if the optionee exercises her option
D. the option agreement must clearly state all the terms and conditions of the sale

102. A licensee can reveal confidential information about his principal:

A. under court order or subpoena
B. under no circumstances
C. when another party asks directly if a certain fact is true
D. when acting as a dual agent

103. A lease is likely to be a net lease if it requires the tenant to pay:

A. a portion of the tenant's business income
B. periodic rent increases based on a measure of inflation like the Consumer Price Index
C. utilities
D. property taxes

104. Through careful management, a property manager increases an apartment building's monthly gross income of $3,000 by an additional $500 per month. Assuming a cap rate of 8%, what is the increase in the building's value?

A. $37,500
B. $43,750
C. $75,000
D. $525,000

105. A home inspection revealed that black mold is present in a home. What should the buyer's agent tell the buyer?

A. That black mold is toxic, and that the buyer should not buy the house
B. That mold is commonplace, and can be cleaned up with bleach
C. To require the seller to remedy the problem
D. To seek expert advice

106. A real estate agent would like to contact a buyer that he previously represented, to ask if that person would be interested in listing her home or if she has any referrals. Under what circumstances could the agent contact that person without having to consult the Do Not Call registry?

A. He represented the buyer within the previous 6 months
B. He represented the buyer within the previous 18 months
C. There is no limit; he can contact the buyer regardless
D. He may never contact the buyer

107. A licensee is criminally charged for stealing prescription drugs on July 2. He tells his designated broker about the charges on July 5. Who must notify the Real Estate Program Manager?

   A. The licensee must provide notice within 20 days of conviction
   B. The licensee must provide notice by July 22
   C. The licensee must provide notice by July 25
   D. The designated broker must provide notice by July 25

108. A property manager needs a real estate license when engaged in which of the following activities?

   A. Managing property owned by the company that employs her
   B. Managing self-owned property
   C. Managing a self-storage facility
   D. Third-party property management

109. L owns a bookstore and the lot it sits on. He hires M, a high school English teacher, to find a buyer for the business and property. He agrees to pay her $5,000. M finds a buyer and L pays her $5,000. Has M violated the real estate license law?

   A. Yes, because selling a business opportunity that includes real estate for pay requires a license
   B. Yes, because she entered into an oral listing agreement
   C. No, because L came to her with the idea of selling his bookstore
   D. No, because business opportunities aren't classified as real estate

110. An unlicensed real estate assistant may do which of the following without a license?

   A. Receive referral fees in some cases
   B. Discuss financing options with a client
   C. Hold open houses and discuss properties listed by the company he works for
   D. Provide full-service property management

111. A real estate agent took a $3,000 cash earnest money deposit on Friday morning. She had another appointment on Friday afternoon and didn't want to misplace the money over the weekend, so she deposited it into her personal bank account. First thing on Monday morning, she transferred the money to her firm's trust account. She has:

   A. acted properly
   B. acted properly if her account was registered with the state as a temporary account
   C. commingled funds
   D. not violated the law because the deposit was only for several days

112. A broker may accept compensation for the services he provides in a given transaction from:

   A. the property owner only
   B. any broker connected with the transaction
   C. the property owner or the broker's designated broker
   D. the broker's designated broker only

113. A dual-state brokerage firm doing business in Washington must:

   A. maintain a trust account in Washington if holding any funds in trust
   B. keep its transaction records on file with the Department of Licensing
   C. only hire out-of-state licensees
   D. maintain an office in Washington

114. An applicant passes the broker's examination and takes the notice to the designated broker where she plans to work. At what point can she legally begin selling real estate?

   A. When the license is hung on the wall
   B. When the application is mailed to the Department of Licensing
   C. When the license is received back from the Department of Licensing
   D. 45 days after the application is mailed to the Department of Licensing

369

115. L's broker's license is issued on October 16. L's license will expire at the end of:

    A. this year, on December 31
    B. next year, on December 31
    C. one year, on October 16
    D. two years, on October 16

116. Who is responsible for preparing and conducting real estate license examinations?

    A. The Department of Licensing
    B. The Director
    C. The Attorney General
    D. The Real Estate Commission

117. Which of the following is EXEMPT from the pooled interest-bearing account requirement?

    A. All earnest money deposits for residential transactions
    B. Earnest money deposits of no more than $10,000
    C. Earnest money deposits of no more than $5,500
    D. Property management trust funds

118. Which of the following statements about a blind ad is true?

    A. It is misleading because it fails to state the asking price
    B. It fails to identify the advertiser as a real estate agent
    C. It doesn't indicate the location of the property
    D. It's an ad directed at low-income buyers

119. Z, a real estate licensee, has been certified by the Department of Social and Health Services as not in compliance with his court-ordered child support payments. What disciplinary action is available to the Director of the Department of Licensing?

    A. Suspend Z's license
    B. Revoke Z's license
    C. File a cease and desist order
    D. File a criminal complaint in superior court

120. Which of the following is NOT a purpose of the Center for Real Estate Research?

    A. Provide scholarly information about real estate to the public
    B. Establish listing prices for properties
    C. Recommend changes to real estate education courses
    D. Perform real estate economic studies

121. When does an active license become inactive?

    A. When it is canceled
    B. When it is delivered to the Director for any reason
    C. When it is revoked
    D. When the licensee discontinues selling activities for any reason

122. Which of the following statements regarding pooled interest-bearing trust accounts is true?

    A. A client who makes a $5,000 earnest money deposit can insist on a separate trust account
    B. Pooled interest-bearing trust accounts are for property management accounts only
    C. Earnest money deposits over $10,000 can be placed in separate trust accounts
    D. All earnest money deposits must be placed in a pooled interest-bearing trust account

123. In the course of business, a firm earns property management fees that are to be paid out of the trust account. The fees must be taken out of the account:

    A. monthly
    B. quarterly
    C. semi-annually
    D. annually

124. A property manager handling a vacant building fails, for several months, to keep out vagrants who damage the property. Who is liable?

    A. The management firm's designated broker alone
    B. The property manager alone
    C. The property manager as well as the designated broker (for failing to properly supervise the licensee)
    D. No one is liable

125. If an agent fails to renew a license within one year after expiration, the license is considered:

A. inactive
B. suspended
C. revoked
D. canceled

126. Broker T explains to her designated broker that she is leaving the firm for a better opportunity with another brokerage. What must T's designated broker do?

A. Immediately send her license to the Director of the Department of Licensing
B. Explain that her license cannot be released until her pending transactions are closed
C. Hold the license until notified by the Department of Licensing that it can be returned
D. Return the license immediately along with a summary of the agent's work history with the firm

127. Addenda to a purchase and sale agreement must be:

A. kept in the broker's home office
B. kept in the brokerage's transaction file
C. kept in the firm's trust account
D. signed by the broker

128. An attorney at law is exempt from real estate licensing laws when:

A. negotiating the sale of any business opportunity
B. arranging the sale of real property while settling a client's estate
C. soliciting real estate business
D. engaging in the real estate business through her licensed law firm

129. Which of the following would be true regarding the designated broker for a real estate company? He must:

A. have a minimum of 10% ownership of the company
B. be paid a percentage of the company's profits
C. follow the directions of the majority of the owners
D. have absolute supervisory responsibility for all brokerage activities

130. In Washington, an inactive licensee may:

A. conduct open houses
B. manage a branch office of a brokerage
C. be exempt from disciplinary actions
D. be an unlicensed assistant to a real estate licensee

131. Which of the following would not be considered a nominal earnest money deposit, subject to the pooled interest-bearing account requirement?

A. $5,000 in the form of a personal check
B. $7,500 in the form of cash
C. $10,000 in the form of certified funds
D. $11,000 in the form of a cashier's check

132. The Director of the Department of Licensing has revoked S's license. Which of the following is TRUE?

A. S must stop acting in the capacity of licensee as of the date S receives the order of revocation
B. S can appeal to district court
C. only the Director can appeal to superior court
D. S has no right of appeal

133. Broker Q is licensed under Designated Broker K. Q negotiated an unusually complex transaction that worked to the advantage of both the buyer and the seller. The buyer and seller agreed to pay Q a bonus for the services rendered. Q can accept the bonus from:

A. the buyer
B. the buyer and the seller
C. K
D. the seller only, because K was the listing designated broker

134. Which of the following qualifications is required for a licensee to be eligible to be a designated broker?

A. Control over the firm's operational and financial decisions
B. General partner in a partnership
C. Five years as a managing broker
D. Five years as a broker

135. Which of the following is TRUE about the holder of an inactive license? This person:
    A. may not perform any acts that require a real estate license
    B. is technically licensed, and may perform certain acts that require a real estate license
    C. can keep the license on inactive status for a maximum of three years
    D. must obtain 30 clock hours of real estate instruction prior to each inactive license renewal

136. J is a designated broker who manages several commercial properties. J also owns a janitorial company. J contracts with her janitorial company to service the properties J manages. Under what conditions is this permitted?
    A. J's janitorial company is competitively priced
    B. J has written permission to select the janitorial company for the buildings she manages
    C. J discloses her interest in the janitorial company and obtains the owners' written permission to use it
    D. J cannot use her own janitorial company, as that would create a conflict of interest

137. Washington state's real estate agency law does not address which of the following?
    A. Definition of dual agency
    B. Creation and termination of agency relationships
    C. Vicarious liability of principal and licensee
    D. Penalties for not disclosing agency status

138. In preparation for appeal proceedings, the Director of the Department of Licensing prepares a full transcript of the original disciplinary hearing and, per the law, submits it to the court along with the cost to prepare the materials. Who is responsible for paying for this?
    A. Buyer
    B. Director
    C. Licensee/appellant
    D. Seller

139. The Real Estate Commission does all of the following except:
    A. prepare licensing exam questions
    B. set real estate transaction fees
    C. advise the Director regarding new regulations
    D. hold educational conferences for the benefit of the real estate industry

140. A licensee is about to change her business location. Which of the following should she do?
    A. Move her license to the new location until the renewal date
    B. Notify the Director of the Dept. of Licensing by phone
    C. Notify the Real Estate Program Manager in writing
    D. Surrender her license, and apply for an updated license with the correct location

Answer Key

1. **B** A court may find that an easement by necessity (or easement by implication) is created where it is reasonably necessary for enjoyment of the property, and there was apparent prior use. This may occur where a grantor divides a property into more than one lot, and forgets to grant or reserve an easement for the benefit of the new lot. A court-created easement doesn't necessarily run with the land, meaning the easement might not be appurtenant.

2. **D** A 203(b) loan is the standard type of FHA loan that most buyers will use. This type of loan may be used to purchase a property with up to four dwelling units, though it must be the borrower's primary residence.

3. **C** When zoning ordinances and private restrictions conflict, the more restrictive of the two prevails.

4. **A** Courts generally grant specific performance only when the object of a sales contract is unique and monetary damages would not be sufficient to put the nonbreaching party in the position she would have been in if the contract had been performed. That's the situation for a real estate buyer, as well as for purchasers of items such as jewelry or artwork.

5. **D** While any of these prior uses might stigmatize the property, none of them are material facts that would have to be disclosed by a seller or a seller's agent. There would be an exception if a prior use adversely affected the property's physical condition. For example, if the property had been used for illegal drug manufacturing, which may leave behind harmful chemical residues, this would have to be disclosed. However, the question refers only to drug sales, not drug manufacturing.

6. **C** The sales comparison approach (also known as the market data or market analysis approach) is the best method for appraising residential property. Replacement cost, which is based upon the idea that a property is not worth more than it would cost to replace it, may also be suitable for a newer residential property.

7. **C** An agency relationship may be terminated by revocation by the principal, without the consent of the agent. Even so, the revocation of a listing agreement is often a breach of contract, in which case the principal (the seller) may be required to pay damages to the agent (the brokerage).

8. **A** A landlord may sell leased property during the term of the lease, but the new owner must honor the lease for the remainder of its term.

9. **C** Only the building itself is depreciated, rather than the land, which cannot lose value due to depreciation. Multiply 1.5% by 10 years (since the question says "an average of" 1.5% per year, rather than saying it depreciated 1.5% each year), which is 15%. 15% of $120,000 is $18,000.

10. **D** An easement appurtenant runs with the land; in other words, subsequent owners of the properties that benefit from or are burdened by the easement will also be subject to the easement. An easement appurtenant benefits the dominant tenant, not the servient tenant.

11. **B** An option agreement, because it is a contract, must include consideration. The consideration can be a nominal amount (like $5), but it must actually be given to the optionor and can't be merely a recitation of consideration.

12. **C** A VA loan borrower who later defaults may be liable to the VA in some situations; in all situations, his guaranty entitlement (which he could use to obtain another VA loan) won't be restored until he reimburses the VA.

13. A Deed restrictions "run with the land," meaning they bind all subsequent owners of the property. A court may find that a deed restriction is no longer enforceable, for instance, if it violates public policy or hasn't been enforced by residents, but it will continue to remain part of the deed.

14. B With a sublease, the lessee is the one who remains liable to the lessor for rental payments. The sublessee (the new tenant) is responsible for making payments to the lessee (the original tenant), who will then pay the landlord.

15. B A quitclaim deed conveys any interest in a property that the grantor has at the time the deed is executed, without warranties.

16. A The buyer and seller can agree in the purchase and sale agreement that certain items of personal property will be included in the sale. Because the furniture is personal property, though, a separate document in addition to the deed, known as a bill of sale, will be necessary to transfer the personal property.

17. D Whenever the duties and powers of a property manager change, the property management agreement (the document that describes the scope of a property manager's authority) must be amended.

18. A A security instrument (such as a mortgage) and a promissory note are both contracts between borrower and lender. The promissory note is a promise to repay money, and the mortgage pledges the subject property as security for the loan.

19. A The tenant's payments under a net lease include a share of the property's operating expenses, such as maintenance costs, taxes, and insurance.

20. D The contract is valid. Since it was not made contingent on financing for the shopping center, Jerry must go ahead with the purchase.

21. D If the listing includes the sale, exchange, or lease of the land on which the mobile home sits, the real estate agent is not required to have any additional kind of license. If the listing does not include the sale, exchange, or lease of the land on which the mobile home sits, an agent would need a mobile home dealer's license (her real estate license would be irrelevant).

22. B By telling the buyer that the seller's walk-away price is $195,000, the listing agent divulged information that the seller would expect to remain confidential and, if divulged, works to the seller's detriment. This is a violation of the agent's fiduciary duties.

23. B Riparian rights are water rights that belong to owners of property that borders a stream or river. (Littoral rights refer to water rights associated with property that borders stationary water, such as a lake.)

24. D The seller is responsible for the taxes for the first four and a half months of the year (January, February, March, April, and half of May). $250 × 4.5 = $1,125.

25. B If the option money is in the form of a promissory note (in other words, the option hasn't been paid for yet), the optionee cannot assign it.

26. C It is legal for an agent to show a buyer homes in the neighborhoods that the buyer has chosen, even if the buyer chose the neighborhoods based on race. Nothing in the Fair Housing Act requires an agent to show buyers houses against their will.

27. C If co-owners are able to will their property to their heirs (instead of having it pass through right of survivorship), that means they hold title as tenants in common.

28. A A buyer who records a deed is giving constructive notice of his interest in the property. Anyone who later acquires an interest in the property is held to know about all previously recorded interests, even if she didn't check the records.

29. C Functional obsolescence includes both undesirable or out-of-date design elements (such as the narrow hallways) and undesirable or out-of-date fixtures or appliances (such as the window units).

30. A A group boycott would include an agreement between two competitors to exclude other companies from fair participation in real estate activities.

31. C Divide the points paid by the loan amount to find what percentage was paid in points ($4,800 ÷ $80,000 = 0.06). Since one discount point is the same as one percent of the loan amount, the borrower paid six discount points.

32. C The alienation clause, also called the due-on-sale clause, prohibits the assumption of the loan. It means that if the property is sold, the loan must be paid off (unless the lender agrees to assumption of the loan by a particular buyer).

33. A A corporation cannot take title through joint tenancy, because of its potentially perpetual existence. Corporate property may be owned in severalty by the corporation itself.

34. D A real estate licensee is limited to filling in the blanks on a printed form drafted by attorneys. Going beyond that, by drafting covenants or trust documents, for example, would be considered the unauthorized practice of law.

35. C Even when property is sold "as is," sellers and real estate agents have a duty to disclose any known latent defects or other material facts. Here, whoever concealed the hole--whether it was the seller, the licensee, or both of them--would be liable for misrepresentation. If only one of them covered up the hole, the other one could also be liable if he or she was aware of the deception and failed to say anything about it to the buyer. Also, even if the seller knew nothing about the problem, in many states the seller could be vicariously liable if it was the seller's agent who concealed the hole.

36. A A special rule, called the doctrine of emblements, applies to crops planted by a tenant farmer. If the lease is terminated through no fault of the tenant before the crops are ready for harvest, the tenant has the right to re-enter the land and harvest the first crop that matures after the tenancy is terminated.

37. B An agent has a duty to disclose not just latent defects, but also red flags that indicate that a latent defect might be present (such as signs that flooding might be a hazard). It is up to the buyer, however, to decide if he wants to investigate further or not.

38. A When Al decided to buy the property for himself, his duty to disclose conflicts of interest and material facts to his principal required him to let Sally know all of the circumstances. If he failed to do so, it was self-dealing and a breach of fiduciary duties.

39. B General real estate taxes are ad valorem taxes; the amount of tax owed is based on the value of the property.

40. B A judgment lien may attach to the property of someone who loses a lawsuit and is ordered to pay damages. (This person is referred to as the judgment debtor.) If the judgment debtor doesn't pay off the lien, the court can issue a writ of execution ordering the sale of the property.

41. B A state government may delegate the power of eminent domain to local governments, and to private entities that serve the public, such as utility companies and railroads. Eminent domain is the right; condemnation is the process.

42. D To determine how much money the seller will take away from the transaction after closing (her net proceeds, in other words), start with the seller's credits and subtract the seller's debits.

43. B Since the furniture belongs to the tenant, the seller cannot promise it to the buyer. The buyer is not entitled to receive the furniture, but the seller might be liable to the buyer for damages for the misrepresentation, if the buyer relied on the seller's promise.

44. B A person can typically rescind a contract he entered into as a minor, as long as he acts fairly quickly. The key detail is what age the buyer was when he agreed to the deal, not the age when he tried to rescind. Here the buyer appears to have acted reasonably promptly.

45. B Mortgage interest rates are primarily influenced by the supply of and demand for funds in the money market. This is determined by many factors, including actions taken by the Federal Reserve.

46. A A real property owner can deduct the property taxes she pays.

47. A The tenants had an estate for years: a lease for a specific period of time. Unless the parties renew the lease, or unless the lease itself provides otherwise, an estate for years simply terminates at the end of the agreed period. No notice is necessary, and the tenants can't be charged a penalty for failing to give notice.

48. B A quiet title action is a lawsuit that is used to remove a cloud on the title to property, by settling questions about the property's ownership or the legitimacy of other claims against it. A quitclaim deed will also clear a cloud, but it requires the cooperation of whoever would need to sign the deed. Thus, a quiet title action is a more complete answer for this question.

49. A The Fair Housing Act prohibits the seller from refusing to sell his property because of a disability of the buyer or a family member of the buyer. The buyer's agent should let the buyer know about her options for legal recourse.

50. B A home protection plan is a short-term warranty that a home buyer may purchase at closing. The buyer will be reimbursed for expenses related to the failure of covered systems or appliances, usually only during the first few years of ownership.

51. A FHA loans require an appraisal by an appraiser who has met the educational and certification requirements for inclusion on the FHA's roster of approved appraisers. Secondary financing provided by a close family member is allowed, but secondary financing from an institutional lender is not allowed.

52. D Once a Section 1031 exchange (tax-deferred or "tax-free" exchange) has been arranged, the parties must close the transaction within 180 days.

53. B An acceleration clause allows a lender to "call" a loan, or demand the repayment of the entire loan balance, in the event of a borrower's default.

54. B Cluster zoning is an approach to zoning that allows developments in suburban or rural areas to have smaller lot sizes and higher density, but also more shared green space. A development cannot exceed the general plan's limits on density, though.

55. D For a valid contract to exist, there must be offer and acceptance. An advertisement (like a listing) is not considered an offer, only an invitation to negotiate. The buyer's offer is just that: an offer, without an acceptance.

56. C A securities license is necessary in a transaction that involves the sale of a security such as an investment contract.

57. C In a loan assumption, if the seller wants to be released from further liability, she must obtain a document called a release of liability from the lender.

58. A The Fair Housing Act has wheel-chair-accessibility requirements for apartment complexes built since 1991. However, apartments on the second floor or above in multi-story buildings do not have to be wheelchair-accessible if there is no elevator in the building.

59. C New information that is material and comes to light after the disclosure statement has been made should be disclosed in an amended statement (higher property taxes are material if the increase is great enough that the buyer might reconsider the transaction). However, material facts that are discovered after closing do not need to be disclosed, and the buyer no longer has a right of rescission. (Note: Some states provide a partial homestead exemption for property taxes.)

60. C First, calculate the year's base rent, by multiplying the square footage by the rental rate (3,000 square feet × $20 per square ft. = $60,000). Next, subtract the amount attributable to the square footage from the total rent, to find the rent attributable to gross sales ($120,000 − $60,000 = $60,000). Finally, divide that portion of the rent by 8% to find the property's gross sales ($60,000 ÷ .08 = $750,000).

61. A A commercial tenant may take trade fixtures—equipment the tenant installed for use in her business—with her when she moves out at the end of the lease. In this case, however, the counters were added by the owner, not the tenant, so they would not be considered trade fixtures.

62. B If another veteran substitutes his eligibility, a veteran's guaranty may be restored.

63. A A partition suit is filed when co-owners cannot resolve a dispute regarding their property and one or more of them wants to end the co-ownership. The court will decide how to divide the property. If physical division is impossible or impractical, the court will order the sale of the property and division of the proceeds.

64. C One discount point is the equivalent of one percent of the loan amount. Multiply the loan amount by 1% to find the cost of the discount point ($88,000 × .01 = $880). The other numbers given can and should be ignored.

65. A A purchaser wouldn't be buying a fee simple absolute interest in the property, only the life estate held by the seller. The property would pass to the life tenant's children at the end of the life estate's measuring life. (Buying a life estate is rare; probably the most common instance is with a property encumbered by a life estate. To get a fee simple estate, the buyer needs to buy the life estate and also the remainder interest.)

66. D A licensee has the duty to disclose material facts to the appropriate party, even if the principal doesn't disclose that information himself. The insulation depth could be a material fact, since insufficient insulation could have a negative effect on the property's value.

67. C A buyer receives equitable title to the property once the land contract (or contract for deed) has been signed. The seller retains legal title. The seller transfers legal title once the buyer finishes paying off the contract/purchase price.

68. C Among the many things that a local zoning authority might determine is the maximum occupancy of each dwelling in a particular area.

69. C A property's location is usually the most determinative factor in terms of its value. A view or a prestigious neighborhood can boost the value of an otherwise unremarkable property.

70. A The Civil Rights Act of 1866 prevents discrimination based on race or color in any real estate transaction, without exception. The 1964 Act is limited to programs where the federal government offers financial assistance, while the Fair Housing Act (a part of the 1968 Act) is limited to residential transactions and has several exemptions.

71. C   To protect against unrecorded encumbrances, a buyer would need something that goes beyond a standard title insurance policy, which is limited to certain defects in title. The buyer would probably want a homeowner's policy, which provides the greatest protection. (Note that a survey doesn't address encumbrances; it only addresses encroachments.)

72. A   Blockbusting occurs when a licensee tries to induce homeowners to list their properties by predicting that persons from a protected class (usually on the basis of race, but also potentially on the basis of religion) will be moving into the neighborhood and that there will be undesirable consequences.

73. B   The first step is to find the square footage of the lot (215 feet × 154 feet = 33,110 square feet). Convert this to acreage (33,110 square feet ÷ 43,560 square feet per acre = 0.76 acres). $40,000 × 0.76 is $30,400, closest to $30,000.

74. B   A lease that has no fixed termination date, but lasts for a specific period and continues until one party gives the other notice of termination, is a periodic tenancy.

75. C   An object that extends over a property's boundary line is an encroachment. An encroachment is not an encumbrance because it is not a right or use held by the encroaching property owner; however, if it is in place long enough, it may ripen into an easement.

76. D   Building codes set minimum standards for construction materials and methods, in order to protect the public from unsafe or unworkmanlike construction.

77. B   Refusing to make loans for discriminatory reasons is redlining, which is illegal.

78. A   First, multiply the property's boundaries to find its square footage (1,320 feet × 1,320 feet = 1,742,400 square feet). Convert it to acreage (1,742,400 square feet ÷ 43,560 square feet per acre = 40 acres), subtract the unusable portion (40 acres - 8 acres = 32 acres), and multiply by the price per acre (32 acres × $2,000 = $64,000).

79. A   The property description is invalid, because it does not return to the point of beginning. A property description may be based on a man-made object as its point of beginning (although it doesn't have to be), but it must enclose the property's full perimeter.

80. D   Deed restrictions are generally valid, so long as they aren't unconstitutional, a violation of a law, or contrary to judicial determinations of public policy. For example, deed restrictions prohibiting sale to non-white buyers are invalid on public policy grounds.

81. B   For a commercial property, the most appropriate method of valuation would be the income approach (regardless of whether it contains an owner-operated business).

82. B   A ground lease is used when a tenant leases land and constructs a building on that land.

83. B   If a person is declared incompetent after signing a contract, the contract may be voidable at the discretion of a court-appointed guardian. As with any voidable contract, though, the person's guardian may decide to ratify the agreement and continue with it. (If the buyer has an appointed guardian, the buyer would not be the one who decides to disaffirm the contract.)

84. A   Ordinarily, all co-owners of a property need to sign an agreement to list the property. However, if the husband has given the wife power of attorney to sign documents on his behalf in his absence, the wife would be able to sign for him.

85. A   If the condition of the property changes or other new information comes to light that makes the original disclosure statement inaccurate, the seller must give an amended disclosure statement to the buyer or take corrective action so that the original statement is accurate again. The seller's agent isn't supposed to amend the disclosure statement himself, but the duty to disclose material facts would compel the agent to notify the other party.

86. B   The Truth in Lending Act applies to consumer loans (for family, personal, or household purposes), including the purchase of mobile homes and the land they're on. It does not apply to commercial loans, such as a construction loan for a developer.

87. C   To estimate the value of the subject property, adjust the comparable's sales price to reflect what it would sell for if it were identical to the subject property. Add $2,000 to the comparable's sales price (to make it more like the subject property, which is newer), and then subtract $1,000 from the comparable's sales price (again, to make it more like the subject property, which lacks a porch). The result is $270,500.

88. C   The Fair Housing Act allows an exemption for the rental of a unit in a dwelling of up to four units, so long as the owner lives in one of the units, employs no real estate agent, and uses no discriminatory advertising.

89. B   Keep in mind that a house's square footage is based on its outside dimensions, but excludes garages and porches. So, you would only need to calculate the area of the main part of the house (30 feet × 40 feet = 1,200 square feet) and the odd triangular foyer (4 feet × 4 feet × 1/2 = 8 square feet.) (Remember, the formula for the area of a triangle is 1/2 or .5 × H × B—you don't use the diagonal or hypotenuse.) Add the two together to find the square footage is 1,208 square feet.

90. C   A feature outside of the airspace of a condominium unit, but that is reserved for the owner of a particular unit, is considered a limited common element.

91. B   So long as Sam maintains continuous, uninterrupted possession for the required period of time, and meets the other requirements, he will be able to take title to the property (although he may need to file a quiet title action to perfect title). The owner does not need to know about the possession, but the possession must be obvious enough to put the average owner on notice that his interest in the property is threatened, and Sam's letter more than satisfies that requirement.

92. A   Jones or any other homeowner in the subdivision can file a suit for an injunction against Smith; it isn't necessary to be a next-door neighbor. However, if other owners in the subdivision have also been violating the restriction for some time, the court might rule that the restriction has been abandoned and can no longer be enforced.

93. C   A contract signed by a person who is temporarily incompetent (through intoxication, for instance) may be voidable, if the person takes action to rescind the contract within a reasonable time after regaining competency.

94. B   The first step is to calculate how much the seller will owe XYZ Realty ($300,000 x .06 = $18,000). ABC Realty receives 50% of the commission ($18,000 x .5 = $9,000). And Suzy will receive 50% of ABC Realty's share ($9,000 x .5 = $4,500).

95. C   Construction loans are interim loans used to finance construction of improvements. The construction loan is replaced by a permanent loan, sometimes called a take-out loan, when construction is complete.

96. D Physical deterioration is a loss in value caused by wear and tear or by damage. The depreciation mentioned in the question would probably be classified as curable physical deterioration (deferred maintenance), since it's likely that the cost of correcting the problems could be recovered in the sales price when the property is sold.

97. A The Fair Housing Act is enforced through the Department of Housing and Urban Development's Office of Fair Housing and Equal Opportunity. Jones v. Mayer upheld the application of the Civil Rights Act of 1866 in sale or rental of real property. State laws are not preempted by federal antidiscrimination laws; in some cases, they may be more strict than federal law.

98. D Multiply the eight units in the building by the monthly rent to find the monthly income (8 × $800 = $6,400). Multiply that by 12 months per year, to find the annual income (12 × $6,400 = $76,800). Calculate what is 5% of that amount ($76,800 × .05 = $3,840), and subtract that amount from the annual income ($76,800 − $3,840 = $72,960). Add the $4,000 in additional revenue (which is not subject to the vacancy factor) to find the effective gross income ($72,960 + $4,000 = $76,960).

99. C An appraiser will estimate the value of vacant land using the sales comparison approach, referring to the sales prices of similar lots that were recently sold.

100. A A lease where the tenant pays a fixed flat rent and the landlord pays most or all of the operating expenses is called a gross lease or fixed lease.

101. D The option agreement also serves as the sale contract once the option is exercised, so all terms and conditions of the sale need to be included in the option agreement.

102. A While a licensee ordinarily has a duty to not disclose confidential information about the principal, it may be disclosed when the licensee is faced with a court order or a subpoena.

103. D A lease that requires the tenant to pay all of the property's operating expenses, including the property taxes, is a triple net lease. (Although a net lease often requires the tenant to pay utility costs, that can also be true of a fixed lease. A tenant with a fixed lease does not pay property taxes, however, so option D is a better answer than C.)

104. C One way to solve the problem is to calculate the value before the increase ($3,000 x 12 = $36,000; $36,000 ÷ .08 = $450,000), calculate the value after the increase ($3,500 x 12 = $42,000; $42,000 ÷ .08 = $525,000), and then calculate the difference ($525,000 - $450,000 = $75,000). Another way would be simply to multiply $500 x 12 ($6,000) and then factor in the capitalization rate ($6,000 ÷ .08 = $75,000).

105. D A buyer's agent typically does not have expertise in environmental hazards. The proper step, for matters in a transaction outside the agent's expertise, is to advise the principal to seek expert advice. In this case, that would be a mold remediation specialist.

106. B If an agent has an established business relationship with a previous client, he may call that person within the 18 months following that person's last transaction, even if that person has placed her name on the Do Not Call registry. (If that person then asks the agent to stop calling, though, the agent must honor that request.)

107. B A licensee must notify the Real Estate Program Manager within 20 days of learning of any criminal complaint or indictment in which the licensee is named as a defendant. (A conviction has yet to occur in this situation so answer A doesn't apply; if the licensee is eventually convicted, he will also have to notify the DOL of the conviction within 20 days.)

108. D A property manager who manages property for third parties must be licensed. Licensing exemptions exist for persons who manage property they own or on behalf of a group they belong to, and for managers of self-storage facilities.

109. A Selling a business opportunity that includes real estate for compensation requires a real estate license. (An oral listing agreement does not violate the license law. It simply isn't enforceable if the seller refuses to pay the brokerage commission.)

110. A A license isn't required in order to receive referral fees, provided the fee isn't contingent on a licensee's compensation.

111. C The real estate agent has violated state laws concerning trust fund handling, by commingling trust funds with her own personal funds.

112. D A broker may accept compensation only from his own designated broker.

113. A A dual-state brokerage must maintain a trust account in a Washington depository institution if holding funds in trust for Washington clients.

114. B Once an applicant has been notified that she has passed the state exam, she may begin working on the date she mails or hand delivers the signed, dated, and completed application form and license fee to the Department of Licensing. The completed form serves as an interim license for up to 45 days after the postmark or hand delivery date.

115. D L's license will expire two years after its issuance on October 16.

116. D The Real Estate Commission has that responsibility, though they delegate it to a professional testing service.

117. D Property management trust funds are exempt. The pooled interest-bearing account requirement applies to earnest money deposits of $10,000 or less.

118. B A blind ad fails to identify the advertiser by including the name of the real estate firm as licensed (or its assumed name).

119. A The Director can suspend Z's license until Z has repaid the delinquency or otherwise complied with the order. The Director's authority to revoke a license or issue a cease and desist order doesn't extend to cases of failure to pay child support.

120. B The Center for Real Estate Research studies local economic conditions and proposes changes to real estate education curricula. It does not have a role in establishing listing prices.

121. B A license becomes inactive when it is delivered to the Director of the Department of Licensing for any reason.

122. C Earnest money deposits of $10,000 or less must be placed in a pooled interest-bearing trust account (property management accounts are exempted from this requirement). Deposits over $10,000 do not have to be placed in the pooled accounts, but they can be.

123. A They must be removed from the trust account at least on a monthly basis.

124. C The property manager is liable for failing to exercise reasonable care in carrying out the duties she took on for her client. The property manager's designated broker may also be liable for failing to supervise the property manager adequately. (Note: a full-service property manager must have a real estate license and work for a brokerage.)

125. D If a license isn't renewed within one year after it expires, the license is canceled. (A canceled license may still be reinstated within two years of cancellation, if certain conditions are met.)

126. A The designated broker must immediately return the individual's license to the Department of Licensing. A summary of the licensee's conduct while employed by the firm would be necessary only if that conduct could result in disciplinary action by the Director.

127. B A transaction file should include all modifications or addenda to any agreement. The transaction file should be kept where the firm is licensed to have an office, not in a broker's home office. The addenda will be signed by the buyer and seller, not the broker.

128. B An attorney at law is exempted from licensing requirements when performing her duties as an attorney. The exemption doesn't apply to an attorney who provides real estate brokerage services not directly connected to a client matter.

129. D The designated broker must have absolute supervisory responsibility for all brokerage activities.

130. D An inactive licensee is generally deemed to be unlicensed, and may not perform activities that require a license. An inactive licensee would still be able to perform the duties that any other unlicensed assistant could perform.

131. D Nominal earnest money deposits are $10,000 or less.

132. A The revocation takes effect when ordered and remains in effect while an appeal is being heard. S, as well as the Director, has the right to appeal to superior court.

133. C Q can only be compensated by K, his designated broker. The buyer and seller could pay the bonus to K, who would then decide what portion of the bonus should be paid to Q.

134. A A designated broker must hold a managing broker's license and must have the ability to control the operational and financial decisions of the firm.

135. A An inactive licensee may not perform any act that requires a license, because she is deemed to be unlicensed.

136. C Even though J has the authority to select a janitorial company for the buildings she manages, she would still have to disclose her interest in the janitorial company, if that's the one she uses, and obtain the written permission of each owner whose building is serviced by J's company.

137. D Washington's real estate agency law is found in the Real Estate Brokerage Relationships Act (RCW chapter 18.86). It addresses the topics listed in answers A - C (definition of dual agency, creation and termination of agency, and vicarious liability), but there is no reference in the law to penalties for not disclosing agency status. Penalties are found in the license law (RCW chapter 18.85).

138. C If a licensee is dissatisfied with the outcome of a disciplinary hearing, she may file an appeal in superior court. The licensee must post a $1,000 appeal bond to cover court costs, and must also pay for a copy of the transcript of the hearing.

139. B The Commission does not set transaction fees. Fees are set by agreement between the agent and principal in each transaction.

140. D If a licensee plans to change her place of employment, the firm's designated broker or the licensee surrenders the license. The Director of the Department of Licensing will then issue a new license for the new location.

Index